AVID

READER

PRESS

LIFE ON THE

MISSISSIPPI

AN EPIC AMERICAN ADVENTURE

RINKER BUCK

AVID READER PRESS

NEW YORK   LONDON   TORONTO   SYDNEY   NEW DELHI

AVID READER PRESS
An Imprint of Simon & Schuster, Inc.
1230 Avenue of the Americas
New York, NY 10020

First Avid Reader Press hardcover edition August 2022

AVID READER PRESS and colophon are trademarks of Simon & Schuster, Inc.

For information about special discounts for bulk purchases, please contact Simon &
Schuster Special Sales at 1-866-506-1949 or business@simonandschuster.com.

The Simon & Schuster Speakers Bureau can bring authors to your live event. For
more information or to book an event contact the Simon & Schuster Speakers
Bureau at 1-866-248-3049 or visit our website at www.simonspeakers.com.

Interior design by Wendy Blum
Maps by Jeffrey L. Ward
Illustrations by Michael Gellatly

Manufactured in the United States of America

1   3   5   7   9   10   8   6   4   2

Library of Congress Cataloging-in-Publication Data has been applied for.

ISBN 978-1-5011-0637-8
ISBN 978-1-5011-0639-2 (ebook)

Photo Credits:
Front and back endpapers: Dan Corjulo
Dan Corjulo: iv, 107, 148, 327; H. David Wright: 5; Robert Mitchell: 36, 49;
Rinker Buck: 44, 171, 238, 316; Scott Olson/Getty Images: 262

The French philosopher Bernard of Chartres is famous for saying that scholars are "dwarfs perched on the shoulders of giants," a reference to the obligation owed to the great minds who preceded them and influenced their work. I have always believed in a variant of Bernard's credo—that we are the continued minds of our best teachers.

I dedicate this book to three superb teachers who guided me through writing, literature, and history: Abbot Gerard Lair, O.S.B., and Abbot Giles Hayes, O.S.B., of St. Mary's Abbey and the Delbarton School in Morristown, New Jersey, and James E. Bland, PhD, a brilliant lecturer and prudent mentor who taught American history at Bowdoin College.

The history of the Mississippi Valley is the history of the United States.

—ALBERT BUSHNELL HART

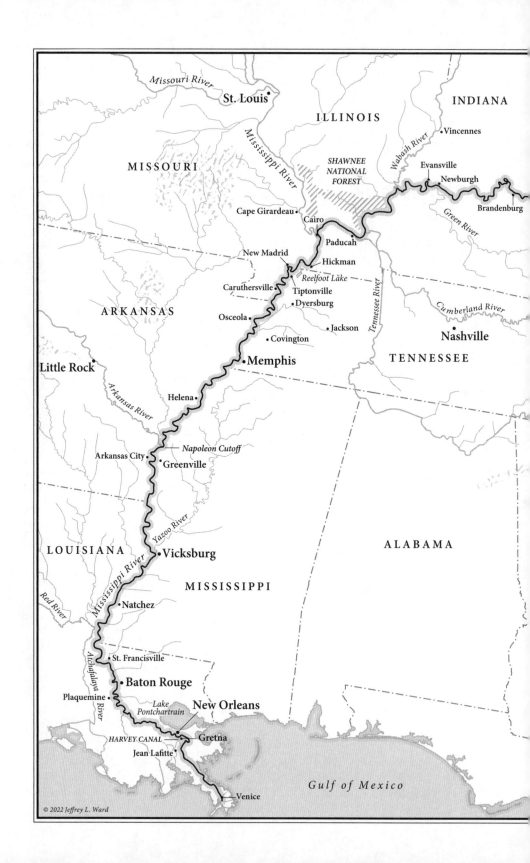

Missouri River

St. Louis•

ILLINOIS

INDIANA

•Vincennes

MISSOURI

Wabash River

Evansville•
Newburgh•

SHAWNEE
NATIONAL
FOREST

•Brandenburg

Green River

Cape Girardeau•
Cairo•

Paducah•

New Madrid•
•Hickman

Reelfoot Lake
Caruthersville•
Tiptonville•
•Dyersburg

Tennessee River

Cumberland River

ARKANSAS

Osceola•

•Jackson

Nashville•

•Covington

Little Rock•

•Memphis

TENNESSEE

Arkansas River

Helena•

Arkansas City•
•Greenville

Napoleon Cutoff

ALABAMA

Yazoo River

LOUISIANA

Mississippi River

•Vicksburg

MISSISSIPPI

Red River

•Natchez

•St. Francisville

Atchafalaya River

•Baton Rouge

Plaquemine•

Lake
Pontchartrain

New Orleans

HARVEY CANAL
Jean Lafitte•

Gretna

Gulf of Mexico

•Venice

© 2022 Jeffrey L. Ward

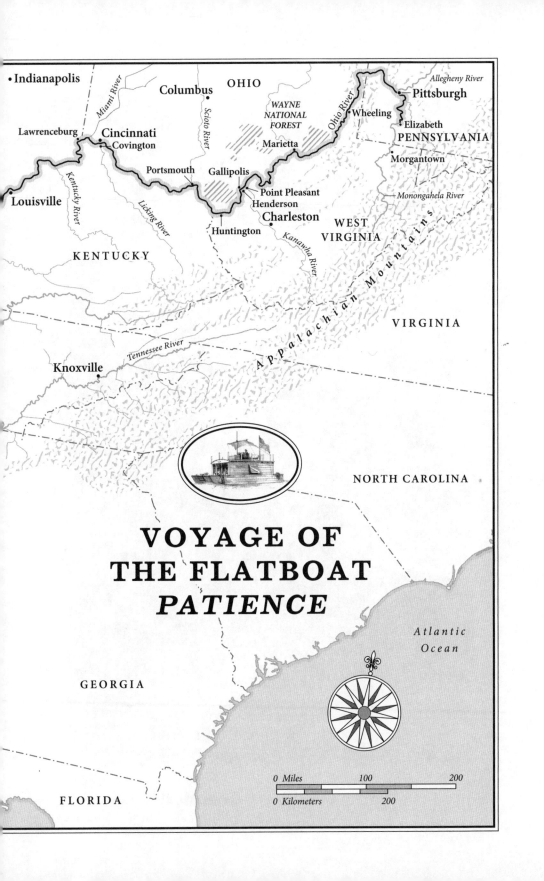

• Indianapolis

Miami River

Columbus   OHIO

Scioto River

Allegheny River

Ohio River

• Pittsburgh

WAYNE
NATIONAL
FOREST

• Wheeling

Lawrenceburg   Cincinnati
     Covington

Marietta

• Elizabeth
PENNSYLVANIA

• Morgantown

Portsmouth   Gallipolis

Kentucky River

Licking River

Point Pleasant
Henderson
Charleston

Huntington

WEST
VIRGINIA

Kanawha River

—— *Monongahela River*

• Louisville

KENTUCKY

Appalachian Mountains

VIRGINIA

Tennessee River

Knoxville

NORTH CAROLINA

VOYAGE OF
THE FLATBOAT
PATIENCE

*Atlantic
Ocean*

GEORGIA

FLORIDA

| 0 Miles | | 100 | | 200 |

| 0 Kilometers | | | 200 | |

Camping on the Levees

1

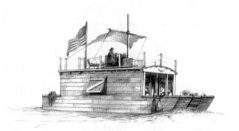

I DIDN'T SPEND A YEAR building a wooden flatboat and then sailing it two thousand miles down the Mississippi to New Orleans simply because I was suffering from a Huck Finn complex, although that certainly played a part. It was hot that spring on the Tennessee farm where we built the boat and I often relieved the tedium of nailing on deck planking or raising roof stringers by daydreaming about spinning lazily down through the muddy boils, exploring remote islands and sandbars, or pulling off at sunset into bayous thick with cattails and cypress stumps. Mostly, though, I was entranced by history. I hungered to see that river country when I stumbled across an account of one of the first boatmen who braved the water route that America followed toward prosperity and greatness.

In the spring of 1782, an enterprising Swiss-German farmer from Reading, Pennsylvania, Jacob Yoder, landed on a novel scheme for marketing his crops that considerably brightened his own prospects and opened one of the most lyrical eras in American history. Yoder faced the kind of economic dilemma that would periodically bedevil his fellow Americans for the next century. The autumn before, General George Washington had accepted the surrender of the British forces at Yorktown in Virginia, effectively ending the American Revolution, but negotiations over the terms of American independence would drag on in Paris and London for another eighteen months. Until a treaty was signed, the transatlantic markets upon which the former colonies relied were closed, and the phenomenal productivity of the German enclave in Pennsylvania had filled the market sheds of Philadelphia and New York with excess produce, severely depressing prices. America, an agrarian society almost wholly dependent on global markets for its crops, was an economic stillbirth.

Yoder was a veteran of the Revolution and accustomed to adventure, and he could hardly have avoided looking west. He had already proved valuable to the cause of independence by organizing expeditions to southern Virginia and frontier Kentucky to gather herds of cattle and horses to supply the Continental army. That made him one of the few Americans to witness firsthand the budding nation's rambunctious and largely unplanned movement west. Throughout the Revolution, settlers, Continental army deserters, and fur trappers had been streaming across the Appalachians, following the Great Valley Road through western Virginia and then across to Kentucky over the Cumberland Gap. Farther north, over tortuous mountain roads in western Maryland and Pennsylvania, packhorse and wagon trains were establishing the first commercial feelers with the rich but barely settled Ohio country.

A more direct water route to the Ohio valley, however, lay just across the Alleghenies, at the majestic three-rivers junction near Pittsburgh, where the Allegheny and Monongahela rivers joined to form the Ohio. From there, just a few weeks' float down the Ohio past the falls at Louisville, lay the great interior prize of the North American continent, the massive, meandering planet of water called the Mississippi. The Mississippi and its tributaries, connecting more than fifteen thousand miles of navigable water, could deliver passengers and product unimaginable distances in every direction, but especially to the south and the most alluring gold pot of all, the Spanish territories of Louisiana. The blockading of northern cities during the Revolution, and Europe's insatiable demand for American beaver pelts, had turned the Spanish port along the Gulf of Mexico, New Orleans, into the third largest city in North America and the fastest-growing export center in the world. Milled grain to feed the bursting city, or for shipment to Europe, was in great demand. Southern Louisiana's appetite for the commodities that frontier America had to offer—lumber, whiskey, barreled salt pork to feed its growing slave population—would prove voracious. A two-thousand-mile float down the Ohio and the Mississippi to

New Orleans seemed highly speculative, even dangerous, but it was Yoder's best route to a market for his crops.

After spending the winter milling his grain into flour and corn meal, Yoder decided to embark along the banks of the Monongahela River at Redstone Old Fort, a wilderness military post and frontier Quaker settlement dating back to 1759. Later renamed Brownsville, Pennsylvania, during the Revolution the landing along the Monongahela had developed into a lively complex of boatyards specializing in building simple rafts and flatboats for local frontier traffic down the Ohio. Yoder paid a local sawyer about $75 to mill two dozen green oak trees into "half-log" gunwales, deck and floor planking, and probably built his long above-deck shed enclosure to protect his barrels from the rain out of poplar or pine. He launched on the Monongahela in May, floated thirty-five miles north to the Ohio, and spent the next three months negotiating the rapids and submerged logs carried down by the spring rains to New Orleans, where he bartered his grain for paper "script" exchangeable in the Spanish port of Havana, Cuba. There, he bought a cargo of beaver pelts, which he then shipped to Baltimore and sold at a profit estimated at almost $2,000, a small fortune then for just a few months' work. As word of his river adventure spread, dozens and later hundreds of farmers and tradesmen followed, turning Brownsville and nearby Pittsburgh into one of the busiest boatbuilding locations in America and, eventually, the center of a booming steamboat business. Yoder floated the Ohio and Mississippi rivers to New Orleans several more times and eventually settled in Kentucky, helping to form the territorial government along the new Ohio valley frontier.

The great flatboat era, which opened the frontiers of interior America to the world, had begun. From a trickle of relatively small forty-foot boats every year at the end of the 18th century, the Mississippi River traffic would swell to over 3,000 eighty-foot flatboats a year by the 1840s. Another 4,000 to 5,000 flatboats plied the tributaries of the Ohio and the Mississippi, transferring cargo to larger boats that traveled all the way to New Orleans, turning sleepy frontier villages like Vincennes, Indiana, and Cincinnati, Ohio, into boomtowns. The explosion of river traffic revolutionized American trade and made transportation, particularly river transportation, a defining achievement of the country. The success of flatboat routes to world markets through New Orleans triggered the explosive growth of steamboat traffic after the 1830s, and by the Civil War more than four thousand miles of canals had been built, integrating the rivers, tributaries, and man-made waterways into a diverse and flexible cargo delivery system that supported America's industrial revolution and the vast expansion of its agricultural economy in the 19th century. Historian David S. Reynolds calls America during this period the "Waking Giant." "What is now called economic globalization," Reynolds writes, "began with advances in water transportation during the two decades after 1815." Jacob Yoder and his many followers unleashed a transportation revolution that opened America to the world.

The exploration of an inland water route to New Orleans occurred just in time, providing the thousands of Scotch-Irish and German settlers streaming into Kentucky and the "northwest territory" of Ohio, Illinois, and Indiana a ready market for their crops. Strangely, the flatboat era and its immense impact on American history is rarely taught in schools, even at the college level, but, of course, a book the size of Edward Gibbon's *The History of the Decline and Fall of the Roman Empire* could be written about the subjects American historians and schoolteachers have failed to bring to our attention. As much as the writing of the Constitution and the Bill of Rights, or, say, Andrew Jackson's bank war in the 1830s, it was the inland rivers that formed America during its first, seminal burst of growth. During the early decades of the 19th century, the massive flatboat traffic drifting down the Ohio and the Mississippi established the westward drive and political outlook that eventually allowed America to straddle the continent from the Atlantic to the Pacific. This riverine movement began a half century before the more celebrated era of the "pioneers" crossing the western plains in covered wagons in the 1850s. The inland rivers—not the wagon ruts crossing from Missouri to Oregon—were America's first western frontier.

The rivers also carried a much larger migration. During the first five decades of the 19th century, more than three million migrants ventured down the Ohio and Mississippi river valleys to the swelling southwestern frontier. In the 1840s and 1850s, a comparative trickle—fewer than 500,000 travelers—crossed the plains west of the Missouri River by overland routes, primarily the Oregon and California trails. Still, the dusty journey via covered wagon remains the dominant image of America's westward spread, a classic instance of popular myth prevailing over fact.

Compared to its trading rivals in Europe and the West Indies, America in the early 19th century was what we would call today a developing country, and the economic impact of the internal river trade was staggering. Economic historian Isaac Lippincott compiled statistics that showed that the commercial receipts for river cargo in New Orleans totaled $22 million in 1830, or about $660 million in today's dollars. By 1840, the New Orleans river trade—swelled by the enormous growth in cotton exports—had

In Drifting Downriver, *artist David Wright captures the combined economic drive and romance of piloting a flatboat—in this case, past the bluffs of the Cumberland River in Tennessee—a seasonal passage that defined three generations of Americans in the 19th century.*

increased to almost $50 million. By the Civil War, the cargo moving south through New Orleans was valued at $200 million, or $6 billion today. Lippincott estimates that, meanwhile, "inland river commerce" hubs like St. Louis, Cincinnati, and Natchez, Mississippi, were also trading cargo valued at $200 million or more by the Civil War. Like the Nile, the Thames, or the Seine before them, the western rivers in America became a floating supply chain that fueled national growth.

This is not just a curious feature of history. In 2019, according to the

U.S. Army Corps of Engineers, which controls twelve thousand miles of inland waterways through its extensive lock and dam system, waterborne vessels carried $80 billion of America's cargo. States like West Virginia and Kentucky still rely on the Ohio and Mississippi for anywhere from $2 billion to $8 billion of their annual commerce. A typical fifteen-barge tow on the western rivers carries as much freight as 1,050 semitrucks. If river barges were eliminated, travel on American highways would become an unimaginable nightmare. The flatboat and its direct successor, today's metal river barge, link 240 years of American history.

The opening of America's vast inland water network went beyond the economic leap that developed a young nation into a global export giant. The river journey down the Ohio to the Mississippi became a shared American romance, a water route that joined the spare, Anglo-Presbyterian frontier to the north with the exotic beauty and opulent wealth of the Creole plantations to the south, opening vast new horizons for the average American. "For farmers in the Ohio valley, flatboat voyages were both a normal and recurrent aspect of economic life," writes historian Richard Slotkin, "and an extraordinary adventure that carried them beyond the bounds of provincial culture." Over time, dozens of roofed leviathans of one hundred feet or more, carrying a hundred tons of cargo each, drifted to New Orleans every year. The flatboat trade annually employed more than twenty thousand "river men" in what became one of America's largest industries. The drifting colonies of young men acquired maritime skills, a language, a music, and attitudes about labor and trade that were carried back north to their disparate farming villages during the most formative period of America. The flotilla of boats drifting every year from Pittsburgh to New Orleans created a peculiar but potent nation within a nation. Wanderlust, and the alacrity with which Americans solved economic problems through adventure, became distinct national traits. Prior to the Louisiana Purchase in 1803, the Mississippi acted as America's western border, preventing expansion into the colonial empires of Spain and France. Over the next forty years, the vast lands beyond the Mississippi were transformed into a thoroughly American space. More than any other factor, flatboat traffic down the Ohio and the Mississippi drove this leap west.

The pattern of life that quickly absorbed four generations of Americans—farming and clearing land all summer, then riding the rivers to markets in the late winter or spring—supported a demographic shift that would determine

American history. At the end of the American Revolution, only 3 percent of Americans, about 130,000 settlers and African American slaves, lived west of the Appalachians. By 1820, abetted by the Louisiana Purchase and the dredging of rivers and the excavation of canals to create the inland water-way system, the Ohio and Mississippi valleys supported more than 2 million Americans, nearly 20 percent of the national population. Thirty percent of the American population would live west of the Appalachians by 1830.

The westerner became the new American prototype and transience became a common lifestyle. Within two or three years of settlement and the clearing of the rich alluvial bottomlands of the Midwest, the hearty pio-neer farmers found that crop yields usually exceeded what they required for subsistence. But America would have been stalled, its farmers trapped by a primitive barter economy, without a trade route south. Now an extraordinary sweep of the North American continent along the vast Mississippi drain-age—from Canada to the Gulf of Mexico—became linked by an intricate network of ports and transshipment wharves that developed into a sophisti-cated market system. River towns boomed and factories to supply the water traffic—barrel makers, ropewalks, foundries to make steam engines, stoves, and ship's bells—mushroomed wherever there was good water access. Hull design, dredging, and navigation and the complexities of an import-export economy became American specialties, rivaling the mercantile prowess of Europe. The pathway for further western movement became clear.

Flatboats were the ideal conveyance for a developing country with boundless energy but little cash. A generation of young frontiersmen who could already build almost anything—a wagon, a log cabin, an irrigation sluice—with just an axe and a manual drill didn't need a lot of capital or specialized training to build a flatboat. With timber from the nearest for-est, often already harvested to clear fields, the simple half-round gunwales and deck planking for a vessel could be milled in just a few days. The long, shedlike structures above the decks to keep the cargo dry were no more complicated to build than a frontier pole barn. The flow of the rivers—inexhaustible and cheap—provided the energy to carry millions of tons of cargo downstream.

The most zealous advocate for cheap water transport was Zadok Cramer, a lapsed New Jersey Quaker and devotee of Benjamin Franklin who moved to Pittsburgh in 1800. Cramer quickly established himself as a bookbinder, printer, and publisher of meticulously researched almanacs. He became famous among the river travelers for his series of navigation books and gazetteers on the Ohio and the Mississippi, called *The Navigator*. Cramer updated his river gazetteer almost yearly and sold hardback copies for $1 at his bookstore in Pittsburgh and at boatyards along the Monongahela. *The Navigator* became the indispensable Baedeker for the thousands of new flatboaters hurrying over the Alleghenies, and Cramer became a kind of Adam Smith for the new inland rivers economy that was pushing the American center of gravity southwest.

In colonial times, and continuing well into the 19th century, the West Indian trade was one of the most lucrative exchanges in the Americas, as the Eastern Seaboard exported tons of timber, salt pork, flour, and cheese in return for Caribbean molasses, rum, and sugar. In his 1814 edition, Cramer quoted studies that showed the sudden and surprising advantages of river transport over ocean shipping. "Flour, corn, beef, ship plank, and other useful articles, can be sent down the stream to west Florida [parts of Louisiana, including New Orleans, Mississippi, Alabama, and the Florida panhandle], and from thence to the West-India islands, much cheaper and in better order, than from New York or Philadelphia to those islands." According to *The Navigator*, it was "at least 50 percent cheaper" to send heavy bulk cargo—baled tobacco or forged iron—down the Ohio to the Mississippi than it was to carry the same products just sixty miles across the traditional overland route, the muddy wagon roads of Pennsylvania. During the "freshets" of rain in the spring and late fall, immense, one-hundred-ton loads of pork, whiskey, and cordwood were propelled downstream at five or seven miles per hour. Boats bound for New Orleans could often make one hundred miles per day—four times the daily mileage of a team of draft horses. Freight delivered as quickly and inexpensively as this was just what the nascent economy of the new republic needed.

Even the original investment in construction timber could be recouped at a profit. At the end of their journey, most of the flatboats were broken apart and sold as the salvage beams, sidewalk planks, and furniture stock that built the boomtowns along the water route. Cincinnati's first schoolhouse, the first residence in Maysville, Kentucky, and countless Creole cottages in some of New Orleans's most charming neighborhoods were built with "bargeboards" from dismantled flatboats.

The boats were called "broadhorns" because the long side sweeps and steering rudders operated off the roofs above decks, outfitted with carved paddles at the bottom to push the water, resembled giant horns from a distance. Flatbottoms no more than 14 feet at the beam were called "Ohio" or "Kentucky" boats, indicating the operator's plan to ship along only the narrow channels of a single river. The "Natchez" or "New Orleans" boats, 20 or 25 feet across and immensely long, were designed to carry large cargoes to the Sugar Coast plantations of Louisiana or all the way to the Gulf of Mexico. The simple crew shanties of the 18th-century boats were eventually expanded into elaborate, dormitory-style structures with bunk beds, cookstoves, and a wide living area with movable tavern furniture for meals and nighttime fiddling parties. The open-air decks on the bow and stern allowed boats to tie up together at night while the rivermen shared meals, news, and information about navigation hazards ahead. Often, four or five large flatboats were lashed together as a single, 500,000-pound fortress drifting in the channel, floating villages joined by elaborate catwalks and sleeping tents. Massive canvas sails were added and mounted from bow masts, catboat style, to give the barges headway around the bends and capture following winds on brisker days. These sails were called "latines," or "lateens," because they were modeled after the forward-mounted, triangular sails of the Roman galleys and the dhows of ancient Arabia. Their color was "tannin," a yellowish-burgundy hue that emerged after the cotton and canvas sails were hardened and preserved in vats of tree bark (tannins), and then mixed with oxblood and linseed oil.

"The river men are inventive sorts who reject the slavery of being obliged to build in any received form," one eastern traveler on the Mississippi wrote in 1820. "You can scarcely imagine an abstract form in which a boat can be built, that in some part of the Ohio or Mississippi you will not see, actually in motion."

At night the lanterns of the joined boats cast spooky beams of light across the water and the caterwauling of the partying crews echoed for miles around the oxbows. By day, from the wharves at Vincennes, or the cliffs at Vicksburg, the pinkish tannin sails luffed around the bends above the tree line, mystically scudding south like pyramids suspended in the sky. Thousands of teenage boys, watching the parade of sails from the grassy banks at Marietta or Paducah, caught the fever and soon disappeared downriver. "No young man could count himself among the elite young bucks of the community," one local history from Indiana read, "without having made at least one [flatboat] trip."

The grand pageantry of American life drifted south and west beneath those sails. Every year there were long caravans of "settlers' boats," often called "arks" because of the menagerie of farm animals fenced in on their decks, plying the lower Mississippi and the tributaries of the Ohio to search for new lands. Many families lived on their flatboats for a year or more until they could stake a claim for property, and then disassembled their craft to build their first cabin in the wilderness. Another common variant was "store boats," or "peddlers' boats," which tied up at the docks of small towns and plantations, their captains selling their cargo for cash or trading for goods that could be marked up for resale farther south. There were print boats for printers, "fire boats" loaded with charcoal and cordwood to sell along the way, floating brothels, for some reason called "gun boats," and "smithy boats" for blacksmiths, even "whiskey boats," also called "distillery boats," with taverns and gambling halls mounted on jaunty rafts. Conversely, dozens of "colporteurs," or traveling Bible salesmen and evangelists, plied the rivers in flatboats fitted out with steeples or high wooden crosses to advertise their mission. In 1847, two of these colporteurs, the Reverends Gideon H. Lowe and Malkijah S. Vaughan, ministers from a breakaway Tennessee evangelical group called the Cumberland Presbyterians, made a five-month trip down the Cumberland, Ohio, and Mississippi rivers on a thirty-two-foot flatboat named the *Bethel.* Lowe and Vaughan were scandalized when a group of rowdy rivermen purchased two dozen Bibles and resold them downriver at a profit to buy whiskey. But by the end of their journey the ministers reported that they had visited ninety-four flatboats, seventy-three steamboats, twenty river towns, and preached at seventy-two public meetings, and had either sold or given away 3,400 Bibles.

By the 1830s, the madcap cultural mixing that became America was enhanced by another commercial development. Shipments of Minnesota and Wisconsin logs, lashed together as "great rafts" a half-mile long and 150 feet across, blocked river traffic for hours as they snaked around the giant, curved oxbows. As they waited their turn on the bend, the flatboats swarmed together against the sandbars. A typical afternoon gathering included peddlers' boats, Bible boats, and—most popular—"band" rafts with bagpipers from

Scotland, minstrel shows, and traveling Irish harp-and-fiddle troupes. The flatboat crews and settler families restocked their larders from the peddler boats and walked down the bars to join the audiences ringed around the band rafts, forming a kind of flea market–cum–Woodstock along the banks. The roots music of every corner of Europe echoed across the waters, making the Ohio and the Mississippi the arteries that created America's legendary multicultural sound. In his 1826 bestselling travelogue about his many trips west, *Recollections of the Last Ten Years, Passed in Occasional Residences and Journeyings in the Valley of the Mississippi,* the traveling minister and diarist Timothy Flint wrote: "Almost every boat, while it lies in the harbor has one or more fiddles scraping continually aboard, to which you often see the boatmen dancing." The popular tunes included "Wind on the Wabash," "Wiggle-Ass Jig," and "Where Is My Pants At?" In his *Old Man River,* Paul Schneider writes that a violin medley "that started out as a Scotch-Irish reel from Ulster might be passed on along the river to a German fiddler from Mannheim, or a Bohemian Jew, or even a wayward Brahmin from Boston." The inland river country, once so barren and uninhabited, had become quintessentially American—slapdash, colorful, ethnically mixed.

For the farm boys of Ohio and Illinois, reaching New Orleans—sultry, crowded with foreigners, and lined with the ornate mansions of the slave-owning South—was a cultural awakening. Downtown slave auctions and the huge bales of cotton lining the wharves symbolized the tragic complexities of a slave-holding South joined by the Mississippi into economic union with the slave-loathing North. The flatboat wharves along the great bend in the Mississippi beside the French Quarter became a riotous open market with rivermen screaming out prices for barrels of corn whiskey, sides of dried beef and hams, and the bang of auctioneers' gavels echoing through the masts as commercial brokers bid for that day's shipment of coal, flour, and cordwood.

The Mississippi's greatest contribution to the American mindset was to define us as a migratory people, radically departed from our European antecedents. In the Old World, stasis, hereditary property rights, and social caste defined prosperity and happiness for the aristocracy and the merchant class, while virtually denying wealth for the common man. Crewing a flatboat on the Ohio and the Mississippi abruptly reversed that, becoming a template occupation for the new western man. At the edge of civilization in North America, at the wharves and bursting river towns of the new territories, social caste and standing belonged to the uprooted, the wayfarers, the self-made men and boys struggling with their oars to land a broadhorn against the current. Ohio or Indiana farm boys, after a river trip or two, became sophisticated travelers, educating themselves for careers as river captains, traders, and merchants. In 1818, Morris Birkbeck, an English writer and agronomist who migrated to America to become an Illinois frontiersman, observed in his *Notes on a Journey in America*, "The condition of the people of America is so different from aught that we in Europe have an opportunity of observing. They are great travelers and in general better acquainted with the vast expanse of country, spreading over eighteen states, than the English with their little island." Birkbeck's traveling companion, Henry Fearon, thought that "the American has always something better in his eye, further west. He therefore lives and dies on hope, a mere gypsy."

They were gypsies, however, with a purpose, a mass economic movement that set a country on its way. The America of contemporary popular myth was built by the western wagon trails, the railroads, and the skyscrapers of Chicago and New York. But in its first decades America was primarily a river culture, built along a vast and rapidly growing universe of inland water. University of Pittsburgh historian Leland D. Baldwin, author of *The Keelboat Age on Western Waters*, may have said it best. "Perhaps it is not too much to say, that out of the womb of the ark was born the nation."

The urge to build a flatboat and follow Jacob Yoder's route from Pittsburgh to New Orleans didn't overwhelm me right away. At first it simply annoyed me that I knew almost nothing about so formative an era in our history, and the yearning to learn more about flatboats wouldn't go away. There was even an intellectual principle involved. I've found over the years that the history that I've either neglected or that has been deliberately hidden from me leads to far more interesting places than the accepted wisdom handed down by textbooks. Like most Americans, probably because of the impact of the Hollywood Western, I thought of "frontier America" as the period that began in the 1850s as pioneers, gunslingers, and cattle barons pushed into the plains country beyond the Missouri River. For me, as for so many Americans, that era and its character types became accepted as a cultural motif.

Devouring all that I could about America's initial western leap down the Ohio and Mississippi was just the first part of the journey. As I pored over 19th-century maps and dipped into seminal works like Michael Allen's *Western Rivermen, 1763–1861*, or Marquis Childs's *Mighty Mississippi*, I began to realize with increasing intensity that the old frontier lands of the Ohio and Mississippi River valleys were calling me personally. I wasn't just curious about what had become of the country that defined America's first century of growth. My lifelong thirst for adventure and learning had mostly been land-borne. Now I would explore the mysteries of nationhood along this most captivating water space, bobbing like a cork in the currents, sharing the romance of my forebears.

I first stumbled upon the importance of the flatboating years while I was researching a book on the later generation of Americans who joined America's ceaseless push west, the Oregon Trail pioneers of the 1850s. I was surprised to discover that fording skills were decisive for these "overland" travelers. When moving their cumbersome covered wagons across the wide rivers of the far West, the ability to fashion crude log rafts out of driftwood and felled trees often meant the difference between failure and success for the thousands of settlers who crossed Nebraska and Wyoming every summer. Flat-bottomed ferries, pontoon bridges, and floatable wagons shaped like hulls became indispensable fixtures on the trail crossings of the Platte, the Sweetwater, and the Green. As many as a third of the covered wagons that finally reached the Columbia River in Oregon were so completely battered by the two-thousand-mile journey over the plains and the Rocky Mountains that the pioneers had no choice but to rip their decrepit vehicles apart, convert the lumber to rafts or shallow-draft boats, and then complete their continental journey by floating the rest of the way to the Pacific coast. The sturdy Midwestern farmers and small-town shopkeepers who made up the bulk of the trail pioneers had inherited their boatbuilding skills from their fathers or their grandfathers during the flatboating era, demonstrating the plucky, hand-me-down ingenuity that built a country. For the average Midwestern farm boy in the 1820s, learning the rudiments of building a flatboat was no more challenging than framing a barn.

I loved how this understanding of frontier carpentry skills changed my conception of history. Traditional historians, when describing the creation of America, love to dwell on the high-sounding ideals of the Declaration of Independence and the Bill of Rights—protections against big government, the promotion of individualism, freedom of speech and religion—but those were principles far removed from the hardscrabble, edgy lives of most 19th-century Americans. They were citizen-farmers, and they built America with logs, laboriously harvested by axe and two-man crosscut saws. First the logs were flatboats descending the Ohio, then they were converted into crude shacks on the frontier. If there was flatboat lumber after that, they used it to build furniture and simple barns. The steamboat boom that revolutionized American travel and cargo transportation in the 1830s and 1840s was the next logical step, and steamboats relied on flatboat hulls for their design. Federalism and the Missouri Compromise are, of course, useful things to understand. But now I felt refreshingly liberated from the conventions of thinking about our past, the composite of high theory and "great man" narratives that we call history. Logs were the national DNA. America was built by adventuresome people from trees.

The flatboat era was also profoundly tragic. Pioneering the inland rivers also joined white Americans in signature, collective cruelty—the extermination of the Native American tribes, and the metastasizing of slavery into an even more brutal system as the cotton economy was pushed south. America's expansion southwest into the inland river country beyond the Appalachians opened up vast acreages of tillable land, which most white settlers believed had to be cleared of the tribes so that the country's agricultural progress could continue. No one pursued the policy of Native American cleansing longer and more zealously than Andrew Jackson, whose presidency began with the Indian Removal Act of 1830, during which more than 125,000 members of the Cherokee, Choctaw, and several other tribes were force-marched across the Mississippi into the arid barrens of eastern Oklahoma. At least four thousand Cherokees alone died during their 1,200-mile trek west, one of the darkest chapters of American history now known as the Trail of Tears. Simultaneously, in another brutal chapter still unknown to most Americans, almost a million African American slaves were marched by foot one thousand miles over the Appalachians from the depleted tobacco plantations of Maryland and Virginia to the next source of American wealth, the sweltering cotton and sugarcane fields of Arkansas, Mississippi, and Louisiana. The slaves were marched south in "coffle lines" that connected them to each other by chains attached to a circular steel restraint locked around the slave's neck. After slavery's

expansion south, brutal quota systems for harvesting crops were introduced, and deaths by beatings, heatstroke, and disease were pandemic.
The common term "sold down the river," and the misfortunes involved in
the expansion of slavery to the Mississippi valley, is another legacy of the
flatboat era.

The rivermen never completely disappeared. The most alluring group
of river people who kept the romance alive were the "shantyboaters" of the
late 19th century and post–World War I era. After the devastating Panic
of 1893, thousands of abruptly unemployed and now homeless industrial
workers, in river towns from Pittsburgh to New Orleans, found that they
could cobble together a livable house on top of an abandoned commercial
barge down on the waterfront, or build a shantyboat from scratch from the
broad selection of cast-off timbers and driftwood lining virtually every mile
of riverbank. Each year, hundreds of shantyboat families simply cast off
from Memphis or Cincinnati and spent the warm months drifting downriver, camping on remote islands, planting gardens or harvesting wild berries. In a land that prized security and forethought, the shantyboat families
were the quintessential Americans living on the fringe. During the Great
Depression of the 1930s, the Works Progress Administration estimated
that as many as fifty thousand Americans lived on shantyboats.

The most iconic of the river wanderers were Harlan and Anna Hubbard, an artist-writer couple who in 1944 built a shantyboat on the banks of
the Ohio in Kentucky and then spent seven years drifting to New Orleans,
living off the land along the banks, fishing for supper, dawdling at attractive river towns like Paducah, Kentucky, or Helena, Arkansas, to catch up
with their mail and send drawings and paintings to art shows back east.
I was inspired when I discovered Harlan Hubbard's memoir about that
trip, *Shantyboat: A River Way of Life*, a mostly forgotten gem of American
nonfiction comparable to Horace Kephart's *Our Southern Highlanders*.
Hubbard's prose is simple but lambent. Landing one evening on the Ohio
River opposite Cincinnati, he wrote: "We landed at the broad sandbar on
the Kentucky side, relaxed, and ate our dinner of catfish which had been
broiling on the fireplace. . . . Strange train whistles were heard, and constel-
lations of city lights shone from the opposite hill." Hubbard faced the same
skepticism about taking on the rivers that I would encounter seventy years
later—one riverman warned him before he left that his shantyboat would

Harlan and Anna Hubbard made a lyrical, seven-year journey down the Ohio and the Mississippi in the 1940s. Hubbard's Shantyboat: A River Way of Life *served as both a practical guide and my inspiration seventy years later.*

be caught in the whirlpools of the Mississippi, spun in circles, and then "sucked beneath the surface never to reappear."

But Hubbard and his wife safely and delightfully made it to New Orleans, creating with a dreamy river trip not only an unusual marriage but a charming story about the diverse possibilities of American life. Reading Harlan Hubbard wasn't just a poetic invitation to cast off and then point myself downriver past the bluffs, sailing for the unknown. Hubbard's "river way of life" was a call for personal independence, an unshackling from the comforting but essentially delusional "conveniences" of modern life.

"I merely wanted to try living by my own hands, independent as far as possible," Hubbard wrote in *Shantyboat*. "I wanted to bring in my own fuel and smell its sweet smoke as it burned on the hearth I had made. I wanted to grow my own food, catch it in the river, or forage after it. In short, I wanted to do as much as I could for myself."

I was startled by my research and realized that I had reached an ironic moment in life. I have always been studious to the point of obsession about America's past, but I had never heard of flatboats, the "Great Migration" down the rivers, store boats, or coffle lines. Before the American Revolution, America's cargo system was predominantly riverine and not overland, and this would have been useful to know as I contemplated my country's origins. But I knew that lacking this foundational knowledge was not unusual. Innocence about our country's true beginnings is woven into the American character. Now it was time to get south and see the inland river country as intimately as I could, to catch up with the truth.

Venturing southwest from Pittsburgh on my own homemade barge fashioned from logs made little practical sense, and could even be dangerous. The modern Ohio and Mississippi rivers are jointly managed by the U.S. Coast Guard and the Army Corps of Engineers exclusively for the benefit of commercial barge traffic and, except for a few weekend recreational areas around major cities like Cincinnati or Louisville, today's private pleasure craft rarely travel more than a few miles from their marinas. I would be sharing the world's busiest commercial waterway, often in a channel just a quarter mile across, with hundreds of six-thousand-horsepower tugboats pushing "strings" of twenty-five or more barges stretching up to 1,500 feet, with an additional six hundred feet of "blind space" caused by the bows of the forward barges. Even if they could see me, the lumbering tugs and their barge strings couldn't possibly steer out of my way. Every day, often at a bend in the river that would prevent me from seeing them until the last moment, I would have to make way for twenty or more of these behemoth barge tows. Once I reached the mouth of the Ohio at Cairo, Illinois, I would face a Mississippi dramatically altered from the 19th-century flatboat days. To improve the river for commercial traffic, the river has been endlessly dredged, and its banks lined with rock "wing dams" and cement revetments that redirect its flow into a deeper, faster channel. I couldn't possibly brave swift currents like that without a motor to help me steer around the massive barge traffic. But there would be three-hundred-mile stretches along the lower Mississippi where I wouldn't find marinas or fuel, and access to nearby towns would be blocked by fifty-foot levees tangled with stabilization cables and "riprap" boulders.

The capriciousness of the river, however, was timeless, and seemed to join me to the fellowship of rivermen that reached back more than two centuries. In 1882, when he was forty-seven, Mark Twain took a month-long tour of the entire river to compile notes for his nonfiction classic *Life on the Mississippi*, which included extensive sketches of his days as a young apprentice steamboat captain in the 1850s. Whole islands that he had once relied upon while navigating at night had disappeared. Cut-throughs made during the steamboat boom in the 1850s and then the Civil War had shortened the river he once knew by seventy miles. "The river is now so thoroughly changed that I can't bring it back to mind even when the changes have been pointed out to me," Twain wrote in his journal. "It is like a man pointing out to me a place in the sky where a cloud has been."

My family and many of my friends enjoyed pointing out that I was comically unprepared for a challenge like this. As a boy, I had crewed on sailboat races on Cape Cod, and later taken several canoe trips in Pennsylvania and the Adirondacks, and kayaked in New Hampshire and Maine, but this merely qualified me as an amateur on the water. Now I was proposing to myself that my first trip as a boat captain would be to negotiate two thousand miles of some of America's most notoriously dangerous waters. Two of my brothers, Coast Guard veterans, laughed hysterically when

I told them about my plans. "Nah, nah, nah, Rink," said my brother Bryan. "You'll sink the boat in the first storm. You're going to die." My brother Nick considers me clinically inept when it comes to practical knowledge of things like pickup trucks and boats. Nick had a lot of experience tying up Coast Guard icebreakers and rescue launches in strong currents. He was convinced that I wouldn't know how to lash to a tree or nearby wharf in strong winds or during a sudden thunderstorm. "Rinker, you don't know knots, and you won't be able to tie up in time," Nick said. "You're going to die." That quickly became the dirge, the theme song written in advance, for my trip. I was going to die.

In the 1820s and 1830s, the raucous, turbulent lives of the Ohio and Mississippi rivermen were celebrated with the popular moniker "alligator horse." The term, reprised in wildly popular plays, paintings, and humorists' newspaper sketches, described the hybrid melding of frontier woodsmen, Indian fighters, and Continental army deserters who took to the water from Ohio and Kentucky to expand the empire southward. The boatmen were also called "Kaintucks," a derisive term referring to their origins in desolate Kentucky and Tennessee and their vulgar, backwoods dress and speech. This amphibious new man became a folk hero of the early 19th century. The alligator-horse rivermen were heavy drinkers, lawless, and courageous, pitching their crude flat-bottoms with abandon over falls and chains of rocks. The most popular of them was Mike Fink, a forester and scout from western Pennsylvania who worked the Ohio and Mississippi as a brawling, self-promoting keelboat captain and degenerate, though his image was largely created out of myth and little about his actual life was known. To early 19th-century Americans, the appeal of outlaw heroes like Fink was similar to later generations' fascination with infamous figures like George Armstrong Custer, Bonnie and Clyde, Al Capone, and John Gotti. I was impressed by how Americans have worshipped these dubious character types, as if we are desperate to escape our own banal, middle-class lives. I was reminded of this when I came across this passage in Michael Allen's *Western Rivermen*.

Jacksonian Americans were fascinated by the western boatmen. The Ohio and Mississippi flatboatmen, keelboatmen, and lumber raftsmen enjoyed a status and mystique in pre–Civil War America very comparable to that possessed today by truck drivers, loggers, railroadmen, and rodeo cowboys. They became folk heroes to frontier squatters and Eastern shopkeepers alike. . . . Whether they were poling their keels against the rushing current of the Mississippi, fighting Indians and river pirates, playing outrageous practical jokes on one another, or drinking, gambling, and fighting in Natchez and New Orleans beer sties, the western boatmen grew larger than life in popular literature.

One of my favorite records of the flatboat years is a refreshingly down-to-earth journal written in 1834 by Asbury Cloud Jaquess, twenty-two, a Hoosier farm boy whose family worked land along the Wabash River drainage in Posey County, Indiana, just above the tributary's confluence with the Ohio. I was attracted to the Jaquess account, "The Journals of the *Davy Crockett*," because I have always loved the comely, winding Wabash and how its vast, moist bottomlands below Terre Haute and Vincennes spill west into southern Illinois. Jaquess's pithy, detailed travelogue evinced the character of the era and how, as Timothy Flint wrote in 1828, the young flatboatmen "experienced that expansion of mind which cannot fail to be produced by traversing long distances of country, and viewing different forms of nature and society." Jaquess was an everyman of America's riverine expansion.

At the end of the harvest season that year, Jaquess and his relatives gathered a cornucopia from about eight family farms along the Little Wabash River. This included 1,700 bushels of corn, fourteen thousand pounds of barreled pork and beef, six live steers, fifteen bushels of oats, forty kegs of lard, and four hundred chickens and turkeys, all of which was loaded onto an eighty-foot flatboat that they built themselves and named after their frontier hero, Davy Crockett. Four other family members served as crew, and young Asbury—bookish, ambitious, and curious about the world beyond southern Indiana—was appointed "Clerk & Journalist of the voyage." The four-thousand-word "Journals of the *Davy Crockett*" unfolds with the wonder and perils of a young provincial seeing the world for the first time. The journals are also a saga about the violence of American life.

The *Davy Crockett*'s crew dodged thunderstorms, immense tree snags, heavy rain, fog, and high-water rapids, barely avoiding collisions with the foundered hulls of steamboats. With young Jaquess supervising most of the transactions, the *Davy Crockett* crew sold corn in Memphis, pork and chickens at plantations in Arkansas and Mississippi, and had only 50 barrels left to sell by the time they reached New Orleans. They lashed with other flatboats sailed by friends from Indiana and "fared sumptuously" on "potatoes, fowls & chicken broth." Jaquess worried, however, about the crewman of one of the boats that the *Davy Crockett* lashed to, a man named Mike, who began to serve as the expedition's cook. Mike was imperiling their journey by stealing chickens and turkeys from other boats, or from houses onshore, to make supper for the crews. A week later, Mike was murdered in retaliation for his chicken stealing, and his enemies among the other flatboatmen rejoiced about his demise by feasting "and drinking toasts merily."

At Natchez, Mississippi, a mini New Orleans legendary for its gambling halls and brothels, Jaquess witnessed the hanging of an African American accused of stealing. He sold a canoe to a drunken Irishman who, when the wind picked up that night, was blown away and drowned. In many other ways the trip became a journey of self-identification, and Jaquess was thrilled by his education in the commodities markets. In New Orleans, with some of the proceeds from his pork and corn sales, Jaquess went on a book-buying binge, acquiring titles that were not available near his rural home 1,500 miles upriver—a biography of Davy Crockett, an anthology of the poems of Alexander Pope, and a life of the Scottish nationalist and freedom fighter William Wallace.

Jaquess was gone for just three months. But his journal pulses with the fullness of newfound knowledge—the joys of learning a trade and discovering new country, a thirst for more adventure, and the heartbreak of adversity and injustice. That was the education that the flatboat era delivered to the first generation of young Americans.

"Before closing this narrative," Jaquess wrote in the last paragraph of his journal, "I will make a few remarks in refferance to boating. This business has much novelty and many charms, hardships and privations connected with it. Men thrown together from all parts of the United States and in deed from the whole world with ther various manners and habits unrestrained by the presence of female influence exhibits a scene of extraordinary novelty and is probaly [*sic*] one of the best places for a man to acquire a knowledge of *human nature."*

By the time I read these lines, I had already decided to include two women among my crew. They would prove to be the most able mates of the journey. But we can forgive Jaquess for his 19th-century gender bias because he was in so many other ways prescient. "The Journals of the *Davy Crockett"* were an everyman's romance, a summons to turn into the rippling channel and point downriver past the bluffs, sailing for the unknown of my country. As I moved south to the Cumberland River in Tennessee to build my boat, I was looking forward to my year of being an alligator-horse. There would be little certainty about my life, no permanent abode or address. But I would shortly and most indelibly learn that the flatboat was indeed an ideal school for acquiring a knowledge of human nature.

2

A MILESTONE IN THE LIFE of my family gave me plenty of time to study flatboats. One October afternoon about six months before I planned to leave for the South, my sister Bridget called from Maine with an unexpected request. My mother, then eighty-nine, had decided to sell the old clapboard house she had lovingly restored along the coast of Maine and move to a smaller, village apartment about fifteen miles away. She was essentially quite healthy but had suffered one mild stroke and the occasional falls typical for her age, and her ambition now was to remain independent as long as possible, to avoid, as she put it, "the purgatory of assisted living." After a long struggle with her children, she had finally given up driving. My family in Maine needed one more sibling nearby to share the chores of taking her shopping, and chauffeuring her back and forth to her exercise classes, doctors' visits, and book clubs.

I had spent the last decade frequently driving from my home in Connecticut to Maine, for long weekends or even weeklong stays, finishing the light carpentry, painting, and gardening chores on my mother's to-do list. I loved the companionship with her and the home-away-from-home romance of knowing every hardware store shelf in mid-coast Maine. I wanted to complete this life's work and welcomed the opportunity to put off my Mississippi trip and move to Maine.

With Bridget's help, I found a quaint, simple log cabin to rent on the old summer camp of a chocolate candy tycoon, scenically perched on the high south banks of the Damariscotta River. The Damariscotta, which the Lincoln County old-timers call "the Scotty," is a lovely stretch of fast tidal water with a unique set of reversing falls at the village itself. The river runs sixteen miles east to the Atlantic along the Boothbay peninsula, its high banks lined with pine forests and craggy cliffs. My cabin was only a five-minute drive from my mother's new place in town. Closing down my house in Connecticut, I loaded the few things I needed into my pickup and enjoyed the familiar ride up through the lake country of New Hampshire, settling into the cabin late one afternoon just before Thanksgiving. As I carried my snowshoes and chain saws down the steep stone steps to the cabin, a sea breeze was whispering through fallen leaves and the setting sun lit the river below into a luminous needle pointing east.

Maine proved ideal for researching flatboats. In the mornings I reported to my mother's apartment to take her food shopping or watch her lift weights at the senior center, and then we'd retire to S. Fernald's Country Store and Deli at the bridge over the Scotty for her favorite meal of red flannel hash or vegetarian chili. I joined a volunteer group down on the Boothbay peninsula, the Woodchucks, that split and delivered firewood for needy families. By night, I immersed myself in the growing pile of books and PhD theses on the flatboat era that arrived by mail every few days. I stored my research materials in cardboard boxes labeled by subject matter—"Flatboat Construction," "River Journeys," "Natchez Trace"—on top of a shipping pallet I had liberated from a dumpster behind the Tractor Supply store in Brunswick. The snows that winter were dreamy and deep, and the wispy spirals blowing up from the drifts whistled and pinged against the windows and obscured my view outdoors. Immersed in my research, I was wonderfully shrouded from the world by the winter storms, isolation that seemed to enhance the romance of the distant age of rivers and boats.

The flatboat era, sandwiched between the end of the American Revolution in 1783 and the beginning of the Civil War in 1861, overlapped with the overland years of covered wagons crossing the plains, which began in the mid-1840s. This period is commonly identified by economic historians as the "first" American industrial revolution. The availability of abundant, rich croplands west of the Appalachians and the young country's penchant for mechanical innovation combusted powerfully to create an ideal model for development. The invention of the automated flour mill in Delaware, the development of the water and then steam-powered spinning jennies and looms of New England, and the introduction of the cotton gin in the South flooded world markets with cheap American commodities and textiles that gradually overwhelmed the "factories of the world" in England and France, in much the same way that the clothing and electronics of China and its low-wage Asian neighbors have saturated the aisles of Walmart today. Swelled by immigration, especially after the end of the Napoleonic Wars in Europe in 1815 and the Irish potato famine in the 1840s, the U.S. population would boom eightfold, from 4 million after the Revolution to 32 million by 1861. America's apparently boundless growth, however, was stalled by a glaring weakness that would astonish foreign visitors for the next century.

The roads were abysmal. In the twenty years after the Revolution, the destitute farmers and Continental army veterans cascading west across Pennsylvania, western Maryland, and Virginia with packtrains of horses and unwieldy Conestoga wagons had no choice but to follow the remnants of narrow, ancient Indian traces or the swampy, overgrown tracks of military routes, like the Braddock and Forbes Roads, named for the British generals whose men cut the paths forty years earlier during the French and Indian War. Leaving settlement behind at the Alleghenies or the Cumberlands, the Appalachian ridges, considered so formidable that 18th-century maps labeled them "The Great Barrier," travelers faced a thicket of hardwood trees and briars that extended nearly a thousand miles in every direction. The uphill climbs over shelves of rock were murderous for wheels and axles. The descents simply lowered the wagons onto streambeds that had occasionally been improved with "corduroys" of logs, which, after a year or two, were pounded by the traffic and the weather into a gumbo of bark, mud, and gravel. These grim sloughs were congested with a maze of cursing teamsters, rearing horses, and bulky Conestoga wagons submerged to their wheel hubs. One of the most important occupations on the emigrant roads was the job of the bugler, also frequently called the "messenger," who ran forward over the hills to sound his horn, or to negotiate with the wagon trains ahead, to clear the road for oncoming traffic.

The most common adjective that early 19th-century travelers used to describe the Allegheny ridges was "interminable." Timothy Flint, the Congregationalist minister from Massachusetts who made a legendary trip down the Ohio and Mississippi in 1815, described the tortuous ridges of the Alleghenies as "a barrier to return almost as impassable as the grave." Flint describes passing dozens of wagons every day mired on the shoulders of what was advisedly called the Pittsburgh Road. "Many of them had broken axles and wheels, and in more than one place . . . teams had plunged down the precipice and had perished." Seymour Dunbar, in his monumental *A History of Travel in America*, describes the settlers from Virginia crossing the Cumberlands into Kentucky and Tennessee in the 1790s, along the equally poor Watauga and Wilderness Roads, as moving "like an army of ants."

The chronically impassable American roads would have a critical impact on the eve of the 19th century, America's golden age, when patterns of development were dramatically shifting. In colonial America, the prevailing settlement routes in the interior portions of the Atlantic Seaboard had moved primarily on a north and south axis—from New York, up the Hudson; from Massachusetts, north to New Hampshire and Maine; from Connecticut, north to Vermont; from Pennsylvania, south through the Shenandoah along the Great Wagon Road to southern Virginia and North Carolina. But the French and Indian War in the 1760s had introduced Americans to the rich possibilities of the Ohio and Mississippi valleys. A quarter century later, the success of the Revolution liberated Americans from the patronizing and politically inept British crown, and by 1790 the compass had shifted in a perpendicular direction. The "Great Migration West" over the Appalachians had begun.

In his epic *The Transportation Revolution, 1815–1860*, Amherst professor George Rogers Taylor explains that, even as late as 1815, "heavy wagons drawn along common roads or turnpikes by four-and-six-horse teams provided the only means of moving bulk goods over appreciable distances by land. It is hard to realize how prohibitively expensive was such transportation." Taylor quotes from an 1816 report on transportation compiled by the U.S. Senate. "A ton of goods could be brought 3,000 miles from Europe for about $9, but for that same sum it could be moved only 30 miles overland in this country."

That was the conundrum of America as its population and the commerce it generated shifted west. By the early 19th century, the first generation of trans-Appalachian pioneers were consistently growing agricultural surpluses, just as they had back in Pennsylvania and Virginia. But the bumpy wagon roads they had followed west were not suitable for shipping product back east. "Not one of the farm products" of early Kentucky and Tennessee, writes pioneer historian Thomas D. Clark, "could pay for its transportation costs overland, not even whiskey." This would never do for a sprawling, new America of plentiful forests and rich bottomlands stretching eight hundred miles west over the horizon. The only route out was the Ohio-Mississippi waterway to New Orleans.

The Monongahela and Ohio River valleys are approached from the east across attractive, mounded foothills that drop sharply to narrow, sandy riverbanks. The rivers below trend north and then abruptly southwest through a series of graceful horseshoe bends that disappear around the forested slopes. Most Americans today see the Mon and the Ohio only from the high interstate overpasses near Monessen and Pittsburgh, briefly glancing below to the Rust Belt tableau of abandoned steel mills, dusty girder bridges, and tugboats pushing dented barges around the bends. But the dreariness of the region is deceptive because not only is the area economically rebounding, it was once one of the busiest and most auspicious locales in America. Between 1800 and 1840, about two million migrating farmers, traders, and mechanics traversed the Mon escarpments, or the Cumberland Gap between Virginia and Kentucky 450 miles to the southwest, exchanging their cumbersome wagons and packtrains for the jaunty new vessel of western movement, the flatboat.

For the weary travelers, the views along the Monongahela banks were as busy as a Pieter Bruegel canvas—welcome visual relief from the dark, sodden tunnel of trees they were leaving behind. Innumerable flatboats, scows, keelboats under sail, and even oceangoing schooners bobbed in lazy clumps at the wharfs or crawled down the navigable channel. Uphill from the banks, water-powered sawmills wailed and threw up rooster tails of hardwood shavings, and the sound of mallets pounding wooden pegs into hulls climbed up with the breeze. On the distant docks, as barrels of grain and ricks of cordwood were transferred from smaller, local boats to larger boats destined for Natchez or New Orleans, the broad-rim hats of the longshoremen skittered around like bees swarming their nests. As Archer Butler Hulbert described it in *The Ohio River: A Course of Empire*, the Mon Valley had become the gateway to the "vast pageant" of western rivers stretching thousands of miles into the American interior. Now there was a new horn sounding in advance of the republic's push west. "And this was the boatman's horn; where it sounded cabins and clearings appeared, hearthstones glowed, and a new nation arose."

Historic periods rarely begin at a single, defined moment, and the flatboat era's antecedents dated back more than forty years. The reason, mostly, was war, and the American passion for cleansing desirable new lands of their indigenous peoples. During the French and Indian War and the Revolution, and then again during Mad Anthony Wayne's Ohio campaign against the Shawnee and the Miami during the Northwest Indian War in the 1790s, agents dispatched by British and then American army quartermasters had sailed southwest on the Ohio and the Mississippi in flotillas of flat-bottomed barges or keelboats, to trade Monongahela flour and whiskey for imported gunpowder, muskets, and bayonets in New Orleans. The bustling munitions trade between the Americans and the Spanish authorities in Natchez and New Orleans during the Revolution set the tone for the next one hundred years, when wartime needs accelerated transportation improvements on the rivers. During the Revolution, Bernardo de Gálvez, the Spanish governor of Louisiana and Cuba, was openly pro-American and even led successful expeditions against British forts at Baton Rouge, Mobile, and Pensacola. His sponsorship of arms smuggling along the Mississippi is still regarded as a decisive contribution to the American cause, and after independence Gálvez was awarded honorary American citizenship.

The success of the arms supply routes along the Mississippi midwifed the new commercial era, opening the Ohio and Mississippi corridor to a fresh, ambitious cast of players. By the late 1790s, French trading firms, mostly backed by investors from Philadelphia, had taken over the old military routes and established a reliable network of shipping agents along the Monongahela, the Great Falls at Louisville, and at Natchez and New

Orleans. During the same period, according to one historian's estimate, more than nine hundred "settler" flatboats bearing pioneers for the Kentucky frontier cast off every year from western Pennsylvania. These rakish boats, measuring fifty or sixty feet long, were particularly colorful, loaded bow to stern with everything a family, or several families, needed to carve a homestead out of the Kentucky forests. A fenced area in the stern carried horses, cattle, pigs, and goats, and the settlers' boats were often called "arks," after the fabled vessel of Noah in the Book of Genesis. A log cabin for the family to sleep in was built mid-vessel, and planting seed and flintlock powder were stowed in watertight barrels on the deck. Pioneers with less money to spend simply threw up a crude canvas tent on the deck and roped their milk cow and horses to the sides. Children romped in play spaces between the tents. After 1788, when the federal government issued the first land warrants in the West for Revolutionary War veterans, more than five thousand veterans from Virginia alone, including Abraham Lincoln's grandfather, headed over the mountains with their families on these floating farms, plying the Indiana and Kentucky banks of the Ohio and its tributaries in search of likely homesites to clear.

Many of the early pioneers anticipated the later cargo designs by building watertight, warehouse-style structures that stretched almost the full length of the flatboat. Thomas Ashe, an Irish immigrant who in 1806 sailed all of the Ohio and stretches of the Mississippi in a forty-foot "Kentucky boat" that he purchased on the Monongahela, described his ark in his three-volume *Travels in America*. "The whole represents an oblong apartment—both ends perfectly square, and nothing indicates the bow but the small open space in the roof, and holes in the sides, through which the oars work." Ashe did most of his living and navigation from the "quarter deck" roof of the apartment that, by raising his vista point by just ten feet, provided panoramic views of the river and the environs beyond the banks. Ashe's floating abode had to be both durable and well-provisioned. "I had a good chimney built in my boat; four windows made . . . I laid in two coops-full of chickens, other kinds of stores, spirits, coffee, sugar, etc. I need not tell you how completely I set off."

The pioneer flatboats had to carry everything a family might need for a year or two on the frontier—they were floating farms, almost floating villages. "We have seen family boats of this description, filled up for the descent of families to the lower country, with a stove, comfortable apartments, beds, and arrangements for commodious habitancy," wrote the frontier diarist and minister Timothy Flint. "We see in them ladies, servants, cattle, horses, sheep, dogs and poultry, all floating on the same bottom; and on the roof the looms, ploughs, spinning wheels and domestic implements of the family."

The Kentucky arks helped promote the idea of salvageability. Taking the boat apart after the river trip and selling the wooden decks and framing timbers as construction lumber became a welcome means of recovering the largest cost that Indiana or Kentucky settlers incurred on the trip—the price of their boat. In his multivolume collection of pioneer narratives, *Early Western Travels*, Wisconsin historian Reuben Gold Thwaites quoted contemporary accounts of pioneers buying arks large enough for four or five families and their belongings at the Monongahela boatyards for $75. The boat "could be sold for nearly its cost six hundred or eight hundred miles further down [the river]." This became an added financial bonus for the captains of flats carrying cargo instead of settlers, and the commercial flats were often called "one-ways" because they were designed to float just one trip south and then be disassembled. Historians estimate that, depending on the lumber market downriver, selling the salvage wood could contribute from 10 percent to 15 percent of the profits of a flatboat trip.

The rough-hewn settlers' arks served in many other ways as design prototypes for the armadas of cargo barges that would soon follow. The weight-bearing capacity of one of these floating farms was considerable, and here the shape of the simple, boxlike hulls was critical. Just the livestock in the rear pens—typically a team of draft horses, a dairy cow, five or six pigs, and maybe some goats—could weigh more than five thousand pounds. A modest log cabin built on deck, frequently fitted out with a stone hearth and chimney, came to another twelve thousand pounds.

To maintain buoyancy under such loads, the flat bottom spread the displacement of water across a broad span at least fourteen feet across, while pushing only about a foot or eighteen inches of hull below the waterline. The modest draft of flatboats allowed them to safely cross the shallow edges of sandbars and banks, and their hefty mass and flat-bottom surface tended to scrape and bounce over submerged rocks and tree snags without grounding. This was critical, considering that on the Ohio-Mississippi transit, boatmen could encounter sandbars and floating islands of trees several times a day. The standard width of fourteen feet, originally established to allow the flats to pass through the narrow chutes of the Great Falls at Louisville, proved fortuitous. As settlement spread beyond the main rivers, the shallow-draft flats remained afloat in the low-water conditions upriver close to the headwaters, and in narrow tributaries and creeks that twisted far into the agrarian hinterlands. This opened up thousands of additional miles of navigable water, and millions of acres of farmland with river access. The settlers' ark and its offspring flatboat should not be viewed solely as transportation vehicles. They were a farm-to-market implement, as common and useful as the family plow or wagon, that exponentially increased the tillable acreage of the new American West.

The simplest calculation propelled America past the Appalachians. The average flatboat could carry one ton per linear foot—a forty-footer would bear forty tons, even more, if you didn't mind water sloshing over the sides in rough weather and a slightly deeper draft. The water displacement of a fifty-footer would allow the disembarking pioneers to take along the in-laws or grandparents, along with their field plows, walnut chests laden with heavy pewter tableware, and the old family stone sink.

Modest, low-income farmers from Pennsylvania or Virginia were not the only ones seeking a new life on the western rivers, and flatboats could be fitted out to suit almost every taste. In 1805, his career in ruins after he killed Alexander Hamilton in a duel, Revolutionary War hero and former vice president Aaron Burr hastily departed for Pittsburgh to pursue land schemes and trading deals along the Ohio and Mississippi. Burr was a notorious womanizer, bon vivant, and social climber, and the description of the flat-bottom he had built at a Monongahela boatyard, in a letter to his daughter, aptly reflects his pretensions.

> My boat is, properly speaking, a floating home, sixty feet by fourteen, containing dining room, kitchen with fireplace, and two bedrooms; roofed from stem to stern; steps to go up, and a walk on the top the whole length; glass windows, &etc. [sic] This edifice costs one hundred and thirty-three dollars.

Flat-boating drove the economy of the new American West, creating a network of inland ports to service the river traffic, just as Boston, Baltimore, and Charleston had grown to service the 18th-century transatlantic trade. In towns along the Monongahela, the Ohio, and the Wabash, basic industries like sawmills and iron foundries were established within a few years of settlement, and boatbuilding in particular sprouted like oat seeds blown into manure. Because of its proximity to the emigrant route along the National Road ruts, Redstone Old Fort on the Monongahela, later named Brownsville for land speculator Thomas Brown, boomed as a construction site for flatboats. Flatboat designs quickly evolved into the hulls for the much heavier steamboats, and after the introduction of the steam engine in 1811, Captain Henry Shreve and his many imitators in Brownsville built more than three thousand steamboats. The new boat works became one of the largest in the country, creating a kind of hyperlocal industrial revolution that fed development far downriver.

In *The Navigator*, Zadok Cramer recorded that, as early as 1810, Brownsville had "two tanyards [tanneries], a rope walk, two boat yards, two tin and copper manufactories, two factories of nails, . . . one scythe and sickle maker, blacksmiths, silversmiths (one of whom makes surveyors' compasses), tailors, shoemakers, saddlers, etc." The next year, Brownsville added a blast furnace for steel, a sawmill, and a glassworks. Just about everything a family needed to get started in the wilderness was available right there, in the cottage industries located on the banks beside their new boat.

The boom along the Monongahela revealed another critical aspect of frontier development—the occupational exodus required to support it. Again, war and its aftereffects played a large role. In the late 1770s, Stephen Bayard, a successful Philadelphia merchant with good banking and trading contacts, was swept up by the American Revolution and received several promotions as a Continental army officer, eventually serving as the second-in-command at Fort Pitt in western Pennsylvania. There, he married the much younger daughter of his commander, Elizabeth MacKay, inherited substantial lands along the Monongahela through her, and after the war opened a store, a land development company, water mills, and, later, a boatyard at a site along the river between Brownsville and Pittsburgh that he named after his wife, Elizabeth-town. The area could be easily reached from the Pittsburgh Road, and Bayard could see the vast commercial potential offered by the settlers streaming through. But initially he feared that a shortage of laborers would

hinder the growth of his new works. In 1787, he announced his new establishment on the river by placing advertisements in the *Pittsburgh Gazette* and
the *Pennsylvania Journal* of Philadelphia, including this plea for workers:

> The proprietors are now erecting a saw mill thereon, where every ma-
> terial for building may be had at a very reasonable rate. Artists of all
> kinds, particularly boat builders, carpenters, joiners, masons, black-
> smiths, are especially invited, and will find it to their interest in settling
> at this place.

Within a few months, Bayard was able to attract four veteran carpen-
ters from the Philadelphia shipyards. The next year he was back as an ad-
vertiser in the Philadelphia and New York papers.

BOATS FOR SALE
At Elizabeth Town, on the Monongahela, may now be had

> Kentucky boats of different dimensions, where also for the future, Boats
> of every construction and size may be had . . . at as low a price as any of
> those on these waters.

Bayard was an entrepreneur who understood the basics of advertising
and marketing, among them, leaving little to chance and creating word-of-
mouth by reaching as many venues as possible. During his three-year ad
campaign in the eastern papers, he pointed out that detailed, printed plans
for his new town and specifications for his boats could be found at the kind
of resting places in the East where investors and adventuresome types were
sure to congregate: "Mr. Oswald's Coffee House in Philadelphia and the
Old Coffee House in New York."

Bayard also crowed about an additional advantage that would tempt
easterners and war veterans desperate to reach the new lands of the
West, but who were understandably leery about the well-known delays in
finding and outfitting boats once they reached western Pennsylvania. He
would offer one of America's first package tours. His residential plan in

Elizabeth-town included extra houses, where settler families could rest and store their belongings while they waited for their boat, "and be supplied with provisions of every kind at reasonable price." In later ads, Bayard said that he charged what remained the standard cost for flatboats until the 1820s—$1.25 per linear foot. This generally meant that a pioneer family could expect to spend about $175 purchasing and outfitting a boat.

Brownsville and Elizabeth-town, later simply called Elizabeth, were only the beginning. By 1820, the Mon Valley was a smoke pot of industry, with the haze from the foundries and sawmills mixing with the river fog to create a dark overcast on still days. Along the river, where major tributaries like the Youghiogheny and the Cheat enhanced the flow and made boat launching possible almost year-round, boatyards specializing in flats, keelboats, steam-powered hulls, and tall mast ships flourished. Wheeling, McKeesport, New Geneva, and of course Pittsburgh all developed as boatbuilding towns to support the new commerce and migration. The Mon Valley shipbuilding towns played the same role in developing western traffic as Bath, Maine, or Marblehead, Massachusetts, played in the whaling and spice trades. Provisioning the thousands of settlers' arks and cargo flatboats now departing along the Mon and the Ohio every year became another engine of growth, and Pittsburgh alone would double in population, from 2,400 people in 1800 to almost 5,000 in 1810. Building flatboats and steamboats and supplying the new export economy from the strategic three-rivers junction helped turn Pittsburgh into a small metropolis of 50,000 by the Civil War.

We should be grateful today that Zadok Cramer was a dogged compiler of fact. In *The Navigator*, Cramer's list of Pittsburgh's business establishments took up four pages in agate type, indicating how quickly the town grew as a manufacturing center to supply the booming Ohio-Mississippi trade route. He reported that an 1810 inventory of local establishments in Pittsburgh included "8 boat, barge, and ship builders, 1 pump maker, 1 looking glass maker, 1 lock maker, 7 tanyards, 2 rope walks, 1 spinning wheel maker, [and] 17 blacksmiths." An "English artist," James Patterson, was forging a line of metalware that was sure to be popular with the departing flatboaters: "Fire shovels, tongs, drawing knives, hatchets, two feet squares, augers, chisels, adzes, claw hammers, door hinges, chains, hackels, . . . [and] plough irons." No, Andrew Carnegie and Henry Clay Frick did not "invent" the steel business in Pittsburgh. As early as 1812, iron and steel foundries around Pittsburgh were already producing four hundred tons of ingots, wire, and beam per year. The annual production of construction lumber and "scantling," or boat timbers, reached over seven million board feet. "The stranger is stunned," Cramer wrote, "by an incessant din of clattering hammers, and blowing of bellowses from morning till night."

And still more wagons were coming. In 1814, the *Pittsburgh Gazette* carried an item about a farmer who lived four miles outside town along the main wagon road. Impressed by the volume of traffic heading west for the boatyards, he decided to record every passing wagon between January 1, 1813, and January 1, 1814. His count over that one-year span came to 4,055. At least another five thousand wagons crossed every year on the National and Wilderness Roads. By then the business of building flatboats was so scattered up and down the tributaries of the Ohio, the Mon, the Cumberland, and the Tennessee—and from farm to farm anywhere west of the Appalachians—that no one could possibly count the number of vessels built every year. A few of these hulls would enjoy brief second careers as store boats or floating docks near town landings. But most of them were quickly recycled into frontier log cabins, the sidewalks of Natchez, or the rafters for Creole cottages in New Orleans, one reason why so little evidence of flatboat construction was either preserved or documented for posterity. History, in this case, was literally destroying a record of itself every time a flatboat landed and was taken apart to build something else.

By the middle of the winter, my flatboat research had brought me to a familiar, wearying place. I was pleased that the early 19th-century exodus to the rivers carried me backward and forward through so many strands of history, but frustrated that there was still so much to learn. I hadn't even found reliable accounts on how to build a flatboat yet. I knew almost nothing about how to navigate a turbulent, obstacle-strewn river like the Mississippi. But my prevailing weakness for learning still more was also an asset. Research that begets more research is deeply satisfying for me. And the chaotic, democratic forces that had contributed to the flatboat era seemed endlessly seductive.

Besides, my times in Maine with my mother were golden.

My mother, Pat Buck, was petite and bookish, with a sharp, dry wit, and a smooth, rosy complexion. She was so sarcastic and hip that none of my friends could believe that she was eighty-nine. One aspect of her character had impressed me over the past thirty years. She had done all of her growing up after the age of fifty-five, when the last of her children had moved out or left for college.

It could not have been any other way—she simply didn't have the time to mature while still young. She was a postwar bride who married quickly and young soon after she met my father in 1947. After the age of twenty-one, she bore eleven children over a span of seventeen years. We were a raucous and maddening brood, and surviving her offspring was itself a miraculous achievement. She had lost my father when she was forty-nine, with three children still in the house. In her early fifties, determined to improve her retirement income and help put the last children through

Pat Buck at ninety-one, eight days before she died. I spent the best eighteen months of my life caring for her in Maine while I researched flatboats, and her spunk and determination propelled me all the way to New Orleans.

college, she decided to start work—her first job—as a social worker. Despite her age, the state of Pennsylvania could not deny her a position; she had scored number one on the state civil service exam. Finally alone in her house with time of her own, she matured into a completely different person from the strict disciplinarian, Irish Catholic mystic, and overworked housewife I had known as a boy.

Now retired to Maine to be closer to her children and grandchildren, she seemed to have the personality of a retired academic who couldn't give up a life devoted to analysis and firm opinion. One book club was not enough for her; she always belonged to two. She attended every lecture that interested her at the local colleges and faithfully demonstrated every Friday against the Iraq War on the frigid green in Brunswick. At the age of eighty, dismayed by the Roman Catholic Church's attitude toward women, and the craven behavior of the bishops during the priestly sexual abuse crisis, she left the Church and was proud and discerning about never going back. "I didn't leave the Church," she said. "The Church left me." Her laughter, trust in a deeper spirituality, and plucky weathering of adversity were all very Irish and fun.

As an octogenarian, especially after she gave up driving, one of her favorite activities was supermarket shopping. It was a once-a-week affair—twice a week if she was expecting children, grandchildren, or guests for dinner—that made her feel independent and still fully part of the workaday world. She liked to be driven to the big, shiny Hannaford supermarket on Main Street and then to be left alone for an hour while she slowly circuited the aisles, using a shopping cart as her walker and stopping now and then with her hand on her chin, pensively examining the prices and ingredients of boxed foods and sauces.

I could see that her weekly strolls through Hannaford did her a lot of good, but still I was worried. She had taken a lot of spills lately, two of them when none of us were around and strangers had to carry her home before we arrived to rush her to the hospital. The first time I drove her to the supermarket, while we were waiting for a traffic light on a snowy day in Damariscotta, I told her that I was concerned about her roaming such a big store all alone.

"Stop being ridiculous," she said. "You're the one planning on building this Huck Finn raft and sailing it down the Mississippi. Nicky and Bryan think you'll sink the thing on the first day. But *I* can't spend an hour alone at the supermarket?"

My sister Bridget, the Big Nurse of the family who was supervising our assisted care program for my mother, had already admonished me about this.

"Rinky, Mom makes all of the decisions about her life," Bridget said. "We don't."

"Okay, Mom," I said in the car. "I won't mention it again."

"It's fine, Rinky," she said. "I just wish people would stop worrying about me. Am I less capable now than when I was raising eleven children?"

At Hannaford's, I pulled into a handicap parking spot and ran around the car to open my mother's door and offer my arm for the slippery walk up to the self-opening glass doors. Safely delivered to the handle of a shopping cart, my mother tossed her walking cane into the cart and gamely padded off through the produce department, gently smiling as she glanced side to side under the generous fluorescent light. I couldn't believe how lovely she still was, so poised and well-dressed.

"I'll see you in an hour," she called back. "And don't worry! I'm happy here."

An hour later, as I nosed into the handicap spot to pick her up, I was relieved to see my mother's serene, attractive profile, topped by a woolen cap, through the frosty glass windows. When I had her safely walked out to the car, and her shopping bags loaded on the rear seat, Mother announced that she would like another of her favorite things, which would become a secret between us.

"Take me to Wasses for a hot dog," she said.

Wasses was a famous old hot dog stand from Rockland, popular with tourists, that had lately opened a new satellite concession trailer in Damariscotta.

"We're not supposed to do that," I said. "Too much salt, the doctor said."

"Oh, what does he know? There's a new study out saying that salt isn't as bad as they thought. I heard it on National Public Radio."

At Wasses, we munched on our hot dogs and chatted while the windshield wipers squeaked against the light snow. Mother was looking forward to the spring, when we could follow the pink and lavender bloom of the wild lupines along the banks of the Sheepscot River, all the way up to Head Tide. She loved bragging about her overachieving grandchildren—one of her oldest, Kitson Jazynka, had a new children's book out and was regularly publishing articles in the *Washington Post*. The partisan attacks on the Obama administration dismayed her, and her recurring pet peeve, the Roman Catholic Church, was acting out again. There were new flare-ups of the priestly abuse crisis from Philadelphia to St. Louis and the College of Cardinals in Rome was, once more, waffling on the subject. The Roman curia, she thought, was "a comic farce."

"Why can't the cardinals just ditch all those silly red dresses and their skullcaps?" she said. "They could act like men."

Once I got her home and all of her packages carried in, I stepped outside to sweep the snow off her deck. I always kissed her on the forehead and told her I loved her before I left because I knew that each parting could be our last. When I drove off, she was sitting at her kitchen table reading Anthony Doerr's *All the Light We Cannot See*, absentmindedly stirring her tea.

3

LUNACY OF MY KIND ENJOYS many advantages. If you're not expecting anything to happen, and then suddenly an opportunity seems to fall out of the sky, the release from uncertainty feels like a major life accomplishment. In March that year I received an email from a talented boat carpenter and logging friend in Maine, Doug Fowle, with whom I had been exploring various ideas about building a flatboat. Doug's subject line read "Check This Out" and the email contained links to a YouTube video and a website for a small family operation called Cooper Flatboats, in Gallatin, Tennessee.

Initially, I wasn't very impressed by the blocky flatboats that Cooper built. They looked like wooden ship containers mounted on giant lowboy semitrailers. The pictures on the website featured the proprietor of the firm, "Captain" John Cooper, in the reenactor period dress of a Kaintuck boatman—a blousy yellow shirt, a cotton sack hung from his shoulder, and a floppy brimmed hat. There were also pictures of some man-boy reenactors on one of Cooper's boats shooting replica flintlock muskets. I am leery of reenactors because I've found over the years that their ranks contain too many odd fellows interested in the bloodletting and jargon of war, not thoughtful history, and their pseudo-military groups harbor too many conspiracy theorists and gun nuts. But Cooper had already made more than twenty flatboat hulls and spent a colorful life riding the rivers on commemorative trips, and he was described in newspaper articles as one of the few flatboat builders, if not the only flatboat builder, left in America.

Cooper and I spoke on the phone a few times and exchanged research in emails. I found him quite personable and his career path had followed charming idiosyncrasies. After growing up on a hardscrabble dairy and tobacco farm in Gallatin, Cooper had worked on the Apollo space program at the Kennedy Space Center in Florida, then drifted into building flatboats after returning to Tennessee and starting a business that installed high-end floating docks and boathouses along a scenic, broad section of the Cumberland River north of Nashville called Old Hickory Lake. Cooper had created an impressive record of river voyages on flatboats he had built, including numerous journeys to build awareness for river-keeping and conservation groups, and a "Journey of Remembrance" between Rockport, Indiana, on the Ohio River and New Orleans to reenact Abraham Lincoln's first flatboat journey in 1828.

In the late spring that year, Doug and I decided to take a road trip to Tennessee, and, when we met Cooper at his ramshackle family farm on the rural outskirts north of Gallatin, I immediately liked him. Portly and bearded, with a long ponytail dropping over his shoulders, Cooper was folksy and hospitable, with the endearing dialect of a southerner. (He pronounced arthritis "arther-itis" and described space nearby as "right chonder," far-off space "chonder there." Height was "heighth.") Cooper didn't have a flatboat in progress at the time and we sat with him and his wife, Gloria, at his dining room table reviewing several large scrapbooks containing pictures of his boats and river trips.

There was one contradiction about Cooper that I enjoyed. He was fastidious about inconsequential details like wearing period dress while running his expeditions downriver, or mounting deer antlers and skinned muskrats, as the Kaintucks did, on his cabin sides and doors. But the workmanship on his boats was haphazard and clumsy, completely lacking in the finesse of mortise and tenon joints or caulked bottoms actually used by pioneers. Buoyancy on his bottoms was provided by polystyrene shipping blocks fished out of Tractor Supply Company dumpsters, and he slapped together his boat sides and decks with common framing nails or deck screws bought at Lowe's. But a side of me liked the idea of sailing down to New Orleans in an ugly duckling. The 19th-century Kaintucks were the hillbillies of their era, often economically desperate, displaced farmers who built simply according to the methods and material available at the time. An unpretentious, rat-bike flatboat built from the dumpsters of Tractor Supply, with clunky, faux stainless steel door hinges from Home Depot, felt appropriate for my trip.

Cooper didn't appear to be very knowledgeable about flatboat sails and didn't even know what a lateen rig was, and seemed surprised when I told him that flatboats rarely carried anchors because they tied up onto trees along the banks. I couldn't get him to understand that I wasn't interested in reenacting, but instead wanted to use a homebuilt boat to explore history and write about what had become today of a fabled riverscape that once defined America. But he was a good start and I felt that I had finally moved my plans along just by meeting him. Before I left with Doug to enjoy the ride back north, I told Cooper that I wouldn't be in a position to order a boat until I was done helping my family care for my mother. Cooper said that he would rough out some plans for me, just in case, and we agreed to stay in touch.

During my hiatus in Maine, I didn't spend a lot of time worrying about how to crew my boat. A lifetime of reporting and writing had conditioned me to trusting a lot to chance. Even in distant places where I didn't know a soul, someone always came along to help me get the story or rescue me from a jam. This wait-and-see attitude would make crewing both my most brilliant achievement and abject failure of the trip, and my first recruit was typical.

Danny Corjulo is a short, pudgy, effervescent burst of energy, one of those people I am convinced that God placed on this earth just to torment me with the knowledge that the bonds of human friendship can yield both our highest moments of pleasure and our deepest pits of rage. Danny and I were old flying buddies and he had flown up to Maine a couple of times to help me make repairs on my truck and install new window screens at my mother's place. Generally, I don't discuss my various plans for junkets beforehand, because a lot of them never happen and I don't want to become known as a nonperforming dreamer. But Danny knew I was up to something and had been pestering me for months about my next project.

First Mate Danny Corjulo. His infectious enthusiasm and haute cuisine were our most valuable assets aboard the Patience.

His persistence can be both obnoxious and endearing, however, and one night, while we were sitting at the bar of King Eider's Pub in Damariscotta, I finally broke down and made the mistake of sharing some details about my flatboat trip. I realized the immensity of my error when his eyes lit up.

"The Mississippi on a flatboat?" Danny said. "I'm in. You can start calling me First Mate Corjulo."

"Danny, no. I'm not making decisions like that yet. Besides, you're too annoying to take along."

"Tell me something I don't know about myself," he said. "I'm coming."

I met Danny years ago in the newsroom of the *Hartford Courant*. I was known then as a dependable reporter who always came back with a fresh angle on a big story, but in a new digital age requiring personal change, my technical deficiencies were legion. From remote locations in the Adirondacks or in Europe I dispatched my stories via email to an editor who had gone home for the night. I couldn't properly code my copy for typesetting and I doused brand-new laptops with hot coffee or wine. Late at night, as the last-edition deadline neared, there was a big hole on the front page waiting for my story, but my calamitous transmission errors had made it impossible to find. I was known around the newsroom as the "Darth Vader of copy."

Danny, a former *Courant* photographer who had transferred to the information technology staff, was the emergency fixer often dispatched to untangle my screwups. Because these disasters usually happened late at night, when I was in town Danny and I would go out for a late dinner at some obscure Somalian restaurant or Jamaican barbecue joint in East Hartford that only he seemed to know about, and over time we began to enjoy that curious bundle of incompatibility and shared interests that draw people together. We were both licensed airplane pilots, loved politics, and Danny's stories about his convoluted, endless girlfriend problems were highly entertaining. Danny and I both suffer from the same psychological syndrome, hypomania, a surfeit of dopamine that produces elevated feelings of self-worth, irritability with slackers, insomnia, and the need to remain feverishly busy all day. In other ways, we are also classically mismatched. I am neat and dress out of the Brooks Brothers catalog. Danny is a bundle of wires, battery chargers and portable disc drives bulging out of his pockets. He dresses according to the hideous style of our times in baggy, polyester cargo shorts, clashing camo belts, and T-shirts lettered with slogans like SCIENCE IS NOT A LIBERAL CONSPIRACY and THINK: IT'S NOT ILLEGAL YET.

Still, I found him irresistible, mostly because he was so intellectually vibrant and diverse in his interests, the ideal weekend companion. A mechanical and technology wizard, he could fix anything and was so hardworking that projects that should have taken days were done in a single afternoon. As a boy, Danny had learned scratch cooking in his grandmother's apartment in Yonkers, New York, and his personal heroes are the food writer Michael Pollan and the late celebrity chef Anthony Bourdain. With just a single pan or two, over an open fire or on an old Coleman stove mounted on the tailgate of my pickup, he could prepare the most elaborate meals—rabbit stew made from freshly caught rabbit, artichoke and chicken in white wine sauce—in just an hour. Long weekends snowshoeing in Vermont, logging in the Berkshire woods, and arguing about home restoration projects had cemented our relationship of opposites.

In grade school, Danny had been identified as one of those truly fascinating students who, while highly intelligent and academically successful, were simultaneously handicapped by hyperactivity, attention deficit disorder, and a bundled "multiple dyslexia" complex so complete that he frequently misspells and mispronounces words. His brain works like an amalgam of penne pasta and burnt-out circuit breakers.

Danny's combination of extreme impatience and dyslexia produces entertaining results. When the word he is searching for refuses to reach his tongue, Danny hurriedly skips to whatever seems close. "North Carolina," for example, is usually "North Dakota," and "Colorado" is "Coronado." Pittsburgh usually comes out as "Pittsfield," "Pittstown," or "Pittsville," and I've heard him refer to the sixteenth president as "Theodore Lincoln" and the thirty-fifth as "Dwight Kennedy." Once, when he was making a road trip across Route 66, Danny texted me from Amarillo, Texas. "I'm in Amaretto," he wrote. When Danny wants to say "foal," he usually says "mare." "Fuel" usually comes out as "oil," and when he means "oil" he says "fuel."

It is a mistake to correct Danny. Once, when I reminded him that "a mare is the mother, the foal is the baby," he replied, "Stop being difficult. You know what I meant."

I happen to love people with dyslexia, or the many varieties of autism symptoms like Asperger's syndrome, because they are so often interesting and even courageous examples of human coping. They compensate for their handicaps with fascinating strategies. Danny has trouble reading, but I'd noticed over the years that he was exceptionally well informed on a variety of subjects—European politics, technology, filmmaking, American history, and Civil War battles. He'd been compensating for reading difficulties for years by taping all of his lectures in college, and using text-to-speech software. Riding with him in his pickup is an educational experience because he is constantly listening to audiobooks. Dyslexia wasn't a barrier for him. He had "compensated" and become one of the most informed people I know.

For all of his technological prowess, Danny is also physically clumsy and maddening to be around. He elbows power tools off ladders, missing my head by inches, and is so distracted by the multiple cell phones, iPads, and tracking systems that he has plugged into his pickup chargers that he can't hold a real-time conversation for more than a minute or two. After we have finished one of our projects, he leaves behind a debris field of discarded parts boxes, hose clamps, and onion peels before he hurries on to the next repair job.

Our friendship had matured with the disappointments of the digital age. In the mid-2000s, dismayed by the layoffs and budget cuts that had reduced the *Hartford Courant* to an emaciated newsletter, Danny became restless and was considering finding a new job, even a whole new industry. At the time, I had noticed that the hot new job title at New England prep schools was director of information technology. Danny's enthusiasm and multidisciplinary zeal would be ideal in this environment, and I liked the idea of his bantam personality disrupting the traditional, stuffy ranks of a prep school faculty. When the job of IT director opened up at the prestigious Loomis Chaffee School in Windsor, I encouraged him to apply, gave him interview coaching, and wrote a letter of recommendation.

Danny got the job and has since thrived at Loomis Chaffee, but I have paid a big price for this. The most lovable and irritating person I know is now my most loyal fan.

"You were the one who showed me how to pull the rip cord at the *Courant*," Danny says. "It changed my life."

That winter and spring, Danny flooded me with elaborate lists and provisioning arrangements for "our" flatboat trip. He was downloading navigation software for the entire Ohio and Mississippi rivers on an iPad, and devising strategies for securing fuel during the three-hundred-mile stretches on the Mississippi where there were no marinas. He could airlift smoked Virginia hams and New England shellfish to the boat. He seemed to have learned overnight everything there was to know about deep-storage marine batteries and river currents.

I finally gave up and yielded to Danny's pestering not because I was convinced that it was a good idea to make him the first member of my crew. I gave up because, by then, I was steeped in the lore of flatboating and the journals of the alligator-horse rivermen, for whom recurrent bedlam was as much a part of the trip as dodging giant driftwood piles or negotiating savage currents. Like Asbury C. Jaquess of the *Davy Crockett*, perhaps I was questing the waters not so much to reach New Orleans, but to acquire a knowledge of human nature, embracing the inevitable personal conflicts of very diverse people cloistered together on a forty-foot boat.

Danny and I soon hatched a plan. At the time, he was owed six weeks of vacation and sick days that he had never taken, and Danny would expend his owed time in two-week stretches on the boat, and then fly back to Connecticut, rejoining me for another two weeks the next month. It was a classic Danny scheme. "Whenever a piece of equipment breaks," Danny said, "I can carry it back in my luggage, fix it in my shop, and bring it back to the boat two weeks later." Besides, my departure still seemed far off—I still didn't know whether it would be this summer or next. There was plenty of time to reconcile myself to Danny Corjulo, first mate.

Several months later, John Cooper called me with favorable news. A production company preparing a PBS documentary on the most noteworthy artist of the flatboat era, George Caleb Bingham, wanted to re-create with live actors Bingham's most recognizable canvas, a classic of American scenic art titled *The Jolly Flatboatmen*. Painted at the height of the flatboat era in 1846, the picture depicted eight crew members enjoying a fiddling and dancing party on the curved roof of an archetypal barge, floating in the slack waters of the Missouri River near St. Louis. Bingham's masterpiece now hangs in the National Gallery of Art, and the film crew wanted to use a forty-foot replica of the boat as the centerpiece of their production. After filming was completed in June, Cooper would finish off and slightly modify the hull for my trip, and the $15,000 that the production company paid for a few days of shooting would be deducted from the price of my boat.

I marveled at how randomly luck seems to fall to those who dream. An image brushed onto canvas 170 years ago was enabling my plan for sailing two thousand miles of the old western frontier. Early that spring, I traded the grimy snowdrifts and brown ice of the mud season in Maine for John Cooper's pleasantly shabby farm in Tennessee, and moved into the small camping trailer that the Coopers lent me to live in while the boat was built, parked just across the yard from my project. Every day I could see the timbers of my new flatboat growing taller against tree lines that glowed with cherry and dogwood blossoms.

The Patience *hull rising on a Tennessee farm. I worked on the boat until the heat chased me away by noon, then spent the rest of the day searching for equipment.*

By the time I reached Tennessee, Cooper had already built the basic frame of what he was calling the "Bingham Boat." Thick oak bottom boards that ran fore-to-aft were buttressed by crosswise joists and vertical studs cut from local poplar. The vertical studs rose a few feet above deck level, where they would form the "kevels," from the Middle English *kevile*, or the Middle Dutch *kavele*, a term still used in early 19th-century America to describe the stout posts used to fasten the boat to a wharf or to hang anchors. The boxy structure stood on immense wooden blocks that raised the bottom almost to knee height, requiring a lot of jumping up and down from the deck level every time I needed a tool or laid down a new board. Cooper and I would spend the next two months scrambling up stepladders to raise and attach the side boards, build the deck and cabin, waterproof the roof deck, and finishing the windows and doors.

At dawn every day, mourning doves cooing from the telephone wires out on Gibbs Lane woke me with an itch for work. We generally tried to put in several hours on the boat early in the morning before the sun and humidity chased us away at noon. After the sides of the boat had reached five feet, we assembled a tubular-aluminum scaffold around the hull to raise the massive two-inch-by-ten-inch side boards, weighing up to 120 pounds apiece. Cooper cut the poplar boards with a circular saw and then we lugged them over together, hoisted the boards up on our shoulders, and tacked them on with a long wood screw on either end. While Cooper went to measure and cut the next board, I walked from stern to bow along the scaffolding, driving the rest of the screws into the vertical framing. We followed the same procedure laying the slightly curved streamers and roof boards over the cabin, which would serve as the high upper deck from which I would operate the boat. By noon, my shoulders and wrists ached from the constant work of raising the heavy poplar boards and drilling in dozens of screws per hour. The sawdust mixing with my perspiration chalked my hair and forearms and made my eyes and neck sting. But this was welcome, fruitful pain. Knowing every piece of the boat as it was built from the ground up would be valuable once I launched and began to move downriver. Hard manual labor is therapeutic. My lingering doubts about the New Orleans trip seemed to recede the harder I worked.

Still, every day, it seemed, someone would make a comment about the difficulty of steering around the tugs and barges on the river, or the brisk currents of the Mississippi jamming the boat into bridge pylons or submerged dams, and I would feel sudden, involuntary pangs of trepidation about the trip. But I could always bluster these fears away by consciously willing myself to display an outward bearing of confidence. The sweat equity of building the boat was beneficial that way, a reminder of how important this phase of the trip was for my outlook. All morning I scrambled around the deck muscling around heavy ten-by-two boards, and in the afternoon I drove out to Lowe's or C&O Marine to search for boat parts and hardware. At night, with a fire glowing beside the boat, I sat on an old Amish hickory rocker and taught myself to splice rope for anchor lines.

I knew that a big, shiny American flag snapping in the breeze on the stern would improve my relations with the tug captains, and make the boat stand out to traffic on the river, and I did want to make a patriotic statement about my trip. Walmart has a pretty good flag selection and I picked the biggest one I could find, made from nylon for durability. I liked the no-nonsense, proletarian utility of that—I would sail to New Orleans with a Walmart flag. The flag sat around my trailer for a few days wrapped in clear plastic while I was busy making other fixes on the boat.

One evening, underneath a pink glow of sunset against the Tennessee foothills, I walked with my chain saw up through Cooper's back fields to the north tree line and found a perfect young cedar tree to use as a flagpole, trimming it to size before carrying it on my shoulder down to the boat. I mounted the pole against the exterior back wall of the cabin, jury-rigging an assembly with PVC pipe, galvanized clamps, and bungees, and hung the flag from the pole with nylon clothesline and Home Depot pulleys. Nylon subtly reflects sunset light, and the breeze picked up. I liked the way that the flag, rippling above the stern, transparently received the nighttime pink.

I was happy about another thing when I was finished with the flag mount. I had grown up on a converted dairy farm in New Jersey. Everything was shit-rigged. When we couldn't reach the high eaves on our barns to spray-paint them, my father built a "paint vehicle" by mounting some playground climbing bars, and an extension ladder, onto an old Buick chassis that we had lying around. It worked great, but he kept running it underneath the telephone wires out near the main road, cutting off phone service for the whole neighborhood. When our front doorknob broke, we replaced it with vise-grip pliers. The horse country of Morris County, New Jersey, was not the place where my family belonged. Our neighbors and friends owned shipping companies, gold mines in South Africa, or were the idle descendants of old robber baron clans whose social life revolved around the autumn fox hunts run by the Spring Valley Hounds. I spent my adolescence deeply embarrassed about our homeplace and did everything I could to prevent my school chums from seeing this hillbilly asylum.

With maturity, however, the social anxieties of family began to recede, especially after I became an accomplished shit-rigger myself. During college, I shit-rigged a cargo rack for my motorcycle out of an old metal milk crate so I could travel with my typewriter and books. To heat my first loft in lower Manhattan, I ran stovepipe out through our eleventh-floor window. I began to appreciate my family legacy and understood that shit-rigging is next to godliness, a vital life skill. I feel sorry today for people who didn't grow up with the character formation of shit-rigging. If you can't freely shit-rig you can't live, you can't dream, you can't really go anywhere worth getting to. Shit-rigging is life's golden diploma.

The sky had turned from pink sunset to blue-gray dusk when I finished with the flagpole. I looked back to the boat as I crossed the grass. She was a shit-rigging masterpiece, my hillbilly *Pequod*, my floating jalopy, my personal *Kon-Tiki*, a gorgeous code violation that would carry me south to New Orleans.

It was almost eleven o'clock when I got back to my camper. I'd been at work on the boat one way or another since seven in the morning. I realized that the novelty of building my first boat by foraging in the woods or at tag sales was important for another reason. I was already practically living on the boat. This was an ideal prelude for the trip, a familiarization program as delightful, say, as building my own house.

Truth, however, always returns at night. At two or three o'clock in the morning I would wake in my trailer in a cold sweat, tormented by recurring anxiety dreams. The mind during sleep is a most exquisitely refined torture device. In one of the dreams, I just couldn't explain to that old girlfriend of mine why I no longer lived in houses, but instead in camping trailers, covered wagons, and boats. A few nights later I dreamed that I had dropped my cell phone overboard and, no matter how many times I dove for it in the muddy Mississippi, I couldn't find it. I had been taunted by recurring anxiety dreams forever, and surprised that they don't go away with age. Over the years, I've dreamt at least a hundred times about flunking eighth-grade algebra. Every time I land an airplane in my sleep I forget to put the wheels down. A lifetime of experimenting with coping techniques has been useless. Now, in Tennessee, the nightmares about the perils of taking on the Mississippi wouldn't go away and I was amazed at the capacity of one very jumbled head—mine—for tormenting me at night.

Liberating myself from the fantasy that I was building an "authentic" replica of a 19th-century flatboat was another important step. Log cabins, timber frame barns, farm wagons, and flatboats are often called "vernacular designs" because the semiliterate farmers who built them rarely saw a need to work from elaborate drawings or specification sheets, or to preserve a record for history. Building methods were passed down by word of mouth from generation to generation, or among the large groups of local men who paused after planting or harvesting season to build flatboats. One of the few written accounts that we have today was written by a lumberman and flatboat captain named John Calvin Gilkeson, who built a dozen or more boats at the height of the flatboat era in the late 1830s and early 1840s along the Little Raccoon Creek, a small tributary that flows into the Wabash River in Parke County, Indiana. Gilkeson's "Boat Building on Little Raccoon Creek" has been preserved by the Parke County Historical Society in Rockville, Indiana. I sat up one night out by the boat project, beside a fire made from oak and poplar scraps, reading Gilkeson's unpretentious, log-cabin prose.

Gilkeson described how tall, straight hardwood trees in the local forests were selected and then felled with long crosscut saws, swept back and forth over the trunk between two men. The logs were split by hand into thick boards with wedges hammered by heavy mauls, and the sides were hewed flat by broadaxes and adzes, a labor-intensive task that could take several days. The heavy finished lumber was then towed to a site near the stream by "from 4 to 6 pretty good yokes of oxen," twelve draft beasts in all, and "wo to the weakly chain that happened to get into the scrape." The basic hull was built upside down on dry land so that the gunwales and cross girders could be securely mortised together without the structure being submerged in water. Building sites were chosen where there were steep banks dropping toward streams or rivers. A gang of ten or more men, assisted by draft horses or oxen pulling the boat sides with winches and rope, then pitched the hull down the slope, "flipping" it right side up into the water. The rest of the boat—side boards, cabins, standing decks—was built up from there as the flat bottom floated in the water. The majority of the boats that the Gilkesons built in Parke County were sixty to eighty feet long, but they built some hundred-ton monsters, too—Gilkeson described craft as long as 102 feet, with beams of twenty-two feet. The Gilkesons waited for the spring rains to swell the Little Raccoon and then floated their boats down to the Wabash for sale in Armiesburg, Terre Haute, and Vincennes.

For me, re-creating steps like felling trees with two-man crosscut saws and hauling timbers from the woods with oxen would be just another reenactor stunt, as preposterously "authentic" as, say, donning a shiny stovepipe hat and attempting to recite Abraham Lincoln's "Gettysburg Address" in his distinctive, high-pitched Kentucky twang. I couldn't possibly reinvent word-of-mouth traditions that had lain dormant for more than 150 years. I was doing something different, more realistic for my times— intellectually stalking, but not slavishly imitating, a formative era in the expansion of America. I was particularly drawn to the way that Gilkeson, an unpretentious lumberman on the Indiana frontier, related the flatboat to the patterns of life that emerged during the economic boom that followed the Great Migration over the Appalachians. He ended "Boat Building on Little Raccoon Creek" with this paragraph:

> Thousands of bushels of corn and tons of pork were in those days shipped down the Wabash River and on down to the city of New Orleans. I well remember when boat hands going down to New Orleans had to trudge back home on foot and thought they done pretty well to get home by the first Monday in August which was then general election day.

In Tennessee, I didn't know which day, or even which month, that I would arrive home. I had no reason to expect that I could negotiate the tree snags and rogue currents described by my doubters. I was departing under a veil of uncertainty, completely ignorant of the rivers that I was about to take on. Still, sitting in my Amish rocker and staring at the dreamy embers of my poplar fire, my anxieties becalmed by bourbon, I was philosophical about my pending journey. Through the trees, the coyotes wailed and the train whistles screeched.

The makers of 19th-century America, the thousands of farm boys of the Cumberland and the Wabash, departed southwest under the same shroud of inexperience. During his 1828 flatboat trip, while sleeping in his cabin below Baton Rouge, Abraham Lincoln was attacked and injured by a band of robbers. Lincoln and his boatmate chased them off with sticks, cut their lines, and drifted south to safety in the current. Another bourbon helped me to appreciate that there was a reason I had obsessed so long on Lincoln biographies. On my shit-rig flat, my hillbilly houseboat, I too would go forth. The downstream flow would deliver me past adversity, and beyond my misgivings.

4

TENNESSEE WAS ALSO AN EMOTIONAL roller coaster. Certain preparations for the trip were falling apart even as others were brightening up. John Cooper was frequently away working on lucrative dock and marina projects in the mansion district along Old Hickory Lake and we lost a lot of days working on the boat. Features that I felt were vital for taking on the Mississippi—long-range fuel tanks, a transom on the stern for a backup motor—never got built. I specifically asked Cooper to build me split "Dutch doors," a colonial design in which doors are cut in half, and then hinged separately, to form two pieces that open. On stormy days I could keep out most of the rain by shutting the bottom door, while opening the top section to look from the cabin for traffic downriver. But Cooper shrugged his shoulders and didn't build them. The clunky doors he eventually built out of two-inch poplar boards were too heavy, and shrank once the wood dried, making them useless.

The codes of southern hospitality, however, prevented Cooper from directly saying no to me. Instead, he just repressed the idea and ignored me. I slowly began to accept that this was the nature of my trip preparations. I would have to sail to New Orleans with the big old clunky doors that John Cooper considered appropriate.

When I confronted Cooper about problems like this, he invariably replied: "We're not building this thing for the Queen of England. Stop worrying. You're going to reach New Orleans on this boat."

I was too accommodating. Screw it, I thought. Maybe Cooper was right. This shit rig growing out of a Tennessee hayfield didn't have to be beautiful, and it only had to accomplish one thing. It had to get me to New Orleans.

There were many other problems. In May, I gave John Cooper $5,000 to cover the cost of hauling the boat to Pittsburgh, but by June he'd already spent the money on something else and sheepishly begged me for another $5,000. I was trapped, and knew it, forced to pay double to get the boat up to the Monongahela.

I was philosophical about this, and comforted myself that Cooper was not as bad as many boatbuilders during the pioneer era. In the early 19th century, the writers of guidebooks on the Ohio and Mississippi rivers railed against common shortcuts taken by Monongahela boatyards, such as using inferior woods below the waterline, hasty mortise and tenon joinery, and slapdash caulking—the kind of defects that were hidden behind the fascia boards in the hull, precisely where rube pioneer buyers couldn't see them. *The Navigator* author, Zadok Cramer, warned against these unscrupulous practices, which often created leaking and structural failure within a few days of the flats disappearing beyond the first bends in the Ohio, and he became a kind of early consumer protection advocate. "This egregious piece of misconduct should long before this time have been rectified by the appointment of boat inspectors at the different places boats are built," he wrote in 1811. But the lax standards in the boomtowns at the head of the Ohio—typical for embarkation points during the pioneer era—were rarely addressed and Cramer advised the river migrants to spend a few dollars having their purchases inspected by experienced boatmen. Cooper had turned me into the same kind of hayseed bound for a long water trip. I was too forgiving about this, and anxious to disembark for New Orleans, no matter the quality of my boat. I justified my lackadaisical attitude toward these details by telling myself that any inadequacies the boat had would just add humor and practical challenges to my journey.

Simultaneously, I was having a lot of luck attracting a promising crew, and finishing out the cabin interior by myself, or with friends, buoyed me with feelings of self-reliance. Two experienced and energetic acquaintances that I had met in Nashville, Cynthia Lee and Debra Satterfield, volunteered to help crew the flatboat later in the summer and drove to Gallatin several

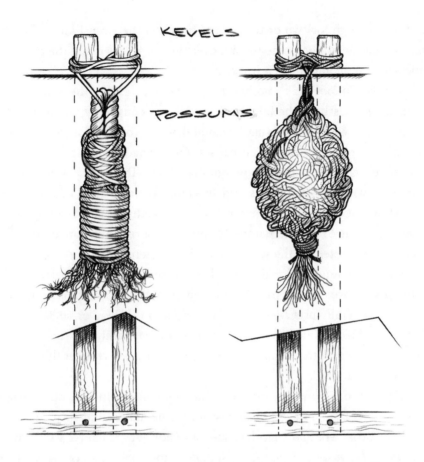

I made our 19th-century "possums"—flatboat-era boat bumpers—out of hemp and nylon rope and hung them from the "kevels" that vertically ran up from the bottom boards and served as tie-up cleats.

times to work on the boat. I knew that bumpers on either side of the boat would be useful for sidling up to other boats and landing against docks in heavy currents. I found in an 1836 journal by a West Virginia flatboater a description of fashioning "possum" bumpers, so called because they looked at a distance like opossums, and built my own possums out of old hemp rope and horse collars found at local yard sales. I even found a way around the problem of the scarcity of marinas along the Mississippi while I was visiting Civil War sites in Franklin, Tennessee, and found a store selling electric bicycles. The "cargo" model that I bought was equipped with side mounts and a front basket capable of holding thirty-six gallons of fuel—enough for two or three days' travel on the river. I knew that the bike might be cumbersome to haul over the tall levees along the river but guessed that I could make it work.

Gloria Cooper was another perpetual burr under the saddle. She meddled endlessly in the boat project and was constantly pestering John to knock off work early so that he could drive her off to shop. She seemed to suffer from a syndrome that causes uninformed people to confidently sound off on subjects they know nothing about. This was fortified by her conservative Christian beliefs and listening to the diktats of right-wing radio hosts. It was Gloria's opinion, for example, that Taylor Swift "couldn't sing," and that President Barack Obama was surely not native-born because "you can tell by the way he talks." I was tempted at first to dismiss Gloria's hidebound regional bias. I'd found that middle Tennesseans are a fun-loving, welcoming bunch and their friendliness and boisterous storytelling generally prevailed over differences in ideology or social values. Political subjects almost never came up and I was rarely aware that I was surrounded by southern conservatives. But Gloria didn't meet this middle Tennessee standard.

I had spent weeks lying awake at night conjuring an appropriate name for my boat. I have a weakness for virtue names, but the usual kind of choices that would depict the stamina required to reach New Orleans—*Resolute, Invincible, Dauntless*—sounded too bellicose or lacking in subtlety. The name *Persistence* might be good, I thought, or *Perseverance*, but they sounded too wordy and lacked subtlety. Finally I landed on the boat name *Patience*, which seemed to depict both the modesty and resilience I would need to have on a long river trip. *Patience* was nuanced, not blaring. When I shared the name with the Coopers, Gloria was appalled.

"*Patience!*" she said. "That sounds like the name for a teacher of retarded kids. Besides, it should be '*The Patience*,' like '*The Titanic*.'"

I wasn't sure myself, my form of ignorance being the confidence that I could always study up on a subject and fill my voids of knowledge. When I checked that night on my laptop, it seemed clear that the article *The* did not precede boat names. But this didn't matter to Gloria. Until the day we launched, she continued to insist that the signs on my boat should read *The Patience*.

My happiness in Tennessee, however, was overshadowed by mixed joy and regret. Back in early December I had been traveling out west on a book-signing tour, and then stayed behind in western Idaho for some trail riding with friends, the first time I had left Maine for a stretch and abandoned my care routines for my mother. During a phone call home halfway through the trip, I learned that she had taken one more bad fall and entered the familiar cycle of a brief hospitalization followed by two weeks in a rehabilitation center. For the past three years, she had fought to stay alive with gumption and humor. "Oh, they say I am doing weight lifting," she said to me when I had visited her during one of her rehab visits the summer before. "But it's a joke. The stupid little plastic dumbbells they give me weigh less than my books."

But now she was losing her strength and her spunk. Rehab was too arduous this time, and she knew that she could no longer will her body back into shape. My brother Nick, who knew how concerned I was and called me every few days with updates, caught up with me after I had returned east and was laying over in the Catskills with friends. We spoke on our cell phones while I was shoveling snow off my friends' deck, enjoying the spectacular views west to the palisade walls of the Shawangunk Mountain Ridge.

"Mom has asked us to take her out of rehab and cut off all food and water," Nick said. "She wants to go home."

I was devastated. I had spent the last eighteen months devoted to her care, emotionally committed to being there for her. I should have been there for her now.

"Bull," Nick said. "We were all saying last night how good a job we've done caring for Mother. That includes you."

I realized later that it was fine, better than fine, that I wasn't there. Everyone in the family knew what to do and I would have just been in the way. My mother had always said that she hoped to die surrounded by her children, especially her daughters, an improbable dream, given how many of us there were, and how she would probably be in some lonely hospital room somewhere. But my mother's best caregiving troika of daughters—McNamara, Bridget, and Ferriss—arrived over the night that she was brought back home, and four of my brothers were wandering in and out until Bridget told the boys to go home and wait. The girls gave my mother a sponge bath, and then carefully dressed her in a fresh nightgown, so that she would feel more relaxed and sleep better.

Bridget arranged for a doctor to visit and, finding my mother confused and wandering in and out of consciousness, he prescribed morphine, to ease any pain or anxiety. Bridget massaged some of it under my mother's tongue. One of the last things I had heard my mother say before I left Maine was "I have a full-time job now—taking care of an old lady," and the circle of daughters around her bed was impressed by how competently she was handling that right to the end. Late that night, Ferriss was alone with my mother when she noticed that her breathing had slowly whispered away to nothing. She stepped into the next room to find Bridget, who returned to my mother and placed her stethoscope on her chest.

Bridget looked up toward the wall while she checked my mother's vital signs, then looked toward my sisters and sighed.

"Let's just be very quiet and still," she said. "Mother's spirit needs space to pass from her body."

Ferriss would later say that, as they quietly stood around my mother's bed, there was more joy than sorrow in the room.

"We were all just blown away by how efficient she was," Ferriss said. "We said to each other, 'Mom, you did it! You came home to die and you did it so effortlessly.' The experience wasn't painful or scary at all. It was beautiful."

Expecting a longer wait, my sisters had brought along their knitting needles and yarn. Now they lifted Mother up to wrap her in a favorite pink blanket and then they sewed it into a burial shroud with their needles and yarn. Before they closed the shroud they placed some dried wildflowers from Ireland on her chest. My son had brought the flowers back the summer before from one of her favorite places, her mother's childhood home in the west of Ireland, at Knocknageeha in County Clare.

Everything that happens to a family that has just lost its matriarch happened to us. I spent Christmas week in my pickup, towing my trailer, ferrying from Rockland to Wiscasset all of the furniture that my mother had meticulously marked for my brothers and sisters. I found among my mother's papers a yellowed manila folder containing every letter I had sent to my parents since I left home in 1969, and was dismayed by how verbose and pretentious a writer I was a lifetime ago. Bridget lit into my brothers

and me for hauling off all of Mother's linens to the Baptist church clothing drive and Goodwill without asking her first. I didn't help matters very
much by offering the pathetic excuse that, while cleaning out my mother's
apartment, I had had "a few"—it was many—drinks. Bridget and Nick put
together a lovely memorial service for my mother at St. Andrew's Episco-
pal Church and, at the reception at an organic restaurant afterward, I was
amazed by how many people approached me just to express how my loud,
raucous, divisive, crazyass clan was "such a nice family."

My mother was fastidious about cleanliness and I knew that she would
have wanted to turn her apartment back to the landlord in perfect shape.
In clearing out the place, however, we had carried in so much snow and
muddy grit on our boots that the wooden floors now resembled the sandy
edge of a beach parking lot. I spent New Year's Day walking backward
through her apartment with a broom, a pail of sudsy Pine-Sol, and a mop.
The lemon scent reminded me of her, and the high ceilings and plaster
walls echoed with small talk as I spoke out loud to myself, conducting im-
aginary conversations with her as I swept the mop back and forth.

When I reached the kitchen door by the porch, I lifted my mop and the
bucket of suds out the door and glanced back inside. It was my last chore
for my mother, my last visit "home" with her, and I was pleased. The sunlight flaring through the windows from the snowbanks outside glowed on
spotless maple floors.

"The floors are done, Mom," I said. "I love you."

I locked my mother's door behind me, stowed my cleaning supplies
in the bed of my pickup, and drove down past the crusted snow berms on
Elm Street and took the bridge over the reversing falls of the Damariscotta.
There were large ice floes racing downriver in the tide with wide spaces of
open water in between. The swirling ice in the frigid, foamy harbor made
me feel lonely. But I also felt complete. Together as a family we had done
such a good job on our last big assignment for Mother.

My original agreement with Cooper had called for him to join the trip for a
week or two on the Ohio, so he could familiarize me with steering around
the commercial boat traffic and negotiating the twenty Army Corps of

Engineers locks and dams on the Ohio below Pittsburgh. But John began to waffle on that after I arrived in Tennessee. Gloria told me that she and John never "spent a night apart," and John must have sensed that I would not welcome her intrusive presence on my crew.

John suggested instead that I take along a prominent reenactor and friend of his from suburban St. Louis, Scott Mandrell. A middle school teacher, National Guard member, and obsessive history buff, Mandrell was well known in reenactor circles for his portrayals of historic figures like Abraham Lincoln and Andrew Jackson. In 2003 and 2004, Mandrell had led a bicentennial reenactment of the Lewis and Clark expedition, acting himself as expedition leader Meriwether Lewis. The trip was cosponsored and funded by the National Park Service, with First Lady Laura Bush serving as an honorary cochairman of the effort, and embodied all of the glaring contradictions of modern reenacting. The replica keelboat used by the Lewis and Clark re-creators was powered by a standard marine engine and hauled from site to site by tractor trailers, with scout cars running ahead every day to check out the river ahead. Mandrell used his contacts in the National Guard to move his keelboat around dams. Police escorts, a lot of chatter on walkie-talkies, and frequent costume changes for video broadcasts to schoolchildren were part of the daily routine. The Discovery Expedition "camped" every night at prearranged stops where they were met by local tourism and town booster groups and fed catered meals. I didn't learn this until I reached the Ohio, but Mandrell had left the expedition under a cloud, and begun a competing expedition. Mandrell said he resigned because the Discovery Expedition was too commercial. But officials at the Discovery Expedition said he was asked to leave because of complaints about his behavior. According to an article in the *St. Louis Post-Dispatch*, several police departments reported receiving allegations of disorderly conduct by Scott. The article on Mandrell ran under the headline "Re-Enactor Has a Growing Reputation—With Police."

"Scott Mandrell is one of the best living history actors that I know, and his knowledge of history is prodigious," said Bryant Boswell, a retired dentist and prominent reenactor from Jackson, Mississippi, who took over as the expedition's Meriwether Lewis after Mandrell departed. "He creates a great first impression, but then you experience his explosive temper, which alienated everyone associated with the project. You learned to stay away from him."

In May, when I drove up to St. Louis to meet him, I missed most of the warning signs. Mandrell was knowledgeable about early 19th-century history, and made several suggestions about equipment I should bring along. But he also seemed to enjoy embarrassing his children in front of strangers, and was so self-involved that he could literally talk for hours about his various accomplishments as a reenactor. Mandrell was particularly obsessed with 19th-century costumes and uniforms and refused to listen when I said that he wouldn't need his considerable wardrobe of "period dress" outfits. It was an obdurate mind block with him—he couldn't conceive of launching on the river without a Meriwether Lewis tricorne hat or a rakish Kaintuck dagger stuffed inside his belt.

For the moment, I ignored this. I'd grown up in New Jersey next door to Morristown National Historical Park and its Jockey Hollow encampment site, where George Washington's Continental army spent the winter of 1799–80, and was long used to the sartorial airs of reenactors I saw there as a boy. Over the years I had seen, when I visited Civil War battlefields, the weekend reenactors gallivanting over the hills in their period dress, obsessing over their McClellan saddles and restored 1863 ambulance wagons. For reenactors it's all about uniform-wearing and fussing over "period" canteens and riding boots—most of them are ignorant of the actual events of the battles they portray, or the deeper significance of Chancellorsville or the fall of Vicksburg. About dressing, reenactors are as vain as prom queens. They are, essentially, throwback fashionistas. I considered these clotheshorses to be little more than battlefield extras, overdressed losers, but essentially harmless. I would have to put up with Mandrell's sartorial obsessions because they came with the package.

The Mississippi still felt like an impenetrable mystery to me and I decided to visit John Guider, a professional photographer and adventurer in Nashville who, beginning in 2009, had spent two months every summer completing a legendary circumnavigation of North America along the six-thousand-mile "Great Loop" water route. The Great Loop journey includes a sail down the Mississippi to the Gulf of Mexico, then across the Gulf to Florida, and then up the Eastern Seaboard to the Hudson River, then north to the Great Lakes and then back down the upper Mississippi. The simplicity of Guider's trip was magical. In a fourteen-foot boat that he had built in his cellar and equipped with oars and a sail, Guider had put into the Cumberland River only a mile from his house, camping on the banks along the way as he braved thunderstorms from the Mississippi to New York. Guider is an extraordinary photographer and one of the most intrepid sailors of his generation. But when I met him at his exquisitely restored home in East Nashville, he was so gloomy and self-effacing that I couldn't believe he was the adventurer who had taken on the Great Loop in a fourteen-foot boat, and I could tell that he was dubious about my trip.

Guider described a gauntlet of weather conditions and obstacles that he was sure would prove perilous. The Mississippi, he told me, is so vast that it creates its own climate, with sharp offshore winds in the morning, when the river heats up faster than the land on the banks. By lunchtime the winds usually reversed to onshore breezes. Weather forecasting can't possibly predict these sudden changes of wind, or the thunderstorms that pop up in their midst, which I would rarely see beforehand on radar. Powerless against these winds, I would be turned broadside and forced into bridge pylons and the massive strings of commercial barges that I would encounter all day. Busy intersections like the confluence of the Ohio and the Mississippi at Cairo, Illinois, would be so congested with barge traffic that I would be lucky to get through without being pincered between two barge tows. Guider's Mississippi was a scorching, floating hell, infested with mosquitoes and strewn with boulders and submerged logs, where even the most trivial mistake could prove disastrous. Under the scorching southern sun, he warned, I would be dehydrated most of the time, but wouldn't recognize it. When my urine turned a deep amber or yellow, or I couldn't urinate at all, it was time to head off to a shady grove of trees on the banks, tie up, and drink a lot of water.

It was a stern lecture from a card-carrying member of the "You're going to die" school. I left Guider's place and drove back to Gallatin feeling downcast and doomed. Perhaps I should return the *Patience* boat signs that I had just received from a sign-painter friend in New England and have them replaced with nameplates that read, say, DEATH WISH or RIVER CASKET. I couldn't tell whether I was a suicidal jackass or just the victim of alarmist advice. There certainly didn't appear to be a lot of space in between.

In mid-April, a beefy ten-wheeler truck mounted with a construction crane arrived from Hendersonville to mount the *Patience* onto the trailer that Cooper planned to use to haul the boat to Pittsburgh. Cooper wanted to drop the boat into the Cumberland River six miles away to test its buoyancy, draft, and maneuverability for a few days in actual river conditions. The crane operators extended the hydraulic load stabilizers on the side of the truck and belayed the boat bottom with heavy lifting straps. As the *Patience* was lifted and swayed over to the trailer, I jumped onto the back of the truck to read the display screen of the digital scales measuring the weight of the boat. The empty weight of the *Patience* came in at 16,400 pounds, or eight tons. With motors, provisions, fuel, and a crew, the loaded hull would probably come in at almost ten tons. This was more than enough heft, I thought, to plow through the tree snags and swirling whirlpools that everyone predicted for the trip.

Cooper's boat trailer had spent the last several years moldering in the Kentucky field of a prior customer, and I could see right away that it was straining underneath the weight of the *Patience*. As I followed in my pickup as the trailer and boat turned onto the paved road, the metal fenders bounced over every bump and pothole with a menacing squeal and puff of smoke against the bald, rotting tires. I could have been driving blind that day. The stench of burning rubber drew me all the way to the Cumberland.

"John," I said when we reached the Army Corps of Engineers boat ramp on the Cumberland. "Is this trailer going to make it to Pittsburgh?"

"This was just par for the course," Cooper said. "The trailer is fine."

As soon as he got the trailer back to his farm, Cooper told me, he would use his welding torch to remove the fenders. He was planning on doing that anyway.

The *Patience* slid down the boat ramp and plunked into the water with a satisfying splash. I waded into the river up to my knees and plunged a tape measure below the waterline. Cooper's calculations about the boat's draft seemed to be accurate—the hull was drawing just eleven inches, and would probably not exceed eighteen inches once it was loaded. The next day, we took along a picnic lunch and pushed the hull down the river a couple of miles with Cooper's workboat. The *Patience* was remarkably agile in turns, and leapt forward against the current with the least suggestion of power. The bottom easily plowed through tree snags and bumped over rocks near the banks.

I felt happy and invincible. The *Patience* floated. She was as sturdy as a Roman galleon and looked as jaunty as a hillbilly monster truck. Along that stretch of the Cumberland, the bends in the river are guarded by a series of majestic sandstone bluffs, rising perpendicular from the water a hundred feet or more. The cabin roof where I would spend most of my time steering the boat commanded a breathtaking view downriver, and the afternoon sun turned the bluffs into luminous pastels.

We tied the *Patience* up for the night in a quiet cove within view of the big north-south bridge carrying the traffic along Highway 109. Driving away, I looked back as I turned onto the highway, and my new Kaintuck cabin serenely bobbed on the river, framed under a giant willow tree. The *Patience* was irresistible. That evening, I loaded my pickup with some camping gear, a cot, and shopped for food on my way back to the boat.

I lived on the boat for the next three days, basking in an alligator-horse trance. The big tugs pushing coal to a nearby Tennessee Valley Authority generating plant sloughed off giant wakes that reached me on the shore as lullaby rolls at night and gentle wake-up calls at dawn. In the afternoons, teenagers from the nearby marina splashed and screamed in the water. At sunset, the river turned lavender and pink as the low rumble of traffic on the nearby highway bridge mixed with the wails of CSX locomotive whistles on the railroad tracks. Life was simple and relaxing aboard my new floating sanctuary. There were no running-water luxuries—no toilet, shower, dish-washer, and sink—to bother me. I read at night under the soft glow of my Coleman lantern while a lamb stew simmered on my camp stove.

I was still worried about John Cooper finishing up all the features that I had asked for on the boat. I woke up one night with my T-shirt drenched with sweat, tortured by the "You're going to die" prophecies of all the river skeptics. In one dream, I navigated downstream in open space toward a girder bridge shining in the sunlight. Two large barge strings suddenly appeared on either side of the boat, closing the space in front of me so suddenly that I could no longer see the bridge.

But then a passing tug on the Cumberland sent some pleasing, stern-to-bow rollers my way, a breeze blew through the cabin, and I was entranced by the sounds of the peepers fiercely screeching from the wetlands nearby. Life on the river felt incurably romantic and hopeful. Screw it, I thought. I couldn't rid myself of trepidation. Anticipating the trip would probably continue to be dreadful. But I wasn't going to let a bad dose of adventure regret turn me back now.

5

HAULING THE BOAT TO PITTSBURGH was an epic fiasco. John Cooper's ancient boat trailer was rated for a maximum weight of twelve thousand pounds. The trailer tires that had baked under the sun in rural Kentucky for several years were as roadworthy as Jell-O. Now this misbegotten assemblage was being asked to haul eighteen thousand pounds of boat and gear, three tons over its limit, 550 miles to Pittsburgh. There were four blowouts on the boat trailer before we even got out of Tennessee, twelve flats in all, and a trip that should have taken ten hours ended up lasting a day and a half. By the seventh or eighth blowout I marveled at my incomparable stupidity. I should have named my flatboat *Calamity*.

I followed the crippled *Patience* convoy on the interstates north, sullenly staring through my pickup windshield at the yellow and black WIDE LOAD sign ahead and watching for the telltale puff of black smoke that announced that another tire was shredding. I was saved from complete depression by Brady Carr, a former marine, logger, and now a successful magazine publisher in Tennessee, who had approached me months before about joining the first leg of the trip. During the ride up together, Brady and I were developing an interesting relationship, a Redneck-Yankee détente that somehow worked. Brady is an outspoken southern conservative who can't resist projecting his political views as a major element of his personality. He was constantly goading me with nasty quips about liberals,

minorities, and immigrants. He loved it when I cheerfully lashed back, calling him a "cracker." But Brady would prove to be so reliable and enduring
in tough situations that it was easy to ignore his rote conservative insults.
Later, I would think of our Pittsburgh run together as another useful dress
rehearsal for the ordeals to come. No matter how much he provoked me, I
was learning to trust Brady.

Brady had spent years hauling timber on sixteen-wheeler log trucks
and had a commercial driver's license. Blowouts didn't faze him.

"Damn," I said as we climbed a hillside in Kentucky and another tire
blew, lofting snakes of rubber up over the chase car and into my pickup
grille. "I've spent ten thousand dollars to get this boat to the Monongahela
and all we're doing is buying tires."

"Relax," Brady said. "I've seen this before. It's part of hauling. That
driver is very determined and he's got a really good helper there changing
tires."

We had decided to launch the *Patience* along the Monongahela at
Elizabeth, Pennsylvania, twenty miles south of Pittsburgh, because of the
critical role the town had played in the early 19th-century flatboat era. The
town's historic boat ramp sloped to the water beside a small park and picnic
area below First Street. The green riverbanks sharply rise toward a horizon
dominated by the steeple of the United Methodist Church, and, below it,
the charming brick and clapboard facades of Stephen Bayard's old river port
faced the river. We finally parked the trailer beside the picnic benches in
the park at ten o'clock on the second night after we left Tennessee. Pangs
of despondency over the dreadful ride north stabbed my chest, but my lifelong ability to censor away bad news about myself redeemed me that night.
While everyone else climbed the Allegheny hills to find a restaurant for a
late dinner, I wanted to be alone for a while. I stood on a grassy spot a few
feet above the river, happy to have the *Patience* within launching distance of
the Mon and elated by the nocturnal views across the water.

To descend the walls of the Mon Valley to the banks of the river is to be
encased in an eerie and historic American beauty, especially at night. The
seedy downtowns and boarded-up bowling alleys of the dying blue-collar
towns perched on the Allegheny hills gradually give way to spectacular
views through the breaks in the trees, or over a cluster of rooftops, to an
industry-scape of intense blacks and browns. The Mon is an immense

woodblock print of reality. The brisk river breezes act as a kind of visual and emotive bellows, enhancing the yellow glow from the lights of famous steel towns—Homestead, McKeesport, Clairton, and Duquesne—that crowd the bends of the Monongahela up to Pittsburgh. The silvery river itself centers the eye on images that are so gritty they seem divine. Tugboats pushing rusty coal barges rumble by, churning up white wakes lit by their running lights. The gantries and stacks of the old U.S. Steel works loom somberly along the riverbanks, markers in a giant manufacturing graveyard, and the endless string of bridges north and south cast spooky shadows lit by moonlight on the Monongahela. All of this is condensed into a narrow corridor of vision by the hills rising abruptly from the banks, which close the river off from the world.

The wind picked up as I stood by the water, carrying the whining of the tugboats downstream. It was chilly on the banks and time to go. I was torn between the rapture of launching my flatboat in a day or two and the misgivings generated by the dispiriting run from Tennessee. I couldn't see much beyond the first distant landmark that I would pass, the Union Railroad bridge at the big bend of the river at Clairton. But at least I had reached the place that I had dreamed about for almost two years, Jacob Yoder country, and the risk was now here to take.

The next morning, the Elizabeth boat ramp hummed with the cheerful mayhem of an expedition launch. By nine o'clock, the wildly mismatched crew that I had collected was racing around the *Patience*, hammering and squealing their cordless drills with all of the unfinished work that still had to be built out on the boat. I was pleasantly surprised that I had managed to attract so many self-motivated worker bees. Scott Mandrell had brought along his fourteen-year-old son, who was working with John Cooper, shaving off the ends of long poplar boards into emergency steering oars. Brady Carr had impressed me back in Tennessee with his organizing skills, consolidating all of our cooking and bedding gear, and now he was busy all around the *Patience*, coiling rope and building hooks in the stern, mounting lantern and light fixtures and sketching out a plan for shelving in the kitchen galley in the bow. He was a true marine, hardworking and cheerfully busy, very fastidious about returning wrenches and screwdrivers to their proper places in the toolbox.

Danny Corjulo had arrived the night before and immediately began applying his manic energy to the boat electronics and running gear, bitching quietly to me about Cooper's construction standards. He compiled a list of hardware and supplies—a backup battery and charger, twelve-volt wiring for the radios and lights, hoses and clamps to install an engine pressure gauge, a radio mount, star drills, and charging stations for our cell phones. We would follow the same boatbuilding regimen that I had practiced in Tennessee. All morning we worked like demons on the boat, and then we spent the afternoon tearing around Pittsburgh to find the equipment we needed. The clangor of us readying the boat mixed in the breezes with the song of the Mon Valley, the din of a nearby foundry, and the diesel whine of the tugs on the river.

I was amazed at the amount of loot that Danny had managed to shoehorn into the luggage he carried to Pittsburgh on his airline flight. He was determined to make the *Patience* a self-sustaining navigation platform, hardware store, and media lab, all floating within one hull. Typically for Danny, he carried three iPads, two for the boat and one for himself, containing a marine navigation system, iNavX, and transponder software that would allow him to remotely track the *Patience* from the shore so he could maintain a real-time website map of our journey. He also carried three GoPro units and assorted mounts for remote photography and video, lithium battery packs, and a police-grade megaphone for communicating with tugboats in case our radio failed. Danny's cooking gear—cutting boards, chef's knives, pasta-making equipment—was elaborate enough for Chez Panisse. We didn't need even half of this stuff, and all of the paraphernalia swirling around him would just induce Danny's attention deficit disorder and infuriate me. But I was ignoring that for now—I would have to ignore a lot to get to New Orleans with the menagerie of personalities aboard the *Patience.*

I could see that first day that Scott Mandrell would become my biggest management problem. He strutted around the boat all morning, trying to engage himself in everyone else's projects, struggling to accept that his Meriwether Lewis alter ego didn't put him in charge of our trip. For Scott, the slightest fixture or repair on the boat triggered long, self-involved soliloquies about his various misadventures with ripped anchor lines or terrifying river currents, which nobody listened to because they were too busy wiring lights or building out the galley. He seemed completely incapable of inhabiting someone else's emotional space and considering his impact on people. The most inconsequential details of Meriwether Lewis's life prompted him to drone on with another story about himself. Nobody met Scott's standards. John Cooper had introduced me to him as one of his best friends in the river community, but Scott spent most of that first day savaging Cooper and his wife behind their backs, deriding the craftsmanship on the boat, and castigating Gloria as "annoying." I tried to silence him by giving him something useful to do. I asked him to study my river charts and find likely refueling points along the Ohio River that we could rely on for the first week between, say, Pittsburgh and Marietta, Ohio. But that didn't work.

"I already know all of the fuel stops on the Ohio," Scott said.

Danny and Scott developed an instant dislike for each other, a true Bobby Kennedy–Jimmy Hoffa mutual loathing, which had begun the night before. Scott's impetuousness could be dangerous. Excited that the *Patience* had finally arrived, he squealed his SUV in reverse across the parking lot above town where we were waiting for the trailer. I saw him coming and jumped out of the way, but still Scott missed me by inches. Danny was livid about it.

"Who is this guy?" he asked me. "He's a total wing nut."

"Let's just be tolerant now, Danny," I said. "We need him to learn the river."

Their personality clash went way beyond the parking lot near miss. Their DNA derived from distant planets. Danny—provocative, sarcastic, and a defiant food snob—radiated Italian Brooklyn. Danny was loud and brash, but he was essentially humble and loved self-mockery. Scott's sole raison d'être was taking himself seriously. Incompatible doesn't begin to describe their feverish animus for each other—they were Sophia Loren on a blind date with Billy Graham. When they first clashed, I thought to myself: *Oh, what a fun trip we are going to have here. Rinker, as a human resources manager, you are first class.*

As a newspaper photographer, Danny had developed a reputation for sharp visuals, with a fine eye for light and color contrasts, portraiture, and moody landscapes. His camera was always nearby and an inseparable part of his antic, multitasking personality. In the middle of conducting simultaneous internet searches on his iPad and cell phone, or wiring a new radio, he would glance over and see a promising visual possibility, grab his camera, and snap.

From the moment he stepped out of the car in Elizabeth, Danny was shooting away, obsessed about documenting the flatboat trip. That morning, the second or third time that Danny poked his long-lens Sony Alpha around to shoot Scott, Meriwether Lewis blushed bright red and the veins on his forehead pulsed like fire hoses.

Scott pointed his finger at Danny.

"You can take all of the goddamn pictures of me that you want," he snapped. "But don't ever show me with a cigarette! My wife doesn't know that I smoke."

Danny knew just what to say.

"Scott, we're separated at birth! I'm a closet smoker, too!"

Scott had brought along an oddball sidekick named Jay, a loyal groupie from his Meriwether Lewis trips. Jay had spent most of his life as a union pipe fitter on large construction projects, working on power plants along the Ohio River, and now supplemented his pension by installing poles and American flags at office parks and car lots. He was tall and broad-shouldered with a bushy white mustache, his head invariably topped off with a filthy do-rag, and he was seriously afflicted with the reenactor costume obsession. He lived for the fantasy life of being a pirate. Before we left the Elizabeth docks, he took off his "street clothes" and donned a pink linen pirate's tunic that dropped almost to his knees, held in place with a large garrison belt and dagger. He wore this getup barefoot, and without underwear. His varicose scrotum flapped in the breeze as we worked on the *Patience* on the Elizabeth wharf. Jay was just about the most foul-mouthed person I had ever heard. But I liked him. His Blackbeard swagger and exhibitionist gonads lent a buccaneer aura to the *Patience*.

The many and evident eccentricities of my crew prompted me to return to a subject I had reflected upon almost from the day I decided to build a flatboat and sail to New Orleans. How would I lead, especially captaining a boat? I had always defaulted toward a laissez-faire approach to leadership, favoring a style that mostly stressed enabling people to make decisions on their own according to their strengths, and not issuing a lot of explicit commands. This preference had been affirmed by my recent experience caring for my mother in Maine, when there were a lot of family conflicts to work around. Talking about this one day with my mother, she had said, "Your family consists of the people you are bound by convention to love but learn to ignore."

My situation on the *Patience* wasn't that different. Somehow, without really trying to, I had attracted a crew of keen self-starters with strong personalities. The exception was the querulous and insecure Scott Mandrell, but I had decided to overlook him for the moment. That first day working along the riverbanks I settled on a strategy of just standing apart and relaxing, enjoying the madcap sampling of humanity I had drawn to the *Patience*.

History seemed to support this approach. Ninteenth-century flatboat excursions weren't elaborately planned, and the choice of companions mostly depended upon happenstance. This theme was stressed by John Francis McDermott, a professor of American history at the University of Southern Illinois, whose influential compilations—*Audubon in the West* and *Before Mark Twain: A Sampler of Old, Old Times on the Mississippi*—I had read that spring. McDermott was known for his reliance on tangible, down-to-earth contemporary accounts by common rivermen and forest guides, and not educated elites. In a 1967 essay in *Proceedings of the American Antiquarian Society*, "Travelers on the Western Waters," McDermott described the accidental hiring practices that more or less guaranteed that flatboat crews would be made up of "a foul-mouthed, rough set of bullies and braggarts—riff-raff and oddments of society—who rapidly became tiresome and inescapable traveling companions."

The trans-Mississippi frontier was a thorough mixing of global misfits. "Long before the first steamboat puffed its way down to New Orleans in 1811," McDermott wrote, "travelers of every sort, class and occupation were abroad on the western waters for a multitude of reasons." The flatboat route along the Ohio and the Mississippi had become an international haven for escaped convicts and political exiles searching for sanctuary. McDermott identified several British army veterans searching for work as mercenaries, Christian missionaries bent on converting the Shawnee or Choctaw tribes, and nobles escaping the Reign of Terror during the French Revolution. The royal botanist of France, André Michaux, conducted several prestigious scientific surveys along the Ohio and Mississippi while simultaneously spying for his government back in Paris. In 1804, flatboat captain George Hunter left Brownsville along the Monongahela with a crew that included "an old Spanish fencing master, a Swiss shoemaker, & a German who [all] worked their passage."

To man a Kentucky boat for the trip downriver, McDermott wrote, "one took in whatever crew was available. Oftentimes there were men hanging around the port of departure hoping to hitch a ride westward." Captains routinely described this grab bag of crew members as "indolent," "profane," "inebriate," and "constantly sleeping all day." They avoided tying up near towns at night because too many crew members would desert.

Historian Charles Henry Ambler, in his *A History of Transportation in the Ohio Valley*, made an important point about this early social mixing and strife on the western rivers. Historians have generally depicted the great migration west as a process of removing the excess energy of the heavily populated East. The unemployed, the dreamers, the swindlers, and gunslingers whose personalities were unsuitable for the settled society of the East found a culture more suitable in the violent, unpredictable West. But Ambler also believed that the rush west performed a valuable service for the more established East. "Eastern capitalists and conservatives," Ambler wrote, "generally regarded it as a good riddance of worthless debtors, incurable demagogues, and insufferable malcontents." The frontier, in this conception, wasn't just a national migration that bumptiously settled the open spaces of the West. It was a *cleansing* process for the East, allowing the more subtle institutions and practices of the industrial revolution to proceed relatively free of conflict.

Reliance on history runs so deep in me that it's not hard to use its lessons as a personal excuse. I probably shouldn't blame myself for the haphazard way that I found a crew, I thought, because many of the original flatboat captains had done no better. The mash of characters that I'd gathered would turn the *Patience* into my own private microcosm of America floating downriver. That would be the adventure. I had gone to see my country in a new way, and wrangling this crazy corral of misfits into a workable crew would perhaps be my greatest challenge.

———

At the end of that first day, we launched the *Patience* on the Monongahela by backing the boat trailer down the steep ramp on the bank until the hull floated off by itself. We knew that the brisk river currents would quickly carry the boat away, and I watched with interest while Scott Mandrell and John Cooper secured the bow and stern with rope lines tied to trees on either side of the ramp. Both lines were taut within seconds of the *Patience* reaching the current and I was impressed with how gamely nine tons of hillbilly flatboat responded to the downriver flow. John Cooper started the Mercury engine, establishing that the *Patience* would make way, and then called for the lines to be cast off. Moving slightly offshore, he made a few gentle turns to test the boat's handling qualities, and then slowly chugged down to the town wharf a quarter mile north. I scrambled along the banks downstream to the wharf, elated by the *Patience*'s. clunky but picaresque profile from the shore. Once more I watched carefully as Cooper secured the *Patience* to the rusty bollards on the wharf.

Nineteenth-century flatboat travelers on the western rivers generally didn't rely on compasses, except for the occasional, relatively prosperous captain who carried a primitive, handheld family heirloom. The farmers who manned most flatboats were accustomed to judging their direction by the sun and local landmarks, and their bounds of movement were restricted by the riverbanks and well-known hazards like sandbars, islands, and rock formations. After 1811, the maps and gazetteers of the Ohio and the Mississippi published by Zadok Cramer and Samuel Cumings meticulously described or pictured the best deep-water channels, as well as the landmarks onshore that helped define the desired "sail line." Until the 1830s, when steamboat traffic began to increase, darkness at night and morning fog weren't serious hazards because boats could always pull to the banks and wait for better conditions. Sudden thunderstorms, drifting logjams, and sandbars that shifted position from year to year were, to be sure, serious hazards to navigation. But in most conditions the boats could only travel between two banks, or between low-water shoals that could be seen at a distance, and the flatboaters didn't need a compass to assess their position against these obstacles, which also served as useful, highly visible waypoints.

The situation I faced on the rivers in modern times was completely different. There are now twenty dams on the Ohio alone, and virtually every mile along the lower Mississippi contains an elaborate lattice of underwater wing dams, cement revetments, and long, curving rock jetties to "channelize" the water flow and increase its velocity for barge traffic. Maintaining consistent compass headings to steer around these obstacles was vital. Barge traffic was my biggest worry. On any given day along the lower Mississippi (below the confluence with the Ohio), there are at least 820 tugs pushing barges, and the typical fifteen-barge string weighs over twenty-two thousand tons, making it virtually impossible for them to alter course quickly. As I was moving downriver and one of these big Ingram or ExxonMobil pushers was emerging from a tricky river bend two or three miles away, I would have to "read" the tugboat captain or helmsman's intentions and forecast the course he would take up the straightaway toward the next big channel buoy. Tugboat captains, like airline pilots, are notoriously unwilling to bother with radio communications with smaller, private craft in their way, and the rule of the river is to avoid needless radio chatter. They can call me; I don't hail them.

My closing time with these commercial vessels would not be especially fast, and I could usually expend several minutes figuring out which way the tug was going to push its barge string. But after that it would be absolutely necessary for me to announce my intentions by dramatically moving my bow to starboard or port, signaling that I was clearing the way for the ungainly barges and tug. At major cities like Cincinnati and Memphis, there were interstate highway bridges where the passageways between the supporting pylons were narrow, allowing enough space for just two or three boats at once. That, I knew, required a compass. The current and winds could always alter my heading, signaling to the tug captain ahead that I was not "reliable traffic," also called "drifting traffic," and that I was inadvertently wandering off my avoidance course. Small-boat traffic is an enormous worry for tug captains. Fast outboards pulling water-skiers and yahoo teenagers out for a beer and a lark in Daddy's cigarette boat can careen wildly in and out of the sail line, suddenly disappearing unseen beneath the visual barrier of the barge hulls. The Coast Guard is legally entitled to pull these boats off the river as a "hazard to navigation," based on just a single captain's report.

Before I left Tennessee, the tugboat crew members that I had spoken with on the Cumberland River had advised me about another factor. Tugs sharing the same ten- or fifteen-mile stretch on the rivers talk constantly with each other, either via marine band radio or by laptop and cell phone text. A boat that is considered dangerous to commercial traffic becomes well known even before the captains can see it. The last thing I wanted, the tug crews on the Cumberland had told me, was a "bad rep" within the fraternity of tug captains on the river.

I didn't know much yet about tying up at night, but I wanted the comfort of a compass that was lit all night. Once all of my lines were secured to shore, and an anchor was laid off the stern to stabilize my position, changing currents and wind could always reposition the boat after the sun went down. The civilian staff that runs the Army Corps of Engineers dams can release enormous amounts of water at night, to improve the depth of the channel underneath the sail line. These nighttime water releases could dramatically affect current and change the position of my boat. If my compass heading changed overnight, it meant that my lines weren't holding me in a consistent position against the banks. I wanted to be able to quickly climb up to the roof deck in the dark and check that my compass heading remained steady. If I went to bed and my compass against the Indiana bank read 280 degrees, it had to remain at that heading all night, or I had to adjust my lines.

None of this impressed John Cooper or Scott Mandrell, "experts" whose attitudes about a compass I was convinced were not dictated by reason, but instead by their backward reenactor mentality. On their expeditions, when they "camped" along the river for a catered meal at a prearranged town landing or marina, their boats were safely tied to a floating dock or boxed in by the slip of a commercial marina. They didn't need compasses for their kind of trip. Even though I had asked Cooper several times to have a lighted compass installed at or near the steering console on the cabin roof, he never got one.

In Elizabeth, when I asked Cooper one last time for a compass, he was very polite about it.

"Well, as I've tried to explain, the old flatboats didn't have compasses," he said. "I didn't get one because you really can't find many of those today. They either come installed with a new boat, or they don't."

Scott Mandrell was aggressively rude about it, equally oblivious of the need to adapt to barge traffic. He was a reenactor, ergo the river belonged to him.

"Meriwether Lewis only carried small hand compasses, and he didn't steer his expedition by them, and he didn't even have maps," Scott said. "He was the first upriver and he was *making* the maps."

I could tell that Danny was upset when I explained all of this to him. His particular verbal dyslexia, a difficulty sorting out place names and proper nouns, tends to return when he's under stress.

"Maritime Lewis!" Danny said. "What's he got to do with it? He's not coming on this trip. Let's go compass shopping! I'm sure I can hook one up."

We tried everywhere around Pittsburgh, in between Danny's long stops at Whole Foods, All-Phase Electric Supply, and Harbor Freight Tools. We checked all of the fancy suburban boat shops in Fox Chapel and Wilkinsburg, and Allegheny Marina Boats & Yachts along the river, where the pretty-boy store clerks in their Nantucket red khakis seemed surprised that we would even *think* about asking for a boat compass. "They come with the boat," they said. "Why would we stock a compass?" The big-box chains—REI, Cabela's, and Dunham's Sports—were just as frustrating. Jacob Yoder country! The flatboat gateway to the old Northwest! But none of these slick vendors sold boat compasses.

In despair, we finally ended up after nightfall at a dingy marine-supply discount outlet in Dravosburg. Danny was disconsolate at this point, and had determined from examining several websites that we could probably jury-rig a digital GPS compass to the twelve-volt system. When we pulled up to the store, the show window out front featured a Day-Glo rubber boat bumper above a sign that read: FITS ALL BOATS! This was definitely our final stop.

"I'm not even going in there," Danny said. "The dickheads of American retailing don't sell compasses anymore."

But when I pushed through the door, I couldn't believe what I saw, atop the first endcap in the store. There was a big magnetic compass, encased in a clunky glass dome that looked like it dated to a 1960s Russian space capsule, with large-type numerals identifying the 360 degrees. The box beside it advertised the special "NiteLite" function, which worked twenty-four hours a day, regardless of ambient light. The compass was perfect for the console on the roof deck of the *Patience*.

I pushed back through the door and waved Danny inside.

"Okay, this will work," Danny said, examining the compass and the electrical probes on the back of the casing. "I can slave this to the power source for the navigation iPad and everything will be fine."

Inside the store, Danny also found a shiny "Special Forces Tomahawk" and fondled it in his hands. The tomahawk was a perfectly balanced carbon steel instrument, powder-coated in black, with a sharp cutting edge on one side and a hammerhead on the other. The labeling on the package said that the hatchet was "Designed by a real Green Beret from North Carolina!" It was capable of cutting through "doors, heavy wiring and metal fencing" and, when the bullets ran out, the tomahawk could also be used for self-defense. The pattern of the glass-reinforced nylon grip was exquisite.

I could tell that Danny really wanted that Special Forces Tomahawk, but he refused to buy it because he was worried that we were spending too much money. He'd been impulsively stopping at convenience stores all afternoon to buy Mega Millions lottery tickets. If we won anything, he said, we could finance the entire expedition to New Orleans.

But I insisted on buying the Special Forces Tomahawk anyway. Screw frugality. It wasn't lack of funds that would prevent us from reaching New Orleans. A lack of enthusiasm or perseverance would prevent us from reaching New Orleans. Danny was already driving me insane. He was obnoxious, hyperkinetic, couldn't stop losing his train of thought while multitasking with his cell phone and laptops, and he wouldn't shut up. But Danny had already made a monumental contribution to the trip, and I just wanted to reward his insufferable ass with something nice.

Danny was jubilant about the purchase and was still fondling the Special Forces axe when we got out to my pickup.

I agreed with him. I was anticipating wonderful outdoor fires along the banks of the Ohio and the Mississippi and the Special Forces axe was going to be great for splitting firewood.

"No way!" Danny said. "You keep your filthy hands off this. The Special Forces axe is a culinary tool. I'm using it to cut up steaks and whole chickens."

It was dark by the time we got back to the town wharf in Elizabeth and I was entranced, filled with the fever for journey, when I saw the *Patience* gently tugging her tie ropes. The light from a streetlamp above filtered down through the trees and bathed the poplar profile with soft lavender and blue hues.

Barry Boucher, a city councilman and future mayor of Elizabeth, drove to the wharf that night and offered to guide us down the Monongahela in the morning as far as Pittsburgh. A big, gregarious Mon Valley native with a pronounced Pittsburgh accent, Barry had fished and taken boats up and down the Mon for years. He told me that just about every challenge we'd face on the Ohio—Army Corps of Engineers locks, barge traffic, channel markers, and buoys—would occur along the twenty-three miles downriver to Three Rivers Point in Pittsburgh. "You'll be a pro by the time I'm done with you," Barry said. I'd been particularly intimidated about negotiating the big government locks, but now I was relieved, anxious to get started in the morning. My backup on the first day would be a local riverman.

Beside the *Patience*, everyone was sorting through their duffel bags and compiling rejection piles of excess gear, jettisoning extra clothing, electric shavers, and shoes, to reduce the belongings they had to worry about for the next month. I was astonished by the piles of Scott Mandrell, who had lugged two enormously long and overstuffed army surplus canvas bags from his SUV.

It was just unbelievable what he had. There was enough period wear in his bags to costume the whole *Mutiny on the Bounty* set—pirate belts and daggers, tam-o'-shanter caps, berets, tricorne hats, French and Indian War officers' uniforms, waist sashes, and several cuts of steampunk pants with suspenders. A Victorian explorer would be embarrassed to own so much crap.

Scott must have sensed from the look on my face that I was appalled, and looked up as I passed.

"Don't worry, Rinker, I'm only going to be doing so much period dressing," he said. "I'm just bringing some calico shirts, duck pants and the right belts, a straw hat, and rainwear. Rivermen usually went barefoot, so I don't need shoes."

"I didn't know that, Scott," I said.

I loaded my own duffel onto the boat and stowed it on the aft wall of the cabin, where Brady Carr had hung stout metal hooks for our gear. An antiques store owner in Elizabeth had donated three spindle chairs and a small pine sideboard, which attractively filled out the cabin.

Onboard, Danny was fussing around the galley in the bow, firing up his espresso pots on my Coleman camp stove. I walked behind and stood outside in the stern and stared down the Monongahela beyond the Elizabeth Bridge. A big white tug named *Connie K* pushed by with coal barges, followed by a tug pushing a work barge filled with scrap metal and a tall, mid-deck crane. Their wakes gently rocked the *Patience* and the diesel residue left behind by their stacks felt like a drug, inducing the romance of travel.

Danny walked back through the cabin smoking a cigar and handed me a cup of espresso. The smell of coffee and Danny's cigar smoke pleasantly mixed in the air with the diesel scent.

"This trip is going to be great," he said. "But it's already getting to be a clusterfuck."

"Get used to it," I said. "Clusterfuck is good. Clusterfuck is our new normal."

6

THE NEXT MORNING, AS I walked down the sloped pavement toward the Elizabeth wharf, the east light rising over the Alleghenies cast an immense shadow from the steeple of the United Methodist Church. A lone tug across the river was pushing three barges south from the fleeting docks of the Consolidation Coal Company. It was a perfect July morning with a low deck of fleecy white cumulus clouds over the Monongahela. The *Patience*, framed by the water and the high hills on the west banks, looked as lovely as the flatboat in the Currier and Ives lithograph *Bound Down the River*. I was flushed with pride and anticipation. That's *my* boat parked on the Monongahela, I thought, my trip down the river.

On the boat, Danny had donned his white chef's apron and was making a breakfast of goat cheese and basil omelets with bruschetta toast. We dawdled on the deck for almost an hour, laughing, drinking coffee, speculating on the day ahead. My crew was already in fine form. Jay was wearing his burlesque pirate's tunic and dagger belt and was telling raunchy stories about life on the river as a steamfitter. Brady teased Danny about his apron and called him Chef Boyardee. Danny laughed and, handing Brady his omelet, said, "Bon appétit, you dumbass cracker." Then he entertained us with his stories about learning to cook in his grandmother's apartment kitchen in Yonkers. Nothing could spoil our launch now.

But, of course, something could. John Cooper had come down to the boat the night before to mark the steering wheel with black electrical tape so that I wouldn't turn too sharply and hang up the Mercury motor's lower shaft against the large wooden box he'd built into the stern to house the motor. Then, using the Mercury's electric trim, he had lowered the propeller to what he considered the right depth against the bottom of the boat.

"Everything's all set," he said in the morning. "Gloria and I are going to drive up to the Elizabeth Bridge and watch you leave."

Barry Boucher joined me at the steering console on the roof deck and, as I started and then idled the motor in neutral, I looked up and down the river. Our only traffic was a tug pushing five barges almost a mile upriver, tracking left of center in the channel.

"Traffic not a factor," I said.

"Correct," Barry said. "You can see from how low his barges are in the water that he's heavily loaded. He won't be here for at least fifteen minutes."

Scott came forward and kneeled beside the steering console, recommending that I follow a long list of launching commands. He insisted that I call out, "Forward Mate! Lines secure? Stern Mate! Lines secure? Prepare to cast lines."

But when I looked down, Brady was quite competently holding the stern line against the rear kevel, and Jay was holding his line on the bow. They were prepared to launch and carefully looking above to me.

"Scott, we'll be fine, thanks," I said.

Scott stepped to the side of the deck and angrily lit a cigarette.

"You're supposed to call out the proper commands to your crew," he said.

"We're good, Scott," I said.

I took one last look to judge the velocity of the current going by the boat and called to Brady and Jay.

"Free the lines," I said, and I was impressed by the way, after releasing us from the wharf, they pulled in the ropes and coiled them into neat circles on the deck.

I could sense that the current would immediately push us downriver and try to turn us broadside, so I gently turned to port into the fast water, easing the throttle forward to about 20 percent power until I could see what the boat would do. The *Patience* quickly responded and made way into the current. I advanced to about half power and turned more to port to make a wide sweeping turn across the river, to test our steering ability before we headed away from the wharf. I leaned over to talk to Barry.

"I know that I'm turning into the current and across the river, but I'd like to be upriver if we need to get back to the wharf."

"You're good," Barry said. "That's the way to do it."

But as my speed increased and there was more water running under the boat, I could feel the steering wheel grow heavy and then almost lock up. It took enormous muscle to keep the boat in its left turn and there was obviously something wrong. I curbed my instinct to panic, looked quickly up and down the river for traffic, and then reduced power to ease the forces on the helm. I steered upriver in an even flatter turn to position the boat to drift back toward the wharf.

"We're going back, Barry," I said. "This steering is definitely not right."

I had never docked anything larger than a canoe, but I felt comfortable using my instincts getting back to the wharf. Once we were straightened out and headed back downriver, I repeated to myself, "Slow, slow, slow." We couldn't get into any trouble if we were slow. And the *Patience* was such a bulky scow, way overbuilt with two-inch poplar on the sides, that even a rough landing with a cement wharf wasn't going to hurt anything.

One hundred yards out I had the *Patience* aligned, tracking a parallel course with the edge of the wharf, and I let the river current do most of the work pushing us downstream. I occasionally feathered the throttle to maintain steering. I called down to Jay and Brady to man their ropes and prepare to dock. When I looked down, they had already uncoiled the lines and were ready to jump off to the wharf and fix us tight to the bollards.

I was calm, relaxed, and loved being at the helm of this hillbilly wooden barge. Mishaps early in a trip are good, I reassured myself, without really feeling that. This is my education. Docking would be no more difficult than landing a plane with an engine that was acting up.

Behind me, Scott spoke up.

"Your crew is supposed to yell back, 'Aye-Aye, Capt'n!'" he said.

I ignored him, but Barry, who'd known Scott for years, could see the problem.

"Rinker's doing fine, Scott. Relax."

Ten yards out, I gently advanced the throttle one last time to pitch us at just the right angle to the wharf, waited three seconds, and then eased us into reverse. The *Patience* sidled onto the wharf as gently as a puppy nuzzling its mother, and Brady and Jay jumped off to the wharf and secured our lines.

"Jesus, I don't have much to teach you," Barry said. "That was perfect."

"Just beginner's luck," I said. "Now we've got to fix this thing."

John Cooper had raced down from the Elizabeth Bridge when he saw us turn back and had diagnosed the problem before he got back to the boat.

"I adjusted the propeller too low last night," he said. "The lower unit of the motor is hitting the sides of the housing. All you have to do every morning is play with the lifter until it's at the right height."

Brady and Danny had already figured that out. They were back in the stern hanging over the edges of the engine housing, fiddling with the electronic tilt that controlled the depth of the propeller in the water. They weren't satisfied with Cooper's proposed fix. The engine was held in place by two stout chains, attached to eye hooks connected to a large transom board inside the housing. It was another installation that needed adjusting. The chains needed to be shortened to make the motor stand more upright, which would create more clearance for the motor in the housing.

"What do you say, Danny?" Brady said. "I think one link shorter would do it."

"Two links," Danny said. "That'll compensate once the transom and the housing begin to sag with use."

"Two links, then," Brady said.

Jay, in his pirate's tunic, sprawled seminude across the motor housing and wrestled a rope around the back of the motor. He looked like the proverbial plumber fixing a lady's sink, baring the crack in his ass as his pants slid too low. Grunting and cursing as they jimmied the heavy motor straight with the ropes, Jay, Danny, and Brady had the chains connected two links shorter within twenty minutes.

After the repair was done, Danny came up to the roof deck and sat beside me at the wheel. He was furious about the snafu with the motor housing, and he had already complained bitterly to me about Cooper's crude electrical wiring, the doors that didn't fit, our clunky poplar navigation console.

"Cooper's a loser," Danny said.

"Danny, stop complaining," I said. "All of the problems with this boat?"

"There's a lot of them on this shit rig."

"And they're all my fault," I said. "I hired Cooper. But this is *our* shit rig now, and it floats. We're taking it to New Orleans."

We tested the adjusted steering while still tied to the wharf. I ran the motor very slowly and rolled the wheel all the way starboard and port, and the lower unit of the engine was no longer hitting the housing.

The tug pushing barges that we had seen before was way downriver now, almost out of sight, and there was no other traffic.

"This may be overdoing it," I said to Barry once we were ready to re-launch. "But I'm going to swing wide across the river again just to make sure."

"Sounds right to me," Barry said.

I felt more confident now as I called for Brady and Jay to release their lines and then briskly turned west into the current, running straight across the river parallel to the Elizabeth Bridge. The *Patience* responded a lot more nimbly than I thought she would as I tried a few S-turns running west and played back and forth with the throttle, to test her response to power. The stiffness of the wheel had disappeared and I noticed only one oddity of handling, which was that there was a brief lag in response coming out of a turn. The *Patience* was just a forty-foot, ten-ton dock attached to a motor, boxy and without a keel, and a certain reluctance to change course was to be expected. The flat bottom slid sideways out of a turn. But I liked this hesitation in steering because it meant that I had to anticipate every maneuver beforehand, rolling out of turns a few seconds early. The brief period of sliding sideways out of a turn created a useful "holding moment," an advantage I could use when docking or steering around tugs.

We were launched. As I steered the *Patience* downriver toward the Elizabeth Bridge, I could just make out, at the big Clairton bend ahead, a collection of massive stacks spewing steam and exhaust, which was slanted almost due north in the wind. Good, the wind is behind us. When I checked my Army Corps of Engineers charts, the site was clearly marked as U.S. Steel's massive coke works at Clairton, and I decided to "cheat" the sail line in the middle of the river by steering for the west banks and then the stacks, cutting my traveling distance a bit.

I was startled by the thunderous clangor once we got under the bridge.

The structure acted as an immense reverberation chamber, throwing down a deafening rumble from the steel span above. Eighteen-wheeler semi-trucks, as they bounced over the grated roadway, shook the bridge girders, and the din from that descended and glanced off the cement pylons, slammed into the water with a metallic roar, and then violently echoed back up. When they strike water, sound waves are bent, or refracted, which magnifies their decibel level. Sound refraction by water is the same principle that makes it possible for boaters to hear voices onshore, or vice versa, or exaggerates the growl of the prop and engine when an airplane flies near clouds. The amplification was so loud that it seemed to penetrate my ribs and rattle my insides. After we passed the bridge, the relative silence and the pristine quality of the ambient noise—now I could hear traffic along the riverside highway and the clacking of Union Railroad cars—was almost like experiencing sound for the first time.

I loved the gritty novelty of seeing the Mon Valley from the water—it was akin to the surprise of seeing the country for the first time from a railroad passenger car. I was navigating through space that had matured over 250 years, the time of my country's being, from pristine wilderness to traveled waterway to mighty American Ruhr. The Mon is a celebration of historic extremes. In his 1826 *Recollections*, Timothy Flint lyrically described rivermen "dancing to the violin on the deck of their boat," and how they'd "scatter their wit among the girls on the shore who came down to the water's edge to see the pageant [of boats] pass." We learn from Flint about the origins of the famed Mississippi River steamboat whistle. To broadcast their position to oncoming traffic, or announce their landing at the next town, the early boatmen used the same kind of bugle that the messengers carried on the wagon trains crossing the Alleghenies. The abundance of whiskey and food on the flatboats were, Flint wrote, "seductions that proved irresistible" to pioneer teenagers watching the boat procession from the banks. "The boats float by their [pioneer] dwellings on beautiful spring mornings, when the verdant forest, the mild and delicious temperature of the air, the delightful azure of the sky of this country, the fine bottom on the one hand, and the romantic bluff on the other . . . all these circumstances harmonize in the youthful excited imagination."

Flint and other early 19th-century observers were traveling the Ohio and the Mississippi at a time when rural views were slowly being altered by settlement and waterwheel industrialization, but their descriptions were still essentially pastoral. As they curved around the bends on their flats, the river travelers encountered crude frontier villages with cedar shake roofs glinting under the sun, docks made from timber with the bark still on, and loggers' huts clinging to the steep inclines of cleared forests. But the intrusions of man along the rivers only added to the bucolic romance of the river environment. Easterners and Europeans in particular were amazed by the abundance of wildlife, especially flocks of birds so thick that they blocked the sun in the middle of the day. During a bird-hunting and sketching trip down the Mississippi in 1820, John James Audubon saw "astonishing" numbers of merganser ducks, bald eagles feasting on deer carcasses, and "sworms" of grackles, purple finches, and broad-winged hawks. In early December, Audubon found the chattering swallows and honking geese following the Mississippi south so loud "that one might suppose the noise over head as proceeded from a violent storm of Wind."

But now the locale that inspired Flint and Audubon, the one I was seeing that morning, was a mosaic of clanking rail yards, frothy wakes of tugs pushing coal barges, and the shuttered hulks of giant blast furnaces. Iridescent petroleum discs from the leaky diesel and gas tanks of boats, and refinery spills, swirled at the dock pilings and against the industrial wharfs. The contrast was inspiring and, for a moment, steering down this much-changed river, with the wind blowing my hair and the low, sunlit clouds suggesting heaven-on-river, I thanked myself for myself. When I reach a landscape like this, a life of too much reading and obsessive reverence for the past prompts inflated feelings of satisfaction and self-worth. The grease-pot landscape along the banks was so ugly it was beautiful.

Barry and I tested the accuracy of the new compass on the *Patience* against our river charts. We found that the indicated north was about five to seven degrees off "true" north. The discrepancy was probably explained by the natural "magnetic deviation" caused by mineral deposits beneath the river bottom, not to mention the dense iron corridor of steel plants, rail yards, and barge fleets stacked against each other on the banks, and not much to worry about. I tested the steadiness of the compass needle by holding a consistent course to the stacks at Clairton, and then the left pylon of the Glassport bridge, and the needle wandered very little, even when we bounced through the wake of an upriver tug. The iNav app on the iPad in front of me was a reliable cross-check with the compass and our "contact navigation" with landmarks on the shore. The iNav also continuously updated our position to the curving sail line, a computation of the best course to the next buoy marking the channel, usually close to the middle of the river, that also accounted for the deepest water.

Barry gave me a tutorial on the Army Corps river charts, and I was surprised by the wealth of information they offered to aid my "pilotage," or navigation using fixed physical references on land. Bridges would prove to be my most reliable waypoints all the way down to New Orleans, and starting in the Pittsburgh area was the best course in Bridge 101 I could find. Because industry and residential areas are so heavily clustered along its three rivers, Pittsburgh is often called "The City of Bridges," and indeed it is the most spanned region in the world, even more than Venice, Italy. Within the Pittsburgh region, there are 446 bridges crossing the three rivers, their tributaries, and the steep ravines of the Alleghenies—we would pass underneath sixteen bridges in all just between Elizabeth and Three Rivers Point in the city, where the Ohio River begins.

But a bridge isn't just a bridge. They vary extensively in the number of supporting pylons, the profile of the suspension arches and trusses, and the grid patterns of their steel girders. The Elizabeth Bridge that we had just passed under has two center pylons that define the navigation channel, a comely, curved suspension arch in the middle, and then two double-pylon struts supporting the ramps on either side to carry the traffic of State Highway 51. The Union Railroad bridge between McKeesport and West Mifflin has seven pylons, three suspension arches over the railbed, and two inverted deck trusses under the rails. The steelwork designs on spans vary greatly in look—there are triangulated Warren trusses, octagonal Parker trusses, Whipple trusses, Baltimore and camelback trusses, and even a common, lens-shaped design called the lenticular pony truss bridge. Most long bridges combine several of these styles. Bridges today are designed on CAD, or computer-aided design. But the variety of shapes that bridges encompass is so great that, even today, young bridge engineers and architects are trained by building models out of uncooked spaghetti and glue.

Best, printed on the back of every Army Corps river chart, each one depicting about three miles of water, there are exact, miniature blueprints of each bridge. Even at night, pilots can't possibly mistake the Elizabeth

Bridge for the Union Railroad bridge in McKeesport, because their pro-files are so different, and instantly available on the back of the Army Corps charts. My heart raced with relief. On foggy days, or in heavy rain, I could always determine exactly where I was by comparing the Army Corps draw-ings to the next bridge downriver.

The charts were a feast for a navigation zealot like me. Every mile along the river, measured from the distance to the river mouth, was marked on the charts and had a corresponding mile marker along the shore. High-tension electrical lines crossing the river, cement plants and fleet-mooring cells, national parks and boat club marinas were all clearly marked. The locks and dams were meticulously portrayed, right down to the "pull chain for private boats," used to alert the lockmaster that traffic was waiting to enter the locks. I planned to be as glued to those charts as a monk to his Bible.

Barry was an insightful but down-to-earth teacher. Everything on the river, he said, was predicated on common sense. When we got below the Mansfield Memorial Bridge, where the Youghiogheny River joins the Mon at McKeesport, a small white tug was pushing three barges upriver from the fleet docks on the east side of the river, tracking a course that would cross ours, but still a mile or so away.

"What can you tell me about that boat?" Barry said.

"Small tug," I said. "Three barges. He's going to be slow because he's pushing against the current."

"What else? Are those barges loaded?"

The barges were clearly empty, and now I realized that it was vital to observe the waterlines on barges—whether they were high on the water, thus empty, or low on the water and full. Generally, load equals speed. Barry explained that while I was correct to conclude that the oncoming tug would be slow, it wouldn't be that slow because the barges were empty and therefore light. About half of the commercial boat traffic I would en-counter on the rivers would be these "local" tugs, particularly in congested areas with a lot of industry. The local tugs were also called "switch boats," to distinguish them from the "line-haul" tugs that traveled much greater distances pushing barges. The local switch boats were mostly used to stage full coal barges for unloading at nearby power plants, or for unloading corn and soybeans at the Cargill or Archer-Daniels-Midland silos, and then restaging the empties at their parking fleets along the river a short distance away. "Fleeting areas" would be another reliable navigation aid along the rivers. They were clearly marked on the charts with purple diagonal lines and could easily be identified by the tall, cylindrical "mooring cells" at either end, where the fleets were secured with heavy ropes.

Local tug captains often have an "attitude," Barry said, because they were constantly having to give way for the bigger "through tugs," or linehaul boats, pushing twenty or more barges long distances on the river, and the locals were paid a lot less money than through captains. Local captains considered their three- or four-mile stretch on the river their personal domain and couldn't care less about private boat traffic. The locals don't talk very readily on the radio and they are prone to make sudden, unannounced turns back toward their mooring fleets.

The locals, Barry said, are "basically forklift operators," squealing around the factory wharfs and industrial inlets with their barges. I would meet a lot of them over the next months. Many of them are kind and fun, but many of them are not the kind of fellows born with an active politeness gene.

Barry stabbed his finger on the map where the Youghiogheny joined the Mon at McKeesport.

"I'm guessing that this guy is going to turn hard left in front of us and steer up the Yough," which he pronounced as "Yock."

An old steel company mill was being torn down, about a mile up the Youghiogheny. A big steel shredder had been staged on the banks and the empty barges were being carried up the Yock to be filled with scrap, Barry said.

"If you can figure out what the guy is doing, which you usually can, you can guess where he's going."

Sure enough, the little white tug swung its barges wide across the river and then abruptly turned back east, aiming for the navigable space between the sediment bars at the mouth of the Youghiogheny. We still had a good half-mile separation from the tug and barges, but we were clearly on a collision course.

"What are you going to do?" Barry said.

When Barry said that, a pretty good life lesson came through, reminding me that journeying isn't just journeying, seeing new water and landscape. Journeying is also a reprise of past life. Fifty years ago, when my father was teaching me to fly, there was a procedure to follow when making "see and avoid" maneuvers around other planes, or to safely cross mountainous terrain. "Do it right away," he had said. "Make your turn or climb. But then talk to me, son. Talk, talk, talk to the other pilot. Show him that there's a logic to what you're doing. It's a way of teaching yourself to fly."

I turned the *Patience* hard left toward the west banks and spoke to Barry.

"I'm going to hug the Dravosburg side of the channel until we're abeam of that green channel marker," I said. "Then I'll head for the buoy straight downriver. I want that white tug to know that I'm giving him all the room he needs for his turn."

"Good," Barry said. "Even if he's the biggest asshole in the world, avoid him. There's no place for road rage on the river."

By the time I had turned back downriver for the buoy, the white tug had finished its sweeping maneuver and was headed straight for the mouth of the Youghiogheny. We had cleared each other by at least a quarter mile.

"And remember," Barry said, "you can always just yank your throttle back and crawl downriver if you can't figure out what the other boat is doing. That'll give you extra time to make the right move and the big through-boat guys will appreciate it."

Scott was the only disturbance we encountered that morning. Whenever a local tug or through boat maneuvered a mile away down the river, he would race up the stairs to the roof, breathlessly chattering away with suggestions for me to follow, launching into another one of his self-involved stories about his Lewis and Clark junket. He grabbed my portable radio transceiver a couple of times and hailed the distant captains, which made me uncomfortable because I knew that wasn't done, and then superciliously tried to engage them in conversations about nothing. He just wanted to play "captain." When the tugs never replied, he took the transceiver below to Danny and complained that it didn't work. But when Danny tested it, the radio worked fine. The captains weren't answering Scott because most tug captains refuse to acknowledge chatterbox boaters on the river. I could discern this trait in their slang and their brief, almost indecipherable replies when they were broadcasting to someone else.

Understanding the radio argot of the tugboats was hard at first, but gradually I got the hang of it. A tugboat captain who meant to say, "Roger, we'll pass on your port side under the bridge," sounded like this:

"Ger passport undee span."

Over time, filling in the dropped syllables became almost automatic.

Every time a tug passed, Scott stood out by the edge of the roof deck and waved to the passing tug pilots, even attempting to talk with them on the megaphone Danny had bought, which was senseless because he couldn't possibly be heard above the roar of the tug motors. Barry was taken aback by Scott's theatrics. He spoke up later in the afternoon when Scott was below.

"You've gotta watch out for Scott," Barry said. "He's too excitable, and excitement doesn't belong on a boat."

But I was still in my benign phase of leadership. For now, as exasperating as he was, it was best to just ignore Scott.

It was a Sunday, and the river was quiet. We wouldn't see much pleasure boat traffic until we got to Pittsburgh. Up on the roof deck, I was pleased by the expansive visibility downriver and the time spent with my mentor. As we rounded each new bend, a new scene of rusty industrial beauty swung into view. The throbbing motor, the low clouds, and the wind and sun on my face infused the tranquility of travel.

McKeesport, Duquesne, and North Versailles went by, their steeples and Eastern Orthodox domes impassive but dreamy, as if the *Patience* was standing still and they were moving by on floating banks. Barry talked about boating on the river during his teenage years in the 1970s, racing downstream at night to the bankside liquor stores in McKeesport, or the abandoned wharfs where he could meet girls. The river was quite polluted then and nobody swam in it, and fishing was poor. But in the 1980s, when the giant U.S. Steel complex on the Mon began to shutter, and the Environmental Protection Agency got serious about cleaning up the river, the Mon's natural advantages accelerated the return of cleaner water. The headwaters of the Mon are in national forests in West Virginia, 130 miles away, with little upstream pollution before the U.S. Steel stretch around Pittsburgh. The Mon's two major tributaries, the Youghiogheny and the

Cheat River near Morgantown, West Virginia, carry clean mountain flow. After the U.S. Steel plants declined, the pristine contribution from the upland headwaters aided EPA efforts to dredge pollutants at the bottom of the river. Noxious chemicals were washed downstream by the Mon. Before the federal Clean Water Act was passed in 1972, the industrial Mon supported only three major species—bluegills, carp, and catfish. But fewer steelworks, improved water treatment plants, and stricter water-release measures, like sealed holding ponds at mines, have vastly improved conditions. There are now more than fifty species thriving in the Mon and most of the edible catch that the flatboat men knew—white bass, rock bass, perch, walleye, and channel catfish—are back in record numbers. The restoration of the Mon is now considered a model of the "healing waters" trend in American rivers. Rivers grow and change. Once protected from the chemical threats of man, their natural metabolism races toward health.

Barry was even more excited about the healing trends for cities and towns. Most of the devastation of the steel plant closings in the 1980s— the grievous population loss, the erosion of the tax base, the blighting of downtowns—was over and, he said, you could almost "smell" the promise of revival in the air. He was dreaming of running for mayor of Elizabeth and redefining the river town as a "greenway community," one just the right distance from downtown Pittsburgh, and just the right distance from the superlative hiking and kayaking country in the Alleghenies. Millennials would discover the cheaper rents and riverside views of towns like Elizabeth and move there. Wine bars and clothing boutiques would follow. Economies and the living areas they support are perpetually mutating, dying, and rebirthing. But the Mon still flowed and people struggled for survival along it. Listening to Barry, I felt the tonic sweep of America, past and present merging.

The beginning is more than half of the whole and, that first day, things were going well. I was afire with thoughts about the knowledge of my country to be gleaned beyond each horseshoe bend. As we passed a large barge fleet tied along the west bank, the twin railroad bridges carrying the Union and the Norfolk Southern railroad lines loomed on the horizon. They were solid navigation fixes. Now I could see the volcanic stacks of the blast furnace at Braddock, good old Braddock, Pennsylvania, an ancient waypoint for me. Pittsburgh was only ten miles downriver. But now I had to get through my first set of locks.

7

I KNEW FROM THE START that the extensive dam and lock network on the Ohio River would be one of the most interesting challenges of the trip. Reenactors like Scott and weekend fishermen that I met along the Ohio loved to repeat tales of peril at the locks, from being forced against the cement walls while sharing the chamber with a coal barge, to the sudden race of water in the exit pools once the gates have been opened. On busy summer weekends in settled areas where recreational boating is popular, the line of boats waiting outside the entrance gates to "lock through" can stretch for a hundred yards and delay river traffic for hours. I would soon learn, however, that safely negotiating the locks is really not that difficult, and the exaggerated tales of danger mostly serve to inflate the egos of motorboaters. It's all part of the culture of fear surrounding the rivers. The stories also obscure the significance of the locks. Descending the "aquatic staircase" of the Ohio is to discover what rivers really are today.

The first principle that it was vital for me to understand was that, on the Ohio and Mississippi, I was only remotely encountering a natural river environment. From the earliest days of commercial steamboat traffic on the western rivers, the 1820s, when a legendary boat captain and inventor named Henry M. Shreve began clearing the floating islands of forest debris along the Mississippi with a new design he called the "snag boat," America's major waterways have been so ceaselessly dammed, trenched, and channelized with levees and jetties that they exist today as man-made lakes. On the Ohio, particularly, the extensive dam and lock system has tamed the river, almost completely eliminating the "wild and free" natural flow of the 19th century. The controlled bodies of water between the dams are called "project pools," or "managed pools," with flow and water depths determined by the amount of water the managers of the dams upriver decide to release during any twenty-four-hour period, depending on rains. This flow management has slowed the currents of the river, making it safer for commercial traffic, especially when large barge strings are passing each other near the bends. These slower river conditions were another reason that I had to install a motor, to help maintain headway and steerage during my "float" to New Orleans. The "improvements" to the river made since the 19th century have also greatly increased the volume of commercial river traffic. I also needed a motor to safely steer the *Patience* around the barge strings.

Negotiating the lock system of the Ohio became another experience that dramatically changed my conception of American history. Nineteenth-century American history returns to us in modern teaching as a series of bitter congressional feuds—the Missouri Compromise of 1820, the Compromise of 1850, the Kansas-Nebraska Act of 1854—over the spread of slavery. But Congress was also feverishly busy after 1820 debating the issue of federal expenditures for the "navigation improvements" on the rivers, principally the Ohio and the Mississippi and their major tributaries. The problems faced by a young country growing increasingly dependent on river cargo were vast, but easy to comprehend, and they determined one of the largest political battles of the 19th century.

The Mississippi River's "total catchment area"—the landmass that feeds a river with distant rain and flowing streams—covers almost 40 percent of the continental United States. The river must accept the rainwater not retained by the soil over a 1.2-million-square-mile area that stretches north as far as New York State and Minnesota, and includes the flow from 250 tributaries. The massive melt of the Rocky Mountain snowpack, arriving above St. Louis via the Missouri and the Platte rivers, is a torrent every spring. In major flood years the enormous burden of water carried south by gravity has to go somewhere, and once the flow reaches the sandy soil and bayous in Mississippi and Louisiana it endlessly fissures into new channels and migrating wetlands that obliterate everything in their way.

The riverbanks are not so much banks as they are nature's moveable containment device, wiggling and jumping around under water pressure, like a garden hose on the lawn that has just been turned on from a spigot.

Without intervention, flood overflow from the Mississippi would push New Orleans and its neighboring Louisiana parishes into the Gulf of Mexico, and carry off hundreds of thousands of acres of prized cotton, sugarcane, and rice lands. During the flatboat era, this giant kettle of water was perpetually poised to tip over onto the very places that 19th-century Americans wanted to be—the booming river towns and croplands of the mid-continent. As John McPhee, in his book *The Control of Nature*, put it: "A nation had developed, and the nation could not afford nature."

The natural debris of cottonwood root balls and cedar and locust trees carried down from the northern forests was another grave hazard, this one to boat navigation. Almost every flatboat journal from before the Civil War recounts the story of a barge being sunk by heavy snags damaging the hull, and many boats experienced collisions with floating trees and "deadwood islands" more than once a week. In April 1847, Theodore Armitage, sailing the flatboat *Whig* from Indiana to New Orleans, recorded that two of the skiffs he was towing were seriously damaged by driftwood near Greenville, Mississippi. Three days later, below Natchez, the *Whig* ran against a snag, which stove in the side of the boat, requiring a daylong layover to make repairs. In *Life on the Mississippi*, Mark Twain identified river snags as perhaps the worst hazard to navigation. "The whole vast space of the stream was black with drifting dead logs, broken boughs, and great trees that had caved in and been washed away. . . . Now and then [when] we would hit one of these sunken logs a rattling bang, dead in the center, with a full head of steam, and it would stun the boat as if she had hit a continent." The threat was particularly severe at night, Twain wrote, when the black tree snags merged into the darkness and couldn't be seen. One U.S. Senate report in 1846 listed 21,681 "rigid snags" that had been removed from the Mississippi, the Ohio, the Missouri, and the Arkansas rivers in the early 1840s. There were an additional 36,840 mostly submerged snags of "roots, logs and stumps." The same survey identified 75,000 trees along the banks that were leaning toward the water and "liable to fall into the rivers."

The rivers were, paradoxically, both early America's highway of cash and the natural enemy of commerce. In slack years, the banks along the turns acted as giant speed brakes, slowing the onrush of water to manageable velocity, and providing a relatively stable, navigable passageway encouraging flatboat and later steamboat traffic. But in years of flooding—so intrinsic to rivers that it has to be considered nature's plan—those same sandy banks endlessly braided to allow the currents to carve new shortcuts or oxbow bends, gouging a huge clear-cut of trees in the wake of each rupture. Every decade, sometimes every few years, the deluge flooding south relocated the sandbars, completely changing deposits of silt that acted as both river hazards and navigation fixes. In other places giant straightaways plowed through thousands of acres in just a few days, dramatically relocating the path of the river and isolating the old bends into giant, curved "oxbow lakes." (Lake Chicot and Horseshoe Lake in Arkansas, popular recreational and fishing lakes, both formed after being cut off from the Mississippi.) Towns that stood in the way of the river's hydraulic wrath—Scuffletown, Kentucky; Rodney, Mississippi; and Cairo, Illinois—were either washed away or economically destroyed.

The banks were acting as banks were meant to. One year they held and gently steered the flow, pushing a sufficient quantity of water into the boat channel in the middle of the river. The next year, when the water crested their tops, the banks parted and redirected the excess water into nature's relief system, the nearby swamps. This dynamic hydrology often made sense, given nature's tendency to endlessly replicate itself and spread biological diversity. Erosion is nature's method for redirecting excess water and redistributing fresh, fertile soil. Trees are supposed to lean over the banks and then fall, collecting as floating islands, one reason that stream restoration projects often include leaving "shade barriers" of growing and fallen trees in place. Any number of important river species—catfish, ducks, turtles, water moccasins—rely on leaning or floating trees for cooler water in the summer. Muskrats, mink, river ferrets, beavers, and even raccoons often colonize large river snags, particularly those beached on islands or sandbars, which are ideal habitats for hunting and breeding. They feast on the duckweed, crayfish, and frogs swarming around the snags, forming a food chain that passes up to the predators, vital to every natural system. Bobcats and coyotes love to feed on the snags stuck against sandy banks, foraging for the smaller mammals inside. Nature works by moving soil, flora, and animals around a lot. It just doesn't always work for the convenience of man.

In addition to the early snag-removal efforts of Captain Henry Shreve, the first barrier to be attacked was the Great Falls of the Ohio, between Louisville, Kentucky, and Clarksville, Indiana. The one-mile stretch of white water, falling over a lovely staircase of fossil beds, was dreaded by flatboat captains because it required a time-consuming portage around the falls by horse and wagon, or hiring a local pilot to steer a flat through the narrow rapids. Plans to build a diversion canal around the falls dated back as far as 1781, but a serious effort, by a private stock company, didn't begin until 1824. The Louisville and Portland Canal finally opened in the 1830s and the response was immediate—through traffic to Natchez and New Orleans increased dramatically, to more than seven hundred boats a year.

But a constitutional problem, federalism, initially stood in the way of more ambitious efforts to clear the rivers for navigation. A succession of presidents in the early republic—from Thomas Jefferson in 1802 to James Polk in 1849—objected to the use of federal funds for what they considered river projects that benefited only individual states. A series of Rivers and Harbors Act bills in the 1830s and 1840s faced the continuous threat of presidential vetoes. President Andrew Jackson, though a former river trader and boatyard owner himself, and one who had made a considerable fortune along the Cumberland, the Ohio, and the Mississippi, condemned public expenditures on river improvements as "corrupting influences." (Jackson, of course, didn't object to bills funding public works on the Cumberland, which flowed directly past his plantations outside Nashville.) Mostly, the Rivers and Harbors Act legislation that survived presidential vetoes were modest measures that funded river surveys, local snag removal, or projects that enhanced military preparedness or the "transportation of public mail."

This changed dramatically after the Civil War, when northern control of the Mississippi had proved decisive for the Union, and the vast sums spent on military campaigns had softened public opposition to federal spending. Coal mining had jumped over the Alleghenies from Virginia and Pennsylvania as early as 1800, and Ohio alone was producing over a million tons of anthracite by the 1850s, generating a major new source of wealth and accelerating industrial growth downriver. Few Americans remember today that the American model of economic growth was once predominantly based on "sustainable" energy, from the grain windmills of New England to the factory waterwheels of the industrial revolution. But coal changed everything, converting America to a fossil fuel glutton. By the 1830s, coal was beginning to replace hydropower and wood as a source of energy all the way down to the Mississippi plantation country. Coal became the dominant fuel for heating American homes, and oil distilled from soft bituminous coal, marketed under the name kerosene, was widely used as lamp fuel. Coal barges were already a common sight on the 4,400 miles of inland canals in New York, Pennsylvania, and the Midwest, and by the 1850s stern-wheeler steamboats pushing three and four heavily loaded coal barges at once—essentially, they were just wooden flatboats on steroids—were plying the Mississippi and its inland tributaries. In antebellum America, the big flywheel driving the economy was cotton, and "Cotton was King." But the same might have been said for coal. By 1880, America was extracting 80 million tons of coal a year, and most of it reached distant markets along the Ohio and Mississippi rivers.

Delivering coal and agricultural products along the western rivers was now a national priority, and, with so much money involved, national politicians were willing to fudge their loyalty to federalism. The first big act passed by Congress was an 1884 bill that supported the building of a dam on the Ohio near Davis Island, five miles below Pittsburgh, to flood waters backward and make the major industrial center emerging in western Pennsylvania more navigable. The floodgates were now open, and by the turn of the 20th century Congress was happily endorsing a succession of Rivers and Harbors Act bills empowering massive channel improvements made by the Army Corps of Engineers. On the Ohio alone, a series of forty-six dams and locks were built in the early 1920s, and improvements to lock designs in the 1960s eventually reduced the system on the Ohio to twenty larger and more efficient dams and locks. The renovation of the Olmsted Locks and Dam on the Ohio, seventy miles above the confluence with the Mississippi, finished the improvements in 2020. Today, the Army Corps, with thirty-seven thousand employees and a $5 billion budget, presides over an inland empire of hydroelectric plants, more than 250 river locks, Superfund mitigation sites, and a fleet of dredging boats that keep the river channels clear by relocating 250 million cubic yards of silt a year.

The earliest locks built on the Ohio and along the inland canals were based on European designs that dated back to the 17th century. The first wooden structures were barely more than a hundred feet long, all that was needed for cargo or passenger craft at the time, but today they have been expanded to concrete behemoths with chambers 1,200 feet long, with smaller, neighboring "auxiliary" chambers of 600 feet, to accommodate private craft or just a barge or two.

The principle of building a moveable "water stair" over falls, shallow water, or stretches where sudden changes in river elevation prevented navigation was relatively simple. A large waterproof box, or lock chamber, is built along the banks, and it is fed by either a diversion wall or dam across the river. The chamber is opened and closed by steel or wooden gates facing both the upstream and downstream sides. Once the upstream gates are opened and the downstream gates closed, the chamber naturally fills to the water level behind it, allowing a boat or commercial tow inside. When the towering upstream gates are shut, and the downstream gates opened, the chamber empties to the height of the "downstream pool." The water races out with a loud gurgle, like a giant bathtub emptying through its drain. The boat can now enter the exit pool and move onto the river under its own power. The process is reversed for boats climbing upriver to higher elevations.

There are a multitude of refinements. Today, cement gantries cross overhead, allowing tractor and forklift travel between the main chamber and the auxiliary chamber, or over to the dam structure nearby. A century ago, captains communicated with the lockmaster in his bridge on the lock via an established code of boat whistles. That has now been replaced by radio, and red, yellow, and green lights signaling the boats to hold or enter the locks. Sophisticated instruments measure water velocity and the amount of flow released into the river each time the gates are opened, allowing the Army Corps to precisely forecast water levels dozens of miles downriver. Floating bollards that rise or fall at the same level as the boat have eliminated the need for long lines to be thrown up to the lock crew on the walls above. The control rooms of the lockmasters are tall cantilever structures elevated over the locks with high tinted windows facing 270 degrees, resembling the control towers at major airports. They command spacious views of the sail line and the barge traffic up and down the river.

The Ohio River locks are lovely structures and the experience of locking through the dams down through the Appalachian ridges is as thrilling as riding Amtrak's *California Zephyr* through the Rockies. But the lock and dam system has fundamentally changed the rivers, transferring control from nature to man. The "project pool" between two dams can extend from twenty to nearly fifty miles, with water levels carefully monitored to benefit barge traffic. When heavy rains far north in the watershed threaten the Ohio with turbulent conditions and fast water, the dams restrain the flow, maintaining the best conditions possible for pushing barges upstream. When rains are slack, more water can be released to raise the channel depths for the tugs. The twenty locks on the Ohio have tamed river flows to just two to three miles per hour, and tug captains no longer have to fear a sudden, unanticipated wall of high water approaching because it rained hard yesterday in Indianapolis, three hundred miles away, or running aground at Gallipolis or Marietta because the Midwest was suffering a drought. Most of the year, the river is a softened, predictable space.

Economically, the Ohio River dam system is far from ideal. America's chronic reluctance to reinvest in its cement-and-girder infrastructure has debilitated a waterway that carries almost $25 billion in cargo every year. Tugs pushing a standard string of fifteen to twenty barges are delayed at each lock and dam because standard barge lengths of 150 feet to 195 feet mean that only five or six of them can be pushed into a lock at once. Tug crews can spend a whole day "splitting" their loads while the push boats laboriously ferry back and forth through the chambers and then tie up their partial loads at mooring cells along the river, and then go back through the locks for their remaining barges. If more than one barge string reaches a dam at once, crews can wait ten hours or more for the traffic ahead of them to clear.

This is complicated by antiquated valves that break, panels ripping off dams, and leaky seals that require expensive, cumbersome emergency repairs. The "wickets" on many dams, which are raised or lowered to change water levels, were built in the 1920s and 1930s out of oak, and hydraulic pumps dating to the same period are so old that replacement parts have to be fabricated one at a time. One stretch between Paducah, Kentucky, and Cairo, Illinois, is so prone to delays that river captains call it "el bottleneck" and dread the forty-eight-hour delays locking through each dam during the busy harvest season in the fall. But their own industry is to blame, at least in part. For more than a century, aggressive lobbying by the barge industry has kept taxes and fees that help pay for the upkeep of the lock and dam system pitifully low, which is good for company profits and also lowers transportation costs, but bad for the aging locks. The Army Corps estimates that at least $8 billion in work is needed on the locks and dams, but receives only a fraction of that every year from the relatively modest levies of the Inland Waterways Fuel Tax.

This was the cosmos of water where I would spend the next two months, a one-thousand-mile watercourse of nature subdued, daily parades of twenty-two-ton barge tows, and the hydrophobia of the people I met along the banks. For me the life lessons would be many. And, from my perch high above the water, the sensation of romance was renewed each time I turned the *Patience* around a new river bend.

As I approached my first lock, the Braddock Dam at Mile 12 of the lower Monongahela, the *Patience* felt miniaturized, a tiny detail painted into a looming industrial tableau. The rounded arches of twin railroad bridges framed the river behind us and the towers of U.S. Steel's Edgar Thomson Works rose beside us, matte black against the green Allegheny hills and the cottony-white sky. I was cheered by the happy work of my crew. Danny was bustling about with a tool belt dangling low on his cargo shorts, making more improvements to the electrical system and building stabilizing legs for the fans so they wouldn't tip over every time we hit a tug wake. Brady came up and explained that, ever since he served in the Marine Corps, he had considered himself a "space specialist." He wanted to do more reorganizing of our kitchen and sleeping gear. Jay was dissatisfied with the state of my pots and pans, most of which had been purchased pre-loved and crusted with burnt grime at Goodwill, and he was shining them up with steel wool and Brasso metal polish. When he saw us pass the angled diversion wall outside the Braddock locks, he called up to tell me that he was ready to man the ropes for hooking onto the floating bollards inside the chamber.

That night I would write in my notebook: "Crew performs well without me giving too many instructions. Just be a gentle manager—enable them, don't tell them."

I maintained a holding position outside the lock gates by running the prop at low power in reverse. I remembered that Army Corps regulations required that all crew members wear life vests in the chamber and was pleased when I looked down and saw that everyone had put one on. Initially, the situation at the Braddock lock was confusing. When I talked to the lockmaster on the radio he told me that the "chamber was clear" for me to enter, but the yellow caution light at the end of the revetment wall was still on. A local tug pushing barges was exiting the locks, roiling up the water, and a yahoo driving a small waterskiing boat was careening around the port side of the barges, racing for the exit pool.

Barry was still sitting beside me, coaching me through my first lock.

"You're good to go," he said.

But I didn't like the way that little ski boat was skittering around and guessed that the tug captain didn't want any more traffic entering his space while he was easing his barges out of the lock.

"Okay, but let me do this first one my way," I said. "Let's let the little boat and the tug pass first."

I radioed back to the lockmaster that the *Patience* would hold until the pool in front of the gates was clear.

"Your call. Come ahead when you want."

The motorboat raced by and, as the tug slowly passed, the captain waved an "A-OK" from his bridge. I let the backwash from his propeller push me toward the open lock gates and steered using a minimum of power. Slow, slow, and I couldn't get into much trouble. As we approached the gates I aimed for the starboard wall inside and noticed three sets of yellow vertical lines painted on the cement sides of the lock, spaced at either end and the middle of the chamber.

"The yellow stripes mark your floating bollards," Barry said. "You want to aim for the middle set."

"I'm taking this very slow," I said to Barry. "We're going to just kiss that bollard line."

I felt like a kid learning to ride a bike with training wheels—we were that slow. But, screw it, I thought. There weren't any boats behind us and there was no reason to show off during my first time through a lock.

At the middle yellow lines, I eased the *Patience* into reverse too late, missing the bollards, but recovered by gently skidding my wooden sides against the cement walls of the lock, scraping the *Patience* to a bumpy but acceptable stop at the final set of lines. Jay held the bow against the bollard with his line, letting out rope as the water level in the chamber was lowered, and I held the rest of the boat against the wall with reverse power and a little steering to port.

While we were waiting to descend in the lock, a couple of men in blue

jeans, grimy T-shirts, and yellow safety helmets, obviously members of the
Army Corps lockmaster crew, rested their arms over the metal railings above
and looked down at our boat. Jay was standing just below them, hideously
clashing in his red bandanna do-rag, lavender pirate shirt, and orange life vest.

"Hey, what are you guys?" one of the Army Corps men yelled. "A pirate
boat?"

*Inside the locks along the Ohio River. The sound of our boat sides scraping against
cement and water racing out of the gates thunderously echoed against the high walls.*

I was about to answer, but Danny cut me off in his shrill soprano voice.
"Flatboat *Patience*! We're taking this baby to New Orleans!"

"Whoa," one of them said. "That takes a set of balls."

"We've got 'em!" Danny shouted back. "We'll be drinking gin and tonics on Bourbon Street by October."

I cringed. The *Patience* spokesperson, apparently, would be my frantic-
antic first mate, Danny Corjulo. Later, I quietly suggested to Danny that
perhaps it would be more appropriate for the captain to speak for the boat.

"You?" Danny said. "The Irish stiff? Forget about it. Just watch me. I'll
be great at flacking for the boat."

A loud buzzer sounded inside the chamber as the lockmaster began
to let the water out. As we descended against the towering walls, it was
spooky inside, especially the noise. Every conversation on the boat, every
scrape of the hull against the cement walls, echoed loudly within the cement

enclosure, the sounds endlessly caroming against the water and each other
and then back, a cacophony mixing in the lock with the whoosh of water
emptying below and the splash of leaks from the gates. On the bow, Jay was
telling Danny a raunchy story and the magnified volume of his words—"IT
WOULD HAVE FRICKIN' PISSED OFF AN ANGEL, I TELL YA'"—
bounced all around and lifted heavenward, like a loudspeaker announce-
ment at a football game carried away by the wind. The deafening sound and
the claustrophobia of being surrounded by walls growing taller and taller
induced panic. I had to consciously fight the temptation of worrying about
what would happen if a wall collapsed and trapped us underwater.

A gauge stenciled onto the wall beside us indicated that we were now
approaching 723 feet in elevation above sea level, approximately the water
level outside the gates in front of us. When we reached the bottom, the
gates began to open and another loud buzzer sounded. The water outside
in the exit pool was placid, gently flowing past the retaining walls in the
narrow channel that led back to the Mon.

The biggest surprise was the considerable amount of debris that had
been trapped inside the lock with us. Truck tires, the root balls of trees,
skittering circles of Frisbees and plastic bottles, and a water ski popped up
through the filthy film of water like a beach ball held under the surf and then
released. The debris pile gently collected against the hull of the *Patience* as we
motored out of the lock. We were traveling in a floating junkyard. America's
record of creating waste that lasts forever is an impressive national achievement. In New England, you can still find acres of slag heaps beside deserted
iron furnaces that date back two hundred years, and the tracks "maintained"
by our slovenly railroad companies are just a giant, aboveground graveyard
of rusting I-beams and creosote ties. From Cape Cod to New Mexico the
underground aquifers below former military bases are now so fouled with
hydraulic oil and B-52 fuel that water no longer flows in them. The corporate
looters and air force generals who have presided over this continental defil-
ing insist that cleaning up this mess is the business of anyone but them, and
would rather abandon their fouled nests than clean them up.

The Ohio and Mississippi River valleys are simply this principle executed at large over thousands of miles of water, practiced both corporately
and by the common citizenry. During low-water conditions on the rivers, especially at places where industrial sites have been shuttered or the

commercial channels have been rerouted, car and truck chassis dumps the size of giant used-car lots poke up above the water level in the oleaginous coves. The moribund mooring cells of tugboat companies and petroleum refineries are stacked three or four wide with steel barges, poked with holes from the acidic erosion of bird guano, which turtles use to climb up to the remaining flat spaces of gunwales to sun themselves. Forests of tree saplings grow in the abandoned barges. The water under the bridges in Cincinnati and Baton Rouge has been carpet-bombed with stainless steel shopping carts. The Army Corps of Engineers, fastidious to the point of despotism about private citizens running electrical wires or waterlines down to their river docks, does nothing about this massive and democratically practiced discarding in the rivers. It would be unpatriotic for the responsible federal agency to curb America's genius for spewing off waste.

I couldn't believe the volume and variety of waste now surrounding me as we exited the Braddock locks. We raced a metal garage door, the blue vinyl roof of a backyard gazebo, and what appeared to be a collection of aboveground pool liners down the exit pool. Our transit through this floating town dump dispirited me, but I didn't need to worry about our safety because the heavy, raked bow of the *Patience* easily parted the rubbish to either side. I could hear an occasional underwater grinding when our prop nicked a two-by-four board or a bait can.

I motored up to cruising speed and picked up our next waypoint, the under-trusses of the Rankin Memorial Bridge. Aside from the revolting spectacle of the floating solid waste, locking through was fun and spooky, and now I had returned to the welcome Melody of America—clanging steel yards, train whistles, and the rumble of traffic on the bridges—along Mile 10 of the river.

"That's it?" I said to Barry. "That wasn't complicated."

"That's it. People like to make it sound difficult, but it isn't."

After another mile, we reached the outskirts of Pittsburgh, and the river became festive, a weekend beer party. This would become a recurring visual and atmospheric clash of the trip. Whole afternoons spent cruising through the forested splendor of Appalachian nature preserves, state parks, or the sprawling Shawnee National Forest would suddenly be interrupted as we approached popular boating areas like Cincinnati or the lake-like stretch formed by the river bends near Aurora, Indiana. The Ohio was a float through two competing American spaces. The deep quiet and scenic contentment of endless conservation forests, with nothing in sight beyond the occasional osprey diving for fish, or a big Ingram tug pushing coal barges, would suddenly be ended by the wail of motorboat engines, island drinking melees, and the smoke of barbecue fires climbing above the trees. The Ohio River is a vast conservation space periodically interrupted by party venues.

Scott Mandrell had warned me that morning that getting through Pittsburgh would be nerve-racking, with pleasure boats cutting us off and big tugs with long barge strings exiting off the Allegheny and then making wide, sweeping turns as they pushed upriver on the Mon or maneuvered for the sail line toward the Ohio. But I was learning that he was just habitually frenetic, a self-important bundle of hyperbole and fuss. Exaggerating the difficulties of navigating the rivers fed his ego but made no common sense. The traffic along this urban stretch of the Mon was busy, but not hazardous.

Handsome, shirtless boys with skinny hips and sunglasses, beside their girlfriends in hot-pink bikinis, raced by in their Malibu and Nautique ski boats, throwing off rooster tails of water and lunging wide as they pulled water-skiers and wakeboards. As we approached Point State Park in Pittsburgh, where the Ohio begins, we could see that the seats of PNC Park were full for a Pirates game, and on Sundays the crowd outside the ballpark includes large groups of people, sunbathing and picnicking on the immense green space between the river confluence and the stadium. Laughter seemed to be the predominant feature of the weekend Mon. People waved from the shore and the waterskiing boats skittered over to see the *Patience*, their hulls plunging low and then gently rocking up and down in their back wake.

The big, multideck tourist boats of the Gateway Clipper line were out, too, crowded with partying passengers. Waiters on board were serving meals and lots of beer. The triple-decker *Three Rivers Queen* and the *Gateway Princess* circled us a few times and everyone on board seemed to be photographing the *Patience* with their iPhones. As the cruise boats swung around us, I angled the bow a couple of times to present the best photo op of Jay. They all wanted an image of Jay in his do-rag, dagger belt, and pirate's tunic.

It was fun out there, not the tense conflict with traffic that Scott had warned me about. This was another early indication that the "guide" I had chosen to help me down the river was ill-suited to my needs and, already, I was chastising myself for my bad judgment.

We dropped Barry Boucher off at a small boat landing underneath the

Fort Pitt Bridge. He told me that he would walk across the bridge and then ride the Smithfield Street bus home to Elizabeth. I didn't want to say good-bye to this decent, gregarious man, my first mentor on the rivers.

"I wish you were along for the whole trip," I told him. "You really helped us."

"Nah, I'm a local boy, don't know much beyond the Mon," Barry said in his thick Pittsburgh slaw. "You'll be fine, Capt'n. All you gotta do is use your head."

As I picked up the sail line on the Ohio River and then passed to the north of Brunot Island, I felt alone up on the roof console. There was still a lot of motorboat traffic and I could see two big barge tows in the distance, moving upriver near the McKees Rocks Bridge. If I had to do some maneuvering down there, I would need to know my position precisely, and I didn't want to both navigate and steer alone.

I called for Brady to come up, suspecting that his penchant for detail would make him a strong navigator. He had told me that he'd had a lot of boating experience. I also liked that he was a retired marine. Military veterans are generally exacting when it comes to following orders, even when they disagree with them, and he was the perfect partner at the helm during a period when I would probably be making a lot of mistakes. All of this proved correct. Brady was an obsessive and quick observer of every mile marker and bridge crossing, and he was good at taking compass readings off high-tension wires and island points, fastidious about keeping track of our position on the river. He was constantly peering ahead through binoculars and then he would place his index finger at each waypoint on my Ohio River chart as I followed along on the iNav screen, and together we discussed the oncoming barges and what we thought the tug captains would do. Fortunately, it was an easy stretch—the sail line moved due northwest as a long straightaway, with plenty of room for traffic.

The lesson of my morning river instruction with Barry was that I should go slow or just coast to a standstill if I couldn't figure out the traffic ahead, and to trust the safest, commonsense conclusion. I was surprised at how quickly I got the hang of river navigation. While researching river cargo, I'd read that empty barges draw three feet of water, at least a foot deeper than my draft, so there was obviously enough water for me off the mooring fleets along the banks. Traveling about forty or fifty yards away from the parked barges along the banks would keep the *Patience* well away from the big commercial through boats out on the sail line, but close enough to the banks so I could always drift toward shore at the first sign of trouble. There was a big fleeting area up ahead on the right bank at the Norfolk Southern rail yards. We hugged the barge fleet down past Neville Island, and the two barge tows coming upriver, one slightly behind the other, passed uneventfully.

At Mile 5 on the Ohio, we were approaching the Emsworth Locks and Dams at Avalon, Pennsylvania, the rebuilt and renamed dam facility built at the original Davis Island site in 1885. I could tell that Brady was going to make a great helmsman, and I wanted him to get some early experience so that our roles as navigator and boat jockey were interchangeable. That way we could spell each other on longer days, or I could go below and rest or take notes while Brady ran the boat.

"Brady, let's have you take the wheel and get us through the lock," I said. "I'll work the radio, you drive."

"Done," Brady said as we traded seats.

I could see that the Emsworth Locks were busy. One of the chambers was closed for repairs and there were two fifteen-barge tows carrying gravel and coal upriver, ponderously moving around on both sides of the dam. The tugs were splitting up their loads to get through the locks, and then crossing the river to tie up their barges at a mooring fleet near some mildly rough water called Little Horsetail Riffle.

When I radioed ahead to the lock, the Army Corps crewman advised that we faced a long wait. The tugs splitting up their loads wouldn't be done for several hours. He requested that I either tie up or anchor clear of the tug traffic, at the mouth of a small creek called Spruce Run, a half mile upriver on the right bank.

Brady motored over to Spruce Run and we tied onto an old creosote piling near the banks, letting the *Patience* drift stern-first in the downstream flow. We wouldn't get through the locks until almost dark, but it was an enjoyable wait. Brady and I sat on the roof deck discussing politics and details of our lives, and I was delighted to find out that he was a competitor in "mounted shooter" events, an equestrian sport during which "cowboy mounted" riders gallop through a corral, plugging away at targets with revolvers or rifles. I had never heard of mounted shooting, but it got my horse itch going. Under the low afternoon sun, Brady explained how the events were organized and we quibbled over the merits and faults of the breeds preferred in the sport—quarter horses and quarter crosses, Arabian crosses, buckskins, and paints.

One contradiction about Brady fascinated me. A dogmatic, obstreperous conservative, he rarely missed an opportunity to gratuitously rant about Blacks, liberals, and immigrants, but personal experience seemed to have rid him of the rote homophobia of right-wingers. A brother of his in San Francisco was gay and had contracted AIDS, and Brady frequently traveled to California to spend long periods helping to care for his brother. Brady also believed that John F. Kennedy had been a great president, "the last Democrat who cared about the workingman." Maybe southern conservatism wasn't as monolithic as I thought.

Waiting on the roof deck of the *Patience* for the Emsworth Locks to clear was a relaxing way to end the day. Light breezes blew downriver and the towers of the U.S. Steel plants rose against an elegant sunset. The river sang the American melody of trains clacking by on the banks and tugs whining in the channel, churning up wakes.

We ended up that night at the kind of place that would charm us all the way down the rivers to New Orleans, a scruffy little shitwreck blue-collar marina in Glenfield, Pennsylvania. The patchy lawns and modest weekend shacks of steelworkers and cops were wedged onto a narrow strip of land running east and west between the Ohio River banks and the Norfolk Southern tracks. Everybody chased around on golf carts littered with empty beer cans. A fun-loving, hospitable crowd met us at the wooden docks and told us that we were welcome to spend the night. There were barbecue pits near the boat and a gracious elderly couple parked one of their golf carts at the dock so that we could use it to drive up the marina lane to the cinder-block lavatory and take showers.

Danny instantly transitioned to his regular evening routine, chasing off on the electric bike to shop for food. As soon as we docked, he heaved the bike over the gunwales and disappeared down the dock for the local Giant Eagle supermarket.

"I won't be long!" Danny called over his shoulder as he raced off on the electric bike.

This was a lie. "Waiting for Danny" to return from shopping tours and beginning to cook became a regular evening vigil on the trip. It was useless to complain about it.

"Rinker, it takes a long time in the supermarkets down here to find the prosciutto and spices I need," Danny said to me a few nights later. "You're such a loser. You don't even know that the Europeans sit down to dinner at midnight."

Later, Danny donned his chef's apron and chopped up a chicken for stew with his Special Forces axe. I made a fire in the barbecue pit in the grove of maples beside the dock, and the pot of chicken seemed to simmer forever over the coals. We were all tipsy with our gin and tonics as we watched the steam lifting from the stewpot.

The subject of politics and the general social conditions now prevailing in America came up. A few weeks earlier, an Islamic gunman had opened fire in a gay nightclub in Orlando, killing forty-nine people. Brady and Jay had conservative opinions, but reasonably argued ones, mostly leaning on the standard talking point that passing new gun laws wouldn't prevent shootings like Orlando.

This was one of the nights when I both loathed and loved Danny. A beautiful day on the river had filled me with Whitmanesque passion for my country. Danny could have equivocated about what Brady said, faking some kind of consensus. Get along, I thought. Build a country. Love a country. Danny, don't say anything. But no. That's not Danny. He is a Connecticut Yankee who condemns the dogmatism of southern conservatives while preaching the party line of the North.

"Brady, you don't have to worry about Congress passing new gun laws," Danny said. "Everybody killed in that nightclub was gay. Conservatives don't mind if you shoot gays."

I stepped over to the portable table on the dock and poured myself another gin and tonic.

Finally, Danny served us his stew, which he ladled over a bed of rice. It was probably the most exquisite chicken I have ever tasted.

A flock of geese, invisible above us, squawked by. The rap music and squeals of the teenagers at the marina youth center floated through the trees against the high turbine whine of a tug out on the river.

"Danny," Brady said, looking up from his stew. "You are a worthless northern liberal. But your ass can *cook*."

8

A RIVER, LIKE A WILD animal, can be tamed, but remnant behavior persists. As we motored down the Ohio through the lovely Appalachian gorges of Pennsylvania and West Virginia, I was amazed by the number of river snags and floating logs bobbing on the river, especially as we exited the locks. When we parked for the night in a quiet cove, the overnight water release from the dam upriver filled the shallows around us with large trees, cast-off terry-cloth slippers, and beautifully weathered two-by-four boards. This was more inspiring than hazardous. Now I was with Asbury Jaquess aboard the *Davy Crockett* in 1834, or Theodore Armitage in 1847, floating from the Wabash on the *Whig*, dodging the river snares with the best of the 19th-century Kaintucks.

The early-morning debris surrounding the *Patience* bonded us with nature. As soon as the sun reached over the craggy foothills, the floating tree snags were busy with wildlife, mostly small aquatic creatures drawn to this ideal habitat—frogs and salamanders scrambled all over the logs, juvenile water snakes slithered in and out of the water, and schools of tiny sunny and yellow perch swarmed below. Throngs of tadpoles raced in circles just below the surface, fast enough to ripple the water. It was a food chain bacchanalia. Great blue herons and white egrets flew in, landed on the snags, and enjoyed a breakfast feast. Giant sandhill cranes stood in the muddy flats and pecked at the edges of tree snares that reached the banks.

I had not realized before that wading birds would approach so close to man. But there was an abundance of food there, and it was a good reminder that we were the invaders in their space, not vice versa. All the way down to the Mississippi, the wading birds were nature's alarm clock. Their guttural calls echoing across the water usually woke me by six o'clock.

The nomenclature for snags used by the early riverman proved quite useful as we moved the *Patience* down the Ohio. "Sawyers" were trees resting on the bottom of the river, usually by their spiderlike roots or crowns, but not firmly, so that they moved back and forth with the current like the swaying of a sawyer with a crosscut saw. Sawyers weren't always that dangerous, and didn't require rapid avoidance turns, because they were pliantly suspended in the water and the heavy wooden hulls could usually plow over them. But they were easy to misjudge and the early flatboat men recorded frequent cases of a particularly heavy sawyer punching a hole in a hull, and the size and variety of sawyers was so great that there were many terms for them.

Popular parlance, of course, intimately follows history, and words borrowed from French dominated 18th- and early 19th-century river terms in English. The colonial New France territory, roughly following the Mississippi drainage, was vast, stretching from Hudson's Bay in Canada south to New Orleans, and the impact of French still resonates. (In the United States, nine state capitals, from Boise, Idaho, to Montpelier, Vermont, have French names. Thirty percent of today's spoken English, about seven thousand words, derives from French vocabulary, although this reflects the considerable impact of French culture on both America and Great Britain.) The French developed one of America's earliest and most lucrative businesses, the fur trade, and terms used to this day reflect that influence—the English word "beaver," for example, derived from the Middle French *baviere*, and the word "pelt" was a corruption of the Old French *pelette*. The early French fur trappers were extraordinarily ambitious explorers, canoeists, and woodsmen, often living in the wilderness of the Rocky Mountains or the Great Lakes for several years, working their traplines, before carrying their pelts south to St. Louis or New Orleans. Their impact on common nouns and place names in American English was enhanced by their willingness to intermarry with indigenous tribes and learn their languages, and then import native words into French that, over time, were assimilated into English. French influence on the inland rivers was still paramount when the flatboat era began after the American Revolution.

The French bateaux men, many of whom served as guides on the first settlers' arks descending the Ohio, used the term *rapides*, which the mostly Scotch-Irish and German settlers pronounced as "rapids," and also gave us such terms as "river" (*riviere*), "bayou," from the Choctaw word *bayuk*, and "barge," which is spelled the same way in French. The generous borrowing of French words extended to one of the most prominent features of the Ohio and the Mississippi, the endless tree snags and other natural obstructions encountered during a typical river journey. The French rivermen called sawyers and other relatively isolated snags *chicots*. The larger obstacles of mixed trees and root balls were called *embarras*, and the French likened them to the large, dried driftwood piles on the banks of French rivers that were commonly used to heat cities. Two major tributaries famed since French colonization for their tree snags, one in Illinois and one in Wisconsin, were given the name Embarrass. The term was still in use during the Civil War to describe rock formations or natural debris that stood in the way of building pontoon bridges across the southern rivers, or conditions on land that impeded the movement of troops and their cumbersome supply chains.

The mostly unlettered Kaintuck pioneers along the banks notoriously garbled this term, calling obstructions along the river "embarrassments," or "harrassments," but mostly they reverted to American-English slang and called the snags "stumps," or "nests," and, when submerged, "breaks," because of the way the water riffled over them. There were many debris subtypes, and their labeling reflected common social conventions. Large snags that bowed up and down with the current were called "preachers." Logs that stove in boats but couldn't be seen at night were called "bandits." In his 1810 *Travels on an Inland Voyage*, Christian Schultz identified an obstruction that he called a "sleeping sawyer," which he considered particularly dangerous because the swaying log was invisibly submerged just below the surface, sometimes firmly enough to hang up or puncture a passing hull.

The big "floater" logs riding buoyantly on the surface also posed a threat, but they were usually positioned parallel with the current and the course of the flatboats, and relatively easy to steer around in clear sunlight. But where the river was shadowed by clouds, the waterlogged, dark trunks were particularly hard to see ahead of the boat. Floaters by the dozens remain along every stretch of the river today. Occasionally, when I was holding a steady course to avoid barge traffic, I was forced to hit the floaters head-on, or at a slight angle, but the *Patience* proved to be a brute against them. The force of the heavy bow colliding with the tree sent the floaters downward several feet, and slowly spinning sideways, and they usually didn't bounce up to the surface on our sides until we were thirty or forty feet beyond them.

I actually enjoyed the sound of floaters banging hard on the bow, and then rolling sideways across the bottom of the boat at midships, before they harmlessly spun out of our way. During a lifetime of logging, I've become a capable estimator of a log's weight, but the ones we glanced off were also waterlogged after several months or even years in the river. As we proceeded downriver, the heavy poplar sides of the *Patience* near the waterline became scarred with scrapes and deep cuts. The *Patience* was a floater plow.

The immobile tree snags that hung up on the tips of islands, against the bends, or in the coves were the bane of 19th-century flatboatmen. These were called "wooden islands" and they were often quite large, clinging tightly against the upstream tips of the islands and sandbars. We encountered a lot of them, considering that there are seventy-five or more islands along the Ohio. High water over the winter and spring had deposited tons of silt, boulders, and gravel on the top of these giant baskets, and while passing in the boat I could actually see how the wooden islands were rapidly expanding at one end, growing into the abutting island soil, and also extending upstream as more floating sticks were added every day to the snag.

This process, which scientists variously call "bar colonization" or "fluvial landscape evolution," can add an acre or more to an island in a single year. In the other direction, the "downstream morphology" of the river also enlarges the sides and the lower end of the islands. As the water parts to flow around the island, the current tends to cling against the underwater shelves on the sides, depositing a lot of silt, and then emptying the remainder of its sediment onto the bars at the downstream tip of the island. Over time, with the right winds and currents, the edge of the enlarged bar attaches itself to the soil on the island. Within a year or two, more sediment carried down by floods supports grasses and first-growth trees, extending the island mass downstream.

John Bradbury, a respected Scottish botanist and member of the Liverpool Philosophical Society, was dispatched by the Liverpool Botanic Garden in 1809 to collect North American seeds and to survey the possibility of improving textile manufacturing by identifying stronger hybrids of cotton. This was the age of the great exploratory and botanical collection tours of the interior Americas by European and American naturalists like Charles Darwin, John James Audubon, and Alexander von Humboldt. After Bradbury arrived in America, President Thomas Jefferson encouraged him to broaden the scope of his travels to include reports back to Washington on how improvements to river navigation could enhance commerce. Bradbury embarked on a great loop of the western rivers, even joining the famed Astorian Expedition to document beaver populations along the Rocky Mountain headwaters of the Platte and Missouri rivers. Bradbury saw almost eight thousand miles of American rivers during his lyrical journey, and his merging of scientific collection and commercial evaluation, typical for the era, made him a keen observer of the interior America that was about to boom with expansion. The snags and wooden islands that Bradbury saw along the Missouri reminded him of the congested tree debris he had seen on the Ohio and the Mississippi.

"The navigation had been very difficult for some days, on account of the frequent occurrence of, what is termed by the boatmen, *embarras*," Bradbury wrote in his *Travels in the Interior of America*, published in 1819. "They are formed by large trees falling into the river, where it has undermined the banks. Some of these trees remain still attached by their roots to the firm ground, and the drift-wood being collected by the branches, a dam the length of the tree is formed, round the point of which the water runs with such velocity, that in many instances it is impossible to stem it. On account of these obstacles, we were frequently under the necessity of crossing the river."

Observing the growth of islands was another reminder of the prudent strategies of nature, and new ways to think about the meeting place of river and land. To most Americans, the islands of the western rivers were isolated and deeply romantic places, like the symbolic Jackson's Island in Mark Twain's *Adventures of Huckleberry Finn*, where Huck could escape his drunken father and the civilizing rules of the Widow Douglas, and the run-away slave Jim found temporary refuge. But the islands were also geologically significant. They grew to immense size because they played a vital role in river ecology, acting as giant filtration barriers. The larger sticks and logs carried by the flow were caught and retained by the upstream end of the island, while the fertile silt was carried below to form more land. Island morphology might even be considered the primeval creator of American wealth. The infinite redistribution of river mud by the islands, the river bends, and the ruptures along the banks built, and continuously renewed, the deep Wabash and Ohio bottomlands that made an agricultural nation rich.

The islands tormented the days of the flatboaters. The extensive network of sandbars along the Ohio and the Mississippi, particularly near the mouths of tributaries, and winter ice, presented additional natural barriers to safe travel. The journals of early flatboat captains are tales of woe rivaling the Book of Job, describing river trips so arduous that it's a wonder the flatboat era ever got started.

In January 1807, a young medical doctor from Rutherford County, Tennessee, near Nashville, John R. Bedford, decided to lead an expedition of two keelboats and a large flatboat barge loaded with cotton and salt pork to New Orleans, to explore new markets for local farmers and to expand his family's considerable plantation holdings and grocery business. The Bedfords had followed a classic family trajectory of the flatboat era. They were "westerers," a term used in the early 19th century to describe families that prospered by following America's expanding western boundaries to the next frontier, often more than once in a single generation. The Bedfords were originally from Mecklenburg County in southern Virginia, along the North Carolina line. Because it was only 120 miles away from the Shenandoah valley and the Appalachian barrier, Mecklenburg became a rich source for Ohio valley pioneers. In the 1790s the Bedfords had traveled west through Kentucky, which was originally a part of Virginia, because Bedford's father was a former Continental army captain holding generous warrants for western lands. They followed the Cumberland River across Tennessee and established a large plantation east of Nashville. Bedford had originally studied medicine, but after his father died in 1804 and he inherited the family plantation, he and his brothers decided to expand their holdings into freighting and trading on the inland rivers. After hiring a river captain and

crew, Bedford and his two brothers left in the middle of January to take advantage of the slow winter period on their plantation. But practical concerns
were only one motivation, and Bedford was filled with the romance of travel
and seeing new lands that so typified the flatboat era. He wanted to create
a travelogue for future generations to read and, as he wrote in his introduction to *A Tour from Nashville to New Orleans Down the Cumberland, Ohio
and Mississippi Rivers in the Year 1807*, "to banish *ennui* and keep at bay the
'*taedium vitae*' of idleness, either of body or mind."

The Bedfords could afford to hire a captain and crew, and meticulously
prepared for the river hazards ahead by installing stone fireplaces in their
boats, investing in expensive buffalo robes, and meticulously stocking their
galleys with smoked hams, dry-stored potatoes, and live poultry to ward
against the hazards of a winter journey. But privilege didn't matter much
out on the river and the Bedford flotilla soon ran into the common plight
of all river travelers: the fickleness of water levels. The "freshets" created by
fall rains and the spring snowmelt made those two seasons the best time
to embark on the inland rivers, but winter flows were generally considered
reliable, too. The winter of 1807 was exceptionally cold, however, and had
followed an autumn of modest rains, and there was no system then of calling ahead to ascertain water heights along their route. Low water and ice
floes would stalk the Bedfords all the way south.

The Bedfords had traveled only one full day on the Cumberland before
they ran into trouble with low water, grounding their heavy barge on the
shoals formed by the mouth of the Harpeth River. The family and their
crew spent three days attempting to extricate the barge from the sandbars and then decided to transfer the heavy cargo from the barge to the
keelboats, and then float the barge, now empty and drawing less water, to
the Ohio. The boats reached the mouth of the Cumberland four days later,
only to learn that a large sandbar at the confluence with the Ohio blocked
their way. They spent the next week laboriously off-loading their cargo on
the south banks of the Cumberland, commuting every day from a local
boardinghouse to rearrange the canvas tarps protecting their cotton bales
from the rain, and sent word back to Nashville that they needed three
more boats with shallower drafts. (The $75 spent to procure these boats
rendered the expedition "destitute," Bedford wrote.) After loading their
new boats, the party once more set off, only to run aground on the sandbar

at the mouth of the Cumberland. It took two hours to free the boats and Bedford fell overboard into frigid, waist-deep water. Once on the Ohio, the crew spent two days reloading their cargo onto their original barge, and pushed off with the water levels still dropping, snow falling, and the winds blowing violently against their bows, reducing their progress to a crawl.

Near Fort Massac on the Ohio, the Bedfords ran a gauntlet of grounded boats along a stretch called Chain of Rocks, the beached vessels acting as a kind of beacon for the low water, and then ran aground themselves, spending a miserable night commuting to shore in their canoe and then camping in frigid winds. They reached the Mississippi only to find it frozen from "bank to bank" in several spots. They ran aground again just above New Madrid, Missouri, extricated themselves and passed another large flatboat that had been beached on a sandbar for twenty days, and then were stalled once more when their bow was stoved by a "large and stubborn sawyer." A passing flatboat refused to pull over and help them free their boat. By this time the Bedfords had lost their canoe and couldn't reach shore to find camping spots or obtain firewood. During most of their groundings the crew slept out on the deck, huddling together against the winds underneath their buffalo robes. The tribulations of the Bedfords were common; in a bad water year, traveling southwest by water was a brutal saga.

We know that the Bedfords eventually reached New Orleans—Bedford sent a letter home from New Orleans dated March 27—but, probably because he was exhausted by the serial calamities of his trip, John Bedford abandoned his diary after the frustrating halts in New Madrid. He was particularly infuriated by the refusal of the passing flatboat to pull over in the current and help his family free their impaled boat.

Inhuman monsters! [They] continued on as if they neither saw nor heard us. No practicable means were untried to loosen her [their boat]—but all without effect. . . . The sadness and gloom on every countenance indicated despondence at ever reaching New Orleans—for it seemed as if our impediments were never to cease. . . . Oh! What perplexity and embarrassment!—are we to stick and ground every 2 or three days? Some fatality seems directed to us particularly, which, after torturing us almost out of life, will sink and drown us! [I] sorely lamented ever attempting the voyage.

Not surprisingly, upon his return to Nashville in October that year, Dr. Bedford promptly advertised in the local papers that he was staying put for a while and returning to the practice of medicine. He went on to make extensive investments in banking and plantation lands along the Tennessee River in Alabama, on richly fertile lands purchased from the Cherokee and Choctaw tribes during the prelude to government-sponsored Indian Removal in the 1830s. In 1818, befitting his status as a flatboat-era pioneer, and quite symbolically for a scion of a wealthy westerering family, Dr. Bedford built a gracious plantation house for his family on land that overlooked the fabled Muscle Shoals along the Tennessee River. He had purchased the site from a wealthy Cherokee leader and warrior, Incalatanga, or Chief Doublehead. Later, to improve his health, Dr. Bedford wintered in New Orleans, where he could live comfortably on earnings from his shares in banks, trading houses, and distant plantations.

By my second or third week on the Ohio, I had bumped my way into the discovery that, on a changed river, with flows relatively restrained, I could harness the snags to my advantage, especially when tying bow-in against the banks in brisk currents.

The snags along the banks had an interesting architecture. The edges of the snags were mostly thin branches and tree crowns high above the water level, allowing them to bake in the sun for months and become brittle. I could slide the *Patience* into this dried barrier and snap the periphery of the snag with the heavy poplar sides, slowing the boat and holding it against the current without doing any damage to the hull. The interior of the snag was a thick, stolid load of mud, heavy logs, and tree leaders, bonded together by the silt of the river. I started to call them "nature's docks." After breaking away the brittle sides, I lodged the boat sideways to this mass to park safely, with the current holding the *Patience* secure. The crew could then scramble across the snag to firm land with lines attached to the kevels on the boat, attaching the ropes to trees upstream. By gently zigzagging the hull upstream with the motor, I could slowly tighten the lines and safely park the boat.

I became particularly fond of tree snags that touched the banks, just below the umbrella of shade provided by overhanging trees. Usually, there was a lot of moss growing on the oak limbs on the upstream side of the snag, which meant that the wood would be wet and partially rotted, thus flexible, a nice, spongy cushion to receive the sides of the boat. Jackknifing into the snags became an early example of my growing self-confidence. But Danny was terrified the first few times I rammed the hull into the tree snags, reverting to this pseudo military jargon that he used in a crisis, probably from watching too many World War II movies.

"Collision! Collision!" Danny would scream from the bow as we sidled into the tree snares. "All hands on deck, brace for crash!"

But most of our impacts with the mossy edges of the snags were as benign as a child's snow saucer coming to rest against a melting snowbank. And Danny grew increasingly adept at scrambling across the snag with a line, lashing it around a tree, and then hauling it in and tying up after I'd inched up to a good parking spot in the current.

The experts were wrong again. The tree snags that I had been warned would sink my boat were in fact conveniently placed cushions that I could exploit to land in brisk currents.

The snags proved useful in other ways. Coming out of the Montgomery locks above Shippingport, Pennsylvania, we were surrounded by a snag pile, mostly smaller sticks that I wasn't too concerned about. But just as we reached the sail line along the south bank, I heard a loud grinding from the rear, like an electric pencil sharpener, and the motor was vibrating strongly enough to send shudders through the hull. Danny raced back to investigate and excitedly yelled up from the stern.

"Neutralize the power plant!"

I cut the power and let us drift toward the shoals near the south bank. While we had been sitting motionless in the lock chamber, floating sticks had crept beneath the motor and the boat bottom and become lodged together in the motor housing, fouling the propeller. Danny managed to remove most of the debris with a shovel, but several of the freed sticks had floated forward under the hull. He was worried that we would jam them back in the motor housing if we, as Danny put it, "steamed ahead." He wanted me to slowly leave the area of the debris pile by moving into the river channel in reverse. But when we did that, the entire stern, including our battery, flooded, because Cooper had drilled large holes to run the electrical wires and steering cables to the motor without installing seals. Water rushed in whenever we were in reverse, or when backflow from tugboat wakes rammed us from behind. The flooding of water through the stern of the *Patience* had been a problem since we launched in western Pennsylvania.

Danny and Brady wanted to make repairs right away. A few miles downriver, I found an abandoned barge company dock on the north bank, surrounded by still water. Raising a din from cordless drills, handsaws, and hammers, Danny and Brady spent the next two hours completely rebuilding the electrical system, adding a second battery and a deep-storage lithium pack that Danny had brought along. They moved the new battery system up to the second step of the staircase leading to the roof deck, where the batteries and wiring would be protected both from river water and rain, and rewired the entire boat with enough outlets to hook up lights, fans, cell phone chargers, even a kitchen toaster. They caulked the stern boards, and Brady ingeniously crafted new seals for the holes in the stern by cutting down the plastic lids from our coffee cans.

When they were almost done, Danny dangled upside down over the stern rail with my cordless drill in his right hand. He wanted to secure the coffee-lid seals into the holes below with Gorilla Glue and deck screws. Danny, however, is no gymnast. Swaying like a beached seal on the stern rail, he pitched forward head over heels and the next thing we heard was "WHOAH!" as he flipped into the Ohio River.

Danny came up laughing, the river water glistening on his hair as he treaded water and held up the drill.

"Man overboard!" he shouted, holding the drill high over his head and pressing the trigger. "But look at this. It still works!"

Danny was pleased with himself when we pulled him back up onto the boat.

"Great fix!" he yelled exuberantly, throwing his arms wide in the air. "Nothing can stop us now."

As he said that, the cordless drill spun sideways out of his right hand and flew behind the boat over the river, disappearing with a splash into the water. A few bubbles rose in the muddy water as the drill sank to the bottom.

"Damn it, that was John Cooper's fault," Danny said. "And now we've lost our drill."

"Danny, stop blaming John Cooper," I said. "He's not on this boat. We are."

Powering up for the next bend, I was contented, resigned to my fate. My bankruptcy plan as a boat owner would continue. We would have to buy a new cordless drill during our next big stop downriver, but we also had a much better boat.

I knew by the fourth or fifth day on the Ohio that I needed to get rid of Scott, but I was procrastinating. It's a personality defect that I have long acknowledged to myself. I am not forthright about dealing with personal conflict, a holdover from being raised in a large family, and recently reinforced by sharing with my brothers and sisters the care of my mother in Maine. The problem, as any psychiatrist can tell you, is that emotional procrastination works, at least for a while. That dubious brother of mine, who is always saying embarrassing things at family weddings, can be ignored for now, because it's too disruptive in that social setting to deal with him right away. Within a few months, one of my sisters is acting out instead, and now my anger at him has vanished behind my anger at her. Coming from a large, complicated family generates an infinite regress of emotional conflict, and then delay, delay, delay. I had taught myself over the years to punt anger, pushing it out of my head for a few days or weeks. But denial has its limits. When the pressure gets too great I blow up at everybody at once and really destroy the family peace. My person-to-person emotions, in short, are repressed, until they go thermonuclear. There are long spells of avoidance behavior in between.

My delay in dealing with Scott also had a lot to do with anger at myself. I was the jackass who had allowed him on the boat.

Just about everything about Scott annoyed me. He overreacted every time a tug and a string of barges appeared downriver, racing up to the roof deck to make suggestions and wanting to use the radio, when in fact I had already figured out the captain's track and had the *Patience* pointed on the right course. His fourteen-year-old son wanted to try throwing the rope for the floating bollard when we passed through a lock, but he missed. It wasn't a problem because we were the only boat in the chamber and his son had plenty of time to lasso the bollard. But Scott raged at his son, his screams echoing against the walls of the lock, which only made it more difficult for his son to throw the line true. Scott strenuously recommended that we plan our descent of the Ohio carefully, to avoid spending the night docked near urban areas like Louisville or Cincinnati, where he was convinced that the "Black kids" from the nearby housing projects would sneak down and rob the boat. (In fact, at Louisville, Vicksburg, and Baton Rouge, where we parked close to African American neighborhoods, we enjoyed many quiet nights. The only Black kids we saw were those who came down to the boat to sell us fish.) Scott never cooked and he never fixed anything on the boat and, most nights, he left his son with us on the boat and then walked into the woods to smoke with Jay. But Scott always had an opinion. He personified a favorite quote of mine, from Ulysses S. Grant. "The most confident critics are generally those who know the least about the matter."

Scott had a number of other peculiarities. For a Meriwether Lewis reenactor, he was surprisingly squeamish about relieving himself in the woods, like the rest of us did when landing in a remote spot. As soon as we tied up for the night, Scott disappeared into the buildings of a marina or up into town to search for a clean bathroom. The state parks or ramshackle marinas where we overnighted usually had a Port-o-Pottie or two. But Scott didn't want to rough it there. Finding a modern, sanitized restroom was an obdurate mind block for him. "That was our biggest problem on the Lewis and Clark trip," Jay told me one day. "As soon as we landed somewhere, the whole expedition stopped while we searched for a clean toilet for Scott."

People who can't shit in the woods annoy me. They are advertising by their fussiness a disassociation from nature and an overreliance on the quite useless and wasteful sanitary standards of a society obsessed with comfort. When I am plowing on an Amish farm and nature calls, or riding the highways, I quite enjoy stopping at the edge of some woods and indulging a good, healthy, gaseous dump. While I squat, birds sing and chipmunks chase around with acorns in their cheeks. I collect napkins from McDonald's or Dunkin' Donuts and store them under my pickup seat so that I always have an adequate store of toilet paper. There is nothing quite so satisfying in the middle of the day as finding a nice, moist, fallen oak trunk, God's toilet seat, and then sitting down on the soft bark to enjoy the act of replenishing the soil out of my own bowels. There is nothing quite so dissatisfying as spending time with a dumbass, pretty-boy reenactor in a calico shirt, pretending to be the man who led an expedition eight thousand miles through the Rocky Mountain wilderness without being capable of shitting in the woods. Scott just annoyed the shit out of me.

In his own way, Scott would occasionally try to be helpful. Because the latest government charts were often ten or more years old, I couldn't rely on them for the location and size of shoals and sandbars ahead of us. When my cell phone reception was good, I could call up Google Earth or a U.S. Geological Survey website to check their data, which was usually only two or so months old. I kept my cell phone lying next to my river charts on the steering console, occasionally consulting these images.

But Scott sniffed and gave me a lecture on the uselessness of technology on a trip like mine. By reading the river for riffles or other disturbances on the surface I could usually identify low water that might threaten the boat.

This was useful, and I got better at it. When I was passing underneath bridges, there were usually defined riffles near the bottom of the pylons, indicating low water. When I steered closer a couple of times to investigate, I noticed that these riffles weren't caused by silt, but in fact many pylons were supported by giant, oblong cement foundations, wider than the pylons themselves. The shallow draft of the *Patience* usually meant that I could clear those foundations. But it was good to know about the low water depths near the pylons because I often met oncoming barge tows near bridges and might need to cut it close to the support structures. The fleet-mooring areas for barges and the company docks along the banks were sometimes rife with disturbed waters. Commercial areas along the rivers, like railroad property on land, are ritually abused by the companies that operate there. To save time and money, old leaky barges are simply scuttled and sent to the bottom, and I-beams, junked barrels, and burnt-out generators are thrown off the docks. I could easily identify these underwater metal dumps by the way the compass skittered around near a mooring cell or a company dock. The obstacles left by commercial America attract a lot of silt and this creates dangerous low water, probably the worst hazards to navigation that I encountered on the trip. I learned to be cautious around industrial sites, carefully reading every indication on the water surface.

Scott's strangest affectation was clothes. Two or three times a day, depending on his mood or the next situation we faced, he would disappear down to the cabin and fuss with the wardrobe department in his big duffel bag, reappearing on the roof deck in canvas trousers and a sailor's striped shirt, or a heavy British admiral's hurricane coat. At Marietta, Ohio, a college and tourist town bustling with riverfront pedestrian traffic, Scott appeared on deck in one of his favorite outfits—skintight duck pants, a colorful ceramic necklace and a bright yellow calico shirt, a dagger and belt with a shiny brass buckle, tall black boots, and a floppy straw sun hat that looked as if he'd borrowed it from Little Bo Peep. Leaping from the gunwales to the dock for a stroll downtown, he furtively looked from side to side as he passed the first group of pedestrians, to make sure they noticed his clothing ensemble. He was a fashion exhibitionist, a period-dress Valentino.

I was embarrassed by Scott's frequent costume changes. The first time Scott appeared on the roof deck in his calico shirt and Bo Peep hat, I must have raised my eyebrows. He already knew that I disapproved of period-dressing. When he felt judged, Scott would revert to a kind of grandiloquent talk that, he thought, aped the speech patterns of early America.

"It's preposterously evident," Scott would say to me, "that you know very little about the haberdashery of men in the late eighteenth and early nineteenth centuries. In those days men wanted to be as pretty as women. Everything in those log cabin towns was boring and drab. Sailing a boat down the river was monotonous. So you dressed to spice up life. It was an age when men were girls."

Scott aspired to be one of these androgynous 19th-century characters. His attitude toward modern women, however, could be quite retrograde, a bent that I had noticed before in a lot of other reenactors.

In West Virginia, we parked for the night at the transient dock of the Wheeling Island Marina, in the middle of the river. The *Patience* always drew a crowd when we tied up at a place like that, and a festive group from the marina and the houseboats in the slips gathered on the dock beside us. Most of our visitors were women who wanted to wander around the boat and finish their drinks on the roof deck, enjoying the views across the river to Wheeling. It was one of Scott's Bo Peep nights and he looked quite fetching in his calico shirt and necklace, sporting a small leather purse hung from his belt, while he smoked a cigarette. Fortified by one of Danny's gin and tonics, I was feeling expansive, enjoying the miscellany of people drawn to our shantyboat and the summer gaiety on the dock.

I had not spent a lot of time before this reflecting on the all-male composition of the *Patience* crew so far. Suddenly I was filled with appreciation for women and I mentioned to Scott that I was looking forward to my new best friends from Nashville, Cynthia Lee and Deb Satterfield, joining the boat in a couple of weeks. Life would be better when the boat was gender-balanced.

"Oh, no, no, no," Scott said, his face turning red with annoyance. "Women are fine on a boat for a party night like this, but not once you're underway. Manifestly, women do *not* belong on a boat."

"I see," I said. "And why is that?"

"Women just have so many problems," Scott said. "They always want everything to be perfect. They take forever to get moving in the morning. And they use too much water."

With that, Scott flicked his cigarette into the river and stalked off down the dock. We didn't see him for the rest of the night.

The next morning, I was cheerfully lamenting one of the critical weaknesses of an all-male boat. If women were aboard the *Patience* right now, Danny and I would have made at least a token stab at washing the dinner dishes last night before we went to bed. But without women around, men tend to revert to their natural, Hobbesian state, flopping straight onto a couch or the floor from the spot where they are drinking or sharing dirty jokes. The dishes could wait until morning. I was laughing at myself as I washed the dishes and pots and pans from the night before in a large Rubbermaid basin on the wooden dock next to the *Patience*.

When we did the dishes together in the morning, I crouched on the dock and scrubbed the pots and pans with a plastic brush and detergent while Danny grunted back and forth to the nearest hose line, carrying back clean water in two-gallon rubber buckets for rinsing. Danny and I enjoyed the dishwashing routine, the same way we loved cleaning our friends' summerhouses or clearing forests when we were invited for the weekend somewhere. To both of us, a vacation or a long weekend was just an excuse to make improvements.

While we washed the dishes, Danny and I chatted about the trip so far and I mentioned to Danny what Scott had said about having women on the boat.

"I don't mind weirdo," Danny said. "My life would be pretty dull without the weirdos. I mean, *I'm* a weirdo. But I can't stand weirdos who don't know they're weirdos."

A few minutes later Scott walked down the dock, cheerfully smoking a cigarette and obviously feeling the promise of a glorious morning, now that he'd found clean restrooms at the marina.

I spoke softly and winked at Danny.

"Here comes Scott," I said. "Let's do this right."

When Scott got to the boat, I had just finished scrubbing a four-quart Revere Ware saucepan, but it was still bubbly with detergent. I held the saucepan up and inspected it in the sunlight.

"Danny, rinse," I said.

While Scott watched, Danny dumped a full two-gallon bucket of water onto the pan with such enthusiasm that a lot of the sudsy water splashed onto his shorts and onto my hair. The pan was completely rinsed, but I held it up again for inspection and motioned to Danny to grab the next bucket of water.

"Nope, not done yet," I said. "Danny, give 'er another bucket."

Danny dumped hard on the saucepan again. Compared to what the pan needed, this was a bath in Niagara Falls.

I inspected the pot again and looked up to Danny.

"Shit, think we need one more?"

"Oh yeah, big time," Danny said, dumping on a third bucket.

Scott looked flustered, appalled.

"Preposterous," he said. "Preposterously asinine. What on earth, may I beg you, are you doing with all of that water?"

"Oh, just getting in touch with my girl, Scott," I said. "It is the responsibility of the captain to make sure that we're using enough water. It's a beautiful morning to be washing the pots and pans. Danny, more water?"

"I love rinsing pots and pans," Danny said. "Using water is the best fucking part of the trip."

Scott threw his cigarette down on the dock and ground it with his foot. He was disgusted with us and stalked back down the dock.

"Preposterous!" he called over his shoulder. "Egregiously preposterous. I'll see you after breakfast."

"Damn it all, Danny," I said. "You just pissed off Scott. He thinks you're a weirdo for using too much water."

"At least I know I'm a weirdo."

Long stretches of the Ohio remain undeveloped and the bluffs that line the banks from Ohio to Kentucky are as scenic today as they were for the frontier Kaintuckers.

9

THE BEAUTIFUL STRETCHES THAT WE were sailing through on the Ohio made it difficult to appreciate that we were descending a valley struggling between life and death. Twisting around the bends, we passed massive electrical generating plants every few miles, sometimes more than one of them crowded together on the banks. Deer and coyotes wandered along the grassy edges of the tracks carrying coal from the river docks to the power plants. A mile above Weirton, West Virginia, the sail line turned south around the left side of Brown's Island, narrowing the channel to just four hundred yards. As we hugged the shoals beside the moribund Weirton Steel works to avoid the commercial traffic, we counted seventy-four passing barges filled with coal, divided between three push boats. A bald eagle dove from the tower of a high-tension line and snared a large fish in its talons, churning up tiny whitecaps with its wing tips as it struggled for height with the load.

But those full barges of coal were deceptive, and the famous works at Weirton symbolized the painful transition underway along the Ohio. In 1983, following several years of declining sales and massive layoffs that plagued the entire steel industry, the National Steel Corporation agreed to sell its aging sheet-steel and tin-stamping plant at Weirton to its workers, creating overnight the world's largest employee-owned company. Weirton was already one of America's most storied industrial enterprises. In 1905, a Pittsburgh barbed-wire salesman named Ernest Tener Weir convinced investors to help him buy the old Phillips Sheet and Tin Plate Company, renaming the steelworks after himself as he quickly expanded his hundred-acre site into a thriving complex of mills, stamping plants, and a coke works. Immigrants from nearby Pittsburgh and southern Europe flocked to the remote West Virginia valley to work at Weirton, eventually swelling the plant payroll to twelve thousand workers. Weir bitterly opposed unionization during the New Deal and his mills and shops exploded with labor protests, but his plant steadily churned out profits through the Great Depression. Weirton prospered through the boom years for steel during World War II, when the steelworks made tank and artillery shells for the war effort, and established national records for ingot production, and continued to grow during the postwar expansion. The sprawling Weirton works eventually covered more than six hundred acres along the river and included a plant in neighboring Steubenville, Ohio. The smoke from the plant, mixing in the narrow valley with the persistent fogs that blew up from the river, created smog so dense that Weirton motorists drove with their headlights on in the middle of the day.

Ernest Weir was a throwback to the split style of earlier steel barons like Andrew Carnegie and Henry Clay Frick—ruthless, but philanthropic. He ran his company town on strict anti-union principles, but he was determined to build an exemplary style of paternalistic capitalism along his stretch of the Ohio. With each new rolling mill and coke battery, Weir built commensurate social amenities to support his expanding workforce—housing, police, and public works departments, a library, parks, and gyms, even churches. In 1937, at the height of the Depression, when he appeared on the cover of *Life* magazine, Weir was called the "presiding genius" of the steel town. By then Weirton had become the largest private employer and largest taxpayer in West Virginia.

The worker buyout of 1983 revived Weirton's fame, mostly because it was briefly and surprisingly successful and appealed to the alternative, pro-labor narrative then popular among opponents of the conservative, business-first administration of Ronald Reagan. Over four consecutive years of employee ownership, profits soared and Weirton steelworkers received annual profit-sharing checks of $4,500, the highest in the industry. But a bungled modernization plan, competition from cheap foreign steel, and expensive joint-venture projects eventually swallowed Weirton in the whirlpool of debt, declining sales, and layoffs that decimated the rest of the American steel industry. Facing mounting losses, Weirton filed for bankruptcy in 2003 and sold most of its local assets to the global steelmaking giant ArcelorMittal. A single rolling and plate mill that produces tin sheet for making soup cans, employing about 850 workers, is all that remains today of this Camelot of the American worker along the Ohio.

I felt winsome for the old Weirton works as we passed its mostly deserted fleet-barge area opposite Brown's Island. Demolition was obviously underway at various locations on the sprawling plant site, and the only sign of life was a large John Deere wheel loader with a grappling hook, dumping scrapped I-beams and tin roofing from a pile on the dock onto a rusty red barge. A showcase of American steelmaking was now being hauled off as scrap.

The Weirton docks were vaguely familiar to me, though changed. In 1983, I had spent a few days in Weirton during the euphoria after the employee buyout, on a reporting tour for *Life* about the collapse of the steel industry in Pennsylvania and West Virginia. I still remember writing in my notes about one of the most memorable sights of the trip. The docks were busy then and the Weirton riggers were racing around in forklifts and giant front-loaders, staging pallets of finished steel for pickup by railcar and barge. The men were brawny and tanned, and they wore grimy red and orange T-shirts, stained jeans, and yellow safety hats. Their work boots were worn down to their steel toes. Their biceps flashed in the sun against the forested ridgelines across the river in the Ohio Appalachians. The flesh against sky and tree reminded me of the imagery in a Diego Rivera mural.

But more than thirty years later the images on the deserted docks amazed me in a new way. Can returning vegetation grow everywhere? Are wild plants and first-growth trees really this aggressive? The wide brick lanes once busy with loaders carrying steel to the docks were disappearing underneath a coverlet of grass. Green bursts of first-growth aspen, birch, and sumac were sprouting everywhere, out of window transoms, smokestacks, metal ore carts, and up through railroad tracks. Virtually every open space in the ghost factory was now early succession forest. This visual paradox would become one of the most dominant images of the trip. Along the Rust Belt landscape of the inland rivers, the persistence of man was dramatically yielding to the persistence of nature.

We decided to stop for gas at a marina just downriver from Brown's Island near Holliday's Cove in Weirton, the site of a Revolutionary War fort and military depot that supplied Continental army detachments operating along the Ohio River frontier. But we needed more than fuel at Weirton—we were desperately short on fuel tanks as well. Even though we were only sixty miles below Pittsburgh, I could see already that refueling was going to be a constant problem. Until Brady suggested that we run a careful miles-per-tank fuel test, which allowed us to reduce power and save fuel, we were pushing the engine too hard, running our six-gallon plastic tanks dry after just two hours of cruising. We had left Pennsylvania with only three tanks, making it impossible to run all day without refueling stops.

This was aggravated by a twin set of issues along the Ohio, which would only become more severe when we reached the Mississippi. The "Great Recession" of 2008 and its massive layoffs had virtually wiped out dispos-able income along the industrialized Ohio. Fishing on the river had always been popular among blue-collar workers, but now most of them were either unemployed or had moved out of the Ohio valley. Water-skiers and other recreational boaters were pinching pennies, too, and the eroding customer base had forced many marinas to close. Three years later, in March 2011, large winter snowmelts and heavy rains pushed water levels past flood stage along many stretches of the Ohio, in some areas raising the river close to the record heights recorded during the disastrous 1927 floods. Many additional waterfront marinas, already marginalized by the 2008 recession, were dam-aged by the 2011 floods and their owners decided not to reopen. The river we were traveling had become a "fuel desert," and we could rely on refueling only at major towns and cities, sometimes more than a hundred miles apart from each other. This was well beyond the range of our three tanks.

I botched our landing at Weirton for reasons that should have been ob-vious to me. As we approached the dock at Holliday's Cove, the American flag that I had installed on the stern was briskly snapping behind me, facing toward the front of the boat, indicating a strong following wind of at least ten or twelve knots. I failed to realize that the wind was pushing the cur-rent, too, and that we were being pushed with it, and that it was impossible to judge speed simply by looking at the water beside us. We felt motionless, but we were fixed in the high-speed flow.

As I angled slightly in to kiss the side of the bow against the dock, the wind caught us broadside and kept us running fast, and even if I had responded earlier and placed the prop in reverse, we were headed for a collision. The bow whacked the dock hard enough to leave a mark on a horizontal apron board and the *Patience* bounced off and slid sideways and was caught again by the wind, whirling ninety degrees, striking the dock again on the stern. I didn't panic, but I was surprised and embarrassed, astonished even, that ten tons of boat on a flat-bottom could be pummeled around so hard just by the wind. As I powered up to regain steerage and to make a wide sweep back into the current for a second attempt at landing, the prop grinded into wood as it hit one of the dock pilings.

Brady was sitting beside me, smiling and unconcerned, and he gave me a "Guess I should have warned you" shrug.

I was turning back upriver, just inching forward at almost full power.

"Okay," Brady said. "Let's try a redo on that. What's the current doing to you now?"

"Pushing me back, pretty hard."

"Right. The water in the channel here is compressed by that island, making the current very fast. What's the wind doing to you?"

I looked behind me at the flag, which was now pointed due aft, snapping strongly. I could feel the force of the breeze on my face.

"Shit, I get it," I said. "We had a following current *and* a following breeze. We must have been doing fifteen knots against that dock."

"No shit, Sherlock," Brady said.

Piloting a boat, I suddenly realized, wasn't that different from flying a plane. The principles were the same and in both cases safe operation required high awareness of natural conditions and a prevailing attitude of common sense. Downwind landings in a plane are dangerous because, even in moderate winds, speeds are too fast and steering inputs either become ineffective or exaggerated and, in a quartering tailwind, the controls are often reversed. But pilots can't sense what's happening to the plane as they are whisked downwind for an encounter with the runway that probably isn't going to end well. I've botched my share of landings approaching downwind, and usually the errors are annoyingly basic. Oh yeah, chucklehead, next time try checking the wind sock first.

As we struggled upriver in the wind and current to swing wide for another attempt at the dock, I realized that I suffered from another deficit of inexperience. I was overconfident, even cocky. During my initial days on the river, my dock landings had been flawless, my steerage around the big barge strings safe by wide margins. I didn't chatter like a "Nancy," the term tugboat crews use to describe overly talkative small-boaters, on the radio. The tugboat captains were obviously pleased because, often, as they passed this odd wooden boat with the big American flag whipping in the breeze, they stepped out to the grated metal walkways beside their bridges, waved their caps, and aimed their smartphones at the *Patience* for pictures.

But this had mostly been beginner's luck, abetted by calm conditions and not much traffic after we left the Monongahela, with very little close-quarter maneuvering required. I realized that river journeys, with the refreshing winds cooling my face, the hypnotic snapping of the flag behind me, and the spectacular views of the hills and distant bluffs, invited complacency. River journeys are a slow, pleasing IV drip of Valium. The sun drenching my face with warmth and the ceaseless murmuring of the water against the sides of the boat made me feel lazy, romantic, freed from the bonds of land. Now I would have to start over again, assuming a base knowledge of zero, constantly goading myself to be alert, remembering to sense what was happening to the boat.

I offered the wheel to Brady so we wouldn't crash into the dock again, but he smiled and declined.

"You can do this," he said.

Brady explained that in following winds and currents, I should pull well upriver, turn on a parallel course to the dock, and then neutralize both the prop and all steering attempts. Letting the boat drift, I could then judge what the wind and the water was doing to me. When I did this, the wind pitched the broad port side of the *Patience*, which was acting almost as a sail now, sideways, at the same time pushing us quickly downstream. We were crabbing, pretty fast, toward the dock.

I used a tall mooring cell on the bank as my speed gauge, judging how quickly we were approaching the dock. We were still moving swiftly downriver, so I brought on reverse power, gradually increasing it until we seemed almost stationary against the mooring cell. Reversing the steering to starboard straightened out the boat and we were now just inching downriver.

"If we hit anything right now, what are the consequences?" Brady asked.

"Almost none. We're too slow."

"Use the wind and current," Brady said. "Make them work for you. With the motor running this strong in reverse, you're practically standing still. Then let nature do the rest, pushing you toward the dock."

I actually increased my reverse power a bit more and gently turned to starboard as we approached the dock, to let the wind do most of the work, easing us slightly sideways toward a landing. I aimed for a set of cleats in the middle of the dock and called down to Danny and Jay to fasten their lines to the cleats from the boat, not jump ashore as they usually did. The current was moving too fast for them to leap to the dock and then swing around in time to secure the cleats.

We hit the dock a little hard and fast, but not dangerously so, and I steered a little more to starboard and held lots of reverse power to lock the *Patience* wood-on-wood to the dock. Danny and Jay had us securely tied in just a few seconds, and we added extra lines to another set of cleats to hold us securely against the current.

Brady's virtues were revealing themselves to me. He was happier to have schooled me through a landing in tough winds than to have performed the landing himself. When we were secure against the dock and I had shut off the motor, he smiled and clapped me on the shoulder.

"Okay, now whatta you do if the same stiff wind is facing you?"

"Pull downwind, far off the dock, and watch what the wind is doing to me. Ideally, I should let the wind push me back toward a soft landing."

"Shit, for a college-educated liberal, you learn fast."

The marina owner at Weirton was tall and polite, with the effortless manners of a southerner. He was captivated by our trip, and wanted to help. "All the way to New Orleans?" he said. "Sounds pretty risky to me, but what a great way to see the country." He also reminded me that southern manners often come bundled with an edge. Before we could get to the subject of gas tanks, he volunteered an observation about the country we were seeing right there.

"The next two hundred miles is coal country," he said. "And we've been destroyed by Washington. Washington and the Clean Power Plan. It has wrecked America. The workingman in this country doesn't have a job anymore."

The marina owner had raised an important point that we probably wouldn't have seen by ourselves. Even with the evidence of Weirton's decline just upriver, it was easy to drone through the Appalachians and ignore the signs that surrounded us along the banks. Moving downriver in an old wooden boat was dreamy. The wildlife drawn to the river environment and the scenic ridges were distracting. Meeting the challenge of steering clear of the procession of barges passing several times an hour was rewarding and made me feel virile and self-satisfied, especially when I remembered the warnings I'd received before we left. We were seeing only what we wanted to see along the banks, subsumed by the relaxing bubble of travel.

When I changed the subject back to the gas tanks, the marina owner told us that business was so slow that he hadn't stocked a big inventory of gas tanks. But he was pretty sure that he had three or four used tanks stored in a shed back at his farm. As I prepared to leave with him in his pickup to see about the tanks, Brady pulled me aside.

"Let me go for the tanks," he said. "I know this type of guy. I can handle him."

Danny was happy about the delay. The marina was scruffy with high grass and piles of hardware outside the shop. Several abandoned boat hulls were resting on their sides, bleaching under the sun. Grabbing some tools from the *Patience*, he disappeared to cannibalize parts from the wrecks that we could use for spares, and every few minutes I could hear the squeak of rusty screws pried loose from weathered fiberglass and wood. He would return later with a very usable pile of rope cleats, hose clamps, battery connectors, and tools.

While Danny worked outside, I sat in the cabin taking notes, and I realized that I had completely missed the clear signs of the death rattle of coal. We had already passed three shuttered power plants, which were easily identifiable because their stacks weren't belching smoke and their coal docks and barge-fleet areas were deserted. All the way down through Kentucky and Illinois we would pass more closed electric power plants, and I would count at least a dozen that were obviously being converted to natural gas. The old coal docks and roofed conveyor lines had been demolished and replaced by connections for natural gas pipelines. At other plants, the coal docks had been supplanted with the metal tanks, pipes, and compressor pumps of gas terminals. There were days when we counted more natural gas barges delivering to the plants than coal barges.

The decline of coal was probably the most dramatic historic shift that we saw on the trip. Hydraulic fracking and horizontal drilling for natural gas over the past decade, mostly just over the mountains in Pennsylvania, had unleashed a massive oversupply of natural gas that was a far-cheaper and less environmentally destructive fuel for making electricity. Energy producers from the Tennessee Valley Authority to the Ohio Power Company had led a retreat from coal that had reduced mining in the Appalachians by 45 percent over the previous decade. Two of the largest electric producers in coal country, Appalachian Power of Charleston, West Virginia, and Dominion Power in Richmond, Virginia, were making business-page headlines across the country by abandoning coal and investing heavily in wind and solar power to create favorable rate packages for companies like Amazon and Microsoft, who had publicly pledged to reduce their reliance on fossil fuels while locating fulfillment centers and cloud computing sites in the region. Vast offshore drilling areas opened by the Obama administration along the Atlantic coast and the Gulf of Mexico contributed to the glut of cheap oil and gas. At the same time, coal-mining executives were their own worst enemy, maniacally devoted to steps that were decimating the industry. Bloated borrowing during a falling market, thoughtless mergers, and expensive settlements over mine safety had swamped the mining companies with debt. By 2017, five of the largest coal companies in America had declared bankruptcy, and several coal company executives were facing federal criminal charges for bank fraud and conspiracy to violate employee-safety rules. Washington hadn't destroyed the coal industry. Management myopia and greed had destroyed the coal industry.

As a result, there isn't a single coal-fired plant planned by an electrical utility in the United States today, and employment in the mines has dropped nationally from just under 200,000 jobs in the late 1980s to barely 50,000 today. At its peak, "King Coal" had employed nearly a million people in the 1920s, making the Ohio River valley an energy powerhouse, vital to the American economy. But today the barges mounded high with tons of sooty black lumps that I saw passing by were remnants, symbols of a dying industry.

Blaming Washington and the Clean Power Plan for the death of coal was a refrain we would hear all the way down the Ohio, and it didn't have to be true to be widely believed. It was all part of the polarization of American politics into slogans, as both major political parties vied for the loyalty of Midwestern blue-collar workers devastated by technological change, and the historic movement of manufacturing jobs to Mexico and Asia. The Clean Power Plan, which grew out of the commitments the United States agreed to in the 2015 Paris Climate Accords, would have mandated that each state implement a program to reduce carbon emissions by either greatly increasing the efficiency of coal plants or converting them to gas-fired facilities. But the legislation was immediately challenged by the state of West Virginia and industry groups in federal court and was stayed by the Supreme Court in 2016, and never went into effect. Multiple studies have shown that the Clean Power Plan probably would have had little impact on coal-mining employment even if it had gone into effect. By the time it was enacted, the large public utility companies were making decisions of their own based on hard financial facts.

Cheaper and cleaner gas had already made it a more desirable alternative to coal, and after 2008 the boom in renewable forms of energy—hydropower, solar, and wind—was dramatically changing electricity generation. On the Ohio alone, three major lock and dam systems were being rebuilt to accommodate hydropower turbines. By 2019, renewables were already generating 11 percent of American power, compared to coal's 13 percent. Natural gas was producing 34 percent. The future was already obvious. There are now 452,000 workers employed by the wind and solar power industries, compared to 211,000 working in the coal mines and gas fields. According to the U.S. Department of Energy, the job of wind turbine technicians, who earn between $43,000 and $70,000 a year, is the single fastest-growing occupation in America.

Along the river for the next few weeks, I would see another, potent symbol of the death of coal, and its impact on both American factories and global markets. At several electrical generating plants and steel mills that were either being converted to natural gas or torn down, huge metal-crushing machines were lined along the banks, rumbling and vibrating all day as they ground I-beams, copper wiring, and aluminum sheets into pellet-sized pieces to be reforged into new construction materials.

Conveyor chutes raced the ground metal down to the waterfront, where it was piled high on old coal barges to be carried downriver for export. Prices for scrap metal had climbed to over $100 per ton, abetted by research showing that producing new metal from scrap was both cheaper and environmentally preferable to making iron and other metals from fresh ore sourced from mines. The American Iron and Steel Institute estimates that about 30 percent of this American scrap is being sent to China to support its economic boom. Several times a day I would see long strings of scrap barges, twenty or more at a time, pushing their way toward the Mississippi for foreign export. The rusty infrastructure of America's industrial revolution was, literally, being shredded into fragments and sent overseas to support the new industrial revolution in Asia. The same barges that once fed coal to the American Ruhr were now carrying America's industrial heritage, piece by piece, downriver.

Later, as we droned southwest through the remote stretches of West Virginia's Washington and Marshall counties, I saw another reason why the deindustrialization of the Ohio valley was invisible to most Americans. In the early 19th century, when the first industrial settlements were built, access to the Ohio was vital both for water power and for carrying away goods on barges. The street grids of towns and most of the factory buildings were constructed to face the river, where most of the growth was clustered, and later there was only room along the banks for a railroad track and a narrow, two-lane state road. In New England, the immense textile mills and shoe factories were built in the same spaces, right on top of the rivers, but they seem to have settled into the landscape as an intended part of the views, with no mountains to hide them. But in the Ohio valley, the 1,200-foot Appalachian ridges on both sides of the river hid this new industrial sector from the outside world and, along long stretches of the river, the towns were small and spaced miles apart. Today, the abandoned mills, shuttered power plants, and derelict coal docks are hidden by the mountains from the busy interstates just a few miles away. Most of the factory abandonment can only be seen from the river itself.

The topography of the Ohio River valley had, ironically, contributed to the groundswell of rage and feelings of displacement felt by hundreds of thousands of workers laid off from the coal mines and steel plants. They felt neglected, abandoned, by both political parties and the majority of

Americans. But it was hard to generate sympathy for deindustrialization that most Americans couldn't see. The same Allegheny ridges that once concentrated industrial growth along the rivers were now hiding the blight from public view.

My trip was changing, and the roof deck of the *Patience* was proving to be an ideal platform for observing economic change. Ever since the American Revolution, generations of outsiders had poured over the ground of the old National and Wilderness Roads to dig in the mines and man the blast furnaces and rolling mills. Now they were dispersing back over the mountains into a postindustrial world of software development companies, big-box stores, and low-paying fast-food franchises that didn't want the kind of muscular labor or engineering skills that these workers had to offer. That is what I was seeing in the corroding and windowless facades of Weirton and Steubenville. The Age of Coal, which had powered the industrial revolution and turned America's inland waters into a colossal chamber of energy, had taken almost exactly two hundred years to move from boom to bust.

When Brady returned with the marina owner, they hoisted four six-gallon gas tanks out of the back of the pickup and carried them down to the marina pumps on the dock. Three of them were in perfect shape and the fourth was weathered and yellow, with a slight leak where the connector joined the fuel line, which Brady was confident he could replace at a marine supply shop somewhere downriver. As we filled the tanks with gas, I asked Brady what we owed the marina owner for the new equipment.

"Nothing," he said. "He's giving them to us, to support the trip."

"How many times did you have to crap all over the federal government to get him to do that?"

"All the way out to his farm," Brady said. "And all the way back."

As we pulled away from the docks, I yelled thanks to the marina owner and he waved his cap. We had just extended our cruising range by almost two days and, after conducting some precise fuel tests and adding a couple more tanks, could easily go almost four days without worrying about fuel. As we passed the beacon at the bottom of Brown's Island and pointed toward the big horseshoe bend at Steubenville, I was alone at the helm on the roof deck. Over the roar of the motor I could hear a clattering of saws and hammering on the stern deck below. Leaving the wheel for a few seconds, I stepped to the edge of the roof and looked down. Brady was building wooden racks to more efficiently stow our tanks. We had left unprepared, and I had been a complete novice about planning for fuel. But perhaps my amateurism was my greatest asset now. I wasn't afraid to adapt, to cobble solutions on the run, or listen to my crew, which I might not have been if I were more experienced and fixed in my ways.

We tied up that night in a small cove inside Buffalo Creek in remote Brooke County, West Virginia, opposite the twinkling lights of Brilliant, Ohio. A mild breeze chased away the insects and the water along the graveled shore was glassine. I saw a pile of aged driftwood upstream and decided to walk up there with my chain saw. For the first time I was experiencing sea legs and I had to drop the heavy saw and practice walking for a few minutes, to recover my balance on dry land. I snipped up several piles of dried cedar and oak, and then carefully selected a few waterlogged trunks to generate a lot of smoke on the coals, and carried them back for a cook fire on the banks.

Danny was contentedly basting ribs, and Brady was slicing potatoes, when I got back to the boat, and later we were all pleased with how the wet logs on hot coals perfectly seasoned the meat.

"Driftwood is the best way to cook that I've ever tasted," Danny said. "Can we do this every night?"

"Whenever we want," I said.

Through the smoke of the fire I could see mackerel cirrus clouds, an intense cobalt blue, just above the river, and pale-fire cirrus off to the west. The weather would be good tomorrow. Living on the river produced an overwhelming sense of relief about leaving the modern living and convenience of cities behind. Simplicity, and living by my wits, were working for me and I loved being a nomad on the river.

10

I WAS ENRAPTURED BY THE rhythms of river life. All night the passing of the tugs filled the air with a pleasing diesel whine, and the wakes that reached the hull a minute or two later hypnotically rocked the *Patience*, coaxing me back to sleep in my floating cradle. From my cot in the cabin I could look forward or aft through the open doors and judge from our distance and position against a nearby tree, or the sweep of the rotating beacon at the next bend, that our tie-down ropes were holding us steady against the bank. The clucking of the herons woke me an hour before dawn and then as the sun rose the river fog rolled in, enveloping the boat in amniotic mist. The sensation of escaping the world beyond the banks lasted all day.

Several times during those first few weeks on the Ohio, I was struck by the prescience of twenty-two-year-old Asbury Jaquess, who had concluded in his 1834 "The Journals of the *Davy Crockett*" that the flatboat was just a vessel "for a man to acquire a knowledge of human nature." Brady and I, for example, were as unalike as two men could be, and would have never met but for the flatboat trip. It would have been easy to dismiss his obstreperous, right-wing views as the ravings of a southern redneck. But he guided the *Patience* through the locks perfectly, and his judgment about steering around the barge traffic was flawless. I could leave him alone at the helm for whole afternoons and retreat to the shade below in the cabin, taking notes, looking ahead for likely overnight stops, or even taking a nap. From the comfort of my cabin chair, I could monitor what my helmsman was doing and judge his steerage around the commercial traffic through the open front door.

I questioned Brady's traffic decisions a few times. One afternoon, as we were approaching the last bend above New Martinsville, West Virginia, I didn't like the way that he was steering inside a twenty-five-barge string pushing upriver along the left banks. But Brady was right—the barge load was so heavy that we easily beat it to the Proctor Landing Light, clearing

Our most challenging task on the Ohio and the Mississippi was navigating safely between the long barge strings.

the traffic by at least three hundred yards. Early one morning three days later, as we were pulling out of the mouth of the Scioto River at Portsmouth, Ohio, I could see that the Ohio River below us was thickly covered in fog. I didn't want to push out into the channel in fog that thick. By this time I had learned that I couldn't trust the channel-marking buoys on the Ohio to be in the right places, and most of our route that morning would be through the Shawnee State Forest, a thinly developed stretch with few landmarks to guide us. Tugs pushing barge strings might be moving in this weather, using their precise navigation systems to remain on the sail line, but I suspected that most of them would be hugging the edge of the channel, unseen, stopped and waiting for the fog to clear, presenting a very real hazard of a collision if we pushed the *Patience* downriver.

But Brady insisted on giving it a try.

"We'll be fine," he said. "It will show you how to handle the fog."

Pushing into the mist that morning turned out to be one of the most educational runs of the trip. As we held at the confluence of the Scioto and the Ohio to listen for traffic, I heard a burst of static garble on the radio, concluding that a barge tug was nearby but probably just around the next bend and out of broadcast range. A few moments later the captain of the *Donna York*, out of Paducah, Kentucky, identified his boat and described his position as east of Portsmouth, moving downriver near a stretch of low water called the Lower Bonanza Bar. When the rusty prows of the *Donna York*'s string of fifteen coal barges emerged from the fog, I called the captain and asked if he minded if we followed his wake downriver. The captain couldn't have been more pleasant and told us that he saw us on his radar at the mouth of the Scioto, and that we were welcome to fall in behind his running lights as he passed. He would follow our position behind him on his radar, he said, and call out steering advice if he didn't think we were following him correctly.

This was new information for me. Although I should have known it, I didn't realize that a tug's radar included coverage *behind* the boat. I hesitated about calling back at first, but then decided that it would be better to learn something new than to worry about broadcasting my ignorance.

"*Donna York*, flatboat *Patience*. Your radar works aft?"

I could almost hear the laughter in the pilothouse when the captain replied.

"*Patience*, our radar paints three hundred and sixty degrees. We've had you on our scope for at least fifteen and could see that you were holding on the Scioto. Just tag along behind us and we'll be fine."

This would prove invaluable for the rest of the trip, especially along the Mississippi, when helpful tug captains volunteered to give us a "follow" from their radar, calling out advisories when we were too close to buoys or shoals. I had also learned that the frequent static bursts on the radio indicated a tug with barges either behind us or downriver around the next bend. The range of our VHF (very high frequency) marine radios was strictly limited by the river topography. VHF radios receive communications on a "line of sight" basis between the two boats, or, technically, between their antennas. On a long straightaway section of river, we could clearly communicate with another boat seven or eight miles away. But for a boat unseen around a bend, obstructions like forests, grain bins, or town buildings reduced communications to static bursts. I wouldn't be able to pick out words until the barge strings emerged around the bend and line of sight was established. But now I knew how to read the static bursts—traffic was coming around the bend, sometimes only a mile away, and I could slow down and wait for the barges to appear to see how the tug and its barge string was playing the channel. I would use the static bursts for the rest of the trip as a kind of poor-man's traffic advisory.

As we followed the *Donna York* through the fog, our only consistent visual reference was the American flag snapping above the white pilot-house of the tug. Mists curled over the conical piles of coal on the barges ahead, and the cottony vapor racing over our roof deck provided the only sensation of moving. Despite the comforting presence of the *Donna York* in front of us, I was nervous and jumpy about the fog. But I was able to make a good fix on a CSX railroad bridge two miles down and kept dogging the red buoys on the Kentucky side to establish our position.

A few miles ahead, at the town landing near Friendship, Ohio, the *Donna York* slowed and the deckhands lowered the tug's metal "john-boat"—a flat-bottom skiff used to run to the banks—to make a prearranged crew change. The fog had receded slightly and Brady and I decided to push on, for as long as we could still see the red buoys on the Kentucky side. Still, I was worried about the accuracy of the buoys. From the radio traffic I knew that a Marathon Petroleum tug, the *Kentucky*, was moving down-river a mile or two away, and probably overtaking us. As we slowly pulled around the *Donna York*, the Marathon tug captain called.

"Pleasure boat *Patience*, the Marathon *Kentucky* has you on our screen. Just stay right where you are on the Kentucky side and I'll pass your starboard in ten."

The red barges of the Marathon tug emerged out of the gloom behind us a few minutes later, casting off vortices of mist as the boat swung wide for the Ohio side of the channel to make the next bend in the river. The white superstructure of the tug faded in and out of the fog several times, but I could always pick up her bright red exhaust stacks, and her whining engines, well off to my right, as she slowly pushed her barges past us. Two or three times, just as I "made" the next red buoy ahead and to our left, I looked quickly back over my right shoulder and could see the *Kentucky*'s red stacks. Out of absolutely no clarity at all, clarity was emerging. In a cosmos of fog, my diagonal vision of red buoy to red stack was defining my maneuvering space.

The fog began to lift by nine o'clock and now we could occasionally see ovals of baby-blue sky painted behind the high Kentucky forests. We had made seven miles running at half power in the fog and by eleven o'clock we'd traveled twenty miles. Sitting together at the roof console, Brady and I debriefed our run through the fog and concluded that we were successful because our map-reading was nearly flawless, and the tug captains, impressed by the accuracy of our position reports, wanted to help. But Brady was quiet and pensive after that, and I was worried that he was annoyed by my questioning his judgment, and I apologized for that.

"No reason to be sorry," Brady said. "You can question my judgment any time—that's why we're here. I totally get how cautious you want to be around these barges. I wanted to try the fog just to test myself, and you. Now we trust each other."

Late that afternoon, we reached the Lively Lady Marina and Campground in Aberdeen, Ohio, and we fell asleep that night with the stern pointed toward the breathtaking views of the Ohio and the Route 52 bridge. We could see across to the steeples of Maysville, Kentucky. Static radio blast to static radio blast, in good following breezes, we were making great progress down Jacob Yoder's river.

Danny's audition at the helm of the *Patience* was one of the big letdowns of the trip. For more than a year he had relentlessly pestered me about the journey, calling me several times a month with suggestions for navigation software, radios, and cooking equipment. He considered the trip to New Orleans his project, too. I was sure that he would be keen to run the boat, and might even feel slighted if I didn't ask him to join me at the roof console. One afternoon early in the trip, I called him up, motioned for him to take the seat in front of the wheel, and explained that I would navigate while he piloted. When he bounded up the stairs to the roof, Danny was carrying his usual personal kit—an iPad, his cell phone, his camera and lenses, and a small duffel stuffed with wire and tools for electrical repairs. I showed him how to follow the sail line on the navigation iPad and cross-check it with what he could see outside, but mostly to concentrate on a consistent course around the tugs and their barge strings.

It was a monumental miscasting. Danny had positioned his iPad beside him on the console and I could see that he was also watching a video on how to change oil in our Mercury engine, occasionally turning his head down from the river and his steering to concentrate on the YouTube video. He was steering with one hand while taking pictures of a large barge fleet moored against the forests on the Ohio bank with his other hand. He also managed to duck his head underneath the console, where several electrical wires met, using his current tester to see if we could install an extra port to power the iPad and charge other devices. He was ignoring steering the *Patience*. Meanwhile, a tug was running upriver with a full string of barges, a half mile away, and Danny was letting us wander across the channel into the tug's course line.

I was infuriated, bursting with silent rage at Danny every time I had to reach over and pull the wheel left to maintain our course. Danny symbolized for me the perpetual distractedness of an entire society. We are spending our lives in a state of extended mental incontinence, addicted to these worthless little boxes perched in front of our faces, constantly jumping between cell phone, laptop, and tablet. Riding the *Patience* downriver showed me the high price we are paying for our mass digital distraction. On our roof deck, we were living the most romantic existence possible, a chapter from Mark Twain's *Adventures of Huckleberry Finn*, or Herman Melville's *The Confidence-Man*, passing wetlands that thronged with wading birds and raptors, and curved sandbars so beautiful and bright that they almost stopped my heart. But Danny couldn't embrace the river and the here. He couldn't focus on steering. He was always off there—on Facebook, or Twitter, or a YouTube instructional video about electrical hookups.

The run should have been easy for Danny. Downriver, a tug pushing eighteen barges was entering the straightaway just above Riley Run Bar, steering for the channel buoys underneath a set of twin bridges, the Bellaire Interstate Bridge and the CSX railroad bridge. All we had to do was hug the red markers on our left and the tug would have plenty of room to pass us under the spans. I was happy about this because Danny would have gained confidence by threading through the two bridges and the barge string at once. But his concentration couldn't hold for more than five seconds and we kept wandering toward mid-channel, an obvious hazard to the tug.

My right hand was now permanently affixed to the wheel, steering us straight ahead toward the red buoys below the railroad bridge. Obviously, my leading by not leading, what the French call *mener par calme*, leading by calm, wasn't working with Danny. But an instinct that I couldn't understand or really trust told me to defer, to wait, to suppress, until the tension built and suggested a solution.

As we approached the Bellaire Bridge I held tight to the buoys with my free hand. The metallic thunder underneath the span startled Danny and he looked up and saw that the barge string was closer now, only two hundred yards off our starboard bow. He was supposed to be steering a consistent course on the edge of the channel, to let the tug captain know that we would maintain safe separation, but now he was letting go of the wheel entirely and reaching down toward the camera bag at his feet.

We were now on a collision course with the barges. But instead of steering to port to give way to the tug, Danny pointed his camera downriver and clicked through several frames of the oncoming barges.

"Damn," he said. "That's a good picture."

"Danny, please, heading, heading here," I said as we drifted toward the center of the channel in front of the barge string. "Left, Danny, left. Hug the left and give way for that tug."

Danny looked up from his camera, half-heartedly yanking the wheel again, but hardly steering on a steady course parallel to the buoys. His eyes flashed with anger and distress. He was livid with me. Impetuously, he wanted to shoot every picture he saw out there, but I needed him in the here, steering the boat. I pitied him more than I was angry with him— Danny literally could not edit out the distractions long enough to avoid a disastrous collision with the oncoming barges. Worse, he generated his own distractions, cluttering his life with a surfeit of digital gear.

I took the wheel with both hands and steered us back to the buoys.

I loved Danny too much to discipline him. We were back on the correct course line for the buoys now, which was good, I thought. *Calm, Rinker*, I said to myself, while still holding the wheel. Don't yell at your crew. *Maintenez le calme.*

As we cleared the first bridge, Danny looked up again at the tug, then back to his camera and up to the tug again, shaking his head in confusion and visibly nervous. He was having an ADD seizure—desperate to take another picture while he knew he should be steering the boat.

Danny was spring-loaded with tension, bursting with distraction. But the pressure, the internal crisis, was building toward solution. When he looked sideways at me and called out, his voice cracked with anger. But he was also uttering a high-pitched plea for help.

"You know I *hate* this!" he said. "*Hate* it."

"Too much concentration?"

"Too much pressure," Danny said. "You're constantly watching how I steer the boat, judging me. But I can't be you, Rinker. Can't we just put the boat on autopilot?"

Danny was steering the boat the way he drove a car, inattentively, and preoccupied with something else. He cooks distracted, grilling meat at a distant fire, racing back to parboil vegetables or bake bread, refilling martinis, all at once. He cleans chimneys while simultaneously texting on his cell phone. That was fine, even a lovable mad-hatter routine, but it was no way to steer a boat along one of the busiest commercial waterways in the world. Focusing on a single goal, accomplishing just one thing at a time? It doesn't exist in Danny's behavioral repertoire.

But anger can often express opposing feelings and my emotions immediately doubled back. I was swelled with sympathy and even more love for him. A century of therapy, a pharmacy full of drugs, was never going to cure Danny's ADD. This moment taught me to give up on that. Instead, plumb his weakness, I thought, find his hidden strengths.

"Danny, isn't there something down below you want to fix?"

"Definitely," he said, standing up and gathering his iPad and camera. "I want to rig the gangplank with pulleys and rope and fix the connection to the charger on the backup battery."

Danny's first time steering the boat was his last. I should have known beforehand that he wouldn't be happy at the helm, but I had to show that to myself first. For the next hour, I was furious at Danny and his inability to gather enough concentration to steer the boat. He could never be my backup at the helm. But as I contentedly steered the boat alone in the falling afternoon light, my anger ripened to reflective calm. I was really more angry with myself than with Danny. I had to curb my instinct to control. I couldn't change someone into being me.

That night, when we discussed what happened earlier in the day up on the helm, Danny offered an explanation.

"I consider it my responsibility to help you get down the river. I want to make sure that every preparation, every system on the boat, is working. At work, I manage systems. I don't run them day to day. I never wanted to steer the boat."

The river was my teacher. Crises beget solutions. People are models of complexity, not perfection, or even expectations. Bend to bend, moment to anxious moment, I was slowly learning how to master a boat. Awareness arrived in the form of mistakes. I was aboard the *Davy Crockett* with Asbury Jaquess, learning that a river journey is really just an exploration of character.

Maintenez le calme was not a management style that worked with Scott Mandrell. His incessant tales about himself, tiresome costume changes, and overreactions about everything from the weather to docking the boat were obviously incurable. Fortunately, I didn't have to wait to see how long it would take me to order Scott off the boat. People like him eventually eliminate themselves.

One afternoon as we passed through the remote national forest country near the confluence with the Kanawha River, my curiosity was aroused by an abandoned lock marked on my charts, just above Gallipolis, Ohio. During the flatboat era, the Kanawha had played a mighty role in the industrial revolution, carrying thousands of barges of a soft West Virginia bituminous shale, called "cannel coal," bound for large refineries along the Ohio at Pittsburgh and Cincinnati, where it was converted into kerosene. Barges on the Kanawha also carried most of the salt destined for the sprawling meatpacking complex in Cincinnati. The old lock was one of the first encountered by the coal and salt barges pressing south for Huntington and Cincinnati and was in use until the late 1930s, when it was replaced by the massive Robert C. Byrd Locks and Dam complex eight miles downriver, during the Depression-era rebuilding of the river navigation system.

The lock at Gallipolis was now a popular fishing spot, connected by a trail through the woods to the highway running north and south along the river. I've always been fascinated by the recycling of deserted industrial sites. Because they are so often located along scenic rivers, repurposed rail tracks, blast furnaces, and old factory locations create beautiful open spaces, demonstrating how some of the best real estate in America became the workplace of the industrial revolution. Once they were abandoned as manufacturing sites and allowed to bloom again, the same ground evinces the stunning recuperative powers of nature. I decided to pull in to see this connection to an earlier era.

The abandoned Gallipolis locks were indeed delightful, reminding me of a sunken garden fashioned out of an old barn foundation. The space between the two old lock walls was filled with shimmering still water and, beyond a colony of stately lily pads at the far end, a brook disappeared downhill into the woods. I could see the worn path leading west up to the highway. A lush growth of high wetland grass swayed in the breeze beyond the locks.

As we tied the *Patience* up to some rusty but stout iron bollards along the west wall, I was enchanted by the peaceful symmetry of the Gallipolis locks and decided that it would be an ideal place to spend the night.

Everyone fell into their usual evening routines. Jay, who for some reason had exchanged his pirate's shirt for a kilt, carried some sleeping gear up to the roof deck and fussed with our tie-down ropes. Danny bounced up the dusty path toward the highway on the electric bike to see if he could find a supermarket to buy food. I took a glass of wine up to the roof deck and, enjoying the low sun on my face, luxuriated in the views out to the river. Secured in the derelict lock, the *Patience* seemed enveloped by an aura of beauty and calm.

Then, from behind the boat, I heard the high-pitched screaming of Scott, and what sounded like the pounding of a hammer against rock. When I looked over to see what was going on, it was clear that Scott had dragooned Jay into a completely worthless project, pounding one of our metal anchors into a deposit of rocks just beyond the lock wall. It was insane. The *Patience* was safely tied for the night and was going nowhere, and the idea of securing a metal anchor to a rock with a large sledge made no sense—it couldn't even be done. I didn't like the way Scott was berating Jay and I didn't like the disturbance of what had been a sublime evening.

My temper, already spring-loaded over Scott, snapped as sharply as a rat trap. I completely lost it as I bounded down the stairs, across the lock wall, and then stalked through the tall grass toward Scott and Jay. I was particularly incensed because I had asked Scott, politely, and almost every day, to stop losing his temper and yelling at the crew. I was mad at myself for tolerating him for so long. My bottled-up rage toward Scott was rising volcanically from my waist up and my voice cracked as I yelled out.

"Scott, what the hell are you doing? The boat is fine, absolutely fine, all right? You can't pound an anchor into a rock."

Scott began to explain that, one night "up on the Missouri," a big wind came up and tore his boat from its dock cleats. He felt that we needed the extra anchor lines.

"Fuck the Missouri, Scott. That's a thousand miles away from here."

"I'm just trying to suitably secure this boat."

"Get the hell out of here," I yelled. "I've talked to you about yelling at the crew. Jay, you're in charge of tying up this boat. Don't listen to Scott."

It was a glorious shitstorm at the Gallipolis locks, full of irony and my own idiotic folly. I was screaming at Scott because Scott was screaming at Jay. But that's what happens when people are angry and temper management circuits become overloaded and fail. Anger is highly contagious and quickly infects an entire circle of people in a kind of raging emotional pandemic.

I grabbed the anchor and line that Scott had hauled out there, coiling the rope elbow-to-palm as I walked back toward the boat, while Jay followed with the heavy sledge. Red-faced and for once saying nothing, Scott moped off for the cabin to retrieve one of those dainty little leather man purses that he loved to hang from his belt, and then walked up the dusty path toward the highway, disappearing into the trees.

We didn't see Scott for the next day and a half. Late on the second morning after he had stalked off, he parked his rental car up by the highway and walked down to the boat, offering the feeble excuse that he needed to return home for personal business. I offered my hand as a token of thanks for what little he'd done for the trip, but Scott refused to shake it, brushing by to retrieve his canoe and his wardrobe duffels. Then he glumly hauled his canoe and heavy duffels up to the highway.

After Scott left, feeling refreshed and unburdened, I made the decision to launch at noon, to see if we could make another twenty miles by nightfall. As we pulled into the river and passed Gallipolis Island, the stone pier and stately brick facades of the old French city glowed under the sun, and I steered southeast for the big bend at Walker Light, and then due south through the beautifully serene Wayne National Forest. My problem child was off the boat and now I could enjoy the river.

The dreamworld romance of negotiating the remote, lazy bends of the Ohio ended abruptly as we approached civilization again at the first major way-point of the trip, Cincinnati, Ohio. It was a Friday evening and the boat'n and booz'n weekend had begun, with all of the folly and excess of America out on the river for the night. Grandparents driving their long, gaudy houseboats and cruisers—the *Spoiled Rotten*, the *Golden Handshake*—were towing the grandkids around in inflated rafts and water tubes, and the bumper-car mayhem of Jet Skis and cigarette boats jammed the waterway east of the city. A brisk following wind made it difficult to avoid all of these yahoos and the colliding rollers kicked up by the traffic rocked us so violently that the timber beams in the cabin groaned. Brady struggled to muscle the boat into the Manhattan Harbour Marina on the Ohio side and then, with a lot of bellowing and cursing between him and Jay, we finally had the *Patience* tied securely in the muddy low water of the western section of slips.

The marina was owned by a developer from Cincinnati who had grand plans to add luxury condominiums, stores, and a new restaurant to his waterfront space, but it was clear that the post-recession decline in private boating had taken its toll. The floating walkways were missing deck boards, and the pilings leaned at crazy angles that made the whole slip complex unstable. As I walked up to the shower stalls behind the marina restaurant, I realized how exhausted and unsteady I was—the twelve-hour days out on the roof deck, the myriad details of feeding the crew and planning for gas stops, or dealing with eccentric characters like Jay, were wearying. After my shower I decided to stop at the marina restaurant for a drink, and then lingered longer to order dinner. The marina owner stopped at my table to say hello and looked longingly out through the large picture windows to the *Patience*, tied down about forty yards away.

"How far are you planning on taking that thing?" he said.

"New Orleans," I said. "We're going to the bottom of the Mississippi."

"That sure takes a big set of cojones," he said. "You know how danger-ous it is out there, don't you?"

"So far, it really hasn't been that bad," I said. "You just have to be careful steering around the barges."

A couple of boaters from the marina joined us at the table and ex-plained why local boaters rarely ventured more than seven or eight miles from Cincinnati. The currents and navigation hazards were relatively mild along the Ohio, they said, but taking on the Mississippi was madness. They were firm adherents of the "You're going to die" school.

Along the Mississippi, they said, swift currents, whirlpools, and the fast water near bridge pylons were notorious for swamping small craft, and everyone knew stories about even professionally run barge tugs sinking, along with their crews, during high-water conditions on the river. I would get my first taste of this in a few days, they predicted, once I got downriver below Evansville, Indiana. Heavy rains that year in northern Indiana had created high-water conditions on both the Ohio and its major tributary, the Wabash, and the confluence of the two rivers would be a gauntlet of white water, whirlpools, and unmanageable fast currents. I shouldn't be afraid to swallow my pride and turn back before I reached the Wabash.

"The currents running out of the Wabash are going to push you right into the sandbars along Wabash Island," one of the boat owners said. "You'll have to be rescued by the Coast Guard."

The other boater had even more dire predictions about the Missis-sippi. The furious, swirling boils of water along the river below Cairo, Illinois, could be larger than a one-acre pond, and even the bigger tugs avoided them. We would encounter a particularly treacherous network of submerged bars and whirlpools opposite Wickliffe, Kentucky, just after we turned south onto the Mississippi. The colliding river currents at the confluence of the Ohio and the Mississippi, he said, made the broad stretch along the Wickliffe revetment a "widow-maker."

"I hope you've prepared your family for the state of the body they are going to be getting," he said. "The first boil in the Mississippi is going to suck you and the boat to the bottom, and then scrape you along the mud for a half mile. I've heard about this. Once you float back to the surface, you won't even have your underwear on."

I walked back to the *Patience* on the swaying walkway dejected and hot, but skeptical about these grave claims. It was a sweltering night and I stripped all of my clothes off and fell onto my cot with just a light sheet covering me. I woke up in the middle of the night watching myself from afar, somersaulting in muddy water with the profile of the capsized *Patience*, sinking upside down, spewing cavitation bubbles nearby. In that foggy threshold between nightmare and waking, I reached down to my waist and realized that my boxer shorts had disappeared. I was dead.

The next day, after we passed the big bend at Petersburg, Kentucky, the pleasure boat traffic disappeared, confirming my observation that the perceived safety zone for recreational craft rarely exceeded five or six miles from large towns. The river was deserted and quiet. The only thing I could see ahead of us was a listless, drifting sailboat near the middle of the channel and the gleaming white facade of the Rising Star Casino on the Indiana bank.

When we got abeam of the casino, the sailboat radioed a panicked "Mayday, Mayday" call. His fuel line was broken and spewing gas into the cockpit and he needed help. The boat pilot was the classic weekend buffoon let loose upon the waters of America. He had described his position as "at Aurora," which was actually ten miles behind him, and in a different county. For the next twenty minutes the marine radio band was a *comédie francaise* of police dispatchers from three neighboring counties— Dearborn and Ohio counties in Indiana, and Boone County across the river in Kentucky—trying to decide who should launch to rescue the distressed sailboat. Through my binoculars, I could see the Ohio County police boat over at the casino ramp on the Indiana side, and the Boone County boat over at the landing at the Rabbit Hash General Store in Kentucky, but both launches seemed reluctant to depart until the police dispatchers completed their radio farce.

I briefly considered turning around and towing the stricken sailboat to the casino dock with the *Patience*, but decided against it when I heard a series of static bursts on the radio. With a sailboat adrift in the middle of the channel, a big commercial barge tow was approaching.

Looking behind me, I could see a clear stretch of water upriver for three miles, with no commercial traffic. I reasoned that a string of barges downriver was moving toward us, and the tug pilot was probably blocked from broadcasting by the thick forest at the large bend below Buckeye Landing Light. The pilot was not going to be able to see around the bend for another ten or fifteen minutes. I steered the *Patience* toward the Kentucky side of the channel and idled the motor while I turned broadside to command views both up and down the river. Somebody was going to have to advise the tug captain about the position of the drifting sailboat.

A few minutes after I saw the first barges emerging around the bend, I could finally decipher a clear broadcast from the tugboat bridge, which was still out of sight around the bend. It was an Ingram tug, pushing a full load of twenty-five barges. The captain seemed concerned about the garbled reports he was hearing about the sailboat in the channel. He would be anxious about it until his tug at the end of the string got around the bend and he could see the channel ahead.

For the next ten minutes, while the tug pushed unseen around the bend, I could feel an intense and even welcome bonding with that captain. The river and the barges and the scene unfolding merged as a single, swirling emotion rising through my chest and then becoming a tingling on my neck and cheeks. My palms sweated while I held the wheel, occasionally jockeying the throttle to hold my position.

I was anxious, but confident. I knew what the captain sensed. He was probably worried that he was talking to an amateur boater who didn't know what he was doing. I would have to reassure him with accurate detail. I wanted him to feel that his eyes around the bend could be trusted.

Meanwhile, I had watched enough tugs maneuver the bends to know that the captain would need to know, fairly soon, which side of the river to play, to position his barges for the next bend upriver, at Middle Creek Light. I was already studying my charts for the best deep water on either side of the channel.

"Captain, the flatboat *Patience* is holding just downriver from Rabbit Hash, opposite the casino. We will keep the sailboat in sight."

"Roger, *Patience*. I need to know where he's drifting. Which direction is he headed?"

"Stand by. I can give you a good read on that in a few minutes."

"The boat will be drifting in the direction the bow is pointed."

That made sense. The current pushed the bow in the direction of drift. Maybe I should have known that already, but now I did. I waited a few minutes, holding the *Patience* broadside to the river and judging the actual drift of the boat against my position.

"Ingram boat, the sailboat is drifting toward the Kentucky side. By the time you get here it will be on the Kentucky side of the channel."

As the high, glinting windshield of the Ingram boat finally emerged around the bend, I guessed—I felt, actually, that I *knew*—what was going on in the wheelhouse of the tug. The captain was peering ahead with his binoculars and could probably just make out the drifting sailboat. He trusted that I was correct about the sailboat drifting southeast toward Kentucky. By now he would have the *Patience* on his radar and might be worried about my movements. I powered gently in reverse to distance myself from the commercial channel, positioning myself in reference to an unmarked inlet on the Kentucky bank. I would hold it exactly on my stern.

"Captain, the flatboat *Patience* will hold here until you pass. The sailboat is a half mile northeast of my position."

"Roger, *Patience*, I have you, but not the drifting boat. Can you hold?"

"Flatboat *Patience* will hold."

"Thank you, sir."

As he broadcast that, the Ingram captain maneuvered his barges from his hard starboard turn out of the bend and turned to port, cross-channel, to favor the Indiana side. That would keep him well away from the sailboat and he would only have to make an oblique turn left to remain on the sail line as he passed the casino and entered the next bend at Middle Creek.

I heard the wail of a twin-engine boat behind and to my right and looked over. It was the Boone County launch heading toward the sailboat— apparently, the Kentucky boys had won the law enforcement palaver over who would perform the rescue. Long before the Ingram tug and its barges passed, the police launch had secured a line to the sailboat and was pulling it out of harm's way toward Rabbit Hash.

The channel was now clear. The Ingram tug was still a mile away. I could turn downriver now and safely pass the tug traffic.

"Ingram boat," I radioed, "the sailboat is being towed to Kentucky side. The *Patience* will pass on your starboard with good separation."

"*Patience*, you can do whatever you want on this river. I sure do appreciate your help, Captain."

The Ingram captain hadn't exactly said it that way, of course. He had said, "Surdo preciate ur hep, Capt'n." I could tell from the tone of his voice that he was happy about encountering the *Patience*, and that would be the word about our boat passed to the other captains on the river.

As the big tug went by, the captain opened his wheelhouse door and stood outside on the grated metal deck, waved his ball cap, and saluted me. I ducked out from under our tarp bimini, waved my hat, and signaled "A-OK" with my hand.

The Ingram boat disappeared behind the stern as we entered the Buckeye Landing bend. To port, we were passing through the fabled "lick country" of Kentucky, where broad inlets marked the creeks drifting down to the river from the interior salt licks that had once drawn dense herds of buffalo and deer, then the Shawnee and the Chickasaw, and finally the invading white pioneers. The licks of Kentucky were where the pioneers lived and built their mills and churches, and now, like the fading coal hollows of West Virginia, they are sparsely populated and impoverished. Alone on the roof deck, I navigated down to the Markland Locks and Dam by fixing our position at Lick Creek, Big Bone Creek, Gunpowder Creek, and Paint Lick Creek. Mild following winds pushed the *Patience* through glassine waters and I finally had a chance to relax and harvest the joys of the trip. I had my old river, and its remote stretches of forests and comely oxbows, back beside me, funneling my journey through the pioneer lands that bloomed a country.

The tug captain had hailed me as "sir" and "Captain"—in the laconic parlance of the rivermen, that was practically effusive. There was a beautiful sunset that night where we parked bow-in, tying to a massive oak, at Big Sugar Creek. I wasn't worried anymore about dying on this river, or any other river.

11

DANNY'S FREQUENT DEPARTURES FROM THE *Patience*, to return to his job in Connecticut for two weeks, became a definition of friendship for me. I could hear myself think now. I could run the *Patience* downriver from my beloved rooftop helm without being sprayed by the confetti of electrical wire and salty food crumbs while Danny sat beside me, mending a hand-held radio while snacking on Sunshine Cheez-Its. I missed my loyal cabin boy, but his absence did deliver a welcome bonus for me.

In the morning, we were always anxious to get started early, a half hour after dawn, putting some miles downriver behind us to get a good lead on the day. Brady and Jay were more than capable of running the boat up top without me, and as soon as we cast off, reached the channel, and identified the first buoy or landmark, I left them at the helm and descended to the galley below. I loved making coffee and breakfast for the crew on the open bow. The slapdash arrangement of shelves and pots and pans hanging on the poplar walls was homey and fun, and the panoramic view down the Ohio allowed me to monitor our progress along the banks.

I wasn't going to feed my crew with the kind of faux-European breakfast—*fromage de chèvre* omelets with basil and Asiago toast—that Danny made. My Kaintuck brethren on the roof deck deserved better than that, real food, trucker chow, good old American breakfast fare that you could identify without feeling guilty about flunking high school French. Brady had already improved my cooking skills by teaching me how to make biscuits and gravy, and to this I added gently simmered scrambled eggs, crisp bacon, and canned Kelly potatoes fried with bell peppers and onion.

After shining their silverware with the tail of my shirt, I loaded the plates high for Brady and Jay and placed them on a plastic tray. Happy with myself, I headed back through the cabin to the stairs in the stern that climbed to the roof deck. I carried the tray over my shoulder with my right palm bent backward and held high, like the best *ristorante* waiter in Rome.

As I reached the steps with my tray, a large Ingram tug with a raised pilothouse, pushing a mixed string of more than twenty coal, gravel, and grain barges upriver, was passing about eighty yards off on our starboard side. Brady was playing the massive barge load expertly, maintaining a consistent heading on the Indiana side of the channel. The view downriver was stunning and my heart raced with exhilaration. While the *Patience* flag snapped in the breeze above me, the mixed aroma of bacon, eggs, biscuits, and gravy filled my nostrils, and the muscular beauty of the big tug lumbering by the King Landing Light, with its tsunami wake of curling white water and foam, merged as one sensate moment that felt like ecstasy.

I felt light, almost levitating over the river, and I free-associated right then to Harlan Hubbard. Harlan Hubbard! In his shantyboat, he was almost at this same spot along the Ohio, Gilmore Creek on the Kentucky side, when he fashioned a net out of a burlap bag and pulled up a mass of silvery shad, which he gutted and cleaned and then cooked on wood coals until the fish were "brown and crisp," a delightful meal pulled from the river for him and his wife. Hubbard and his shantyboat. I was living that life now.

It didn't occur to me that the tall rollers radiating in a V from the big Ingram tug would threaten the Roman waiter now climbing the stairs of the *Patience*. I felt immune to the big wakes from the tugs because I was usually sitting at the helm with my hands braced on the steering wheel as the heavy *Patience* seesawed over the waves. Rocking in the tug wakes was uncomfortable, but not especially hazardous.

When the first roller from the Ingram boat hit, I was thrown up and then violently down. I winced from the pain of my knees pounding the poplar steps. But I was desperate to save the crew's breakfast and I quickly genuflected on the stairs, balancing the tray level to save the grub, and then I stretched back up when the boat violently rocked up. On the second or third roll I managed to lower the tray and grasp it with both hands, continuing to maintain a level axis of food against the sharp roll of the boat. I was just a human gimbal now, determined to keep the tray level while inching up the steps. No waiter in Rome could balance a trayful of breakfast as skillfully as this. Then, above the whine of our motor and the tug's, and the sprays of water climbing above my head, I pitched right and I could hear and feel the sharp *crack*.

The *crack* was the sound of my right side banging hard, once, and then twice, against the sharp edge of the railing on the poplar staircase. I knew the sensation well and could tell immediately that I had broken my ribs. It's a perverse admission to make about myself, but this was the fifth time I had fractured my ribs and I have progressively enjoyed each break more than the last. Perhaps athletes experience the same mixed pain and euphoria after repeat injuries. I like what being a champion rib-breaker says about my life. I first broke my ribs when I was ten, falling off a horse. I was playing hooky from school that day and of course couldn't tell my parents what happened, and I was proud about the way I stoically disguised my pain for two months. I broke my ribs twice more in my twenties and thirties, logging in the forest. I had broken them the last time in my early fifties, when I slid off an icy ridge while snowshoeing the Taconics in western Massachusetts. So, broken ribs again, this time aboard the *Patience*. Good. In the bizarre and foolish ways that we celebrate ourselves, broken ribs have defined me.

I wasn't worried for the moment because I had saved the crew's breakfast, and broken ribs don't hurt at first. When ribs are fractured, the cartilage banding the front of the rib cage stretches like a bungee, allowing the broken pieces to comfortably dangle out on the perimeter of the chest cavity for a day or two. But then the bones fight to fuse again at the break, pulling on the cartilage, and the cartilage fights back to resume its old shape. The orthopedic tug-of-war is akin to having a pulled muscle, which simultaneously pinches all the local nerves. Every small expansion of the chest—coughs, sneezes, laughs, lifting light objects—radiates pain on that side of the chest. The body compensates by transferring a lot of the stretching to the other side of the back and chest, especially while sleeping, so a rib fracture on the right often reports as sharp pain on the left. There is no cure, except for a lot of painkillers or whiskey, and broken ribs cannot be set with a cast. After six or eight weeks you begin waking up realizing that the first deep breath of the morning is hurting less every day. After as many episodes as mine, you begin to experience rib fracturing as a lifestyle, not an injury.

I wasn't even thinking about that now as I struggled to reach the roof deck on my knees, jubilant about saving the breakfast for my crew. I waited at the edge of the deck, crouching to more easily balance the tray, and then inched over to the helm console as the tug wake dissipated. Jay and Brady were grateful for the bacon and eggs.

"Mother of Jesus," Jay said, rubbing his hands together, "I'm happy as a hound on a biscuit."

"Ma-a-a-velous, Captain," Brady said. "Didn't know you were such a galley queen."

I went below and fixed myself a plate and a cup of coffee, carried a chair from the cabin out to the bow, and sat contentedly eating with my breakfast plate on my lap, staring downriver. Low, fleecy cumulus were already forming to the west and mist was climbing off the hollows in the forests above the Kentucky and Indiana banks. Squaw Creek, Knob Creek, and the postcard-perfect village of Bethlehem, Indiana, went by. I knew what my next month would be like. I wouldn't be able to carry anything, pull an anchor line, or exert myself with a load of firewood without constantly adjusting my stance against the pain. I would be awake a lot at night, cursing my poor judgment. Every rock of the boat would unleash more ripples of pain.

But after a month the pain would be manageable and, against the constant torture on my sides and chest, I instinctively would be fine-tuning my gait and my distribution of weight when lifting anything. For reasons that I can't quite explain to myself, I enjoy this regimen. Rib breaks and their pain are a reminder of my foolhardiness, perhaps, or my addiction to adventure, or my need for comeuppance for having led such a fortunate, happy life. I was on the *Patience* bound for New Orleans and my broken ribs once more made life challenging and good.

Moving down the broad, curving stretches of the Ohio below Cincinnati, I was impressed by the interior beauty of riverine America, and touched by the lives of people I met in the river towns. When I was alone on the roof deck of the *Patience*, navigating and steering around the barge traffic, the monotonous engine noise and the relentless sunlight glinting off the water often made me feel drowsy, drugged with the passing beauty. Along the banks I could see old pioneer stone walls and the black shadows of small girder bridges on the back roads.

Days like this stoked an old fantasy of mine, my identification with the glorious vagabondage of my favorite American, the poet Walt Whitman. A year or two earlier, I had been excited to read, in David Reynolds's *Walt Whitman's America*, about a fabled trip down the Ohio and the Mississippi that the poet took in 1848. That year, Whitman accepted an offer to leave New York to help open a newspaper in New Orleans, the *New Orleans Daily Crescent*. Traveling with his brother Jeff, Whitman followed the traditional route west by stagecoach over the Alleghenies to Wheeling, West Virginia, where he and Jeff boarded the steamboat *St. Cloud* on the Ohio, reaching the confluence of the Mississippi on a cold February morning that year. Except for the dramatic bluffs at Memphis and Natchez, Whitman found the shores of the great river "monotonous and dull," but, once reaching New Orleans, he reveled in the opportunity to flex his immense talent as a prose stylist and social observer. He wandered the French Quarter and the "bustling markets" of the levees, soaked up the lore of the river while befriending stevedores and boat captains, and was dazzled by the urban parade of "Indian and negro hucksters," oyster vendors, prostitutes and con men, and a "Creole mulatto woman" selling delicious coffee from a large copper pot. He was delighted by the drinks topped with strawberries in the "splendid and roomy and leisurely bar rooms."

Whitman's essays on New Orleans were mostly published in the *Crescent*, and not widely circulated at the time, but his vivid take on the city's glamorous cultural mix captures the appeal of the port city to a generation of restless northerners and Midwesterners. His 1848 trip also birthed several poems that were later included in his signature collection, *Leaves of Grass*. For Whitman, like so many of his contemporary Americans, the trip over the Alleghenies and down the inland rivers was transformative. He fell in love with the South ("O magnet-South! O glistening perfumed South!"), a passion he could never fully surrender even as an ardent Unionist during the Civil War. Whitman enjoyed a brief, intense love affair in New Orleans, though no one seems to know whether it was with a man or a woman, and indulged his lifelong passion for walking by wandering out to the distant bayous at the edge of the city. Literary scholars have concluded that his New Orleans period broadened Whitman's interests beyond his native New York and contributed to a marked enrichment of his prose work. The Creole melting pot at the bottom of the Mississippi convinced him that America's future lay in diversity, not provincialism, and that the westward push unleashed by the Louisiana Purchase would join clashing but complementary regional societies into a single, larger nation.

I get carried away with Whitman sometimes, overreaching myself with a sort of combined time-traveling and impersonation, imagining that I am him. On that stretch of the Ohio below Louisville, I was afloat with Whitman's soul. *The boatman singing what belongs to him in his boat, the deckhand singing on the steamboat deck,* and the *slow, sluggish rivers where they flow, distant, over flats of silvery sands or through swamps,* felt as dear to me as they did to him. The people I was meeting along the banks were Whitmanesque, too.

At Brandenburg, Kentucky, a lovely town with porched houses and comely brick commercial facades that slope downhill to the river, we tied up at the public wharf for two nights. After the Civil War, because of its favorable location below Cincinnati and Louisville, Brandenburg had grown with the river trade and become a combined regional transportation hub. Tug-and-barge crews, after spending a month on their boats, frequently disembarked there and were replaced by new crews, making Brandenburg known as "the crew change capitol of the Ohio." A rail spur built down to the river from the main tracks of the "Old Reliable," the Louisville and Nashville Railroad line, had turned the town into a busy, gritty transshipment point for grain and lumber cargo. But from the river the town also looked romantic and prosperous, evocative of a bygone, gracious river life. The tall white porticos of a couple of mansions up on the bluffs shined brightly under the sun as we pulled into the wharf, and I used the American flag on the lawn of one of them to read the winds that were pushing the *Patience* toward the bank. Over the next two days I hiked the steep sidewalks several times for exercise, enjoying how almost every vista in town swept downhill to the gentle bend in the Ohio, so that the river filled my eyes everywhere I turned.

The townspeople of Brandenburg fell in love with the *Patience* and visited in groups in the evening, each family or cluster of retirees bringing us gifts of six-packs of beer, chilled bottled water, and boxed dinners from an excellent local restaurant that occupied the ground floor of a restored brick building above the waterfront, Jailhouse Pizza. My favorite local was a soft-spoken old river rat with a handlebar mustache, Ron Richardson, who wandered down to the wharf at the foot of Main Street every morning to have coffee and chat aboard the *Patience*. Richardson was in his early seventies and epitomized the life of river town people who have spent several generations on the Ohio.

"River rat" Ron Richardson of Brandenburg, Kentucky, came down to the boat every morning to regale me with his stories about growing up on the Ohio and dispense advice on how to negotiate the next stretch of bends.

Richardson was worried about us navigating the next stretch of river, which curved sharply northwest and then southeast, and then due south, through about fifty miles of remote state and national forests. Gravel mining in the area below Brandenburg had eroded the banks in several spots, making our maps inaccurate, he said, and we couldn't trust the navigation buoys, either, because many of them had been dragged by large tree snags in the spring rains and no longer marked a safe channel. We sat on the galley deck of the *Patience* poring over my Army Corps charts, and I made notations on the maps along the bends up past Leavenworth and Wolf

Creek, where Richardson predicted that rogue buoys and tree snags would make conditions hazardous.

Richardson suggested that I follow a simple navigation practice, especially in places where the water was high and fast and the edges of the channel ahead were strewn with sandbars and tree snags. When I saw a tug and string of barges approaching from a distance ahead, I should immediately slow down, carefully observe the way the tug captain "played" the bends, and sketch with a pencil on my charts exactly where the lead barge passed the banks and the buoys. When the tug passed, he advised that I immediately turn into the channel and follow its wake until it dissipated, and then consult my penciled route from there. "That barge string that just passed you didn't run aground, right?" Richardson said. "Just follow that captain's route downriver." I found this guidance quite useful, especially at congested spots with a lot of local tug traffic like Paducah, Cairo, and Vicksburg. Within a month, "channel-sketching" the water ahead became so habitual that I didn't need it anymore. At Brandenburg, Richardson was really teaching me to memorize the tug paths as the best way through.

I learned a lot more than navigation from Richardson. He was almost a moral philosopher about river life, describing how the cycles of families, generation to generation, were determined by the cycles of the Ohio. He reminded me of another one of my favorite passages from Harlan Hubbard's *Shantyboat*. In Hubbard's estimation, meeting people who had spent their lives on the banks was perhaps the most pleasurable and edifying reward of drifting down the river.

"I cultivated the acquaintance of old-time river people whenever possible, and listened to their yarns almost with reverence," Hubbard wrote. "The simplicity and naturalness of their way of living fascinated me, and gave a definite shape to the vague longing which the flowing river had inspired."

On the second morning when he came down to the *Patience*, Richardson settled into a comfortable chair in the cabin and told me about his life.

Richardson had grown up in Brandenburg during the 1950s and early 1960s. His father was an auto mechanic with his own garage in town who picked up extra work when the riverboats needed repairs. He loved organ music. The best place to listen to organ music was on the "showboats," like the *Delta Queen*, which still toured the river towns all summer and were particularly known for their steam-powered organs. This was just about the only luxury Richardson experienced. He and his parents often spent their summer nights attending the vaudeville varieties and Broadway musicals on the showboats, afterward climbing the steep streets toward home as the band music from the late show was blown uphill by the river breezes.

"The showboat play that I remember best was *Uncle Tom's Cabin*," Richardson said, "probably because it was all about a stretch of the river near us. The showboats sold boxes of soft taffy wrapped in wax paper. It was a big deal when my parents bought me taffy on a showboat."

Entertainment on riverboats had begun relatively early in the 19th century, and their legacy was one of the most lasting cultural impacts of the flatboat era. The large family of William Chapman, a Shakespearean troupe from England, spent the 1830s drifting downriver every summer, stopping at river towns, or the floating villages of flatboats bunched together along the banks, performing *Othello* and *The Taming of the Shrew* in an amphitheater with a capacity of 120 seats, built on top of a hundred-foot barge. The Chapmans sold their barge for scrap in New Orleans every fall and then built a new one in Pittsburgh every spring, until they modernized with a steam-driven boat. The Chapmans were wildly popular and were followed, in the 1850s, by the 250-foot Spaulding and Rogers' Floating Circus Palace, which could hold an audience of over three thousand and included an act of fifteen waltzing horses, food concessions, and bars. Performing on the river was interrupted by the Civil War and then resumed in the 1870s as the great showboat era, a cultural phenomenon that spread the influence of vaudeville and variety shows, Stephen Foster songs, calliope steam organs, and, eventually, blues and jazz.

The Richardson family has been sustained by the river for three generations. From the turn of the 20th century until World War II, Richardson's grandfather, Allen Richardson, worked the Ohio in a small packet boat, a term used to describe a variety of mail boats, small-cargo haulers, or ferries. The Richardson boat, the *Daisy*, was a low-draft wooden boat powered by a tiny Neptune outboard engine. The *Daisy* performed a function completely forgotten about in today's America. In those days the consumer society, especially in remote areas that the railroads didn't reach, was largely served by traveling salesmen—the Fuller Brush man, the Copper Maid man from Revere Ware, dry-goods sellers, men taking orders for shoes, precut suits, life insurance, hardware, and even car parts from the thick catalogues they carried on their trips. There were garden seed salesmen and traveling knife and axe sharpeners. River travel was more direct, and more dependable, than riding the remote washboard roads that climbed over the steep hills above the riverbanks. When the machinery at sawmills or quarries along the river broke, specialized mechanics traveled by boat to overhaul engines and gearboxes.

These itinerant salesmen and mechanics were called "drummers." The term had carried over from the 19th century, when the ubiquitous salesmen traveling the countryside by stagecoach or horse and wagon carried large cases, or "drums," of goods. They "drummed" up business by banging wooden spoons on bells or pans. The drummers usually traveled to towns like Brandenburg by train, disembarking for a day or two to peddle in the region, providing a strong economic base for the local restaurants and lodging houses. Richardson's family made a reliable, if not lucrative, living ferrying the salesmen to the farms and towns along the Kentucky and Indiana riverbanks. The drummers were dropped off in the morning at river landings in the small towns. The *Daisy* returned at night to ferry them back to boardinghouses along the river.

"Grandaddy slept on the boat, and sometimes he was gone for the whole week," Richardson said. "The *Daisy* might go fifty miles downriver to all of the small towns, and when the boat got back on Friday night with all of the drummers, they would take the Louisville and Nashville back out of town and spend the next week in a packet boat on another stretch of the river."

As a boy, after school, Richardson would walk down to the river and pick up odd jobs on the commercial boats docked at the town wharf. He earned a quarter or fifty cents by coiling rope or painting anchors, and worked carrying boxes between the delivery trucks parked at the wharf and the waiting "cargo packets." One year he had a regular job as a "counter boy," carefully recording on a loading slip the number of boxes of goods carried from truck to boat. When he wasn't jobbing on the wharf, he was fishing from the banks or from a small johnboat parked in the weeds at the end of River Road.

"A lot of days, when I got home from school, my mother would say, 'Hey, we don't have any meat. Go down to the river and catch us some fish.' You were ten years old and putting dinner on the table for your family."

Richardson usually caught more fish than his family needed those nights, and this made him popular with the neighbors. He walked his hilly neighborhood every evening, selling his surplus catch to the families nearby. He had learned to clean fish by the time he was twelve and had a thriving business as a teenager. The satisfaction of providing fish for the neighbors filled him with pride.

"I grew up feeling that everything came from the river, including my sense of self-worth."

Richardson was ambitious and wanted to go to college. After high school, he took a summer job as a deckhand on an Ohio River tug pushing coal barges to an electrical generating plant a hundred miles upriver. He worked day and night for three months, helping the captain "split loads" at the locks, manning the motor room, chasing up and down the tug's metal steps as the "galley hoss" carrying coffee and meals to the crew. With overtime, he earned enough to pay for his first year at Western Kentucky University, where he studied industrial arts. For the next three years he worked on the boats all summer and during his Christmas vacations to pay his tuition.

"The Ohio River," Richardson said, "gave me my college education."

Richardson spent his first five years out of college working as a shop teacher at an Indiana high school, traveled around the region servicing the machinery at local factories for several years, and then spent twenty years at what is considered a plum job for the Brandenburg area, as a design draftsman at the nearby U.S. Army base, Fort Knox. But the river continued to call him and he still loved the brawny, modest work along the water. Nights and weekends, he moonlighted as a deckhand on a popular excursion and dining boat, the *Belle of Louisville*.

He's retired now, but only officially. Richardson still works a pretty much full-time job as the wharf geezer of Brandenburg. He tries to make every crew change down on the river, just in case there's a disembarking crew member who needs a ride to the bus station to get home. He checks the waterfront early every morning after a storm to make sure there aren't any loose pleasure boats or barges drifting in the channel. He runs errands into town for any boater in need. I could tell that he loved being aboard the *Patience* not only because he was entranced by the romance of our trip. He considered me a neophyte boatman and wanted me to take on the river below under the care of a veteran river rat. Just before we cast off from the town wharf, Richardson stood with one leg perched on the gunwales of the *Patience*.

"They're calling for more rain tonight and the dams will all be releasing water. The river will be fast and will want to push you into low water. You can't trust the buoys. If a big string of barges is coming around the bend at Jennings, just pull over, wait, and then follow the captain's wake into the right channel."

As we pulled away from the town wharf, I looked behind from the roof deck as Richardson stood at the edge of the river and waved, watching him shrink to a miniature as we moved down the channel. As we passed under the cantilever span of the Matthew E. Welsh Bridge, I waved back and sounded my portable air horn to say goodbye. His words would stay with me for the rest of the trip.

The Brandenburg wharf geezer was correct. The next two nights were rainy and windy, but I enjoyed the sensation of falling to sleep in my poplar nest, warm and dry under my quilt, while the rain pattered above on the roof deck. The wind whistled through the *Patience*'s mast and the trees onshore groaned with each blast. I could feel the tension of the boat pulling against its tie-down ropes in the current and the wind, vibrating up through the legs of my cot. The *Patience* quivered and released, quivered and released, a comforting sign that the extra "spring line" I had set between the shore and our kevels was arresting our drift at just the right point, then letting us swing back gently against the current.

The second night, I was in a lot of pain from my broken ribs. I woke up several times, once or twice walking out to the deck to check the lines. I noticed that the constant pulling of the boat against the current was cutting into and fraying the hemp rope where it was wrapped around the sharp edges of our poplar kevels. Releasing one line at a time, I wrapped a towel around the kevels and reset the ropes.

I actually enjoyed the occasional stab of pain in my ribs when I pulled the lines against the boat because, instinctively, I'd become a decent contortionist and was constantly adjusting my gait and balance, compensating against my injured ribs. To pull the set ropes or haul the anchor, I leaned hard and low, bracing against the gunwales with my knee, triple-wrapping the rope on my right forearm, and pulling only from the elbow. I became gyroscope boy again when the deck rocked, bending my knees and lowering my center of gravity to ride the deck up and down with the swells.

On the third or fourth night, when I rolled from one side to the other to avoid a sharp stab of pain, I woke suddenly and realized that I had been dreaming about my mother. She kept falling, falling, and I was unable to catch her in time, before she fell against the sharp edge of a coffee table, opening up a gash in her arm, or slipping on the ice while I was loading her into my car for a trip to the supermarket. The recriminations were crippling. I was failing my mother, not living up to my obligations as a son.

Dream interpretation is not that difficult and, when I woke abruptly that night, I realized that my own fall on the *Patience* had simply opened the memory vault labeled "Falls" and then randomly inserted some memory data about what was really bothering me. Mother falling—it was more or less a constant refrain of our relationship up in Maine. Mother stumbled and fell on the tree roots growing through the sidewalks when she decided to go down and watch the Pumpkinfest parade in Damariscotta alone, even though she'd promised to let us escort her. There was a lot of denial involved. "I didn't fall," she said. "The roots tripped me. The town of Damariscotta is to blame for not fixing the sidewalks." I accepted this as an expression of her determination to remain ambulatory and continue her social life in town.

When she fell one afternoon and opened up her arm against the sharp edge of her coffee table, she called me at home and asked if she could "borrow a Band-Aid," even though she needed six stitches in the hospital emergency room. I knew that none of these tumbles were my fault—they were the late-stage mishaps of aging. Her balance, like her eyesight and hearing, was beginning to fail. But emotionally, especially in my dreams, it was always my fault. I was sleeping on an Ohio River flatboat, nocturnally lacerating myself with guilt.

Lying awake in the swaying boat, I wondered why dreams so often reflect negative, menacing emotions—guilt, past events I would like to revise, insecurities about my character. The truth was so much more comforting. Often, after her hospital visits, Mother just wanted to be taken home for a rest or a long reading spell, savoring her most treasured asset—privacy. I would enjoy my afternoon off, going snowshoeing along the coast, or cutting firewood for my family.

Just as often, Mother and I took day trips together. Several times, in June, when the spiky lupines bloomed in profusion along the high, natural levees of the Maine rivers, we took a long drive together, following the brilliant lavender trace up the East River Road along the headwaters of the Sheepscot and the Damariscotta, up past Head Tide and Coopers Mills. I am an inveterate wildflower picker and always carry my equipment—garden clippers, harvest baskets, jugs of water, and Goodwill vases protected by bubble wrap—in my car. I treated my lupine trips with Mother like an expedition, packing the sandwiches she liked and a thermos of tea and cheese and crackers. Mother read her novel in the front passenger seat while I ranged out through the fields of wildflowers. Afterward, the perfume of lupine filled the car as we talked, taking in the lovely views of the grassy wetlands along the Sheepscot.

One June afternoon, just after she had turned ninety, my mother surprised me with a subject I never expected her to bring up.

"Rinky," she said. "There's something I've always wanted to say to you. But I never do. So now I'm going to do it."

She took a deep breath and then exhaled, nodding her head with the determination of someone who was going to say what had been long withheld.

Oh no, I thought. She was winding up to upbraid me for the mistakes I had made in my marriage, or my drinking. But what she wanted to discuss was different, unexpected.

"I've always wanted to apologize to you for telling Daddy so many times that you used that word."

"What word, Mom? Do you mean 'shit'?"

"You don't have to say it, you know. But yes, that word."

It wasn't an especially painful memory for me and I was surprised that her long-ago reporting of me to my father meant so much to her now. It was the usual drill of a 1950s boyhood. Coming in from the barn or from swimming in the pond, I would stub my toe on a door threshold and say, within earshot of her, "Shit." My younger brothers had borrowed my tool kit again and misplaced my wrenches, and I slapped them around and called them "little shitcakes."

There were eight or nine siblings by now and keeping track of our misbehavior was practically a full-time job for Mother. She notated the time of day and the offense for each child on a yellow legal pad so that my father could mete out lectures or punishment when he returned from work. But I was usually the main offender, the family Barabbas. The list of infractions under the column labeled "Rinker" ran all the way to the bottom of the page.

As soon as he got home at night, my father would call me into his library and motion for me to stand in front of his Franklin stove.

"Ah shit, Rinker," my father would say as he looked at the yellow legal pad. "You said 'shit' in front of your mother."

"Dad, I say 'shit' in front of you. You say 'shit' all the time. Why can't I say 'shit' in front of Mother?"

"Ah shit, son. It's different. You said 'shit' in front of your mother. Go upstairs and pick out your belt."

The long walk upstairs to the belt rack on my father's closet door was supposed to represent torture, but it wasn't really that much of an ordeal. Adolescent boys were regularly whipped by their fathers then, and my friends and I would compare notes the next day in school, laughing about it. Getting a thrashing didn't say anything about you because all the boys, depending on family tradition, got the belt, the paddle, or the dog leash.

But my mother had held in all that guilt about those beatings for nearly fifty years and now I could see that she was relieved to be letting it out. She exhaled noticeably again as we talked.

"Rinker, I'm sorry. I've wanted to say that so many times. I knew perfectly well at the time where you learned to say that word. You learned that word from Daddy, down in the barn."

I thanked my mother for apologizing to me and explained to her that my memories of learning how to curse from my father, and then being beaten for it, had faded over the years. Incidents like that are actually my favorite stories about growing up, and they seem humorous to me today.

I had dealt with all of this baggage years ago and understood it as just another by-product of growing up Catholic, and growing up in the 1950s, when most parents were emotionally clueless about raising children. The double standards of Roman Catholicism and the times were rigidly enforced. While we were still young, a great deal of verbiage was devoted to the subject of priests being holier than the rest of us because they lived under the vows of poverty and celibacy. But all of the priests we knew lived in comfortable, roomy brick rectories, belonged to country clubs, and drove Cadillacs given to them by rich parishioners. They drank too much and flirted with teenage girls. My grandmother and my father were chain-smokers who insisted that we never smoke. I learned to say "shit" down in the barn with my father, and then he whipped me for saying "shit" in front of my mother. But now I was grateful for this upbringing—my experiences as a boy had gifted me with a bent for sarcasm, a skepticism and appreciation of irony that had immeasurably helped me as a writer.

"Mom," I said. "I almost like the way Daddy kicked my butt. It made me a better person. It made me a tougher person."

Our conversation branched into other subjects—the madness and clamor around the house while she was raising us, my father spending too much money on motorcycles, horses, and airplanes, how the younger kids always felt that all of the family money had been spent on the older kids. We were sharing the rich, layered, Big Family 101 course that we had needed for years.

I realized that it wasn't my job to make her feel better about what had happened so many years ago. It wasn't my job to impart any feelings at all. My mother had spent nearly thirty years raising children, then another thirty years raising herself into the independent, freethinking person she had become. There had never been time to indulge the emotional ghosts of her past. It was my job to just sit and listen.

While we sat and talked in the car, the fields of lupines along the Sheepscot had filled the view out the windshield, swaying in the Maine breeze while they radiated lavender, pink, and white. Now, along the Ohio below Brandenburg, the hills along the banks were filled with brilliant profusions of wildflowers. They were mostly loosestrife, bluebells, and coneflowers, and they must have been part of the prompt that made me think of my mother.

For some reason that I couldn't explain to myself at the time, I had brought along a framed photograph of her, taken over Christmas the year before. She was so lovely, her skin still flawless and unwrinkled at age ninety-one, her expression calm and cheerful. Not thinking about it much, I hung the portrait above the small, built-in desk along the port wall of the cabin that I used for navigation planning and taking notes.

But now, below Brandenburg, I understood why I had placed the portrait of my mother above my desk on the *Patience*. I wanted her along so I could gaze at her face while we twisted through these lonely places on the river. The synapses of the brain are delightfully connective, just as all nature is connected.

All rivers flow into other rivers and my memories of being with Mother on the Sheepscot merged with my time on the Ohio. I surrendered to that feeling and, several times a day, when I saw her calm, irresistible photo above my desk, I thought of the *Patience* as a floating shrine of feelings, carrying me southwest to my past.

12

AFTER DANNY GOT OFF THE *Patience* at Huntington, West Virginia, to return to his job in Connecticut for two weeks, and Brady and Jay got off in Louisville, Kentucky, I found myself alone on the *Patience*, twenty miles below Battletown, Kentucky, waiting for my next crew. I was fatigued and dehydrated, tired but elated from the stress of running the boat twelve hours a day. My ribs pierced with pain every time I adjusted a line or got off my chair. But life on the boat without anyone else on board was also delightful. I finally had time to read, luxuriating with some of my books on the lower deck while the big commercial tugs churned by. As the sun fell, the fleecy cirrus clouds behind the hardwood stands of the Hoosier National Forest glowed pink, and I loaded up on Tylenol pills, begging my ribs to settle down and give me a decent night's sleep.

I was parked bow-first in shallow water against a private dock at Cloverport, Kentucky. The Army Corps crews at the dams below Louisville were regularly releasing water, which lifted the *Patience* a couple of feet as the extra flow moved downriver, usually after dark. I trained myself to wake after midnight to check my lines, so that I could reposition the hull against the dock. But one morning in early August I woke to find the bow firmly stuck in the thick Kentucky mud beside the dock. An hour later the bottom of the *Patience* was beached all the way to the middle of the boat. There must have been a dry spell in central Indiana and Kentucky, and the lock and dam crews had stopped releasing water.

With a start, I realized that I might be trapped on this remote bend in the river. My hull was rapidly settling into the mud and I could be stuck in Cloverport for days. I was a 19th-century flatboater now, stranded at the low-water banks until it started to rain hundreds of miles away. Harlan Hubbard had been beached or iced in along this stretch of the Ohio during his long flatboat journey in the 1940s. But the riverbanks were more populated then and dozens of men from nearby farms had materialized with teams of horses or tractors to pull him to safety.

I didn't have that advantage, or even time to think. I was alone on the boat and had to launch and quickly find a safe berth in deeper water. I ran up to the roof deck, started the motor, and dropped the lower unit partway into the river, and there was just enough water underneath the stern to give the propeller some pull against the stuck hull.

Everyone who had advised me on the trip warned me against this. I couldn't possibly sail the *Patience* solo, doing all of the work of pulling lines and anchors, establishing landmarks onshore while steering the boat, and then docking alone.

But I knew that I had to. I left the motor running in neutral and raced down the stairs to the stern, pulling up the heavy cement anchor that John Cooper had made for the boat. This chore usually required the muscles of two, but I was desperate and just pulled through the raging stabs of pain from my ribs. I cut the shore-line rope with my hunting knife—it would have to be sacrificed for now, and there was plenty of extra rope aboard. My ribs twinged in agony every time I moved, but the adrenaline rush from panic mostly quelled the pain.

I tried to sort out my situation. I couldn't just firewall the throttle and reverse the boat hard. That would sink the bow in deeper and, probably, foul the prop in mud. I would have to jockey the bottom back and forth, gently reversing and then forwarding the gearshift at low power, to use the weight of the boat for some momentum, like rocking a wheelbarrow loaded with heavy soil back and forth a few times to get it to move.

As I played with the throttle and the gearshift, the *Patience* ponderously moved a few inches forward and backward, and the murky plume of water radiating behind the boat was tan, not dark brown, which meant that I was agitating as much water as mud. I could feel the oak bottom boards easing out of the muck, the bow becoming slightly buoyant. Slow, slow, I thought. This was the *Patience* after all.

While still at one-quarter power in reverse, when the boat was consistently moving backward, I counted to ten until the speed in reverse was perhaps one knot and then I advanced the throttle to half power, still in reverse. Good. The plume of river water mixed with mud was mostly behind me now. I was churning up clear water and could lower the propeller to full depth. I held a steady course backward into the river for another ten seconds and then eased into the channel, slowly reversing the bow sideways until the rusted hull of an abandoned barge, stuck in a sandbar on the Indiana side, fanned into view. I will never forget that half-submerged barge because, by the time I was facing it directly on a heading west, I was throttling back to cruising power to save fuel. I had reached navigable depth. There was plenty of water below me.

As I moved downriver, I was filled with the most glorious feelings of freedom and self-love. I knew how to do what I didn't know how to do, what I had been told I couldn't do. The sunlight on the trees over in the Hoosier forest shimmered in abstract shapes, moving sideways and upslope, and the water downriver was roiling up V-shaped ripples as the current ran into a sandbar at the next bend. I was laughing at myself, too, about all of the earlier warnings that I had taken at face value. Everyone had told me that if I woke up with the bow stuck in the mud I would probably be there forever, and John Cooper told me that I couldn't free a beached boat without a lot of crew.

I wasn't gloating about disproving the "experts," but in the soft inner glow of fading adrenaline I did enjoy my newly discovered confidence. Pure, unknowing stamina and persistence was releasing me from fear. Screw the experts, I thought, just go, and move downriver. I had allowed myself to be myself. The inner knowledge of what to do was there, and not much of it was complicated. Barry Boucher had told me this, all the way back on the Monongahela, and now his prescience impressed me. Go slow and trust common sense. The practical coping invited by the river had once allowed hundreds of thousands of 19th-century boatmen, former farmers, adventuring preachers, out-of-work schoolteachers and printers, mostly amateurs like me, to float through and find the new America. Now, by my own fault, stranding myself in rural Kentucky without a crew, I had inadvertently created the need for a solution and liberated myself to man the *Patience* alone.

I wanted to be as unfettered as possible. I didn't bother turning on all of Danny's electronics, and I navigated just by shore references and my Army Corps charts, occasionally consulting the compass, easily picking up the daymarks and creek inlets marked on the maps. I didn't need crew or GPS signals from outer space right now. The isolation of being alone on the boat, sailing solo beside the river and the trees, and the wind on my face, was salvific.

As I rounded the big bend, turning due north around Hudson Hill Light, I looked ahead on my river chart. I could see that there was a marina ahead at Rocky Point, Indiana, which twisted around the wide inlet formed by the combined flow of Deer Creek and Little Deer Creek merging into the Ohio. The marina was close to the safe channel and fed by the water of the creeks. Rocky Point would be a good place to dock for a few days and catch up on the country I was passing through.

Near Pond Run, an inlet on the Indiana side, an immense yellow cloud of butterflies—thousands and thousands of butterflies—arched over the river ahead. The butterfly swarm was commuting south to Kentucky and reached bank to bank as I approached. Now I was looking ahead to a crystalline sky of hard blue and scattered cumulus clouds through a diaphanous screen of yellow butterflies. *Beauty, beauty, beauty, such gossamer yellow beauty*, I thought, *I will never witness a natural event like this again.* The immense yellow parade above was as populous as an ancient buffalo herd and, as I passed, the butterflies parted to make way for my flagpole and mast.

Seventy yards from the dock at Rocky Point, I throttled back and let the boat drift in the flow pushing from the bend behind me. I was finally learning how to manage the boat in currents. From head to toe I was bathed with tranquility, a deeply peaceful inner state where concepts like confidence or safety didn't intrude. *Surrender. Just surrender yourself and your boat to the flow, and steer from the point where the water has delivered your hull. Surrender and let the boat and the current find the marina dock by itself.*

The *Patience* gently drifted sideways and kissed the dock with the port side. The marina dock was right there now and my poplar side was resting comfortably against it, held against the boards by the current. I shut off the motor and walked down from the roof, stepped off the *Patience*, and cleated the lines myself.

Rocky Point became my oasis, my unplanned rest, a brief sabbatical away from running the boat every day. Every morning, while the herons and white egrets browsed for food in the tall-grass marshes nearby, I made breakfast and then retired to the shade of the cabin, where I had fashioned a snug study carrel out of a small wooden table, some bookends, and a comfortable captain's chair. My academic hiatus was supremely relaxing and I soon discovered that I had made two incorrect assumptions about the flatboat era.

I had traveled south because I was intrigued by the way that a primitive technology, a simple wooden box called the flatboat, had quickened America's journey from a provincial, postcolonial society into a major global exporter. The early 19th-century boom along the Ohio and the Mississippi captured the American imagination because the broad river channels twisting southwest appealed to the new nation's penchant for size, volume, massive amounts of everything. Rapid progress against a large obstacle—massive rivers, the great plains, the Rocky Mountains— was fast becoming an American value. But as I delved into the histories of the tributaries that I was passing on the Ohio, I discovered a more nuanced reality. Geographically, the young nation's riverine frontier was widely dispersed. The republic's runaway expansionism was also highly dependent on the smaller rivers. By the 1820s, America's specialty had become tributary growth.

I also quickly discovered that it was a mistake to regard the flatboat as a discrete design created after the Great Migration over the Appalachians had begun. In fact, boxy, flat-bottom workboats were imported from Europe during the earliest days of colonization, and then endlessly perfected and refined on the American tributaries of the east during the 18th century, almost as if the colonists already knew that one day they would need a reliable river vessel once they separated from England and were free to

pour over the mountains to the west. Since then, the flatboat was inseparable from virtually every facet of American development.

Beginning in the 1650s, initially to haul building timbers from distant
forests and hay harvested on remote salt meadows, the New England colonists began building a flat-bottom cargo boat called the gundalow, a name
carried over from Europe and probably derived from the Italian word *gondola*.
Gundalows were as broad as eighteen feet across and as long as seventy feet,
drew only four feet of water when fully loaded with upward of forty tons, and
were usually outfitted with large, forward-mounted lateen sails, which gave
the clunky-looking crafts surprising maneuverability and the ability to catch
the puffy, on-again, off-again winds of New England. Gundalows contributed
mightily to colonial development, and later the industrial revolution, along
the rivers throughout New England, particularly along the Piscataqua River in
New Hampshire, which stretched northwest toward a wide navigable channel
called Great Bay. The waterway connected a region of interior rivers in New
Hampshire and Massachusetts that joined the towns of Newmarket, Exeter,
and Dover into a bustling inland port called the "Tidal Basin Empire."

After the American Revolution, the discovery of deep, alluvial beds
of "blue clay" in the river valleys of New Hampshire, ideal for brickmak-
ing, solved one of New England's most persistent problems—the urban
fires that whipped through the wooden North American cities virtually
every decade. Building methods dramatically changed after the New
Hampshire blue clay was aggressively mined in the 1790s. The millions
of bricks eventually pressed from the clay deposits were fire-resistant,
and rapidly transformed the residential districts of Boston, Portsmouth, and Providence into the stately facades we know today. (When
the bricks are heated in kilns, the blue tint of the clay recedes and the
iron fragments in the clay give them their distinctive salmon or brown-
ish-red color.) By the 1830s, the tidal basin of New Hampshire was
turned into a vast brickyard of more than forty major establishments
manufacturing 5 million bricks a year, production that would grow to more
than 50 million bricks a year after the Civil War. New Hampshire and
neighboring Massachusetts became economic giants, and the portabil-
ity of bricks, and their utility as a building material, were major factors
in the explosion of textile and shoe manufacturing in New England by
the 1830s. In the span of a single generation, New England had grown

The gundalow flat-bottoms of the Piscataqua River in New Hampshire were the "semi-truck of New England," and endlessly copied throughout the colonies in 18th-century America. They often carried hay from marshes upriver.

from a scenic, dispersed incubator of cottage industries into a humming industrial complex that was supplying markets all over the world.

The "workhorse" of this center of America's industrial revolution, as historian Richard E. Winslow III called it, was the highly mutable Piscataqua River gundalow. In colonial times the New Hampshire rivermen had gradually perfected their flat-bottom design with broad, spacious decks, side rails to hold the cargo, and small cabins so that crews could make long round trips up and down the river on rainy days. The long narrow rudders were hinged so that they could easily bump over rocks and shallows in low water. Running with the tide and a following wind, the beamy, indestructible gundalows could make the twenty or thirty miles to Portsmouth in a single morning. Returning upriver, the gundalows carried manufactured products from abroad, Shaker furniture and seeds, iron wheel rims and tableware from the forges of Massachusetts, to be sold in the Merrimack valley towns.

The rapid growth in cotton textiles that revolutionized global trade in the 1820s bonded the American North, South, and England into a lucrative triangular trade route across the Atlantic. Hundreds of bales of ginned cotton, weighing five hundred pounds each, were loaded onto a single ship in New Orleans, Charleston, or Savannah and then sailed to the giant spinning and weaving mills of New Hampshire, Massachusetts, and Rhode Island, or to Bristol and Liverpool in England. The ships sailed home loaded with bolts of cotton and linen for remanufacturing, and finished rugs and clothing. Even after the introduction of steamboats, the simple gundalow continued to be the major freight hauler of the New England waterways, and hundreds of them operated in the tidal basins every day. A simple, democratically shared technology, a wooden rectangle that almost anyone could build and sail, cemented America's new role in the global economy.

FLATBOAT USED IN SOUTH HADLEY CANAL
1795 – 1845

The "fall boats" of the Connecticut River valley, also called "beam boats" and "canal boats," carried grain, hay, and iron ingots from Vermont to Long Island Sound. Their hull design and "lateen" or "galleon" sails were carried over the Appalachians by New Englanders during the post-revolutionary migration.

The sight of the tall lateen sails catching the sunlight, and the broad decks laden with barrels of Boston ale or Alabama cotton bales, was so common a feature along the riverbanks that the Piscataqua gundalow, according to Winslow, became an American "literary convention," celebrated in the novels of writers as diverse as Kenneth Roberts and Sarah Orne Jewett. In one of his most famous poems, "The Countess," John Greenleaf Whittier describes the cargo boats he could see from the banks of the Merrimack River in his native Haverhill, Massachusetts.

The river's steel-blue crescent curves
To meet, in ebb and flow,
*   The single broken wharf that serves*
For sloop and gundelow.

As gundalow designs migrated north to the Maine rivers and then south along the Atlantic Seaboard and merged with local designs, the flat-bottom barges often took on other names. Along the Connecticut River, flat-bottomed freight scows were called "fall boats," or "beam-bottoms." In the middle states, ninety-foot Susquehanna River arks with

The flat-bottom, raised-end Durham boat was famed along the Pennsylvania rivers, carrying iron ingots and flour barrels from Easton to Philadelphia, and played a prominent role during the American Revolution.

pointed ends carried lumber and wheat hundreds of miles from New York State and central Pennsylvania to Baltimore, providing, according to an 1827 article in the influential *Niles' Weekly Register*, about half of the products exported from the Maryland port. Farther east on the Lehigh and Delaware rivers, the sixty-five-foot Durham boat was named after the colonial Durham Iron Works and the Durham Grist Mill at Riegelsville in Bucks County. The flat-bottom Durham boat often had a raised, pointed bow, and sometimes a pointed stern, to improve its handling qualities in the shallows near iron foundries and gristmills. The sturdy Durhams drew only two feet of water when loaded with up to twenty tons of iron ingots, or 170 barrels of flour. With their lateen or square galleon sails billowing against the Pocono foothills, the Durhams were a familiar sight along the 18th-century cargo route between Easton and Philadelphia.

The widely dispersed Durham design demonstrated the democratically shared building style, and the diverse naming patterns, of 18th-century life. Although the boat was eventually named after the Durham Furnace district along the Delaware, the design was probably first introduced in the early 18th century by Dutch and Finnish colonial boatbuilders in northern New York, where the boats were used to carry passengers and cargo, particularly heavy barrels of salt, along the Hudson and Mohawk rivers. Though identical in design from river to river, the name of the boat changed according to place. The Durham was variously called the Schenectady boat, the Niagara boat, the Mohawk boat, the Erie boat, and the St. Lawrence boat as its use spread from Albany and New York City to the Great Lakes. Long before variants of the Durham design were carried over the Appalachians for use on the Ohio, the flat-bottoms were projecting the nascent prowess of American manufacturing. By 1750, the American colonies were already exporting nearly five thousand tons of pig iron to Europe every year, most of it carried downriver on Durhams to exporting hubs like New York, Philadelphia, and Baltimore.

The use of the name "gundalow" was even more widely dispersed. Because so many small farmers from Pennsylvania migrated to Virginia—the families of Davy Crockett, Daniel Boone, and Abraham Lincoln initially followed this settlement route, south through the Shenandoah valley—usage of the term "gundalow" was also common on the rivers of the Old Dominion, including major waterways such as the Potomac, the Shenandoah, and the James.

Temple University historian Seth C. Bruggeman has established that there were at least forty regional variations of spelling for the boat. By 1809, Bruggeman writes, "gundalow" in the United States broadly referred "to a large river-going flatboat." Pronunciation and spelling standards in the 18th century were notoriously lax. It is not surprising that alligator-horse Kaintucks often called their Ohio River flats "gandaloos" or "gunlos." Flatboat transport had followed settlement down the Atlantic coast, through the green valleys of the Shenandoah, and finally leapt over the Appalachians, spreading like evangelical Christianity, or Scotch-Irish roots music, or even democracy itself.

In 1809, when the cargo boom after the Louisiana Purchase was well underway, roughly 670 flatboat landings were recorded in New Orleans. The
number of flatboat arrivals in New Orleans continued to rise sharply every
year from 1820 to 1840 and the cargo traffic reaching the bottom of the Mississippi "peaked" at 2,800 vessels in 1846. But these numbers, relying on "official" records like landing fees levied on flatboats arriving in New Orleans, are
suspect. During the riotous expansion of the economy during the Jacksonian
Era, tributary towns in Ohio and Indiana exploded with growth, often because they specialized in a single, high-volume product that had to be carried from interior farms to the through-haul boats traveling to New Orleans.
The number of flatboats traveling on just one of these tributaries could exceed the total yearly traffic on the main stem of the Ohio.

In the 1820s, Cincinnati, where Kentucky's Licking River joined the
Ohio, river trade and slaughterhouses turned the bankside town into the
"fastest-growing city in the West," with the population swelling from 2,500
in 1810 to 115,000 in 1850. In 1845, the completion of the 274-mile Miami
and Erie Canal, which connected the Ohio and the vast interior farmlands
to the north to Lake Erie, accelerated the growth of the meatpacking industry. Almost 2,000 laborers slaughtered and preserved 450,000 hogs a year,
and the city was officially dubbed "the pork capital of the world," and pop-
ularly known as "Porkopolis." (Frontier Indiana was hog crazy and became
the major supplier for the Cincinnati slaughterhouses. In the 1860 census,
Indiana had 1.3 million residents and 3 million hogs.) After the American
Revolution, Vincennes, Indiana, along the Wabash, became an important
reprovisioning and repair stop along the main wagon road from Pennsylvania to Illinois, the Vincennes Trace. By the 1830s, after the agricultural
development of Indiana, more than two thousand flatboats were entering
the Ohio from the Wabash every year and Vincennes gradually converted
its wagon shops and forges to building flatboats, anchors, and chains.

In *Western Rivermen, 1763–1861*, Michael Allen, a former deckhand on
Mississippi River push boats who is now an emeritus professor of history at
the University of Washington, Tacoma, points out that transporting cargo by
flatboat was heavily dependent on the delivery routes along the tributaries.

"In the commercial year 1852–1853 in Cincinnati, for example, an estimated 5,000 flatboats landed at the city wharf, and many of them traveled no farther," Allen writes. "About half that number arrived in Pittsburgh from the Allegheny and Monongahela rivers. When one factors in the continuous local traffic on the Muskingum, Scioto, Kentucky, Green, Tennessee, Cumberland, and Wabash rivers, the great magnitude of the non-Mississippi trade becomes apparent."

Depending on the needs of a particular industry, or the unique conditions on a tributary, the basic flatboat design endlessly mutated after it was carried over the Appalachians. The Kanawha River in West Virginia, for example, was critical to American growth between the Revolution and the Civil War. The Kanawha joins the Ohio River at Point Pleasant, West Virginia, about 150 miles upriver from Cincinnati. The river flows over the rich underground salt deposits left behind by an ancient body of salt water that geologists now call the Iapetus Ocean, which left behind the famous salt "licks" that drew herds of buffalo and deer and later the hunting parties of the Cherokee and Shawnee. After the American Revolution, the early white settlers acquired salt-harvesting skills from the local Native American tribes and then rapidly expanded the business by introducing well pumps powered by waterwheels and steam engines to bring salty water to the surface, where it was boiled in massive coal-fired evaporation pans to render it down to finished salt.

By the 1850s, the Kanawha supported more than fifty saltworks producing four million bushels of salt a year, about half of which was sent to the sprawling Cincinnati meatpacking complex downriver on the Ohio, turning the "Salines" along the Kanawha into America's largest salt-making region. The Kanawha was jammed with immense flats carrying salt to market, called "Bitter Boats" or "Bitter Heads." (In the 19th century, many rural Americans used the term "bitter" as a synonym for salt, a vernacular carried over from English and Scotch-Irish farming villages.) More than two thousand barrels of salt, weighing 350 pounds apiece, were jammed onto the decks of a single Bitter Boat, which were sometimes as long as 160 feet. Massive salt scows from the Kanawha were soon traveling as far south as New Orleans, distributing throughout the frontier territories and the new southern plantations an ingredient critical for food preservation and animal feed, liberating America from the cost of slogging heavy salt over the Appalachians.

"When discovery was made of the salt springs of the Kanawha and the Holston [in Tennessee], and Kentucky," Frederick Jackson Turner wrote in his famous frontier thesis, "the West began to be freed from dependence on the coast. It was part of the effect of finding these salt springs that enabled settlement to cross the mountains."

The Kanawha salt mines are controversial today because, under brutally inhumane conditions, slave labor was used to work the pits—one of the few instances where the southern plantation system was adapted to an industrial or mining setting. Life was cruel for the roughly three thousand slaves who worked the Kanawha Salines. The saltworks were run twenty-four hours a day most of the year, to avoid the inefficiency of shutting down and restarting coal furnaces every day, and a "task system" established strict quotas for how many bushels of coal, or baskets of salt, each slave had to produce. Dozens of slaves were killed or maimed every year by scalding at the evaporation pans, steam engine explosions, and falls down salt and coal shafts, and cholera epidemics were common.

Well before the Civil War, the Kanawha River and its flatboats became a microcosm of America's conflict over slavery. Because of the proximity of Ohio, a free state, just across the river, slave escapes from the Salines were frequent. Many runaway slaves hid on the Bitter Boats to reach Ohio, where they then posed as freedmen to obtain jobs on the steamboats, and the problem became so common that many Virginia planters, before they sent slaves over the mountains to work in the Kanawha pits, required contract clauses stipulating that their chattel could not work on boats or river wharves. The numbers of slaves escaping to freedom across the Ohio turned the Cincinnati area into a seething cauldron of sectional conflict. The Ohio River country teemed with southern bounty hunters in search of runaway slaves, who in turn were harried by determined abolitionists bent on secreting escapees into the safe houses of the Underground Railroad, many of them supported by antislavery families from the North who had moved west for adventure and to start new lives. The writer Harriet Beecher Stowe spent almost twenty years living in Cincinnati, befriending many escaped slaves and abolitionists, and she used the Ohio River country as the setting for her antislavery narrative, *Uncle Tom's Cabin*, perhaps the most influential novel in American history.

The Bitter Boats jamming the Kanawha became an ironic symbol of the firestorm awaiting America. The flatboats bearing salt to the Ohio were vital to the bursting economy, but they also threatened the foundation of the southern plantation system, slavery. Writing in the *Journal of Negro*

History in 1974, historian John Edmund Stealey III described how the traffic between the Kanawha and the steamboats on the Ohio River undermined slavery by harnessing the vital advantages delivered by the flatboat era—social mobility and freedom of thought.

"The steamboat, the primary vehicle of upriver transportation on the Great Kanawha, was a corrosive influence on the institution of slavery at the Salines," Stealey wrote. "It furnished the possibility of quick mobility that overland flight did not. Steamers frequently employed slaves as stewards and cooks. Such slaves obtained a degree of freedom unavailable to the laborers at the salt furnaces. The presence of steamboats would explain why slave-owners would attempt to keep their chattels away from river craft. Contacts with 'liberated' slaves could corrode discipline when knowledge of distant ports on the Ohio and elsewhere was transferred. Steamboats transported ideas as well as merchandise."

The flatboat played a pivotal role in another famous moment for America, but its role was almost completely eclipsed by one of those distortions typical in the recording of history.

In the middle of a northeaster on Christmas night, 1776, George Washington stealthily crossed the icy Delaware River from Bucks County, Pennsylvania, with 2,400 troops. The next day he routed a mercenary force of German Hessians in Trenton, New Jersey, taking almost one thousand prisoners and several cannons, establishing a strong position for defeating the British a week later at nearby Princeton. After months of defeats, the colonial cause was revived and the weaknesses of the hidebound British officer corps, who endlessly drilled their troops in traditional battlefield formations but were unprepared for the surprise attacks and unconventional tactics used by American soldiers, were revealed. Washington's rise as a trusted military leader, who relied on the slow hemorrhaging of the enemy by a war of attrition, had begun.

In 1851, the German-American artist and portraitist Emanuel Leutze immortalized the surprise Revolutionary War attack on Trenton with his inspiring oil painting *Washington Crossing the Delaware*. The Leutze painting is considered a masterpiece of historical art, and versions of it now hang in New York's Metropolitan Museum of Art and the White House in

Washington, D.C. Leutze, an enthusiastic follower of the uprisings against monarchy that swept through Europe in 1848, wanted to create an image from the American Revolution that would inspire reformers in France, Germany, and Holland.

Art undertaken for the sake of ideology, however, rarely sweats the details. Leutze's famous tableau is a stirring depiction, with shafts of crepuscular light stabbing through the low clouds and, impeding the boats, immense blocks of ice that appear to turn the Delaware into a giant punch bowl. But Leutze rescheduled the crossing as a daytime event, portrays a dignified Washington much older than he was, and, fluttering behind him, the American Stars and Stripes that Betsy Ross hadn't made yet. The rowboat carrying Washington has shiplap sides, a curved hull, and carries ten men, hardly realistic considering the demands of moving 2,400 troops across the river. The eighteen cannons that Washington is known to have crossed with, some of them six-pounders weighing over 1,700 pounds apiece, not to mention the ammunition, caissons, and draft horses to pull them, are nowhere in sight.

In 2011, Mort Künstler, who is known as America's foremost historical painter, was commissioned to paint a more accurate image of the crossing for an unveiling at the New-York Historical Society. Künstler is known as a meticulous researcher, and he already knew that large flatboat fleets carrying troops and artillery had played vital roles in several decisive battles—at Staten Island and Brooklyn, during the Battle of New York, and then at Lake Champlain, both in 1776. Künstler was also able to determine from contemporary documents that Washington had in fact requested from the governor of New Jersey the sturdy, sixty-five-foot Durham gundalows used along that stretch of the Delaware to haul iron ingots and wheat to Philadelphia. The crossing was actually a considerable engineering and intelligence feat. Washington dispatched a large quartermaster force to seize every local flat-bottom along the Delaware. Men experienced with flatboats—local Delaware boatmen, and gundalow sailors in a regiment from the famed port of Marblehead, Massachusetts—were selected to steer the flotilla across to a point four miles above Trenton.

Künstler's canvas, which won raves from historians and art critics alike, depicts a less heroic but still determined Washington standing on the square bow of a flatboat, his arm resting on the wheel of a cannon, which is lashed to the side rails with rope. Leutze's immense chunks of ice are replaced with the thin, pebbly sheet ice typical for the Delaware during the winter. The sixty shivering Continental soldiers on the low deck behind Washington are either kneeling or standing. Künstler's research indicated that on the notoriously leaky Durhams, especially on a rough, rainy night, the decks would be too wet for sitting.

How we remember history is as important as history itself, and the story of the two paintings, created 160 years apart, shows how the hoarfrost of mythmaking and edited detail can obscure our real past. Authenticity matters. With his painting about Washington's crossing, Künstler replaced the glorification of the Revolution in the Leutze rendering with the glum hardship of engagement that is the reality of a soldier's life. The American Revolution wasn't only an ardent, high-minded stand against an imperious British Crown. Washington's struggle was a miserable, eight-year slog, rife with mutinies, mass desertion, and the despair of poorly supplied, disorganized winter camps. While an estimated 6,200 Americans were killed on the battlefield, more than 17,000 Continental soldiers died of malnutrition and disease.

Künstler's canvas also indicates why the flatboat era took off so rapidly after the Revolution. The colonists already had long experience with the gundalow and its sibling flat-bottoms, and all of the required elements— how to build a flat, how to load and sail one, how to dispose of them at a profit downriver—were in place. By 1800, Americans had been rehearsing the water marathon to New Orleans for almost a century.

And the lore of flatboats performing military work on American rivers might also explain a caprice of dialect in the early 19th century. A high percentage of the alligator-horses drifting down the Ohio and the Mississippi were Revolutionary War veterans, or the sons of veterans. They pronounced "gundaloo" with the emphasis on the first syllable, as in *gun*dalow. Their memories of the boat that helped to liberate them from the British Crown, freeing them to push west, were potent and fresh.

After several days at Rocky Point, cloistered in my study carrel on the *Patience,* I felt refreshed. My evenings were especially memorable. A group of union workers and their wives, from the Century Aluminum plant across the river, lived on their boathouses at the marina during the summer, and now they were my river community, my Harlan Hubbard clan. They dropped by for drinks every night, brought me casseroles, and raced the electric bike down State Road 66.

But mostly, I was lazy and recuperative, recovering from a month of stress on the river. At Sunset Park in Tell City I found a picnic table along the riverfront where I could relax on cool nights with my books. The river I was reading about, and its sensations of river life, was right there. The mildly brackish smell of the still water at the banks, and the far-off squeals of children playing behind me in the park, completed my sense of being at rest beside the historic waterway that had carried America southwest.

In R. E. Banta's *The Ohio*, which was published in 1949 as a part of the popular Rivers of America series, I came across a reference that amused me. Growing up, I had always loved the 19th-century murder ballad "The Banks of the Ohio," a classic country-western song so durable that virtually everyone in country and folk—Johnny Cash, Dolly Parton, Joan Baez, Pete Seeger, and Arlo Guthrie—had recorded versions over the years.

But now I learned from Banta's book that a different song titled "Banks of Ohio" was the centerpiece of a popular frontier musical that was performed in the inland river towns as early as 1812. Frontier musicals and individual ballads like "Cumberland Gap," "Fare You Well, Polly," and "No Irish Need Apply" were a kind of national media at the time, an itinerant, shared narrative performed by wandering troupes at natural amphitheaters along the banks, or from the "theater flats" tied up to the docks, and they were often the only entertainment that Kaintuck settlers saw all year. "Banks of Ohio," Banta wrote, evoked the "wanderlust of youth" that inspired a generation to float southwest.

As I read the lyrics of "Banks of Ohio," the sun falling behind me warmed my neck and time moved back and forth in glimmery waves. I indulged the fantasy of being an alligator-horse in the time of my great-great-great-grandparents.

Come all young men who have a mind for to range
Into the western country your station for to change
For seeking some new pleasures we'll altogether go
And we'll settle on the banks of the pleasant Ohio.

STORE BOAT

OATS

50¢

13

THE LIVELY BANDS OF PIONEERS boarding flatboats in Pennsylvania and West Virginia in the early 19th century would soon share a particularly dreadful memory of the inland rivers. The thunderstorms in the Ohio and Mississippi valleys were unavoidable, and just about the worst environment to encounter while riding in a wooden flat-bottom that steered like a bathtub. Most 19th-century journals about river trips include descriptions of at least one or two perilous encounters with thunderstorms, which often ended with a collision against submerged trees, sandbars, or wooden islands. Mark Twain, famous in his day as a seasoned world traveler, said that even the legendary fury of storms in the Alps "were not the equal of some which I have seen in the Mississippi Valley." In 1842, the frontier naturalist and writer Thomas Bangs Thorpe, in an essay in the *Spirit of the Times* of New York, employed the literary technique of recurrence-repetition to stress the most harrowing aspects of the Mississippi storms—their intensity, frequency, and duration.

In the essay, "A Storm Scene on the Mississippi," Thorpe describes how he and two companions, a Native American guide and an old woodchopper, were crossing the swampy edges of the Mississippi by foot when they were forced by a violent storm into an abandoned squatter's cabin that sat on a point jutting into the river. While lightning flashed outside, the woodchopper was inspired by the weather to tell the story of a trip he had made as a younger man, steering a flatboat loaded with bacon from Pittsburgh to New Orleans. About three hundred miles north of New Orleans, after an eerie quiet, "all of a sudden it [the weather] changed, the river grew as rough as an alligator's back, thar was the tallest kind of noise overhead, and the fire flew up thar, like fur in a catfight." During the thunderstorm that followed, the captain of the boat insisted that it was safer to remain on the river than trying to tie up on the banks, and the flatboat was soon carried by runaway currents into a submerged tree.

"The boat broke up," the woodcutter continued, "like a dried leaf would have done, pork and plunder scattered, and I swum half soaked to death, ashore. I lost in the whole operation just two shirts, eighteen dollars in wages, and a half a box of Kentucky tobacker, beside two game cocks; I'll tell you what, a storm on that ar Mississippi, ain't to be sneezed at."

While the woodchopper was yarning away, the Native American guide cocked his head to listen and warned his party that the river was rising and coming "too near." The men decided to flee the cabin and run for high ground, and just after they exited through the door, the "weighty unhewn logs" of the structure, and everything around it, crumbled and disappeared into the rushing current of the Mississippi. After spending a miserable night in the forest, Thorpe and his companions woke in bright sunlight to see that the entire promontory where the squatter's shack once stood had completely disappeared. The river had massively rerouted itself right where they had sheltered the night before. "The caving banks had obliterated all signs of humanity," Thorpe wrote, "and left every thing about in a wild, and primitive solitude."

Thorpe's essay was the tale of a storm wrapped in the middle of another storm, interrupted by a storm-tossed river carrying the whole scene away. The meteorological rages of the Ohio and the Mississippi valleys were inescapable, in Thorpe's telling, whether travelers were on land or huddled in the cabin of a flatboat. This presented a supreme and ironic challenge for early 19th-century westering Americans, given that the river valleys beyond Pittsburgh were where millions of people wanted to be. Thunderstorms along the inland rivers epitomized the irony of America's thirst for western settlement. Every week, hundreds of additional pioneers and cargo-boat crews were scrambling over the Appalachians to join the flatboat procession, and every week, a dozen or more flats were wrecked during storms along the water route to New Orleans.

Long experience on the rivers didn't seem to make much of a difference. One of the most poignant tales of a storm's wrath was delivered by Timothy Flint in his *Recollections of the Last Ten Years, Passed in Occasional Residences and Journeyings in the Valley of the Mississippi, from Pittsburgh and the Missouri to the Gulf of Mexico, and from Florida to the Spanish Frontier*, a bestseller published in 1826 that inspired many Americans and European immigrants to join the migration over the Appalachians. Flint was one of the most interesting figures of the flatboat era and typified a character type frequently drawn west: the lovable, entertaining misfit who reinvents himself on the frontier. The son of a Massachusetts farmer, Flint was born during the American Revolution in the North Shore country above Boston. After Harvard, where he studied theology, Flint lackadaisically served as a supply minister at Congregational churches around the North Shore and soon became renowned for his incompetence. On the grounds of poor health, he refused to deliver the traditional second, Sunday afternoon sermon, and he neglected to record the marriages at which he presided, or the births and baptisms of parish children, including his own. His sermons were outrageously sophomoric—sometimes his homily consisted of a long reading of everyone in the North Shore towns who had died, been married, or accused of crimes over the last month. Flint preferred to spend most of his time conducting scientific experiments and reading adventure and travel books, like Daniel Defoe's *Robinson Crusoe*. He dreamed of following the trail of the famed Revolutionary War explorer and militia officer George Rogers Clark through the northwest frontier. But Flint was dashingly handsome, a colorful raconteur, and he married well, to Abigail Hubbard of Marblehead. She was related to the Peabodys of Salem, a wealthy shipping family that proved willing to bail the Flints out whenever Timothy got fired from another church.

Failure gets quite boring after a while, especially in the staid environs of North Shore Boston, and in 1815, when he was thirty-five, Flint decided to head west over the Alleghenies and repackage himself as a traveling "frontier missionary." His waywardness quickly proved to be an asset once he reached the Ohio River and found his voice as a writer. He failed at farming in Missouri and Arkansas, frequently moving with his growing family, which exposed him to a wide swath of country south to the Mexican line. He also moved east into present-day Florida, where he could observe the terrain and the social development of frontier towns, providing him with convincing details for the newspaper articles he had begun to write. During his wanderings, there was always a church that needed a minister, however maladroit. Flint, apparently, was capable of making strong first impressions, by slyly alluding to his Harvard degree, for instance, or the fact that he spoke "fluent French," which appealed to churches in the polyglot river towns of the former French territories along the lower Mississippi, where many residents still spoke the language. His French, in fact, was mediocre. But everybody loved listening to a Flint sermon on Sunday because his wild mispronunciations and verbal antics were so entertaining. From Louisiana to Missouri, the Flint myth grew every time he moved on to a new church. Though forgotten today, he became one of the great literary voices of the trans-Mississippi frontier.

The vagabonding family eked out a precarious living at various parishes in the river hamlets, and Flint became one of those literary figures who gravitated toward writing because nothing else had worked out for them. Between residences, Flint endlessly voyaged the rivers on flatboats and keelboats, and his keen observation skills and high tolerance for the eccentrics found on the frontier helped launch his writing career. He wrote several well-received novels about the frontier and, after meeting and interviewing Daniel Boone, published a much-embellished account of Boone's life that became one of the bestselling biographies of the 19th century and helped spread Boone's mystique. After its popular success in North America, Flint's *Recollections*, adapted from letters sent to his cousin back in Massachusetts, was widely translated and reprinted in Europe. *Recollections* is credited with introducing the American public back east to the rigors of pioneer life, and improving the image of the Kaintuck frontiersmen, and scholars have also credited Flint's two-volume *The History and Geography of the Mississippi Valley* with "materially advancing" the settlement of the Ohio and Mississippi River valleys.

In the fall of 1819, when his wife was eight months pregnant, Flint decided to move again, this time from Arkansas back to an earlier haunt along the Missouri River above St. Louis. Undertaking an early-winter boat trip with young children and a pregnant wife was not a particularly good idea, and the journey was a classic Flint fiasco. His hired boatmen quit and sneaked off in the middle of the night, requiring Flint and his young sons to manage the boat alone. The Flint boys, Micah and Ebenezer, shivered with malaria, and the water that year on both the Arkansas River and the Mississippi was low, forcing father and sons to laboriously haul their six-ton boat over sandbars. The Flints ran out of food and were gouged by the crew of a passing boat, who charged them $30 for one barrel of pork and one barrel of flour.

Early one sultry morning in late November, while the Flint boat was parked against a sandbar opposite the Second Chickasaw Bluff, a remote, uninhabited stretch of the Mississippi above Memphis, the family heard distant booms of thunder to the southwest, and the wind picked up. Abigail Flint had just entered labor and was huddled inside the boat cabin under covers while the Flint children wrapped themselves in blankets out on the sandbar.

As the wind began to howl and the rain hammered down, Flint panicked about his family's predicament, but Abigail Flint was a model of saintly composure. "She was so perfectly calm, spoke with such tranquil assurance about the future, and about the dear ones that were at this moment 'biding the pelting of the pitiless storm' on the sand bar, that I became calm myself," Flint wrote. By noon the ferocious winds of the storm had torn a hole in the roof of the cabin on the boat, and Flint wrapped more blankets around his wife to protect her from the rain. The storm began to subside at four in the afternoon and at five the sun came out. Mrs. Flint would struggle in labor for six more hours before a baby girl was born at eleven o'clock that night.

But the Flints had not been delivered from torment. The storm baby was "feeble and sickly" and died two and a half days later. The children cried while Flint said last prayers over the dead infant. Flint and his sons placed her body in a small traveling trunk and laid the makeshift coffin in a grave dug near the tall grasses at the edge of the sandbar.

The tribulations of Job continued to wrack the Flints' winter journey. By December, their boat was often frozen in when they woke in the morning, and finding food and firewood along the deserted banks of the Mississippi was a constant trial. Finally, the Flints limped into New

Madrid, Missouri, about seventy miles downriver from the Ohio River confluence, and, typically, decided to spend the winter there. The capricious decision-making of the Flints, however, was a gift to history. New Madrid was a fascinating and important river town and Flint's writing about it became one of his best frontier portraits. In the spring, the family moved fifty miles upriver to Jackson, Missouri, and lived there for a year while Timothy continued to travel, preach on weekends, and began his first novel. The Flints seem to have been reasonably happy there. Ebenezer and Micah found some pretty girls to court. But the disappointment of burying their infant girl at the Chickasaw Bluffs would always haunt the family.

Eight or nine years later, on a clear spring morning, Micah Flint was traveling the Mississippi on a steamboat. He was now almost twenty and studying the law, but he would eventually jettison these career plans after one of his earliest poems, "The Mounds of Cahokia," was published to high praise. (The star of the delightfully named Micah Flint would soon burn as brightly as his father's.) As the steamboat approached the timbered bottomlands opposite the Second Chickasaw Bluff, Micah stepped to a quiet place on the upper deck, away from the other passengers, and stared down to the bar along the banks where he had helped his father bury his newborn sister in 1819. He was overwhelmed with emotion when he recalled the stormy scene of years before.

The elegy that Micah Flint later wrote, "Lines, on Passing the Grave of My Sister," was still recited by American schoolchildren up until the 1950s. William Cullen Bryant considered it worthy enough to be included in his influential *Selections from the American Poets.* By the time it was published, Micah had become the editor of the highly respected monthly his father had founded in Cincinnati, *The Western Review*, and enjoyed a large following as a poet.

Here are the first and last stanzas of Micah Flint's "Lines, on Passing the Grave of My Sister":

> *On yonder shore, on yonder shore,*
> *Now verdant with the depth of shade,*
> *Beneath the white-arm'd sycamore,*
> *There is a little infant laid.*

Forgive this tear. A brother weeps.
'Tis there the faded floweret sleeps.

She sleeps alone, she sleeps alone;
But yearly is her grave-turf dress'd,
And still the summer-vines are thrown,
In annual wreaths, across her breast.
And still the sighing autumn grieves,
And strews the hallow'd spot with leaves.

It seemed amazing to me, when I read about the Flints, that the rocky wagon road over the Alleghenies, then the unpredictable rivers and the vagaries of a rough, unplanned frontier life, not to mention the demands of growing up in a crazy, unstable family, could produce such character, such stanzas, such expression. Micah Flint's "Lines, on Passing the Grave of My Sister" delivers to us something important. From the rudiments of tragedy and suffering, the frontier, so often, produced brilliant flashes of beauty.

I had flown and motorcycled across the Mississippi valley every few years since I was fifteen and thought I knew exactly what to expect from the legendary "Dixie Alley" storms. The most common progression of weather in the thousand-mile river corridor of the lower Mississippi begins with the development of "maritime tropical" systems, moving north from the Gulf of Mexico, which pick up moisture and energy as they race toward the Gulf Coast between Galveston, Texas, and New Orleans. The systems moving from the south typically carry high temperatures and high humidity, and the "high precipitation supercells" embedded in the air mass can generate rainstorms dropping two or three inches per hour over Louisiana, coastal Alabama, Mississippi, and East Texas.

The maritime tropical storm systems generally track north by northeast up the Mississippi valley, roughly following the river's course toward Cape Girardeau and St. Louis. The maritime tropicals generally create broad bands of weather, stretching all the way back to East Texas and lower

Arkansas. Systems that wide and heavy with moisture take several hours to pass over any single spot, lingering while they continue to drop heavy rain. This is the primary reason why the bayous of Louisiana and Mississippi are so prone to flooding.

Once or twice a month, or even more frequently, the wet air mass from the South collides at the top of the Mississippi valley with the prevailing westerly flow across the Rockies and the plains. The westerly "continental" flow is slightly cooler and dryer than the maritime tropical flow. When the edges of the two air masses meet, the differences in the temperature and moisture gradients generate large storm fronts that explode northeastward through the Ohio River valley as far as Pittsburgh. The collision of the air masses also stalls the tropical front moving north, prolonging the rain and winds along the Mississippi.

The result can be clusters of storms from Indianapolis to Pittsburgh, spreading south to the banks of the Ohio, raging almost weekly in the summer. As a consequence, southern Ohio, Indiana, and Illinois, along the Ohio River valley, receive about ten inches more rain every year than the northern areas of the states. In pioneer days, except for veteran captains who were good at reading clouds, the majority of flatboaters were virtually defenseless against these storms because they couldn't see them until the rain and high winds were almost on top of them.

Modern weather forecasting and radar have greatly improved things, of course. For fifty years now I've flown planes or driven motorcycles, even mule teams, across the Mississippi valley storm belt. I've learned over time, especially when traveling west, that it's best to hold short just shy of the Appalachians, and then again just shy of the Missouri, to check ahead for Gulf storms moving up the Mississippi. If there is also a strong continental flow in the airspace ahead, the storms will be hellacious.

That was my plan for the New Orleans trip. Every night, or perhaps early in the morning, I would give myself a full radar and forecast weather briefing from my cell phone or laptop. In remote spots where cell or internet reception was poor, I knew that I could rely on my favorite radio show, the detailed forecasts broadcast on VHF bands by the National Weather Service and the National Oceanic and Atmospheric Administration (NOAA). When I saw that a big maritime tropical from the Gulf was moving up toward Memphis, and about to collide with the westerly continental flow, I could lay over in a marina or a protected cove, tie up well, and enjoy an afternoon of wind and rain in the cozy poplar cabin of the *Patience*.

It was a good strategy, backed by years of travel experience, and totally erroneous. As soon as I left Pittsburgh in July and began to regularly check the weather ahead, I could see that a new and unfamiliar weather pattern had established itself for the summer. A large and unusual U-shaped dip in the jet stream over the Great Lakes was drawing the continental flow north of the Ohio River, and pushing the tropical flow slightly west of the Mississippi. Every morning, the radar maps looked the same. A long, crescent-shaped front of storms, parallel to the Mississippi but usually about fifty miles away, curved up toward southern Illinois, and then bent east, paralleling the course of the Ohio. On the weather radar, a curled line of dark green, indicating steady rain, stood just off the rivers, like a two-thousand-mile privet hedge stretching from the Louisiana coast all the way north to Pittsburgh.

This initially seemed favorable, because the unique weather formation was mostly keeping the big, slow-moving fronts off my course on the rivers. But the volatility of the air masses north of the Ohio River was often creating a series of relatively small but fierce "pop-up" storms that peeled off from the main front and then raged south and east to the Ohio and the Mississippi. One morning, I listened carefully to a "Special Alert" on the NOAA band while a government meteorologist explained that these pop-up storms often quickly emerged and then disappeared, only to re-appear twenty or thirty miles away, making them almost impossible to see beforehand or follow on radar. I would know that one of these fast-tracking storms was headed for my position on the *Patience* only a minute or two before it got there, when I could see it. I had never seen storm formations quite like these before. But I knew that aberrant jet stream formations, once established, tend to remain embedded for the whole season. It was going to be a hell of a summer for pop-up storms along the Ohio and the Mississippi.

I welcomed these conditions. The constant threat of unannounced storms would only draw me closer to the experience of the 19th-century Kaintucks. Only rarely could they see the raging meteorology lurking just over the horizon, about to pounce on their boats. The unique conditions of my summer aboard the *Patience* would produce the same results. I wouldn't be able to see the storms until they were literally just off my bow, and my days as an alligator-horse on the inland rivers were going to be challenging and fun.

I ran into my first pop-up storm along a remote stretch of the Ohio just past Grandview Light, about ten miles upriver from Owensboro, Kentucky. I couldn't have been better situated for the event. By far my best crew member all summer, Mike Binkley, was sitting beside me at the rooftop steering console when I felt a sudden blast of cold air on my right shoulder. When I looked west past the inlet of Honey Creek, the sky had turned anvil black with shadings of deep purple and green, the colors swirling in a kind of cyclonic barber pole behind a thick screen of rain that was falling about two miles away. The smaller trees on the Indiana side were already bending low and swaying from the wind. The storm was nearly on top of us.

Mike was an interesting fellow. A successful furniture store owner and real estate investor whom I met in Gallatin while I was building the boat, he had spent most of his free time for the past thirty years racing motorcycles in the United States and Europe, mountain climbing, and making weeklong bicycle tours through the South. He is tall and blond with movie-idol good looks, so fit that he looks ten years younger than his sixty-four years. He couldn't join me at Pittsburgh for the launch of the *Patience* because he was hiking the Grand Canyon in Arizona with his children, but had first joined me in Kentucky, then returned home for a few days before rejoining the boat at Rocky Point in Indiana.

Mike had spent most of his life boating on the Cumberland River, particularly the Old Hickory Lake stretch near Gallatin. The Cumberland is a great training area for learning the inland rivers. The Army Corps of Engineers does not consider it a major commercial waterway like the Ohio or the Mississippi and only occasionally maintains the channel and riverbanks with dredging and improvements. The banks of the Cumberland are littered with runaway buoys never returned to marking the channels, and the river is strewn with tree snags and wrecked boats. The Old Hickory Lake section is only an hour's drive from Nashville, making it a popular destination for water-skiers and bass fishermen, but its numerous and tempting coves are generally unmarked, and treacherous with shallow water. "On the Cumberland," Mike says, "you can go from having sixty feet of water below you to less than three feet of water in a matter of yards." Few conditions we encountered on the Ohio or the Mississippi intimidated him. To this experience, Mike added two valuable attributes as a sailor. He enjoys a great sense of humor and is wonderfully sarcastic, and this is leavened by a deep, abiding calm.

Upriver, Mike had been on board when fishermen and marina owners had punctuated their dire warnings about the treacherous boils and tugboat wakes ahead of us with the rote omen "You're going to die."

When I looked back from Honey Creek, the advance winds of the storm were already pushing against the starboard sides of the *Patience*, turning us broadside.

I motioned my head west and spoke to Mike.

"Look at that thing. We're about to get blasted."

Mike looked over my shoulder and nodded.

"We're going to die, Rinker."

"Damn. Do I have time to get below and write a last note to my family?"

"Make it quick," he said. "Then we'll have more time to die."

By now, the whitecaps were kicking up on the river ahead of us and the hardwood bottoms on the Indiana banks were a swirling, watery rush of pale green against green as the underside of the leaves flipped in the wind. Large branches and even the crowns of some of the trees were cartwheeling in the air. The wind was shifting, too, turning to blast us from the south and pushing toward us a somersaulting wave of surface water.

Mike's imperturbability was reassuring.

"What do you want to do?" he said, without indicating that there was an urgent need for me to know. His tone was "Let's turn this into a teaching moment."

The situation was a classic example of how an amateur like me, whose only knowledge arrived from reading books, didn't have much to go on. In a sudden storm like this along the Ohio, Harlan Hubbard had thrown an anchor behind his shantyboat and laboriously hauled himself downwind into an inlet, and then tied himself to a tree, but he still got beached by the storm onto a mud bar. But Hubbard's shantyboat rarely remained aground for long—the local farmers, or a commercial boat with a motor, always came along and either poled or pulled him out. In the 19th-century Kaintuck journals I had read, captains had either steered or desperately poled for shore and tied to a tree, or tried to point into the wind as much as possible and remain with the current. Both strategies had worked most of the time, until they didn't, and the journals tended to favor lurid accounts of ropes snapping in the wind, or disastrous rides over sudden white water onto rocks, submerged sawyers, or sandbars.

Initially, I elected for the tie-up-on-the-shore approach, because I was desperate to escape the chaos out in the current. But as soon as I turned for the Kentucky banks and looked for a likely tree to catch with a rope, I could see the futility of my choice. The strong southwest winds had turned us sideways and almost motionless, and I could see that there was no chance of safely handling the boat near the banks. The wind was still picking up and both of the riverbanks were turbulent with high whitecaps and even waves. The hardwood stands on the Kentucky side that I intended to reach for protection were a blurry mass of flying limbs, swirling leaves, and airborne spray.

Mike had stood up and quickly removed the bungee cords attached to our convex bimini cover, then stowed it on the roof deck beneath a pile of lawn chairs and a sleeping cot. We were both yelling over the roar of the storm.

I told Mike that I had concluded it was madness to try and tie up on the banks in a maelstrom like this. Now I knew that this wasn't the preferable option. After asking me if I minded a suggestion, Mike yelled above the wind.

"Give me full power and point the bow of this crate directly into the wind."

Of course. Pointing into the wind would at least stabilize the direction of the boat and prevent us from turning broadside, at which point we would be pushed either backward or in circles.

I knew that the heavier rain that was about to arrive would reduce our visibility to almost zero, so I picked a clump of trees at the next bend on the Indiana banks and looked at our compass for a heading that would probably keep us in the navigable channel. In the rough water, the compass was skittering around about thirty or forty degrees in both directions. But it looked as though an "attempted heading" southwest, about 220 degrees, would keep us upwind and away from the banks.

Wrestling with the wheel of the *Patience* to keep her tracking southwest required a lot of muscle, and sometimes I had to pull in a single direction with both arms. The wind was blowing so fast past our ears that there was really no sound to hear at all, just the white roar of the storm, and the rain pounding against us came in massive sheets, like the flow off a barn roof. My ribs shuddered with pain every time I pulled the heavy wheel around to correct our heading against sudden gusts. But by jamming my knees and feet against the wooden console I could at least bear the pain and avoid wandering too far off 220 degrees.

The rain was now banging on the roof deck as loudly as a hammer echoing against nails. I was reveling in my contrarian personality. I loved this storm and the thudding pain in my ribs and the wetness and blindness of being on the turbulent river. I guessed but really didn't know that by holding my heading we were safe because we were almost motionless against the wind and couldn't hit anything going very fast. The obsession of holding 220 degrees was comforting and kept me focused.

The sky was so dark now that the binnacle light on the compass had automatically switched on and I stared ahead, fixated on the lit dome. It was the only thing I could see inside this typhoon of water and wind. The distant riverbanks had disappeared, and I could barely see our own bow. I grunted against the pain in my ribs. The only thought or action that existed was to steer 220 degrees southwest.

Two hundred twenty degrees southwest. I was possessed by that heading, like a dog looking for sex.

The adrenaline rush from the storm erased most of the pain from my ribs, and the highly oxygenated air from the rain induced a strange euphoria. This was a random pop-up event, moving quite fast, and it couldn't last long. It would blow itself out in ten minutes. As the *Patience* rocked violently in the waves I was still steering blind into the vapory nothingness all around me. But in my mind's eye I could imagine the image of a radar screen showing a green and yellow blob of rain racing northeast for the river, and then quickly disappearing out over the Kentucky foothills. We just had to hold our heading of 220 degrees and bear the wind and rain for a few more minutes.

After about twelve minutes, the storm blew out over Kentucky and daylight returned almost as quickly as it had disappeared, reminding me that weather is so starkly fickle, an abrupt mood disorder of the sky. The Ohio River, bank to bank, was now calm and glassine, the air as fresh as bleached linen on a clothesline. My 220-degree course had been true. We emerged in clear air right over the sailing line just past the cooling towers of a large generating station near Rockport, Indiana. Two miles ahead, the suspension cables of the William H. Natcher Bridge were shining under bright sunlight.

Mike skipped down to the cabin deck for some fresh towels and we vigorously rubbed our heads and backs, letting the sunlight warm us and dry off our clothes. I gave the wheel to Mike and went below to make coffee.

Getting past the storm filled me with self-glory and affirmation. I had done well during my first storm on the Ohio not only because Mike was there. I got through my first big weather event because my father had insisted that his sons be tough. As we resumed our course in calmer water toward the Natcher Bridge, I realized that I missed that complicated, hard-ass man. Toughness was next to godliness for him. In the winter we pushed our sleighs and teams so hard and so far that afterward we had to light fires in the stove in the barn to warm our hands before we could unhitch the horses. In the summer he made me fly the Cessna or the Beechcraft all the way across New York State to Lake Chautauqua at one thousand feet, where the turbulence on a hot day was brutal, with the avionics turned off and just an airman's map in my lap. We flew the Chautauqua route round trip several times a year, carrying our family doctor up to the lake for her vacations. I can still fly the route blind and without a map, by heart, from anywhere, Great Barrington to Chautauqua, Sullivan County to Chautauqua, Lancaster to Chautauqua. Dead, I could fly my ass right up from hell and climb through purgatory to Chautauqua. Morristown to the Clinton Reservoir to the Delaware at Frenchtown to Easton to Wilkes-Barre to Elmira. At Ithaca, we flew 240 degrees past the bottom of the Finger Lakes, and then we dropped down to the headwaters of the Allegheny, descending into Jamestown. My father was a good, demanding flight instructor. He was also a glorious control freak who could imagine so many bright futures for me. Someday, he would say, as we bounced past the Alleghenies, I would be as good as "Saint-Ex in *Wind, Sand and Stars*, or Ernie Gann in *Fate Is the Hunter*." I believed this and my father's regimen of hard travel filled me with adolescent arrogance, good arrogance. I *was* as good as Saint-Ex. Age fifteen, July 1966, 2,400 miles direct to L.A. in less than a week. That shitwreck Piper Cub had a top speed of eighty-five miles per hour and I could feel parts failing in the tail section as we bumped through the thermals. My brother was the pilot and I was the navigator and we had only a shopping bag full of maps, no radio, and a compass that barely worked. But I knew rivers, blacktop, and railroad tracks, even ones that I had never seen before. We never once got lost, not through the overcast Kentucky Swale, not all the way across sweltering, turbulent Texas, not through Lindbergh's 1927 route over the treacherous Guadalupes. Sunburn and exhaustion feel good to me. Arrogance and overreaching produce results. Domineering fathers are quite a goddamn pain in the ass at the time you are subjected to them and you only know later how good they were for you. On November afternoons, when I came in before dark after logging the Jockey Hollow ravines, he was sitting beside the warm, crackling fire in his library. He would tell me that I probably wasn't tired enough yet because I had come in early, while it was still light. He was joking, but I still lacked sarcasm awareness. Supreme dumbass that I was, I went right back down to the barn, harnessed a fresh horse, and climbed up Tea Mountain for some more logs.

Now, on the Ohio above Rockport, I was happy about my miserable, obsequious, workaholic, puddingheaded, and incomparably fucked-up youth. Hard travel dredges up some pretty good realizations. Nothing in my life would ever be as harrowing as climbing through the Guadalupe Pass, and that torture dated back to age fifteen. The Ohio and its storms were just rehearsed behavior for me.

And Mike had given me the best tutorial of the trip. The meteorological template was there now. The major weather challenge of the summer would be the pop-ups radiating off the main storm fronts about fifty miles away. They would arrive with little warning and never last more than ten or twelve minutes. All I had to do was point into the wind, obsess on the compass, and revel in the blind and bumpy ride.

———

Mike and I enjoyed the next day together on an enchanted stretch of the river winding into Owensboro. We were now two-thirds of the way down the Ohio and the eternal flow of centuries had accreted the ancient tree snags into mature, gracious islands, often as large as several hundred acres curving around the bends for over three miles. The islands were green eco-spheres with full forests, sandy beaches, and high open spaces thick with calico bush, wild berries, and Indian grass. Deer browsed in the high clearings above the banks and stared at the *Patience* as we passed.

At night, we tied up to a tree on the banks and sat on folding chairs before our fire, grilling steaks or chicken for dinner. Mike and I talked about our lives, our politics, the mixed joys and disappointments of family, and it was a relief to spend time with a genteel southerner and gifted conversationalist after so many months of unending redneck chatter in Gallatin. One night, when my younger brother called from Maine, I kept my cell phone on speaker because there was nothing to hide from Mike, and we talked about some problems Adrian was having at work and a friend of his who was dying from cancer. But he had joined a mindfulness group that seemed to be helping. When we said good night, Ady and I both said "I love you" to each other. Mike had told me that he almost never spoke with his only brother.

"Boy, I sure wish that I came from a family where brothers said that they loved each other," he said.

Crickets screeched from the banks and, a half mile away, the Rockport Light cast a pale triangle on the river. Night breezes rippled the water. Just before I went in to sleep, a beaver slapped its tail on the water and I stood on the galley deck watching it pull a small island of sticks past the bow.

14

AS I STEERED THE *PATIENCE* around the scenic bends along the Indiana and Kentucky banks, everything I was seeing and reading confirmed that the impact of the flatboat era was vast and enduring. By the end of the 19th century, the growth unleashed by the wooden flats had mushroomed into a 200,000-mile network of rivers, tributaries, canals, and railroad connections that made America a colossus of transportation. But that was all about the epic America of accepted myth, Horatio Alger's America. That was the America of fortunes being made from the humble beginnings of a single slaughterhouse beside the river, or a Monongahela boatyard evolving from building scrappy little pioneer arks to turning out two-hundred-ton paddle wheelers capable of carrying a thousand bales of cotton and a full complement of 175 passengers downriver.

But there was another America created by the flatboat era. The land rush unleashed by the transportation boom between the Revolution and the Civil War ignited a frantic national campaign to annihilate the Native American tribes throughout the inland river country. The Trail of Tears–forced relocation of the Cherokees and other southeastern tribes in the 1830s not only cleared the frontier of traditional peoples so that the one big event that drove America's industrial revolution—the rise of King Cotton—could proceed. The template for clearing the rest of the West of native peoples became embedded in our national character. That is the burden of the 19th-century, trans-Mississippi frontier. Our thriving as a people depended on our destruction of the people who were already here, and were now considered in America's way.

The clamor to occupy the rich new soils of the inland river country began even before the American Revolution was over. Squatters, Continental army veterans anticipating land grants for their military service, fur trappers, and even organized-church groups had been trickling through the Cumberland Gap and down the Ohio in flatboats as early as the 1770s. This trickle became a flood by the 1790s. Skirmishes between the scruffy bands of white pioneers and the indigenous tribes over land use boiled over into massacres, and then revenge massacres committed by both sides. The chaotic situation in the West, and the federal government's realization that it couldn't restrain its own citizens as they streamed over the Appalachians, ignited the Northwest Indian War, a bloody conflict against a confederation of Shawnees, Delawares, and Creeks that would drag on for ten years after the Revolution, by default determining American policy toward the native tribes. The precedent for development of the West was established. As soon as the disruptive waves of white settlers got into trouble, the central government intervened on their behalf, sending troops, building forts, and militarily subjugating the tribes. The defeated chiefs were forced into signing treaties that ceded vast reaches of their lands to white Americans. During the War of 1812, Shawnee chief Tecumseh briefly revived organized resistance to white settlement with a broad confederation of tribes, but the Native American defense of their lands collapsed after his death at the Battle of the Thames in Canada in 1813.

The rivers became bloody scenes of conflict. During the Beaver Wars fought between the Great Lakes and the Ohio River, which had begun as early as the 1630s, the tribes had been fighting each other, or European trappers, for two centuries, endlessly forming new alliances between themselves and with the French, Dutch, and British traders. The tribes of the Ohio country were extraordinary watermen and experienced warriors. They were master canoe builders whose smaller boats glided over the worst rapids as if they were flying carpets, and their longboats, up to thirty feet, were capable of effortlessly carrying more than fifteen braves, or a two-ton load of furs, over the same white water. The big dugouts were easily emptied of their cargo, then filled with weapons and warriors, to join fighting expeditions. For more than a century, new battles to protect fur territories broke out every few years and violence via tomahawk or flintlock was a way of life.

The inland river tribes had long been accustomed to the presence of non-native Europeans. But these were mostly French trappers, who traveled in small, nonthreatening groups of canoes, and who were more than willing to intermarry with the tribes, live together, and share both the work and the bounties of building fur-trading villages together. For a generation or more, the inland river country of Indiana, Illinois, and Kentucky became a network of mixed-race fur-trapping hamlets generally free of conflict. But this changed dramatically during and just after the Revolution, when large expeditions of flatboats began to arrive south of the Ohio River. The new arrivals were predominantly English-speaking Virginians, intent on permanently settling the land for farming. In 1779, land speculator John Donelson led a large flatboat group that founded Nashville, Tennessee, along the Cumberland River. In 1785, Revolutionary War captain Richard Spurr led a group of thirty Virginia veterans and their families who floated down the Ohio and then traveled overland from Maysville, Kentucky, settling the Lexington area. The white man was now arriving in massive arks that resembled floating farms, and these newcomers were determined to own the land themselves and to live far apart from the tribes. They cleared the forests and carried diseases that were often fatal for the Shawnee, Cherokee, and Creek villagers whose land they were now claiming. The flatboat became a potent symbol of a new kind of white invasion, and the pioneer flotillas were vulnerable because they were so identifiable and restricted to the course of the water, where escape was nearly impossible. This produced tragic results for both the white settlers and the tribes.

In the spring of 1779, as the twenty flatboats and supply scows of the Donelson Party proceeded down the Tennessee River from the Cumberlands, smallpox broke out on a few boats and, to prevent a larger outbreak, the expedition leaders decided to quarantine everyone showing symptoms on a single boat, which trailed at a safe distance behind the flotilla. The drifting Donelson boats approached their first Native American villages, occupied by the Chickamauga tribe, along a winding, breathtaking formation of limestone cliffs now known as the Tennessee River Gorge, near present-day Chattanooga. A few years before, the Chickamauga clans had broken off from their Cherokee relatives and moved downriver to escape the white settlement streaming over the Cumberlands, and were known to be hostile to flatboat groups. When a group of mixed-race villagers and Chickamauga braves approached the settler flotilla and warned the settlers about approaching the native villages, Captain Donelson hurried his boats to the rapid currents on the north bank of the Tennessee and swiftly left the villages behind. But the smallpox boat, lagging behind the main group, was defenseless and a Chickamauga war party in canoes soon overtook it, killing or capturing the twenty-eight pioneers on the boat.

The Chickamauga had inadvertently allowed themselves to be lured into an epidemiological trap. The warriors returned to their villages infected by smallpox, and the disease quickly spread not only through their villages, but to the upstream villages of their neighbors and close relatives, the Cherokee and Creeks. The pandemic that raged afterward in the native villages along the Tennessee might have killed only hundreds of Chickamauga, Cherokee, and Creek, but it was probably thousands. Disease, and the fear of disease carried by white settlers, became a major disruptive force along the west face of the Cumberlands, which was now a mixed space comprised of the old Native American lands and the new wilderness roads of the white pioneers. Recurrent epidemics of smallpox and rubella sweeping through tribal lands turned initially friendly villagers into hostile warriors, and the decimation weakened tribal resistance to the white invasion.

As they continued down the river into Alabama, the Donelson group skirmished with several more bands of Cherokee and Chickasaw warriors, losing six more settlers during attacks. The boats reached the Ohio and then turned south to follow the Cumberland River, finally reaching the large bend in the river at French Lick, now Nashville, by the end of April 1780. About thirty-five members of the original two hundred travelers in the Donelson group had been killed during the thousand-mile flatboat journey. For years afterward, sensationalized accounts about the casualties among the Donelson settlers, circulated widely in the eastern press, contributed to suspicions about the safety of flatboat migration and fueled a growing national hatred for the western tribes.

Historian William Heath has estimated that between the late 1780s and the early 1790s, more than five hundred settlers were killed along the Ohio when their flatboats were ambushed by Native American warriors. The deadly mayhem on the frontier was clearly not working as a development program, and the response of the interim government in Philadelphia, the Confederation Congress, was contradictory. A series of land acts passed after 1785 established a clear path for the new territories to apply for statehood.

Congress also settled the problem of retiring the country's Revolutionary War debts by establishing the economic model America would use to push west for the next century. The government sold large parcels of frontier property to wealthy investors and land companies, who in turn were authorized to resell parcels at a profit to pioneers, or to issue deeds to the war veterans and their heirs who held warrants for farmland. Treaty after treaty during the long Northwest Indian War and Tecumseh's rebellion delivered the bulk of western lands to white settlement, while relying on the tribes to vacate their traditional space, generally by disbursing northwest across the next river or two. There was no specific policy, no consistent plan about where the tribes would go, except that in several cases the government paid token amounts for the land, or agreed to fund the cost of moving. There was simply the practice of native retreat. It came to be called "voluntary removal."

By the turn of the 19th century, the first Kaintuck subsistence farmers, and slaveholding planters making excursions into the alluvial plateaus west of the Cumberlands, had discovered that the limestone-rich, loamy soils of Kentucky and Tennessee, and the Mississippi Delta farther southwest, were ideal for cultivating row crops like cotton, hemp, sugarcane, and rice. Westering Americans were anxious to leave the exhausted land east of the Appalachian barrier behind for the better soil over the mountains. The early surveying parties sent into the inland river country in the 1790s discovered another critical benefit that accelerated the march of settlers southwest toward the Mississippi. Tributary rivers like the Wabash, the Kentucky, the Cumberland, and the Yazoo were navigable deep into the interior, sometimes for hundreds of miles, providing reliable cargo routes to the Ohio and the Mississippi and thus to New Orleans, the gold pot of global trade. The race was on to join America's agricultural bonanza.

Thomas Jefferson's Louisiana Purchase in 1803, encompassing 828,000 square miles west of the Mississippi, which would provide enough land for fifteen new states, also provided a convenient bonus. Now there was plenty of new land west of the Mississippi, and that was where the tribes should be sent. Successive American presidents assumed an attitude of paternalism toward the native people. The American presidents were also notably unembarrassed about misstating the facts to their own political advantage. In a letter to Andrew Jackson written from his plantation, Monticello, in 1803, Jefferson offered the comforting thought that the Louisiana Purchase would benefit the tribes. "It [the purchase] will also open an asylum for these unhappy people, in a country which may suit their habits of life better than what they now occupy, which perhaps they will be willing to exchange with us: and to our posterity it opens a noble prospect of provision for ages." In fact, the southwest tribes were aggressive and quite successful farmers, and the barren land where they were sent—the "Indian Territory" of Oklahoma—was vastly inferior for both farming and hunting.

It is significant that Jefferson addressed these sentiments about Native Americans to Jackson, who rose in Tennessee politics as a loyal protégé of Nashville powerbroker Governor William Blount. Jackson was then a former U.S. senator and congressman who had returned to Tennessee to build his fortune, eventually riding his fame as an Indian fighter and the hero of the Battle of New Orleans to national prominence. As historian Sean Wilentz has pointed out, "Jackson's deepest passion was for the military." During the Creek War of 1813, after a violent faction of the tribe called the Red Sticks massacred more than five hundred white settlers at Fort Mims in southern Alabama, Governor Blount ordered Jackson to mount an offensive with one thousand members of the Tennessee Volunteers, to protect the state's southern border. During two decisive battles at the Creek villages of Tallushatchee and Talladega, Jackson surrounded the Red Stick warriors and slaughtered about five hundred of them, suffering modest casualties of his own. Jackson's rampage against the Creeks, Wilentz writes, made him look "like a military genius. But the reality was more prosaic: Jackson, when provoked, was an unterrified and accomplished killer."

Authorized by President James Madison to "negotiate" a treaty with the Creeks, Jackson imposed an agreement on the humiliated tribe that ceded 22 million acres of native land to the United States—most of present-day Alabama and western Georgia. Jackson would spend the next six years fighting a complicated series of battles against the remnant British and Spanish colonial forces, and their Seminole allies in Florida and Alabama, culminating in the Transcontinental Treaty of 1819, under which the United States purchased the entire Florida peninsula. Jackson's bloodthirsty tactics were controversial, but he was lionized by southern settlers and plantation owners for extending American territory from Florida to Texas. Thanks to Jackson and his treaties, southern cotton and sugarcane growers had obtained millions of new acres to plant. Within a decade, Jackson, now the most celebrated American general since George Washington, would ride his military fame into the White House.

During the 1820s, as white settlers continued to crowd the Ohio and the Mississippi with flatboat convoys, American attitudes hardened toward the remaining indigenous tribes in the South. Since colonial times, the southern native peoples had been called the "Five Civilized Tribes" because settlers found large groups of them unusually willing to assimilate and adopt white ways. (They were the Cherokees of Georgia and North Carolina, the Seminoles of Florida, the Creeks of Alabama, and the Chickasaw and Choctaw of Mississippi and Louisiana.) The five tribes adopted Euro-American styles of dress, built log cabins in villages, frequently intermarried with frontiersmen and settler families, and often converted to Christianity in large numbers. Most impressive to the rude Scotch-Irish settlers and the desperate, tidewater planters converging en masse on the Deep South, the Cherokee, Creeks, and Choctaw cleared large forest tracts for cotton, tobacco, and indigo and owned African American slaves to work their plantations. But this just proved to the white settlers congregating on the frontier that the Ohio and Mississippi valleys were ripe for large-scale plantation development. The American agenda was now clear. As long as the tribes occupied cotton country, they were in the way of white settlement.

The year 1828 proved fateful. Andrew Jackson was elected president, shortly after gold was discovered in northeast Georgia, on land guaranteed by treaty to the Cherokees. Overwhelmed by the anarchy of a gold rush on Native American lands, the Georgia legislature promptly passed legislation establishing a lottery to distribute the native land to the white miners, and forbidding Cherokees from claiming legal title to land or mining for gold. The Georgia legislature had endorsed a massive land grab.

Jackson wasted no time affirming Georgia's actions. He spent his first year as president, 1829, methodically laying the groundwork for what would eventually be called the Indian Removal Act of 1830, which provided for native lands in the southeastern states to be exchanged for lands in a new "Indian Territory" along the arid plains of Oklahoma. The usual "pensive nonsense about noble savages," as one historian put it, was spouted

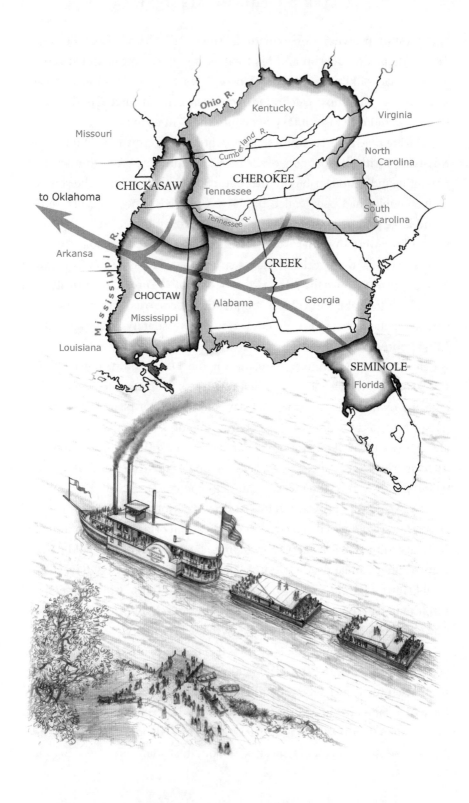

to defend the forced transport of the tribes to the West. The Cherokees, the Creeks, and the Choctaws, even though most of them were farmers by now, would be happier as hunters and foragers on the dry Oklahoma land, and the tribes would enjoy the "advantage" of having their transportation costs paid for by the federal government. In 1829, when Jackson delivered his Indian Removal Act to Congress with a letter of intent, he was blunt about his intentions. The inland river country populated for centuries by the southeastern tribes would now become, by deliberate government action, the exclusive preserve of white settlers and plantation owners.

"What good man would prefer a country covered with forests and ranged by a few thousand savages," President Jackson wrote, "to our extensive Republic, studded with cities, towns and prosperous farms embellished with all the improvements which art can devise or industry execute, occupied by more than 12,000,000 happy people, and filled with the blessings of liberty, civilization and religion?"

The Indian Removal Act was narrowly passed in March 1830, largely on regional lines, and the forced relocations to Oklahoma during the Jackson presidency and that of his successor, Martin Van Buren, were undertaken by a ruthless series of forced marches and water passages that stretched more than a thousand miles between Florida and Oklahoma. At rifle point, U.S. Army troops and state militia forced between 80,000 and 100,000 members of the five tribes from their homes, usually without notice, to prevent the tribes from organized resistance. All of the river resources developed over the past forty years would be devoted to the removal effort. The tribes were "escorted" into unsanitary, diseased wooden stockades that served as holding pens, or concentration camps, before they were herded along combined flatboat and land routes west. During an era before bridges were built across rivers and large streams, water crossings during the Trail of Tears were made on open ferries, or fording by foot, which often meant that large bands of Trails of Tears travelers crossed barefoot on the ice. Thousands of Trail tribal members died from exposure and starvation. Some flatboat expeditions were assigned a single doctor, but a lack of government funds prevented the hiring of nurses and medical assistants who could have cared for tribal members during the inevitable outbreaks of disease. Cholera, dysentery, and whooping cough raged through the flatboats and camping spots along the journey. Overall,

The sinking of the steamboat Monmouth *above Baton Rouge in 1837, which killed over 350 Creek tribal members, symbolized the horrors of Indian Removal.*

among the five southwestern tribes, almost a quarter of the marchers, an estimated 16,000 to 24,000 people, died.

The worst disaster along the water route to Oklahoma occurred in October 1837, when a 135-ton steamboat, the *Monmouth*, was steaming upriver past Baton Rouge with seven hundred Creeks crammed on its decks, part of a three-boat removal convoy contracted by the U.S. Army. During their land march to the Mississippi, the Creeks had already lost one hundred members to yellow fever. On a rainy, cold autumn night with low visibility, as the *Monmouth* rounded the Profit Island Bend, it collided with the sailboat *Trenton*, which was being towed downriver by another steamboat. More than two hundred Creek were thrown overboard into the frigid waters by the initial force of the crash. The steamboat, now broken in two, floated downriver with the rest of the Creeks and the crew, eventually breaking up and sinking. At least half of the Creeks on the *Monmouth*, between 360 and 400 souls, drowned in the Mississippi that night. The high death toll was blamed on overcrowding, the ineffectiveness of kerosene running lights in foggy conditions, and a failure to observe navigation rules on the river, which required boats moving downriver to remain in the middle of the channel, while upriver boats were supposed to travel closer to the banks.

One of the Creeks, David Barnett, later wrote an account of that night on the *Monmouth*. The Creeks, like most of the five civilized tribes, were experienced canoeists and water travelers. Barnett and his father, Timbochee Barnett, warned the crew of the steamboat that it was unwise to steam upriver on a stormy night when the Mississippi was obscured by fog. But the crew insisted that "the boat is going tonight."

"The ship was the kind that had an upper and lower deck. There were great stacks of boxes which contained whiskey in bottles. The officers in charge of the ship became intoxicated and even induced some of the Indians to drink. This created an uproar and turmoil." The Creeks begged the crew to take more care as the *Trenton* moving downriver was seen through the fog, but the Native American passengers were ignored. Barnett could never forget the mayhem on board once the *Monmouth* collided with the towed boat, which severed the steamship about thirty feet aft of the bow.

Then there was the screaming of the children, men, women, mothers and fathers when the ship began to sink. Everyone on the lower deck that could was urged to go up on the upper deck until some of the smaller boats [from the banks] could come to the rescue. The smaller boats were called by signal and they came soon enough but the lower deck had been hit so hard it was broken in two and was rapidly sinking and a great many of the Indians were drowned.

Some of the rescued Indians were taken to the shore on boats, some were successful in swimming to shore and some were drowned.

The dismembered remnants of the *Monmouth* drifted downriver and sank. By dawn, the storm had passed over and the fog had cleared. The impact of one of the great disasters of Indian Removal, and American history, was now clear to everyone.

"The next day," Barnett wrote, "the survivors went along the shore of the Mississippi River and tried to identify the dead bodies that had been washed ashore. The dead was gathered and buried and some were lost forever in the waters."

One of the more remarkable tales of the Trail of Tears was told by John G. Burnett, a young U.S. Army private in a mounted infantry unit that was sent to the Smoky Mountains in May 1838 to help escort a large party of Cherokees to Oklahoma. Burnett recorded his memories of being a Trail of Tears escort soldier fifty years later, on his eightieth birthday, because he wanted his children and grandchildren to know the truth about a shameful period of American history that he had witnessed firsthand.

Burnett was an interesting fellow, a multicultural archetype of his day. He had grown up in the 1820s in a white settlement in Sullivan County in eastern Tennessee, near several Cherokee villages along the Tennessee–North Carolina border, in the prime hunting country on the west face of the Cumberland ridge. He was reared according to the assimilationist values on the frontier. As a teenager he was devoted to hunting and fishing and, while roaming the forests, he befriended many Cherokee tracking parties, "hunting with them by day and sleeping around their camp fires at night." He became fluent in Cherokee and beloved by the tribe after he rescued a young Cherokee who had been seriously wounded while hunting in the Cumberlands, building him a shelter in the woods and nursing him back to health on a diet of chestnuts and roasted deer meat. Later, when he was a U.S. Army recruit barely twenty years old, his military superiors learned that Burnett spoke the language of the tribe and assigned him to the troop removing the Cherokee.

Burnett spent the fall and winter of 1838 acting as the interpreter for the mounted unit escorting a group of Cherokees from the Smokies on the North Carolina border to Oklahoma. The forced transportation was massive—the captive Cherokee train that Burnett helped escort was 645 wagons long. (During the fabled Oregon Trail migration of the 1850s, a fifty-wagon train was considered large.) It's clear from his account that he would have been an unusual soldier anyway, but Burnett's earlier fellowship with the Cherokees made him particularly sensitive to their plight. He often worked guard duty at night in just his government-issue blouse because he had lent his overcoat to a sick Cherokee child who needed extra warmth. Along the trail to Oklahoma, Burnett assisted at Cherokee burials and at night he enjoyed flirting with the Cherokee girls, often sitting up with them while they sang traditional songs. He was disconsolate about the "cargo of suffering humanity" that he witnessed along the long journey through the inland river country to Oklahoma and felt violated as an American soldier assigned to the duty.

"I saw the helpless Cherokees arrested and dragged from their homes, and driven at bayonet point into the stockades. And in the chill of a drizzling rain on an October morning I saw them loaded like cattle or sheep into six hundred and forty-five wagons and started toward the west. . . . Many of these helpless people did not have blankets and many of them had been driven from home barefooted." The route west, Burnett said, "was a trail of death," especially after the winter sleet and snowstorms began to fall on the Cherokee party while it crossed the Mississippi. Most of the Cherokees slept in their wagons or on the ground without fires. During a single night that winter, Burnett said, twenty-two Cherokee died of pneumonia. He saw a Cherokee widow with one infant child strapped to her back, and holding the hands of her two older children, forced by his fellow soldiers to cross a creek at high water. She drowned with her three children in the icy rapids. Burnett was briefly detained and threatened with court-martial after he intervened when he saw a government teamster whipping "an old feeble Cherokee" into a wagon and knocked the teamster to the ground.

Burnett was wistful about his years with the Cherokee and often reunited with them as an older man. Fifty-two years after his participation in the forced march of the Cherokees to Oklahoma, Burnett wanted his children and grandchildren to know about Andrew Jackson's genocide against the five tribes. Burnett is still revered among the Cherokee as a lonely voice of decency during the tragedy of the Trail of Tears.

"At this time," Burnett wrote, in 1890, "we are too near the removal of the Cherokees for our young people to fully understand the enormity of the crime that was committed against a helpless race. Truth is, the facts are being concealed from the young people of today. School children of today do not know that we are living on lands that were taken from a helpless race at the bayonet point to satisfy the white man's greed.... Murder is murder, and somebody must answer. Somebody must explain the streams of blood that flowed in the Indian country in the summer of 1838.... Let the historian of a future day tell the sad story with its sighs, its tears and dying groans. Let the great judge of all the earth weigh our actions and reward us according to our work."

Today, along the inland rivers and the highways of Kentucky, Tennessee, and southern Illinois, it is hard to miss evidence of the Trail of Tears. In 1987, Congress enacted the Trail of Tears National Historic Trail, under which the National Park Service has designated about thirty locations along the major routes, which are supported by dozens of highway trail markers, and artfully designed and informative interpretive signs describing the various phases of the forced migration. But this is highly curated evidence, designed to appeal to modern-day tourists and visiting school groups. At major trail stops, paved roads beside manicured lawns twist through the woods to clusters of attractively designed "interpretive centers" and restored barns and log cabins. I ran into several of these during brief stops or layovers at Golconda, Illinois, along the Ohio, and at Helena, Arkansas, and Memphis, Tennessee, along the Mississippi. But I found that the attractive signage and carefully worded government narratives at these trail crossings, like those at so many historic sites, mainly seemed to sanitize the past and convert these trail locations into textbook landscapes that showcase the National Park Service's undeniable skills at presentation. The tragic drama of the Trail of Tears, and its sharp abnegation of America's constitutional values, is mostly lost.

I felt a stronger attachment to what was lost during Indian Removal in the middle of August, when I made an impromptu Huck-and-Jim camp along a lovely island below Owensboro, Kentucky. Mike Binkley had left the boat and Danny wouldn't be back for a few days, but I was comfortable enough on the *Patience* by now to navigate alone downriver, at a modest pace of just fifteen or twenty miles a day. In the afternoon, simply because it looked so idyllic, I pulled into a small cove on Scuffletown Island, tied up to trees, and then savored an evening of solitude along the river. The random stop introduced me to a brief hiatus during the flatboat era. At places like Scuffletown, America seemed to pause and consider a kind of rough-hewn but peaceable multiethnic future before descending into an all-out war against the native tribes of the southwest.

The term "scuffletown," more or less equivalent to "redneck town," was an 18th-century description carried over the mountains from colonial North Carolina and Virginia. It referred to rude settlements in the mountain wilderness with just a dry-goods store or two, a blacksmith, and a tavern, famous for their "scuffles" because their remote locations were beyond the pale of the law and harbored cockfights, moonshine stills, and gambling. Because the mountain streams attracted a lot of beavers, the scuffletown hamlets attracted French trappers who intermarried with the Cherokee and Choctaw. The secluded villages also drew large numbers of runaway slaves who sought protection by melting into the sparse local population, relatively protected from the bounty hunters. Marriage between runaway slaves and members of the southwestern tribes was common, and each tribe had their own name for the children of these unions—the Cherokee "maroons," the Seminole Blacks, and the Chickasaw Freedmen. Scuffletowns were rough, hard places, but they were also idyllic, forested refuges where the quilt work of mixed-race peoples knew they were safe from reenslavement or being hauled back to civilization to face the law.

Scuffletown Island derived its name from nearby Scuffletown, Kentucky, a small but busy flatboat landing on the Ohio, nine upriver miles from the confluence with the Green River, a sizable tributary that reached more than three hundred miles into interior Kentucky, abundant trapline country that drew Cherokee, Creek, Choctaw, and also French trappers in profusion, spawning the mixed villages of the 18th-century wilderness. The frontier settlement was founded around 1800 by the Scotts, a mixed family of Cherokee, Shawnee, and Scotch-Irish blood typical on the postrevolutionary frontier. By the 1820s, the Scotts were known along the lower Ohio for running a lively trading post and tavern popular with the residents of the mixed-race Kentucky hinterlands, as well as the swelling ranks of Kaintuck flatboatmen drifting down the Ohio every year. The Scotts' tavern became a popular rendezvous point and drinking spot, famous for hundreds of miles upriver and down. The "French Islands" just upriver had become busy cargo ports and a half dozen or more flatboats left the Frenches every day after unloading and cruised downriver, their crews flush with cash. During low-water periods or at the end of the traditional drift seasons in the fall and spring, a riotous mix of French trappers, wandering Shawnee and Cherokee, and alligator-horse flatboaters would camp for weeks, even months, often wintering over until the water rose again.

Despite Scuffletown's rough-hewn environment and reputation for lawlessness, traces of civilization slowly emerged, and the town soon enjoyed the economic benefits spread by flatboat traffic. A school was built in 1813 and a church was built in 1830. Scuffletown became famous for two unique local products. The Cherokees and the Creeks taught the white settlers pecan husbandry and by the 1850s the Scuffletown groves were legendary for their quality throughout the South. By the Civil War, the surrounding swamps of Henderson County had been drained and the land cultivated for a "dark tobacco" strain that became famous throughout the world and was particularly prized in the capitals of Europe. Stripping barns for tobacco leaves, called stemmeries, were built in the 1860s, and Scuffletown eventually shipped more than five hundred barrels of tobacco to European markets every year, a significant export for an area with only two hundred inhabitants. Water-powered and later steam gristmills were built in the 1870s, and Scuffletown had two blacksmith shops and a barrel factory.

Scuffletown briefly achieved national fame after 1893, when the descendants of Cherokees exiled to Oklahoma during Indian Removal in the 1830s traveled back to the Ohio River valley and declared themselves a "returned tribe." The state of Kentucky, now chastened by its past, quickly recognized the "Scuffeltown Cherokees," and two other repatriating groups, reacknowledging them as lawful tribes. These returning groups, and the thousands of Cherokee who never left, spending the 19th century hiding in the mountain hollows and intermarrying with whites and African Americans, eventually formed the nucleus of today's Eastern Cherokee band.

But the river that once so generously gave could savagely take away. In

1913, a massive flood wiped out most of Scuffletown and its pecan groves, and the town was largely abandoned. The great Ohio River flood of 1937 obliterated all Scuffletown remains. The Scuffletown Bottoms area on the Kentucky banks, and Scuffletown Island, are now a preserved space of natural wetlands and cypress groves maintained by the U.S. Fish and Wildlife Service. The sandbars and mudflats along the Ohio and its confluence with the Green, where the Scotts once ran their lively drinking hole, are now considered vital habitat for several species of rare terns, bats, and mussels.

I didn't know about the ghost town of Scuffletown the night I parked alone on the Kentucky side of Scuffletown Island, just across the inner passage on the Ohio where the Scotts' old tavern and the famous pecan groves once stood. I only knew that I was enjoying my solo camp lashed to the trees of an idyllic island on the Ohio, grilling some chicken and sliced summer squash on my Coleman cookstove while a refreshing breeze blew over from the Scuffletown Bottoms. The winds from the Kentucky banks gently swayed the *Patience* on her lines and I enjoyed how the simple pleasures of a river trip could deliver such deep satisfaction. As the *Patience* rode the winds, my hickory rocker effortlessly tilted back and forth on the bow deck.

Downriver, over the next few days, I read more about Indian Removal, and the one-century rise and fall of Scuffletown, in the local history rooms at libraries on both sides of the river. Reading about the tragedy of the five civilized tribes, and imagining it in my head, seemed to recast it more powerfully than visiting the tastefully designed National Park Service sites. When I left on this trip, I had anticipated that descending the inland river country would be a lyrical journey following Jacob Yoder's route to New Orleans. But now, on the middle Ohio, I realized that I was making a passage through the darkest chapters of American history. Strangely, I felt good about that, more profoundly informed about the country I love.

And I realized that Scuffletown represented something even more important. For a brief interlude, just one hundred years, the descendants of the Cherokees and the Chocktaws, and the descendants of the alligator-horses, had paused to pursue coexistence, building a school and a church, discovering prosperity in tobacco, and collaborating on pecans. Then the river rose and carried it all away, obliterating all evidence of accord, but the experiment had been a lot more interesting and fruitful than removal.

15

BY THE MIDDLE OF AUGUST, I had become fond of one particularly beautiful, visual reward along the Ohio. The late-afternoon sun bearing down on the river and the droning of the engine created a drowsy, melatonin half-state between wakefulness and sleep. We spent hour after soporific hour following the sail line between Indiana and Kentucky, drenched by the soothing power of the immense green walls of forests climbing the hills beside us. Then we'd round the next bend and the bank square of Gallipolis, Ohio, or the limestone columns of the county courthouse in Lawrenceburg, Indiana, would sharply come into view, as if waking me from a dream. Encountering the 19th-century Greek Revival and Victorian facades of these towns from the perspective of the river was mesmerizing. The curving expanse of water in front of the steeples and mansard roofs miniaturized the town, and idealized it, fixing the skyline as a distant Fabergé egg.

Our stop at one of the loveliest of these river towns, Newburgh, Indiana, was the longest of the trip, and there was a good reason to be there. We were now two hundred miles above the confluence with the Mississippi at Cairo, Illinois, only a week away, and I'd been warned all the way down the Ohio that the stronger currents and more treacherous shallows of the bigger river made us particularly vulnerable to engine failure. If we lost our engine on the Mississippi—or, just as likely, temporarily fouled it with mud or sand—even a short float without power risked running aground on one of the river's immense sandbars, or would leave us drifting in the navigable channel, like the hapless sailboat back at Rising Sun. That would instantly establish us as a "hazard to navigation" on the river, and a threat to its gargantuan tows of forty barges or more along the Mississippi, and both the Army Corps of Engineers and the Coast Guard were known for pulling such hazards from the channel and then banishing the boat from the river. The long distances between towns on the Mississippi, where we could find help and make engine repairs, and the paucity of marinas only made our situation more perilous.

I would later conclude that these worries were just the exaggerations of the "You're going to die" pessimists. The solution to the absence of marinas, for example, was as simple, if arduous, as bringing along an electric bike and being willing to haul it up over the steep levees close to a town where we could buy gas. I would soon become reasonably adept at extricating the *Patience* from mudholes and sandbars, even at muscling the boat upstream against strong currents. My nerve-racking fears as I approached the Mississippi, however, epitomized the irony of my trip. Most of the fearmongering that I heard was delivered by river town residents who had been raised to be terrified of the river because they had lost relatives or friends to barge accidents or floods. If they did get on the river themselves, they rarely traveled beyond the familiar waters around the next bend. But I wouldn't understand most of this until I reached New Orleans.

I was also, once more, a victim of my own stupidity, a combination of foolhardiness and an unwillingness to confront. It was my boatbuilder, John Cooper, who had originally warned me not to take on the Mississippi without a backup motor. Typically, when I asked him to build a transom mount for one, he didn't and, just as typically, I was too polite and didn't insist. Still, Danny and I were confident that we could find a YouTube video on outboard motor mounts, build it out of driftwood lumber, and then somehow scratch up enough money to buy a used backup motor to hang on the *Patience*. But now we were almost to the Mississippi and the fix had not been made.

Curtis Wasmer, a home remodeler and driftwood furniture maker in Newburgh, had heard about our trip and followed our progress down the Ohio on the moving map display that Danny was regularly updating on Facebook. I had mentioned in one of my posts that we still hadn't resolved the issue of backup power and he called me one day while we were still upriver near Louisville, offering to build us a transom mount for a backup motor. I liked him right away on the phone and we discussed several fixes I wanted to make to the boat. Curtis sounded like a unique river rat—he'd been prowling the lower Ohio for years for driftwood, and building exquisite, artful coffee tables and benches from the logs and root balls he found along the banks. He seemed to know where and how the latest winter storms had altered the bends for miles around. He turned out to be one of the great finds of the trip and a gorgeous bundle of personality.

Curtis had arranged for us to tie up the *Patience* about a mile below Newburgh, just downriver from a combined industrial complex of sand and gravel pits and grain elevators, where a friend of his from church owned a large, comfortable dock complex with running water and a roofed area for camping and cooking. When we arrived at Newburgh in early August, Curtis, a short, balding man with a ready laugh and a smile as broad as a plate, met us at the dock and helped us tie up. He dressed fashionably in Patagonia hiking shorts, spiffy nylon T-shirts, and Keen sandals. He told us that we would rarely see the owner down at the dock and that we should make ourselves at home for as long as we wanted. We could take showers at his house, and just about everything we needed was down the road in touristy Newburgh. I was relieved about the break from the hot, droning boat and marveled at this unexpected gift of river hospitality.

Danny had now arrived back at the boat and ferried my pickup truck forward from Pittsburgh, and he and Curtis took to each other right away. They immediately sat down at a table on the shaded deck above the dock and drew up plans for a transom mount, new cabinets, and storage space in the galley and the fuel bay in the stern, drawing up long lists of the supplies they would need for repairs. Danny and Curtis formed an instant rapport as a boat repair crew and for the next five days, laughing and chattering all the time, splurging on new power tools at the hardware stores, they disappeared early in the morning together to buy hardware and wood. They spent the rest of the day building fixes for the *Patience* in Curtis's shop across town, or on the dock, happily bromancing as new best friends while the big push boats lumbered by on the river.

I now had another antic, Monongahela-style boatyard, and all afternoon the dock echoed with the whine of power tools and the thud of

Dan Corjulo and Curtis Wasmer formed an instant bonding as a Huck Finn pair.

mallets. Danny's liaison with Curtis quickly matured into a kind of cheerful mutiny aboard the *Patience*. They didn't want my help on any of the repairs they were making on the boat and, indeed, seemed to prefer that I vaporize. I was rebuffed every time I offered to help them with the boat repairs.

"Get lost," Danny said to me the morning after we arrived in Newburgh. "I'm sure they have a good local history room at the library."

"Danny's right, Captain," Curtis said. "Take the week off. If you don't, we're hanging you from the yardarm."

At Newburgh, I learned a lot more about the symbiotic relationship between the flatboat traffic and the growth of 19th-century river towns. Though hardly known today, Newburgh was once the busiest river port between Cincinnati and New Orleans. The area was settled just after the Louisiana Purchase by a classic merging of flatboaters—John Sprinkles, a German-American blacksmith, Abner Luce, a merchant from Muhlenberg County, Kentucky, and Washington Johnston, a land speculator from

Vincennes—who built the first sawmills and warehouses along what is now called Water Street. Their town plan took advantage of the high elevation of the banks on the Indiana side of the river, which allowed flatboat and later steamboat landings even during high water. Because it was only a few days' float above the junction with the Mississippi, and just a few miles downstream from the French islands and the confluence with the Green, the town quickly grew as a convenient transshipment point. A ferry was established over to the Kentucky banks in 1818 and wooden plank roads were built into what became the rich, agricultural interior of Warrick County on the Indiana side and Henderson County in Kentucky. By the late 1820s, Newburgh was emptying a considerable portion of the Ohio's agricultural commodities from hundreds of miles away, hosting as many as fifty flatboats a day during the high-water seasons in the spring and the fall. One memoir of the era describes the wharves on Water Street constantly being emptied and then refilled with new barrels and shipping crates, stacked on top of each other, filled with "pork, hominy, tobacco, ginseng root, beeswax, and feathers."

After 1850, when coal was discovered east of town, the wharves were extended even farther downriver to accommodate the increased traffic. The Newburgh pit was Indiana's first deep-shaft coal mine, and coal became an important economic multiplier in several ways. Steamboats towing huge, flat-bottom barges now regularly departed to supply factories and coal dealers as far south as New Orleans, and at the time both passenger and cargo steamboats were converting from wood to coal to fire their boilers, a technology upgrade that helped turn Newburgh into a bustling refueling stop. In the 1860s, several New York and Pennsylvania mining entrepreneurs followed coal baron John Hutchinson to Newburgh and quickly binged on a typical American excess of the 19th century, outdoing each other with their Italianate and Greek Revival mansions built on the bluffs above downtown, many of which remain today. As Newburgh prospered from the river trade and coal, the downtown area just below the mansion district filled with stylish hotels, five churches, a Presbyterian seminary, tobacco warehouses, a harness factory, and a cooperage turning out one hundred barrels a day.

Coal delivered another lucrative opportunity for riverfront towns. The steamboats became a kind of drive-by economy along the river, like the Caribbean and Key West cruise ships making the "port calls" of today. During the heyday of the Ohio River steamboats after 1850, several large paddle wheelers a day pulled into the Newburgh wharves to spend an hour or two refueling while their passengers disembarked to sample the shops and hotel restaurants just a block or two uphill. Steamboat landings were such an event in town that children gathered at the foot of State Street above the wharves to compete at identifying the inbound, triple-decker boats— the *Grey Eagle*, the *Little Grey Eagle*, or the *Cincinnati Belle*—while they were still too far off on the water to read the names painted on their bows.

Newburgh's new merchant caste, many of whom graduated to retailing and hotel building after creating successful coal and river-trading businesses, were desperate to attract shoppers off the riverboats, especially female shoppers. A Newburgh writer, Adah Jackson, called the passing riverboats a "tangible link to the world of wealth and fashion." In 1851, a prominent local businessman, Thomas Floyd Bethell, who had moved to Newburgh from the frontier settlement of French Lick, Indiana, and prospered as a river trader on the French islands at the Green, advertised the new downtown emporium he had established just a block up from the river, Bethell and Brothers. Nineteenth-century women rarely bought finished dresses at stores, but instead purchased fabrics and all the trimmings to be carried to a dressmaker, and Bethell was determined to be known as a fabric merchandizer of the first rank, probably because he had recently married a young Englishwoman familiar with London fashion. The advertisement, placed in the Warrick County *Democrat*, boasted that Bethell and Brothers carried "100 dozen ladies buttons," lace capes, Turkish satins, French silks, Swiss muslins, trimming and ribbons, a large selection of fine jewelry, and "Hayes and Craigs New Style Mole Skin Hats for 1851." Like the immense brick mansion that he would build a few years later on the high waterfront of the Ohio, Bethell's store ad reflected the prentensions of the times.

By the 1850s, the old river frontier beyond the Appalachians had become socially bifurcated. Around the bend just upriver, the Scuffletown and French island trading posts were still scruffy with the look of new settlement, with fresh log cabin homes, pigs roaming the streets, and raucous taverns frequented by French-Choctaw trappers and Kaintuck rivermen. But the new merchant class in towns like Newburgh wanted to repress all evidence of the river's lowbrow, frontier past. They were determined to prove that their new commercial districts were as sophisticated as the shopping blocks of Boston or New York. "In point of beauty and quality," the ad for Bethell and Brothers read, "we confidently assert that our goods cannot be surpassed by any house west of the mountains."

More ordinary shoppers continued to rely on the old broadhorn store boats drifting into Newburgh every day or two, demonstrating how economic eras and merchandizing trends rarely supplant each other entirely, but instead overlap. The retail flatboats, Adah Jackson writes, "were fitted with counters and shelves like a store. They made the smaller wharves, or the straggling settlements on the tributary rivers, carrying such necessities as bar iron, nails, cards (for combing wool), hemp cord, gunpowder, saltpeter, sugar, tea, and country linen."

The store boats before the Civil War also carried a lot of glassware, mostly carried downriver from factories in Pittsburgh and Wheeling, and a glazed pottery called "queensware" that was imported from Europe. For this reason, all along the Ohio, the jaunty, shantyboat-style stores were called "glass boats." The families that ran the boats and lived on them most of the year were called "glassies." The glass boats identified themselves by running a calico flag on the bow, and they alerted shoppers at the settlement towns and tributary wharves of their arrival by blasting a tin horn. The glass boats were also lively recycling centers. When the tin horn of a glass boat sounded, the town children exploded onto the streets and hurriedly gathered rags, stray buttons, and candle stubs from their mothers, or, carrying baskets or sacks, combed the street corners for castoff bottles. The ragamuffin bands of children then ran down State Street to the waterfront, to exchange their bundles to the "glassies" for pennies. Afterward, as they drifted downriver, the glassies laundered and bundled the fabric into "rag buns," washed the bottles, and remelted the wax stubs and poured them into molds for new candles, selling their secondhand goods to customers at their next stop.

Newburgh was not immune to young America's vicious business cycles and the town was eventually eclipsed in the 1870s when the major Ohio valley rail lines decided to join at a large hub in nearby Evansville. But the new generation of steam shovel magnates, coal mine owners, and lumber barons in Evansville preferred the breezy heights of Newburgh to the lower, sultry plots in their own residential districts, and after 1870 the Newburgh mansion district swelled as a Gilded Age summer retreat, with still more extravagant mansions rising every year on the bluffs. During the World War I coal boom, the Evansville-Newburgh area expanded farther, becoming known as the most elegant coal region in the country.

Newburgh was a milestone for the *Patience* in another respect. Debra Satterfield and Cynthia Lee, the friends from Nashville who had helped me finish off the boat, were finally done with their other travels and had joined the crew. They would come and go for a week or two at a time for the rest of the summer and were so sensible about organizing the boat that they stretched our running time by a couple of hours a day. At a camping and hiking store, Deb found a set of inexpensive but very effective solar lights, which she hung above the decks and the stairway in the stern, making it far easier to see my way around when a big tug wake woke me in the middle of the night and I circuited the *Patience* in the dark, checking our lines and our compass bearing. Cynthia is a descendant of the Lee family of Virginia and her forebears had traveled to Tennessee with the Donelson Party in 1779. She is an experienced adventurer who has canoed, kayaked, rafted, and fly-fished most of America's major rivers. An experienced "reader" of river currents and white water, she is also an excellent boat handler, and she and Deb made a competent helmsman-navigator team.

I was jubilant, during the middle of that week, when Curtis asked me one evening if he could take some time off work and join us for a week on the boat. I realized that, while holding for repairs at Newburgh, I was breaking in a backup crew as pleasant, adventurous, and capable as having Mike Binkley aboard. For the rest of the summer and the fall, as the *Patience* made more than a hundred miles a week down the Mississippi, Danny, Cynthia, Deb, and Curtis were my dream team.

The stop at Newburgh wasn't simply educational. Tied up on the lower Ohio for a week, we had finally remained in one place long enough to receive what the river had to offer, a healthful, restful, visually stimulating deliverance from the stresses of the outside world. We bathed in the river together and cut driftwood for fires every night, enjoyed Danny's elaborate cocktails, and stayed up late sharing the stories of our lives. By day I dawdled in the coffee shops, visited the Paleo-Indian site at Angel Mounds and Abe Lincoln's old cabin site at Little Pigeon Creek, and browsed the shelves at the used bookshop at the foot of State Street, the Book Nook. Newburgh was home for me, deep home. From the town landing down on the water I imagined packs of children running over the cobblestones, their arms filled with bundles of rags for the glassies.

Dan Lomax, the captain of the tugboat that maneuvered all of the barges for the Mulzer Crushed Stone company next door, drifted in beside the *Patience* every morning, handing us down melons, fresh eggs, and vegetables that he'd bought at the farmer's market in Evansville on his way to work. He was an unusual and fascinating man who devoured history books while he was tied up for his lunch break every day, and was particularly interested in Native American history, and I traded him back with biographies of Crazy Horse, Red Cloud, and Sitting Bull that I either had along or found at the Book Nook. Lomax is tall, strikingly handsome, and tanned, with long blond hair, and when he piloted by every morning in his sprightly blue and white harbor tug, the *Kristin J*, he was usually wearing a sleeveless shirt. Deb and Cynthia nicknamed him "Fabio."

That week, Dan took us for rides in the *Kristin J*, making his rounds above the Newburgh Locks and Dam as he ferried grain and gravel barges between their mooring cells and the Mulzer works, readying large strings of barges for their transit to the Mississippi, or jockeying huge work barges towering with tall cranes and Caterpillar heavy-equipment lifts. He gave me a lesson in barge pushing, teaching me how to swing the long metal control paddles in the wheelhouse, attached to both the rear and forward rudders, adjust the throttle, and to correct for yaw and drift with a barge attached. At night, when he came for dinner with his wife, Dan told us harrowing stories about managing his mooring cells when winter storms raised the water levels more than forty feet and the raging currents pushed the *Kristin J* around like a child's swimming tube.

At Newburgh we lived as shantyboaters, rapturously high Harlan Hubberites. We existed only for the day at hand and had no purpose beyond enjoying whatever pleasure or surprise drifted by the boat. When I read my history books in the library, occasionally looking out the windows to the river traffic, or hiked back to the *Patience* on Water Street, the Ohio was always flowing beside me, indolent and scenic, a visual drug delivering me to the sublime, guilt-free dopamine of pure happiness. Hubbard had written about this when he contrasted the river wanderers of his day with the original flatboat pioneers.

"The true shantyboater has a purer love for the river than his drifting flatboat predecessors. These were concerned with trade or new land. To him the river is more than a means of livelihood. It is a way of life, the only one he knows which answers his innate longing to be untrammeled and independent, to live on the fringe of society, almost beyond the law, beyond taxes and ownership of property. His drifting downstream is as natural to him as his growing old in the stream of time."

At Newburgh, I learned that river travel extended beyond steering around the barges or tying up to a tree on the banks for the night. I was luxuriating in the stream of time.

16

AS WE MOVED DOWNRIVER TOWARD the big Wabash confluence, I began to feel like Mark Twain in 1897, or Ernest Hemingway in 1954. My death was being prematurely reported, or, to be more accurate, prematurely forecast. Everyone we met in the river towns along the Ohio was convinced that the *Patience* and her crew would soon perish. To the north of our position, at Indianapolis, and to the south, around Nashville and Florence, Alabama, heavy rains during the second week of August had turned the Wabash, the Cumberland, and the Tennessee into raging tributaries, and the rising water levels and debris flow had created treacherous "fans" where they met the Ohio. Everyone said that the fans—mixed deposits of sand, rocks, and trees that formed barrier islands at the mouths of the tributaries—would impale our hull as we moved downriver.

One particularly uncomfortable detail about my impending death was endlessly repeated. The maelstroms at the fans would be so severe that the *Patience* would be briskly spun about and then pulled underwater, grinded so violently along the muddy bottom that the crew members would lose their clothes and eventually float to the top of the river in the nude. We were cautioned once more to warn our families. Our loved ones would have to identify us in a naked state. The agitation of the water and the sand around our waists would be so severe that even our underwear would be ripped off.

But there was favorable news buried inside this upsetting fate for me. At Mount Vernon, Indiana, where we didn't have cell phone service, I pulled the *Patience* into the dock of a barge-cleaning company to inquire about notifying the Coast Guard about the hull of a pleasure boat, which had capsized and was now drifting in the middle of the navigation channel near Diamond Island. The current was brisk near the end of the Mount Vernon Towhead and a helpful worker on the docks caught our line in the air and nimbly pulled us in and secured us to cleats. (The term "towhead" dates back to the 18th century. Towheads are large sandbars or lightly treed islands along the edge of the river that periodically appear and disappear, depending on water levels.) The worker was curious about our trip and expressed concern about the high waters this week, and the capsized boat back at Diamond Island confirmed his fears. He repeated the rote prediction that we would run into trouble at the mouth of the Wabash. We were going to die, he said, but our demise wouldn't be painful.

"They say that the boat gets to spinning around so much that you pass out before you're sucked under," the helpful fellow said. "You will be unconscious, so you won't even know that you're dead."

I was happy for myself. Still, I couldn't believe that the Wabash would do this to me.

If it is possible for a man to be in love with a river, the Wabash has been my lifelong affair. I love the Wabash, I love its unique light, I love the spongy Wabash bottomlands spreading west into southern Illinois, and I love what the Wabash has meant to me for fifty years. I fell for her the first time in 1966 during our California trip in the Piper Cub, when I was fifteen. On our second day out, we arrived early in the morning at Indianapolis to refuel. The weather ahead was not favorable. A low overcast covered most of the upper Mississippi valley and light rain was forecast over our route through southern Indiana and then over our southwest transit to the Mississippi, known as the Kentucky Swale, where we would follow the old Illinois Central tracks down through Mayfield, Wingo, and Fulton, Kentucky. I still remember that Sunday morning in Indianapolis. I was sitting on the asphalt near the fuel ramp at the Sky Harbor Airport, staring down at my maps.

It is emotional even today, recalling how young I was but how my barnstorming instincts were already so mature. "Follow the highways, son," my father would say, "or pick out a river. They're taking you right where you're going and they're as good as a compass." There, on the Cincinnati Sectional Chart, I could see State Highway 40, which was just below the airport, bearing southwest to Terre Haute, where it intersected with a river called the Wabash. The Wabash was infinitely serpentine, winding back on itself in a long series of oxbows that stretched for almost two hundred miles, but its overall bearing tracked due south to the Ohio River, forming the border between Indiana and Illinois. The mouth of the river pointed straight to the Kentucky Swale. The map indicated several small grass strips every ten or twenty miles along the Wabash, where we could always sneak in to land if the clouds got too low or the rain too heavy. After we got the engine propped and we were taxiing out to the runway, I leaned forward from my rear seat and spoke with my brother.

"Steer two-four-zero down Highway 40 to Terre Haute. At the Wabash, turn left to due south. Then I want you to keep that mother in sight off my left wingtip, all the way to Kentucky."

Oh, the Wabash that day. The river, my safety line, was so lovely below. The low overcast bosomed me to the ground and the snarling rain clouds beside me along the Illinois line were nasty and frightful, but they couldn't keep me off the Wabash oxbows, the comely, endless, hypnotic, twisting congeries of her waters, and I followed them as faithfully as a monk chanting Latin at lauds. Two hours later we emerged in bright sunlight on the Ohio, with Paducah and the swale in sight to the west. For the first twenty-five miles of the swale I could push my left rudder pedal to get the tail out of the way and look back out the window for the mouth of the Wabash, using it for a reverse bearing across Kentucky. That night, we made the pinewoods of middle Arkansas, and by forenoon on Monday we were past the Red River and circling in to refuel at Texarkana. Texas, big, expansive, anvil-cloud Texas, 860 miles of hard-ass flying across the dry washes, was ours. I always felt that the Wabash had delivered us to safety in the West and I could never forget her or stop going back.

During college spring breaks, when I would motorcycle down to New Orleans or Galveston, I always turned south off the interstate at Terre Haute, to follow Highway 41 along the Wabash. On the way home, I made architectural pilgrimages along the Wabash to see the covered bridges, and, later, for twenty years, I crossed and recrossed the Wabash dozens of

times on the way toward visiting friends at the Stauffer Mennonite settlement in southern Illinois. The old girder bridge that crossed the Wabash at
Vincennes, delivering me onto Highway 50 and then to the lovely bottomlands of Illinois, was my gateway to the West, and I always drove the span
slowly, savoring the Wabash transit.

I have always been someone much in need of deliverance, and over the
years the Wabash delivered so much for me. I studied the Wabash to learn
river morphology and hydrology, and my lifelong passion as a weekend
forester and firewood vulture began along the river, because I was always
looking to fill my pickup bed or trailer with cured hardwood to bring to
the Mennonites for their cookstoves. I self-educated in botany along the
Wabash. I was fascinated by the way that the silty loams along the Wabash
drainage, a region that soil scientists call the Southwestern Lowlands Natural Region, hosted such rich stands of hackberry, red oak, sycamore maple,
and the rare plains cottonwood tree (*Populus deltoides*). The slightly higher
ground along the streams feeding the Wabash main stem, like the Bonpas
Creek bottoms near Grayville, Indiana, support discrete, thick groves of
the highly prized black walnut (*Juglans nigra*). The roots of black walnuts
secrete the poisonous chemical juglone, which kills all neighboring plants
and tree seedlings, allowing the dominant species to thrive without com-
petition in the highly desirable riparian soil. Today, the black walnuts that
thrive on the creek beds of North America, from the Atlantic Seaboard to
Missouri, are considered some of the world's most valuable hardwoods,
aggressively harvested for furniture board and veneer. A single *Juglans
nigra* trunk, of just "run-of-the-mill" quality, can sell for well over $1,000
per tree. Walnut trees with three-foot base diameters and perfect grains
often sell for $20,000 apiece, and the species is the source of a $200 million
annual export business to China, where most veneers are made.

Several times during my trips west, the Wabash was flooding and I
couldn't get across to Illinois, so I lingered for a couple of days at Vincennes, spending most of my time at the Knox County Public Library,
reading learned tracts on local history or about riparian forests by University of Indiana or Purdue professors. The Wabash at Vincennes became
one of my favorite places, a home away from home. I wanted it to rain hard
before I got there so that I would be trapped for a while by the Wabash
floods. Someday I will take my grandchildren there. They need to see this

old fur-trapping capital and wagon ford on the river, the terminus of the Vincennes Trace, which during the 18th and early 19th centuries was also called the Pennsylvania-Illinois Road, another vanished track through the wilderness that helped create the land of their birth.

The Wabash is classified by hydrologists as an "upstream storage" river, meaning that it tends to flood broadly across thousands of acres along the main river stem, releasing the fast-water energy created by heavy rains horizontally across the land. During major storms, the volume of water is spread sideways and then stored in natural wetlands, which act as flood-control reservoirs, keeping the navigable channel along the river, even if fast-moving, relatively stable. The "flooding regime" of the Wabash is also a kind of natural, mobile land bank. The ground along the vast flatlands or rolling hills adjacent to the river is perpetually renewed with rich deposits of nutrients, valuable minerals, and bottom mud, creating an ideal, permeable surface that soil scientists call "young," or "transient," topsoil. After the annual floods recede, transient topsoil retains moisture quite well and can be returned to high saturation levels even by light rains. Transient soil is so moist that just the natural process of condensation during the summer—the act of nature that creates morning dew—helps retain water. That's advantageous for farmers, and one of the reasons that the Wabash bottoms are considered some of the best agricultural ground in the world.

Wet ground is also ideal for reflecting and refining light. The light along the Wabash is unique, incandescently moody. In the morning, the moist soil along the Wabash valley, and the moist row crops of corn and soybeans, emit pale, rising bands of mists. These usually clear by noon, but in a few hours the rapid temperature inversion of the evening creates new mists. Meanwhile, during the middle of the day, the low-hanging boughs of the oaks and the cottonwoods along the river and its creek bottoms, and the lush understory of ironwood, hazel, and mayapples, retain the mist and seem to push the fuzzy light outward as a soft focus of vegetation. The effect creates days with a perpetual vagueness of the air, an opaqueness, that makes me feel lazy and dreamy. Conversely, solid objects that emerge from this pale light, such as trees or bluffs or fence lines, seem comparatively etched and defined by hard lines. The Hudson River painters called this same quality of light the "river light effect," or the "water lucence" of riverine landscapes. The pastel mists over the Catskills in the background of Asher Durand's *Kindred Spirits*, or the foggy sky merging with indistinct trees in Jasper Cropsey's *Autumn on the Ramapo River*, are examples of this. During his famous painting tours of the West, Albert Bierstadt found this same water lucence at Lake Tahoe, or along the north branch of the Platte.

But to me, the water lucence around Vincennes was the best. Yes, she was running hard that week, racing toward her confluence with the Ohio. Her waters were high. But the Wabash's upstream storage system, dissipating the hydraulic energy by spreading floods across the vast flatlands to the north, would protect the lower channel at the mouth. The lower river would be swift but defined, easy to read at the mouth, and I knew what to do. At the fans, I would turn directly into the confluent wash, "yaw-dampening" the boat, and then nature would push me sideways to safety downriver. I wasn't going to fail to reunite with my beloved Wabash, and her unique light, just because some jackass up at the Mount Vernon Towhead said that she was threatening to rip off my Brooks Brothers boxer shorts.

I wasn't afraid, too, because of what Harlan Hubbard wrote about crossing the Wabash fans during his fabled shantyboat trip downriver in 1944. In February that year he, too, had stopped briefly at the last town in Indiana along the Ohio, Mount Vernon, "an attractive place on high ground with a big hominy factory on the waterfront." After the Hubbards launched the next day, however, their Wabash approach was a series of near disasters. The water was high and the winter winds were brisk. At Slim Island, trying to make the inner passage on the Kentucky side, Hubbard lost control of his shantyboat in a gust of wind and crashed through a grove of willow trees. But he was able to tie up. The next day, at Uniontown in fast water and high winds, he was trying to make a lunch stop at the bend around the Highland Rocks by tying a line to a small tree. But somehow the line got looped around his wife's leg, pinning her against the shantyboat's kevel, and the current was so fast that the line pulled the tree underwater. Hubbard was trying to manage all of this from his johnboat skiff out on the water, and he couldn't hear his wife's anguished cries for help. "She had to endure the pain until the boat swung into dead water and the tension was relaxed. No severe injury was caused."

The next day, nearing the Wabash fans, Hubbard had to turn off at the last moment from the safe inner passage around Wabash Island because another boat was blocking his way, forcing him into the windy, turbulent right channel that ran directly past the mouth of the Wabash. For more than an hour, the Hubbards had to row hard on the shantyboat to stay off Wabash Island as they roller-coastered over the waves at the confluence, barely in control of their boat. "The Wabash flowed in through low ground," Hubbard wrote, "and again we had the feeling of limitless inundation." In brisk currents and a strong following wind, and still rowing hard to stay off Wabash Island, the Hubbards screamed past the Raliegh Bar and finally made a rough landing on the Kentucky side, crashing through a screen of locust trees. They tied up for the night with little protection from the wind. When they looked from their shantyboat porch over to the Illinois side, the Hubbards finally realized how bad the flooding was that year. The forest ground across the river in Illinois, three miles from the Wabash, was completely submerged.

Barely, the Hubbards had survived the Wabash fans. Their lovely marriage survived, too, all the way to New Orleans and back. After World War II, the Hubbards built a simple log cabin on the banks of the Ohio at Payne Hollow, Kentucky. They devoted their lives to simplicity and frugality, becoming almost as known as Henry David Thoreau for making an existential stand against industrialization and its corruptions. They made a lot of art, published journals, and lived off the berries they harvested in baskets in the Kentucky woods, their garden, and the catfish they caught in the river. They mentored to success their young friend and protégé, the next holder of the Henry David Thoreau chair, the incomparable Wendell Berry.

The Hubbards were together and working their Payne Hollow garden until their marriage's peaceable end. In 1986, Anna made her final passage out of Payne Hollow, aged eighty-four years. Harlan left the banks of the Ohio his last time two years later, at eighty-eight. What a couple they were, what an example they set, what a marriage they had. Harlan's *Shantyboat* and *Payne Hollow Journal* will be regarded for millennia as American classics.

I loved the story of the Hubbards taking the Wabash fans and what it meant. Harlan Hubbard! The shantyboat adventurer, the sage of Payne Hollow, Thoreauvian man and writer, nonpareil. The great riverman and his book were my mentors for this trip. He didn't completely botch the Wabash fans. But Hubbard wasn't in full control or command of his shantyboat either. He just pushed past Poker Point, frantically rowing, skittering in the gusts, trusting the waters to carry him to safety down past the Raliegh Bar.

It would have to be the same for me. To reach the great waters, I had to make another Wabash transit, damn the torpedoes and this year's flooding. And no dockside jackass back upriver was going to talk me out of it.

After we got below Evansville, Deb Satterfield often steered the *Patience* alone for long stretches. She was an excellent addition to the crew because her helm management was flawless. She was the *Patience* compass maven and map boss. She always knew where we were on the daymarks and the mile markers and her demeanor at the helm was vigilant but relaxed.

Deb had one quality in particular that is vital when running a boat. Her "cockpit composure" was very sound, verbal, and direct. She clearly enunciated her intentions when we were facing busy river traffic, and she possessed the modesty to accept my advice if I disagreed. The water on the lower Ohio was fast that week and busy with commercial traffic. Often, we had one or more long barge strings overtaking us from behind, and then a big tow moving upriver would suddenly appear at the next bend, swinging wide across the channel with its forward barges to make the long turn around the curve in the river. At Dutch Island below Evansville, a long sandbar curved southwest for almost a mile along the Indiana banks, narrowing the channel.

Deb pointed backward with her chin to the traffic behind, and then motioned with her free hand toward the curving line of buoys and the barge traffic two miles ahead.

"Okay, so that traffic behind us is playing the Indiana side. I'm going to cheat the buoys on the Kentucky banks to stay off that incoming."

She didn't have to say more. I understood her plan. We wanted to stay as far as we could off the Indiana banks and the bars at Dutch Island, to avoid the barges coming downriver, but the barges coming upriver were now pretty much covering the Kentucky side, too. For the moment, we were pinched for space. But we knew that the captain moving upriver would gradually straighten his load for the middle of the channel as soon as he got past the buoys opposite Dutch Bend Light. When we got there, if the fit still looked too tight, we could always reduce power and "cheat" the buoys by steering for the shallows just outside of the channel, indicating to the captain ahead that we knew he was there and that the *Patience* would remain safely out of his way until he passed. Five minutes later, as the Kentucky side cleared of his barges, the captain of the oncoming tug would sound his horn. Then we'd know it was safe to sneak back into the channel and slowly pass his line of barges.

This practice is also called "cheating the bars," and it is essential at the river bends in heavy traffic, so that the captains could "paint" us with their binoculars or their radar and conclude that we were a reliable boat. When the upriver push boats got abeam and we were all comfortably passing each other with a safe separation, the captains sounded two short blasts—"Thanks, wooden pleasure craft"—and then they walked out to their wheelhouse decks, waving their ball caps and taking photos of the *Patience* with their cell phones.

Within hours of her first day on the *Patience*, Deb was perfect at cheating the bars. She seemed to instinctively understand the most important principle of navigating around the long commercial barge strings—always being "a mile ahead of your boat." The barges a mile or two ahead might be blocking the channel for now, but that wasn't a threat because you weren't sharing space with those barges yet. But you had to be able to "see" where those barges were headed, planning ahead for your separation space in fifteen or twenty minutes.

Deb was so good at this that, when we were on the roof deck piloting together, her mind was mine and mine was hers and our river odyssey was joined at the brain.

Deb and I spent hours together up there, talking and laughing, one of us running down occasionally for food or ice water, enjoying the passing landscapes and the roar of the boat horns. Our lives were in similar places at the moment and this was a big part of the *Patience* journey for me, sharing recent experience with Deb.

Like so many baby boomers, Deb had taken a sabbatical from life to manage her parents' eldercare. Her stepfather, a distinguished, retired U.S. Army general, was ninety-five, but still maintaining a busy schedule in military affairs, traveling to seminars, making videos about leadership, fund-raising for conservative political groups. Her mother, a gracious southern belle, was twenty years younger but beginning to experience the forgetfulness and frailties of old age. Deb completely managed their lives in Nashville, including the general's busy travel and speaking schedule. When she came onto the *Patience* for a week or so, Deb hired eldercare workers or asked family members to take over at the house with her parents. Deb was also close to her daughter, who was just finishing nursing school and enjoying life with a boyfriend who was an interesting, fun industrial engineer. She considered her time on the *Patience* a vacation, a mental-health break.

When I told her about my own recent time living in Maine helping to take care of my mother, Deb was particularly interested in the complex dynamics of my large family, and impressed with how my mother had bravely faced change after my father had died when she was forty-nine. My mother still had three children in the house, problems managing the difficult launches of a couple of my brothers, and she was even raising a couple of her grandchildren for months at a time. Yet, in quick succession, in her early fifties, she had gone back to classes to upgrade her education as a social worker, sold her large Victorian house, fixed up a new place, and was beginning to ask all of the right questions about the capons in the red dresses who run the Roman Catholic Church. She was politically active and busy with her book groups and spoke with most of her children on the phone once a week. Now that she finally had a life of her own, not a barracks of unruly children to run, she had become a completely different person from the mother who raised us. But I didn't fully understand the significance of her brave midlife transition until I talked about it with someone. My times on the *Patience* bridge with Deb provided valuable talk therapy.

In the last thirty years of her life, Pat Buck was a gray-hair on fire. Slowly coming to terms with that, and missing her, was as much a part of my trip to New Orleans as learning how to play the sandbars or scrambling over the levees with the electric bike to run for fuel.

"She changed, Rinker, she changed," Deb said. "Not many of us can say that about our mothers."

One night, on that last stretch of the Ohio before the Wabash, my ribs were particularly painful and I dreamed about my mother again. My reveries had turned to a memory about one of my best weeks in Maine with her. There was a shortcut from town, through an orchard of apple and cherry trees in front of my mother's porch, that had become overgrown with vines and Virginia creeper, and I wanted to clear it so that she had better afternoon light and the pedestrians had an easier time cutting through the woods. The town library stood just through the neighboring parking lot and the used book store was on my mother's side of the fruit trees, and she seemed to enjoy sitting on her porch and watching the traffic, chatting with the people cutting through. My brothers didn't want me to trim the trees. An overgrown path would discourage people in town from coming through and bothering my mother, they thought. But my mother had other plans.

"Trim the path," she told me.

My mother considered "her shortcut" good for the town. Young boys could wander through the trees from Main Street and shoot their slingshots. There were a lot of new mothers in Damariscotta and when they came through pushing their strollers she could see their babies and inspect the books they had borrowed from the library. When it came to the path from town, she didn't care about her privacy. She wanted to sit on her porch and greet the traffic passing through.

I carried an orchard ladder and my pruning saw over to her house in my pickup and worked for several afternoons clearing her new path. From the orchard, I could stare down from my ladder and see my mother at the kitchen table, drinking her tea and reading her novel. The windows were open to the salt breeze from the Damariscotta and occasionally she stood up, walked to the sink, and washed a few dishes or filled her teapot. Then she walked out to her porch, sat on her rocker, and greeted a few babies, sometimes holding them in her lap. The brittle branches of the cherry trees lightly scraped my face as I looked at her through a screen of leaves.

Now I was on the Ohio on the long straightaway after Diamond Island. In the far depth of field stretching toward Long Landing, I could see that same, fixed image of her, content in her kitchen or on her porch as I glanced over from my orchard ladder. I was giving her just the mixture of companionship and privacy—distant, but shared—that she enjoyed. I wondered whether it was the dreaminess of the river, or the romance of the kind of travel I was doing, that helped deliver that image of her to me. Perhaps that

portrait of her would have reappeared no matter what I was doing. Or perhaps it was the time of year—it was just one year ago, in mid-August, when
I trimmed her trees. But then I realized that factors like that didn't matter. I
wasn't thinking of her and her death with remorse any longer. I was joyfully
happy for her. We can't possibly see where our mother is just now or how
she is doing. We settle instead on a happy image that pleases us forever. I
was freezing in time a moment when we were both purposeful and content
together. I was on the lower Ohio between Indiana and Kentucky and the
mother who had changed so much was blissfully content in Maine.

The river rats along the Ohio continued to insist that the *Patience* crew was
doomed. Danny was back on the boat now and every time we had to endure another conversation about our pending deaths we looked into each
other's faces, not sure whether we should be laughing or crying.

Six miles above the Wabash, at Uniontown, Kentucky, we pulled into
the cement town ramp to refuel. As we stowed our gas, a middle-aged man
in a dark green johnboat puttered over from the channel and coasted to a
stop against the side of the *Patience*, tying up to one of our kevels. He was a
local sport fisherman who traveled the river upstream past Slim Island and
Mount Vernon, sometimes even up to Diamond Island, but never downriver
past the Wabash. He was concerned that we had ignored the urgent weather
reports about three days of heavy rains in Indianapolis, all of which was now
fiercely running downstream on the Wabash, with specific instructions to
find the flatboat *Patience* and remove the underwear of her crew.

"You're not going any further today, are you?" he said.

"Sure," I said. "I'd like to get below Old Shawneetown."

"Well, I wouldn't," he said. "You don't know the river around here. No one
moves past the confluence in conditions like this. The Wabash is running like
a banshee. The currents at the mouth are going to push you into the bars along
Wabash Island. Even the barge tows don't run in conditions like this."

While the himbo in the johnboat was saying this, a tug pushing a short
string of grain barges was coming around Lost Creek Bend, just below the
Uniontown landing. The tug had obviously come upriver that morning,
right through the Wabash fans. I was tired of dealing with these dumbass

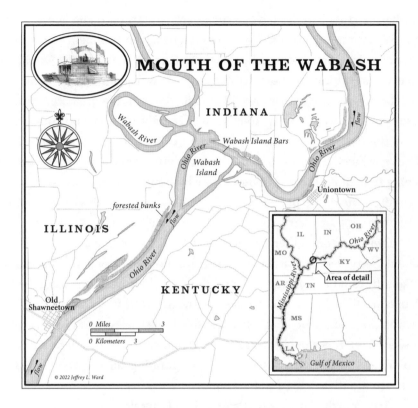

Hoosiers. I was angry. I started our motor and told that dullard angler to untie from my kevel and cast off.

"Danny," I said. "Pull in the lines. Get below and stow everything securely. We're taking the Wabash, *now*."

I knew exactly what I wanted to do because I had been thinking about it for several days, reading my Harlan Hubbard and studying my river maps. The sail line at the top of Wabash Island hugged the Indiana banks and then curved along the bars past the mouth of the river, continuing to hug the starboard side for three miles to the bottom of the island. When I could see the main navigational fix at the river mouth, the Wabash River Light, I would reduce power to judge the current and then power back up, turning the bow north-by-northwest. The flow at the mouth would be torrential and I would have to yaw-dampen—turn directly into the current—a lot more. I wasn't even going to consider remaining with the dominant Ohio River stem because I didn't have enough power, or the right hull, to cut through the confluence wash and keep off the bars along

Wabash Island. I would have to turn hard to starboard and actually enter the Wabash mouth in a sideways crab, letting the confluence flow do the work of carrying me downriver past the bars on the island. It would look like we were pointed northwest straight toward the Illinois banks, but our track over the bottom would actually be with the greatest volume of water, which was moving southwest. My only job that morning was to hold the *Patience* into that hard crab, to ride the fastest water on the top banks, which would keep me off the Wabash Island bars below. I wasn't going to fight nature and flood-regime hydraulics here. I was going to surrender to them. My plan was to surf the Wabash mouth sideways, letting the oncoming tributary flow carry me to safety along the Illinois banks.

There was one other problem that I had to anticipate, which I knew about from reading Harlan Hubbard. The flooding near the mouth of the Wabash would be considerable and the bars along Wabash Island, and the banks on the Illinois side, would be covered with water, depriving me of distinct references on land. My maps would be useless and I wouldn't have a second reference to check against my compass. I just had to be confident, holding a north-by-northwest bearing, pointing all the way across the Wabash mouth toward a watery Illinois.

"Steer northwest, ignore the rest," I told myself.

Danny came up to the roof console to watch me steer just as Wabash Island came into view. The river conditions ahead of us didn't look that bad yet, and he was fascinated by the contradiction between what the locals said about the river and what we were actually finding.

"We're going to die," he said.

"Have you prepared your family for this?"

"Don't worry," Danny said. "I've secured my underwear with duct tape."

Passing the Wabash River Light and then plunging into the confluence was visually thrilling. The south flow from the Wabash, brown from the muddy turbulence churned up by the rains, slammed into the west flow of the Ohio and immediately plummeted downward, forming a beige undercurrent that eddied out into the channel and then abruptly kited west with the stronger Ohio flow. The high closing speed of the Wabash flow set up a large V of ripples that ran diagonally toward the bars on Wabash Island. The wind was pushing hard from the west, momentarily raising the ripples and churning them into whitecaps.

When I pushed the throttle all the way forward and racked the wheel over, pointing directly into the brown Wabash, I deliberately turned harder than I had to, swung the bow to the right more quickly, then briskly turned the wheel halfway back to induce some adverse yaw, pivoting the *Patience* broadside into the west breeze.

The hull was buffeting a lot now in the turbulent flow, but I could see that the *Patience* wanted to hold her heading if I just pushed my wheel hard. *Steer northwest, ignore the rest,* I kept repeating to myself. *Bearing 320 degrees. Just hold this baby at 320 and hang on through the waves.*

The gyrational swing of the bow against the green Indiana banks was beautiful. The wind slamming in from the west pushed us toward the Wabash mouth, but then the ripple flow from the tributary pushed us away from the mouth, a pincer effect that held us solid at a 60-degree angle to the banks, seemingly motionless. The *Patience* just stalled beautifully into the current right there, a big old poplar bathtub sliding sideways through the confluence.

I held her hard. It was difficult figuring out what was happening as we crabbed across the mouth because there were so many distractions. The hull was bouncing up and down in the rough water. The firewalled engine was roaring and I was afraid it would overheat. The cavitating prop was screaming every time the stern rose and fell. My apparent wind indicator, the American flag behind me, was snapping and skittering around on its pole. Beside me, Danny gripped the console with his free hand, staring down to his multimedia display of cell phones and laptops. Every time a new wave banged the hull, he looked like he was about to deliver a baby.

My plan seemed to be working. We were pointed northwest into Illinois, but I could gradually discern that we were tracking due southwest. *Hold that 320 degrees.* In the rough water, the bow sometimes bounced over to 340 degrees, and then back toward west to 300 degrees. But I couldn't worry about every swing of the compass needle. It was our trending that mattered, and we seemed to be trending well, safely inside the river mouth and well off the Wabash Island bars.

As we neared the far edge of the Wabash mouth, a greenbelt of tall trees flashed by us sideways—we'd "made" Illinois. The west wind was now blocked by the trees and the muddy mosaic of Wabash water was beginning to dissipate into the stem current of the Ohio. I gradually turned off

my northwest heading. By the end of Wabash Island our bow was confidently pointing downriver and we were right over the sailing line.

We were now well past the fans and I retarded the throttle to quarter
power to see what the extra current from the tributary was doing to the
boat, and we were still booking eight or nine knots past the Illinois banks.
It was thrilling being on that boat now. The breeze off the Kentucky side
was brisk, refreshing against my face, and the sun's glare off the water made
it hard to read the compass. But I didn't need a binnacle now. Accelerated
by the massive Wabash flow, the current was running strong and direct
toward Old Shawneetown, and the *Patience* almost steered itself. I was
elated to be past the Wabash and now my mind was a spinning jumble of
thought and complementary thought, time and timelessness, memory and
memory enhanced, the souls of everyone who had brought me here to this
river and the souls of the people I had not yet met. I was a joyful riverman
with a mind that was wandering through time.

I kicked the rudder hard and looked back to the Wabash mouth for
a final bearing across Kentucky. In the turbulence, the Piper Cub tail was
bouncing hard and the flying wires wailed the river stanzas from *Leaves
of Grass*. When I turned back forward, our bearing across the water to the
Raliegh Bar was 220 degrees. Harlan Hubbard! That old barnstorming man
who taught me to use the rivers didn't know the half of my takeaway from
that. The coefficient of toughness is sensitivity. Micah Flint at the Chickasaw
Bluffs. I needed to find a place ahead to weld better anchors. I looked back to
the Wabash once more and thanked her for another good transit.

Now I had resumed my journey on the main stem of the Ohio. The sun
and the wind were refreshing against my face. My brain was swimming in
dopamine. Walt Whitman licensed me to sing songs to myself.

Oh, my river, my love, my princess, my raging Wabash, thank you
again. Over and out. I will be back.

We camped that night in the placid waters along the Illinois banks behind
Sturgeon Island, about twelve miles below Old Shawneetown. Danny made
us another one of his great dinners and I built a fire from driftwood. We
drank wine until late.

I was giddy about passing the Wabash, overjoyed that we were nearing the great waters of the Mississippi. I suddenly remembered an old Tin Pan Alley tune, "On the Banks of the Wabash, Far Away," which was one of the most popular songs in America in the years before World War I. The songwriter, Paul Dresser, was a legendary performer and sheet music publisher who had grown up along the Wabash in Terre Haute. He became rich and famous in New York and wrote the song to express his longing for his boyhood home. The song came to represent an industrialized America's wistful memories of an earlier and simpler agrarian life.

I found the lyrics to "On the Banks of the Wabash, Far Away" on my cell phone and decided to sing its famous chorus to my crew. Danny and Deb laughed at me as I stood before the driftwood fire and performed. But I didn't care. I pitched my voice into the river breeze and loved myself and this trip and all the people who make their Wabash transits.

> *Oh, the moonlight's fair tonight along the Wabash,*
> *From the fields there comes the breath of new-mown hay.*
> *Through the sycamores the candle lights are gleaming,*
> *On the banks of the Wabash, far away.*

The congested mouth of the Ohio at Cairo, Illinois, looking from the Kentucky banks toward the Ohio River Bridge. Threading through the steel gauntlet of barge strings at Cairo was one of the most difficult navigation challenges of the trip.

17

THE MOUTH OF THE OHIO at its confluence with the Mississippi, at Cairo, Illinois, is almost one mile wide. The merging of the rivers spreads a massive, triangular fan of rippling water and sandbars to the banks of three states—Illinois, Kentucky, and Missouri. The green Ohio waters closing against the muddier, brown Mississippi form a sharp beige line that points due south right over the best sailing channel. The Ohio is actually considered the main stem of the Mississippi because its discharge after moderate rains, at 300,000 cubic feet per second, exceeds the flow of the Mississippi moving south from Thebes, Illinois, which is roughly 200,000 cubic feet per second. At Cairo Point, the view across this cosmos of water, from the tip of the Angelo Towhead to the north, to the sandy banks of the Mississippi at Wickliffe, Kentucky, is majestic.

But the hydrological wonder at the confluence is deceptive. The riverway leading to the Mississippi is actually a narrow, man-made chute. More than 50 percent of America's agricultural exports, corn, soybeans, and vegetable oils, and 35 percent of America's basic industrial products, finished steel, scrap iron, crude oil, sand, and cement, passes through this space to reach the great global port one thousand miles downriver at New Orleans. The Ohio-Mississippi confluence is one of the globe's busiest cargo hubs, like the Suez and Panama Canals, or the great switching yard of the Northern Pacific Railway at North Platte, Nebraska. The confluence at Cairo is a giant switching station on water, and every day it is frantic with commer-cial traffic.

More than 1,500 barges, often packaged in strings of forty-two or more, move south along the Mississippi during an average week, while more than a thousand mostly empty barges pass them going upriver. Most of the nine-thousand-horsepower tugs moving barges down the Missis-sippi, and many of the tugs pushing cargo upriver, make huge, sweeping turns—called "flanking out"—into the Ohio, penetrating the mouth at Cairo to split their loads up for various destinations across the inland waters. Additional barges are picked up at Cairo for the long tow down to New Orleans, or for trips north up the Mississippi to St. Louis and St. Paul. Simultaneously, a dozen or more long strings moving down the Ohio are backed up all the way to Mound City, waiting their turn to switch out their loads at Cairo and then flank out of the mouth and into the Mississippi.

As we approached the last big turn on the Ohio, at the Future City Light, the four-mile view down the straightaway to the Cairo Highway Bridge at the mouth looked almost waterless—there was no sense of traveling a river anymore. The commercial channel below was a cluttered expanse of rusty barges and tugboat wakes. On either side of the river, massive "anchor fleets" of barges, with upward of one hundred hulls apiece, crowded the channel. The navigable space in between was clogged with tugs pushing barge strings, maneuvering around each other, stopping at the edge of the channel to receive or off-load barges, switching crews, loading supplies, refueling from river tenders. In the midst of this melee, thirty or more nimble switch boats were darting back and forth, bumper cars at an amusement park, separating a barge or two from the anchor fleets, setting them free in the current to race around to push them from the other end, skittering them over to another anchor fleet position, or to a waiting barge string. The crisscrossing of the tugboat and switch boat wakes was a confusing, Jackson Pollock whitewater mélange. Often, the clearances between the switch boats and the barges were just fifty or sixty yards—from afar, the boats and the barges appeared to be colliding. The clear space in between them was narrow and fleeting. For thirty seconds or more I could see a clear path down to the highway bridge at the mouth, but then my field of vision was suddenly closed by barges and switch boats moving diagonally across the river from the anchor fleets. The Ohio River below the Future City Light was no longer the serene, scenic space between the national forests that I had known for the past two months. The cargo thoroughfare before me was menacing and seemingly impenetrable, a steel gauntlet of constantly moving hulls.

Still, I felt euphoric that morning, almost mystically drawn to the congestion I had to cross to reach the great waters. After so many people had told me that I couldn't safely push the *Patience* through Cairo, my determination was manic. For one thousand miles along the Ohio I had seen only a few private pleasure boats—fishermen, houseboats, water-skiers—and then only in safe, recreational pods around urban areas, where the boaters could rely on the convenience of marinas, fuel pumps, and waterside restaurants. Except for the tugs and barges, or the occasional professional fisherman, the river was deserted. Nobody could possibly know whether or not the Wabash fans were dangerous, or about the obstructions at the big confluence at Cairo. They had never been there. Still, they were convinced that we were doomed.

Mike Binkley had come aboard just upriver at Metropolis and we were the only two on the *Patience* as we approached the Mississippi. Mike's presence was reassuring, a tonic that relieved my worries about the difficult stretch of river ahead. Mike had also heard the predictions about the *Patience* being sucked under by the whirlpools and all of our clothes being torn off. We were navigating together at the roof console as we passed the petroleum docks at Urbandale and then rounded the shallow bend past the Future City Light. Mike nodded downriver to the wall of barges ahead.

"Everyone says we are going to die here," he said. "Are you prepared?"

"My family has been advised."

Financially, Mike is bipolar. He thinks nothing of laying down $4,000 to overhaul a motorcycle engine, or spending $20,000 for a mint Infiniti convertible hardtop, but he is miserly about everything else. The upholstery in his pickup and on his pontoon boat is a grimy patchwork of duct tape and sunburnt plastic. He hates the idea of spending money on new clothes.

"What kind of underwear are you wearing today, Rinker?" he said.

"Brooks Brothers boxer shorts. They're the only ones I can wear."

"Jesus," Mike said. "How much are they running nowadays?"

"It's ridiculous," I said. "The last time I got them it was twenty-six dollars apiece. I have a love-hate relationship with Brooks Brothers."

"That's an awful lot of money to be leaving at the bottom of the Mississippi River, Rinker. Why can't you just shop at Walmart?"

"After today, Mike," I said, "it won't matter."

"Right," Mike said. "When you're dead, it's pretty hard to worry about your boxer shorts."

Just above the flood walls at Cairo, I powered back to see what the current was doing to the *Patience.* The water was fast, but not dangerously so, and I planned to linger at the edge of the channel for a few minutes to stare downriver and figure out the traffic. Ahead, approaching the Cairo Highway Bridge, there was a big white Ingram tug in the middle of the channel, pushing a string of twenty or more barges toward the Mississippi, not yet committed to its flanking-out turn, so I couldn't tell whether it would angle wide to starboard to enter the Mississippi going upriver, or angle to port at the mouth, to push south. Switch boats with barges darted back and forth across the river, temporarily blocking my view of the big Ingram string. But then, for a minute or two, the switch-boat traffic cleared and I could see ahead of me again. The Ingram wake was placid and wide, very inviting, and I considered just powering up and catching the big white boat. Either way it was turning after the bridge, I could use the Ingram to block for me at the mouth, following it through the narrows until I was clear of the traffic and safely embarked on the Mississippi.

But when I looked behind the *Patience,* I could see that I would have to decide right here what to do, and decide quickly. Three oil tenders were moving downriver in what the tug captains call a "unicorn formation"— one tender ahead, cutting the water, with the other two behind, side by side. They were rapidly bearing down on our position. Apparently, they were navigating the mouth together as a party of three, for mutual protection, creating an obstacle big enough for the other traffic to have to clear their way. The unicorn tenders were moving fast and would overtake me soon, either forcing me aside into the shallows or into the tangle of traffic ahead.

I considered pulling off to the flood walls and waiting at the edge of the channel, to let the tenders pass first. But then an instinct that would

rule that day and rule the rest of the trip suddenly gripped me, a combined response that felt at once like both panic and calm.

Don't wait. Don't linger. Yes, you can let the tenders pass and then decide, but the space ahead of you might be even worse after that. Take the opportunity you have, now. Do it, go for the mouth.

I didn't think about it any longer. I didn't enunciate my plan to Mike or ask for his opinion. I firewalled the motor and pointed straight for the protection of the Ingram wake. I was going for it purely on instinct. The red tenders behind me weren't going to tangle with the big Ingram boat and I could own the space between them. To reach the mouth, I would be married at the stern to the Ingram boat.

As I gained on the big white rig and the alluring whitewater pond behind it, I was elated to not have a plan. I was indulging purified action, moving downriver by fiat, by impulse, by believing in myself and what the waters were going to do with me and the *Patience*. As I got closer, the Ingram stern trembled and yawed sideways to port. Her stacks were flooding out

black exhaust now. The wake was transitioning from still pond to turbulent rapids. Good. The captain was readying his flanking turn, pointing his
forward barges toward the Illinois banks, which was slowing his load and
allowing me to catch up. I still didn't know whether he was turning north
to flank-out of the mouth upriver, or just gaining every last yard of space
along the Illinois flood walls to give him more room to suddenly flank
south, downriver. But it didn't matter because I was closing on the boat and
I was committed now, married to the Ingram rig and its wake, and I would
turn behind him whichever way he flanked and be in protected white space
from any other traffic.

I quickly looked back and the red tenders behind were falling away.
They were giving maneuvering space to the Ingram string, which was giving maneuvering space to me.

The switch boats were still darting back and forth between the anchor
fleets all around me. The Illinois side was busier. The captains didn't seem
to care a whit about traffic and pointed straight at me before suddenly
turning off forty yards away. Sometimes they were pushing a barge or two
and sometimes they were racing by unhitched. But I filtered them out of
my attention, out of my peripheral vision. They didn't matter because they
were certainly not going to mess with the Ingram string.

When I entered the Ingram boat's whitewater pool, I throttled back to
maintain a forty-yard separation from the stern ahead of me. The curling
wake lightened the *Patience* on her hull and I could feel that I was actually
surfing the nine-thousand-horsepower wake, buoyantly riding it, like a kite
in warm winds, or a small car drawn forward by the suction of a speeding
semitrailer. I felt the perfect union of boats. I throttled back more to let
the tug wake carry me and avoid getting too close to the stern. I was the
caboose to the Ingram string now, effortlessly riding the wake.

Coasting in the Ingram wake, I learned another maneuvering trick that
would help me the rest of the way south along the faster water of the Mississippi. I was zigzagging a lot, making small, gentle S-turns in the bumpy
wake of the tug, to maintain a consistent follow of the tug without gaining
too much on the stern. Forty yards out, maintain that forty. Push hard to
port for three or four seconds, then hard back to starboard, and I was continuously presenting my bow and gunwales to the wake sideways, slowing
me against the stern ahead. The wake was carrying me. The gentle turns

were keeping me positioned in a slight yaw on top of the foam, at just the right distance from the screaming turbines ahead.

The harder I pushed to starboard, then back to port, the better the *Patience* turned. I realized that the induced yaw of my turns considerably improved the handling qualities of my poplar tub. Each time I swung back to remain on top of the bouncing foam, my stern swayed out and wallowed, transferring my center of gravity forward toward the bow, which dipped low and cut the water better. Induced yaw turns. To turn left, I pushed hard to the right and then quickly turned back to the left, shifting my hull weight to the bow. The boat turned better with the extra bow weight and that is how I sailed the rest of the way south. *Turn against yourself and then back.* The *Patience* responded briskly each time and gained a better purchase in the turn.

I still couldn't tell which way the Ingram captain was going to turn out of the mouth. He continued to play the Illinois banks hard and pointed the forward barges of his string toward the sandy beach at Cairo Point, but he was not yet directly facing the brown Mississippi flow. I couldn't see much ahead of me, except the stern of the Ingram boat and the wake I was surfing. The tall pilothouse of the Ingram boat sat atop two lower decks, blocking my forward view, and the thousand-foot line of barges obliquely pointing toward Illinois blocked my view of the Mississippi. If there was a downriver string out there, coming past the Angelo Towhead, I wouldn't see it.

It was glorious riding the frothy carpet of the Ingram wake now. The captain was angling his load away from Cairo Point, but just a little, and I could tell that he was beginning his turn, which would be north, upriver. A film of white heat was rising from his stacks, tremulously scorching the air above, signaling that he was powering up for his big turn toward Missouri. The noise from the tug was thunderous and the wake was bouncing back at me in high, peaked waves, but it was amazing how well the overbuilt *Patience* held in the rough water. The captain looked back from his helm, through his rear window, a couple of times. I knew that he had me on his radar, but he kept checking to see that I was there, trusting me, perhaps, to know what I was doing. I felt joined to the captain and that Ingram boat. He knew that I was riding his wake to the mouth, using it as protection from threatening traffic.

Physicality and emotion fused into pure excitement behind that tug. The *Patience* bounced and yawed in the choppy wake and I kept wrestling her sideways to maintain my forty yards and to prevent the undertow of the wake from pulling me toward the stern ahead of me. *Present sideways, present sideways.* The wheel returning from each yaw flew over my hands, burning new calluses into my palms, and I wished I had thought to put on leather gloves. I couldn't see forward now at all—the swaying Ingram stern blocked everything ahead—but, inexplicably, I felt confident and jaunty. *Ride it, boy, just ride that wake and endure, presenting sideways to the stern.* The Ingram wake was coming back at me now in huge waves, forcing my bow up at a steep angle, then plunging us down the back side of the wave. Hope and prayer and confidence and defiance of peril fused as one now. Every emotion on the continuum was joined and the same.

I didn't want to turn from the protection of the Ingram wake, but the beige sail line curling down the Mississippi was forty-five degrees off my port bow now, and I knew it was time to make my turn away from the mouth. Just as I turned, however, the forward bows of a string of barges coming down-river were turning into the mouth just off our starboard side. The downriver string was angling around the Ingram string to come inside the Ohio, a magnificently beautiful maneuvering of two passing loads curling around each other, one entering the mouth from above, one exiting the mouth from the Ohio. The down-coming string would soon block my path to the Mississippi, but the enormous wake from the Ingram tug was crashing against the distant Kentucky banks, curling up against the sandy river sides, and then racing furiously back toward the middle of the river. The lifting water racing back from Kentucky was being fed by more wake from the Ingram boat, creating a constantly rising level of good water between the *Patience* and the Kentucky bank. The down-coming barges had to turn against this powerful wake, which was slowing them in their turn, giving me more time to race in front of the barges. The sluice created by the nine thousand horses of the Ingram turbines was offering me a brief window of opportunity.

I firewalled and turned hard to starboard, held that position in the bouncing wake for three or four seconds, and then let go of the wheel as the adverse yaw flew the helm past my hands. I gripped hard again when we were facing south and pointed straight toward the Wickliffe bars in Kentucky. The Ingram wake overran my stern and I could hear water splashing down there, but this was good because I could feel my prop biting better in the deeper water. Everything about this sudden contingency was working for me.

We were flying south now, gaining, gaining on the down-coming barges and winning the race to safe space in the middle of the river. I had to turn fairly soon because I knew that the barges turning into the mouth would kill my water from the Ingram wake. I swung wide at first because the captain turning into the mouth probably had me painted on his radar and I didn't want him to worry about the crazy pleasure boat skittering around the mouth directly in his path. I was almost outside the channel buoys once I made the turn west toward Missouri, but it seemed like there was plenty of water ahead. When I was safely past the front bows of the barge string entering the mouth I turned away from the Wickliffe bars along the Kentucky bank and slid due west along the barges as close as I dared. But now I could see the beige sail line of the Mississippi and I powered back and slowly turned south again, downriver.

We were clear of the confluence, with good separation from both barge strings. When I looked at the compass, my heart surged. My bearing for New Orleans, one thousand miles away, was due south 180 degrees. We were on the great waters, safe.

Cairo came to represent for me a vital milestone of the trip, and not simply because at the big confluence of the Ohio and the Mississippi I had reached my halfway point. I realized at Cairo that I had been traveling all summer in an almost complete vacuum of information—actually, it was a zone of complete misinformation. My boatbuilder and original adviser, and the onboard river guide he recommended, were useless because they were reenactors and thus unfamiliar with authentic river travel. All of their stops were prearranged with marinas, state tourism officials, sponsors, and caterers, who met them every night at safe berths with truckloads of supplies and assistance. They were protected from the true vagaries of the river, and neither of them knew much about the weather, tributary flow, or even how to pick a good campsite. The situation was no better once I had launched on the Monongahela. Almost all of the advice I was receiving from people along the river, except for the occasional well-informed river rat like Ron Richardson at Brandenburg, Kentucky, was wrong.

I would see even fewer pleasure boats on the Mississippi—over the next two months, traveling one thousand miles, I passed a total of four pleasure boats on the river. But there were *stories* about how dangerous the river was. Everybody living along the Ohio or the Mississippi had distant relatives, or old family friends, who had lost someone on the river. The memories of the 1927 flood, or the 2010 flood, were potent but largely unexamined. Day after day I met farmers who had tilled or raised cattle along the river for all of their lives, Mississippi Delta residents who worked every day at fuel storage depots or grain elevators along the river, merchants and distributors who delivered supplies to the town landings along the river for the commercial tugboats, but they never ventured out on the river themselves. The Mississippi was deemed to be unsafe because it was *rumored* to be unsafe.

On the *Patience*, I wasn't sailing a river that endlessly twisted in oxbows a thousand miles south to New Orleans. I was negotiating a culture of misinformation. Initially, I wouldn't always be able to separate truth from half-truth, or sound advice from misguided advice. I just had to plunge forward and fend for myself. After Cairo, I realized that I was growing increasingly comfortable and even joyful about that.

Mike and I spent a delightful, educational time on the Mississippi for the next two days, learning our new waters. I could see right away that we were on a different, faster river now. The sail line hugged the Kentucky shore and then crossed the river and ran close to the Missouri side, and the stone revetments holding in the banks seemed to fly by. The water rippled and raced over the underwater wing dams, which reached almost into the navigable channel, forcing me to take the buoys quite seriously on the Mississippi. This river was fast, with the current scurrying past the buoys and the wing dams in underwater swirls and cavitation bubbles, which ascended swiftly from below and then broke through the surface, where they were caught by the wind and threw off a spray.

Above Pritchard Point there were several long barge strings loitering in the shallows, waiting their turn to flank into the Ohio River mouth, and I realized that my swift calculation back at the Cairo flood walls had been correct. There was no good time to take the confluence. Barge strings were flanking into the mouth every fifteen minutes. I just had to chance it and go. In bright sunlight, after clearing the Putney Bend, I could see down the long straightaway toward Belmont Point. From our roof deck the Mississippi before us was an oceanic ribbon of water shining against blue sky and the massive sandbars on the Kentucky and Missouri banks. The river was magnificent, a massive, churning chute of water racing so powerfully south that I felt airborne. In the telescoped view downriver, before the

Mississippi disappeared around the next bend, the shining water appeared to ascend vertically into fleecy cumulus sky. I was sailing into clouds.

Several times, we cheated as close as we dared to the channel markers and the edges of the sandbars, literally scraping the buoys with the *Patience* bow, and then staring straight down over the side to see how much water was left at the edge of the navigable space. On the Ohio, we could cheat the bars all day like that, especially when making last-minute corrections to avoid the commercial barges, and there was almost always a few feet of extra water left if we had to depart the channel and go outside the buoys. But the channel-marking on the Mississippi was shockingly precise. When we skirted the buoy by just a few inches, or even tipped it sideways with our poplar bow, the sand-bar was *right there*, with no water left for transit. The edges of the channel were a cliff—water here, and then a sandbar or rocks just inches away. The rock piles of the wing dams stretching underwater out toward the channel, labeled on the charts as "dikes," were generally not marked with buoys. We could only tell where they were by the current rippling over the surface of the rocks. They, too, were *right there*, adjacent to the deep water channel.

The lower Mississippi was a killer, a thousand-mile invitation to run aground. I realized within minutes of reaching the larger river that my confidence in steering around the commercial traffic, based on predict-ing how a tug captain would play his string around the twisting channels, now had to be considered arrogance. On the Mississippi, the challenge of maintaining safe separation from the barges was magnified by the sheer volume of water, and its swiftness, falling toward the Gulf of Mexico. My traffic-predicting skills had to be especially good for the long strings moving upriver. The Mississippi tug captains, fighting fierce downriver flow, were just inching around the bends at slow speeds, and curling their forward barges as close to the buoys as they could, because they needed every last foot of maneuvering space to make the tight bends. Often, the huge tugs lumbering around the bends with a string of forty barges occupied the whole channel—they were no longer moving targets but stationary ob-structions. On the Mississippi, especially at the edges of the channel, where I would have to pass most of the barge strings, there was no room for error.

The ground stretching east and west of us was low and vast, and even the forests were changing. Cypress trees with boughs hanging low over the water and conical trunks grew in swampy wetlands that gradually thinned inland into bayous that were moody and dark. The birdlife disappeared because the faster currents of the Mississippi made it difficult for the wading egrets and herons to forage while wading in the shallows, or the eagles or osprey to dive from the trees on the banks, and we only saw birds again if we wandered deep inside the coves to camp at night. The banks of the Mississippi were sandy and low—we would not see tall bluffs again for one hundred miles.

But the change in topography only enhanced the sensation of speed and movement. The sun was bright and the Mercury motor droned. The current raced us past the Pritchard revetments and the American flag snapped behind my right ear, pushed hard by a trailing, northeast wind. Destiny was pushing us south.

We ran into the first of the fabled Mississippi River boils during our second day on the river, just south of Columbus, Kentucky. A massive, two-mile beach at the bottom of the Wolf Island bar forced us toward the Missouri banks, up against a series of five wing dams directing the flow away from nearby Moore Island. The channel between the sandbar and the wing dams was exceptionally narrow, providing very little maneuvering room, and a large barge string was moving upriver two miles ahead at the Williams Light, diagonally blocking my path as it turned to make a bend in the river.

The conditions presented a classic Mississippi River navigation challenge. I couldn't just power back and linger at the sandbar, waiting for the barge traffic to pass, because the current was fast and was going to push me into the barges ahead anyway. I couldn't cross the channel for the revetment along the Kentucky banks because the tug captain was clearly positioning his forward barges there to make the next bend. I was on the Mississippi now, and learning. There were no ideal choices.

I instantly firewalled and pointed the *Patience*'s bow toward the north tip of Moore Island on the Missouri side, praying that I could get there and past the wing dams while the tug captain was still maneuvering his load for the Kentucky side.

It looked like I was going to make it. But right there, in the middle of my route past the wing dams, was a big, monstrous, hull-swiveling, boat-swallowing, underwear-removing Mississippi whirlpool. It was uglier than

Hades and reminded me of the mud volcanoes at Yellowstone Park in Wyoming. River whirlpools are formed by the circular motion set off by clashing currents below the river surface, often accentuated by massive holes or convex piles of mud at the bottom, and this one looked very angry. Huge cavitation bubbles broke the surface and set off a mad tangle of colliding, concentric circles, and mud, sticks, and even pea gravel from the bottom of the river swirled around on the surface, like a stew left to burn on too hot a fire.

I couldn't turn off from the whirlpool without ramming the bottom of the *Patience* into the wing dams. Mike stared intently at the whirlpool, grimaced, and looked over to me. Surely, we were going to die.

"Mike," I said. "My brief passage with you on this earth has been heavenly. Thank you for your friendship."

"I am praying for the repose of our souls, Rinker," he said.

I guessed from the look of the whirlpool that it would pull us violently from the bow to port, so at the edge of the snarly, spinning water I pushed hard to starboard, to throw us into a more or less benign yaw. I braced my knees against the console. *Crap*, I thought. *This morning, I should have remembered to put on my life vest.*

We got there. We penetrated halfway into the whirlpool in a second or two. Nothing happened. No yaw, no bouncing of the hull, not even the slightest suggestion of the dizzying, boat-rotating centrifuge that would black us out before we were pulled under. Nothing. I couldn't feel a single indication of trouble on the helm. My first Mississippi whirlpool! My promised death! Would I cry out for my mother before I was sucked under? Would I have one last vision of my Brooks Brothers boxer shorts swirling away from me in the sandy undertow? I would never know. This thing was about as significant as the distant, downwind fart of a small cat.

Nothing. I was speeding through the big river boil and past the final wing dam, starting my turn slightly west to stay with the channel, passing the forward bows of the barge string with a hundred yards to spare. The *Patience* handled beautifully.

We passed the barges and then the tug near the entrance of the bend and now we had an unrestricted view of the vast, open river ahead of us. We looked back a few times to the whitewater gauntlet of the Moore Island dams, where the boil was, and laughed about our folly. We were idiots to have even listened to the exaggerations of the boneheads back on the Ohio.

"It feels good to be alive," Mike said. "How are your boxer shorts doing?"

"They're disappointed," I said. "Brooks Brothers advertises these things as made of the best imported cotton, with snug elastic at the waist. My boxer shorts feel that they weren't given the chance to prove themselves."

"I know how they feel," Mike said. "Life is like that."

Mike and I camped that night at a state park along the Kentucky banks. There was a nice breeze blowing over the river from the Missouri side and a brisk current in the shallows where we parked the boat, and a lot of barge traffic. The boats in the bottleneck at the Ohio mouth fifteen miles upriver were flanking out into the Mississippi in waves, like the congestion along a highway when a light at a busy intersection turns from red to green, and they would be throwing heavy tumblers toward the banks all night. I dropped one of John Cooper's clunky cement anchors off the stern and then waded ashore to tie a bow line to a tree.

The "riprap" embankment at the edge of the water, placed by the Army Corps of Engineers to protect the banks along the state park from erosion, was constructed of large stones, almost as big as boulders, dumped at a sharp incline that climbed almost forty feet in elevation to the open fields of the park. The edges of the rocks were sharp and there were deep depressions between the mounds of stone, making the embankment almost impossible to cross. The only way to climb the embankment toward a tree at the top was to loop my bow line through my belt and then crawl almost vertically on my hands and knees—it was like bouldering in the Catskills. About halfway up the embankment, however, I noticed something useful. The riprap stone was held in place by a series of stout, threaded metal cables, more than an inch around apiece, that ran in parallel lines across the embankment. The cable was incredibly strong but still relatively flexible, a perfect tie-up hitch, and I climbed almost to the top of the bank and tied the bow line to one of those. (Along the Mississippi, these are often called "barge cables," because tug crews can use them to secure their barges in an emergency.) My hands and knees were bloodied and bruised by the time I had scrambled back down to the water, but I was delighted to have found the riprap cables as tie-up points.

I stood in the sand to watch how the *Patience* was handling the current and the tumblers from the tug wakes, not really knowing what to do but devising a plan that I would later read about in a boating manual. It was called a "spring line" hitch, for securing a boat in strong currents or waves. On the upriver side, I ran a line from the kevel on the stern to a boulder just below the banks, securing it relatively snugly, but not tight. From the opposite kevel on the stern I ran a line on the downriver side to another riprap, but set it so loosely that the middle of the line drooped into the water. The triangulation allowed the *Patience* to sway gently upriver every time a large tugboat wake angled toward her, and then she swayed back downriver when the waves dissipated, "springing" against the tighter line. This relieved the tension on the lines and allowed the boat to move back and forth with the currents, while maintaining a relatively consistent position against the banks. If a line broke in the strong current, I would still be tied up in three places.

The riprap banks and their restraining cables were also an example of how the Mississippi, maintained by the Army Corps solely for the benefit of commercial barge traffic, was both a barrier and a boon for my kind of travel. The crews of the big commercial tugs, who spent thirty-day shifts aboard their boats and never stepped ashore, benefited from the erosion protection and "flow enhancement" of the precarious rock banks and wing dams, but they never had to encounter them on foot. Few private boaters, however, wanted to bloody their hands and knees climbing the riprap to level land, and thus the river was cleansed of pleasure traffic that would only bedevil the safety of the tugboats. For the Army Corps, whose only priority was maintaining the river for commercial traffic—public boating be damned—the hazardous banks were the perfect solution.

That night, I was amused that I had thought to pack, before we left on the Monongahela a month ago, a pair of stout, canvas knee pads, reinforced inside with durable plastic foam. I had no idea why I had brought them along, but now the contingencies of the Mississippi provided an answer, and I fished them from the bottom of my duffel in the cabin of the *Patience*. For the rest of the trip to New Orleans, whenever we parked for the night against the riprap, I strapped on the knee pads and put on a pair of work gloves before I climbed the embankments to tie up against the cables.

Mike thought that I should tie the lines tighter. He had a lot more experience tying up a boat, but I was pretty sure that he had rarely tied up in the combination of currents and tug wakes that we faced that night. But that's what made Mike such great crew. He wasn't rigid and bound by convention. He was open-minded about my solution and, later, as we sat on the banks and watched the *Patience* gyrate back and forth on the lines, we agreed that she was secure for the night.

Mike and I were determined to enjoy the views downriver and across the Missouri and Kentucky farmlands from the high banks that night, and we spent forty-five minutes climbing the riprap with portable chairs, a cooler, and some food. I lashed my chain saw to my backpack so that I could cut driftwood for a fire above. Carrying everything up the bank was arduous but pleasant, welcome physical activity after sitting all day at the navigation console on the *Patience.*

On the high banks, we cooked steaks on the fire. The *Patience* looked beautiful and romantic from the shore, swinging from her lines under the light of a full moon. I drank bourbon and Mike drank iced tea. I was looking forward to reaching the fabled towns that I had read about for years— New Madrid, Tiptonville, Vicksburg, Natchez—that lay downriver. The wind from the west picked up after dark, and I threw on my knee pads and gloves and waded back to the boat for our jackets. The breeze fanned the coals of the fire and sent a shower of sparks into the leeward sky.

I felt dreamy that night and I remembered an important detail from Harlan Hubbard's *Shantyboat.* When they reached New Orleans, he and Anna weren't ready to return home yet, so they rowed their shantyboat into the bayous out past the Harvey Lock and lived on it for a year, wandering the remote Cajun waters south of New Orleans. They sold paintings and drawings at art galleries in New Orleans, wrote articles for small magazines, and feasted on smoked catfish and vegetables from their garden on nearby dry land. Hubbard began a series of line drawings and watercolors that established him as a major American artist. His written scenes, collected in *Shantyboat on the Bayous*, became celebrated as classics of naturalist writing. They didn't return to Payne Hollow for over a year.

The *Patience* swinging on her lines below was my home now and I could do that, too. Once I got to New Orleans, perhaps I could find a mooring out on Lake Pontchartrain, or a quiet cove in the bayous down below Belle Chasse, where I could live for a year. I didn't want this trip to end.

18

THE MISSISSIPPI WAS A FASTER, busier river, with four or five barge strings crowding toward the sharp bends at once, and the current so brisk that I didn't have the choice of slowing the *Patience* down and carefully negotiating the shallows and the commercial traffic ahead. The strong flow was always forcing me to boldly plunge forward between wing dams on one side and massive sandbars on the other. All of these obstructions were funneling me into a narrow channel without room to spare. I wasn't navigating the river. The river was navigating me.

But the Mississippi was also a happier river, and some of the tugboat captains decided to adopt us. We ran into this the first time near Chute of the Island, ten miles below Hickman, Kentucky, where the channel suddenly narrowed as it turned west around the bottom tip of the massive Island Number Eight. The channel below the big switching confluence at Cairo was busy with commercial traffic. There were tugboats with long strings everywhere around us, pushing both upriver and downriver, all of them churning up enormous wakes as they pushed toward the narrow chute at the same time—one of the most perilous gauntlets of steel I had seen so far. Just behind us to starboard, a massive white tug with red trim, pushing a full string of thirty or more barges, was bearing downriver on us. Two petroleum tenders were passing around the tug's port side and were now headed directly toward our position. In front of us, a long stick of coal barges was pushing upriver, less than a mile away. A second stick of coal barges was just behind it. For two miles in both directions there was nothing but moving barges, all funneling toward the same slender chute below Island Number Eight.

Deb Satterfield had come back on board at Hickman and was dogging every buoy and mile marker on the map for me, so I knew exactly where I was and what I had to do, but I realized that none of the tug captains lumbering around me had any reason to be confident that I would stay out of their way. I could just barely decipher out of the radio chatter the name of the big tug behind me, the *Caroline N*, and I decided to break my radio silence to hail the captain, advising him of my intentions and hoping that he could somehow referee the crazy flow of traffic crowding toward the chute.

"*Caroline N*, wooden boat *Patience* is at mile nine-ten-point-five at Chute of the Island. We're going to hug the red buoys along the Kentucky bars and remain clear of traffic."

The *Caroline N* came right back and acknowledged my call.

"Wooden boat *Patience*, roger from *Caroline N*. Traffic at the chute, the *Caroline* has this big old wooden thang with wide planking and an American flag just below Number Eight. He seems to know what he's doin' and he's going to be edge of channel. Kentucky side."

A couple of brief microphone clicks interrupted the radio static as the other boats at the chute acknowledged the *Caroline*'s broadcast.

Within a few minutes, the two petroleum tenders and the *Caroline N* were passing me on my starboard side. The oil barges were riding high in the water, empty, so they were fast and raced by quickly, churning up huge wakes and high rollers when they passed. The turbulent water racing toward me rocked the *Patience* from side to side, making it difficult to control the boat, and I had to push the throttle all the way forward several times, and then turn sharply for induced yaw, to gain enough purchase in the water to steer around the next buoy and stay off the bars to my left.

Meanwhile, the two coal strings moving upriver were curling around the revetments along the Missouri banks. The coal strings were so long that their rear barges were close to the buoys I was hugging on the Kentucky shore. The curve of the river coming up past Kelly Landing was forcing them into my path, but the downriver current behind me was moving so fast that I couldn't slow down. There was very little room to maneuver.

The Kentucky bars were right there, just a few feet off my port bow. But I knew the upriver captains needed to be reassured that I would remain out of their way. I would run aground outside the buoys if I had to, just to stay out of their path.

As I was about to broadcast that, the *Caroline N* blared on the radio instead. The captain and I were sharing the same thought.

"Coal at nine-twelve-point-five, the *Caroline* passing your port. Ahhhh . . . That wooden thang there with the American flag will be on the Kentucky markers. He's good. You're okay."

I powered up right away to give me more steerage, cutting so close to the buoys that I could literally see my wake churning up sand along the bars. But I was clear, by thirty yards or more, of the upcoming coal barges.

The precision required of me now must have involuntarily emptied my remaining stores of adrenaline and dopamine. I spent that stretch caroming between panic attacks and elation. I had to steer exactly on a track for the buoys, passing them so close that my port bow was almost glancing them, but still remain free of the bars. Along stretches where the river curved, my arc toward the next buoy had to be perfect—a curvature that kept me at the edge of the channel, while still guessing where the bars were in between. At the same time, where the river curved, the wing dams on the Missouri side were redirecting the current into the channel at an angle, which was also pushing me toward the sandbars on the Kentucky side, and I had to anticipate that, too, with a course correction and some extra power before I got there.

Bouncing through all those wakes at once, while still remaining close to the channel buoys, was thrilling. The *Patience* was yawing all over the place from my flat-bottom receiving so many tug wakes at once. Just as I turned into one wake to gain steerage in the water, I had to turn away from the next one. At one point there were two down-coming strings and two upriver strings in the channel beside me, almost a hundred barges in all, so I just wrestled constantly with the wheel and the throttle to remain close to the buoys on the Kentucky banks. My obsession was complete. *Stay on the Kentucky bars. Stay on the bars.*

The captains seemed to appreciate my struggle with the traffic and the ones from the coal strings moving upriver came out to their pilothouse decks to wave as they lumbered by. The captain of the *Caroline N* radioed that the *Patience* had "done good at the chute."

Now I knew why private-boat owners dreaded the Mississippi and stayed off it. Still, I couldn't sympathize with their fear. It was enormous fun cheating the shallows along the Kentucky side, with the barges only forty or fifty yards away, and feeling the surge of power and displaced water from the wakes pummeling sideways against the *Patience*. The danger suited me and was even pleasurable, addictive. I had to block out the confusion of boats and barges all around me and concentrate on a single, simple task, purifying life down to a sole mission: Stay on the Kentucky bars.

The traffic was thinning ahead of me and now all I faced was the diminished wakes of the tugs slowly disappearing down the straightaway toward Donaldson Point. The huge, fabled bend north toward New Madrid, Missouri, called the "Kentucky Bend," was just ahead. The few upriver barge strings in sight were still far off and I eased the *Patience* back into the middle of the channel. I enjoyed the endless vista of flat croplands stretching east and west and the vast sandbars on the Kentucky banks, and there was time to think. I sat at the helm, pensive and reflective.

I was supremely unprepared when I began this trip, but now the challenges of the journey—the confluences, the fast water racing the *Patience* by the wing dams, the crowded chute below Island Number Eight—were hardening me. The river itself was my education, my preparation. I had to trust my wanderlust, my urge to travel. I had to trust adventuring into the unknown. My personal enemy has always been boredom, stasis is my bane, and I had spent decades wandering and loving and learning my country. Now I had to trust the coping skills I had acquired from that. Nobody could possibly have prepared me for the challenges I had faced over the last three days. I had to discover it myself. The sense of achievement riding south from the chute, the sense of destiny pulling me toward New Orleans, was at once wearying and rapturous.

The captain of the *Caroline N* seemed reluctant to leave us behind. For the next two hours, all the way down the ten-mile straightaway to Donaldson Point, and then all the way around the giant Kentucky Bend that curved 180 degrees on the compass toward New Madrid, the captain was tracking us with his stern-facing radar and calling back advice.

"Flatboat *Patience*, give me er like twenty points more off your starboard to stay off that bar."

The captain later explained that heavy rains that spring, which arrived after the Coast Guard had relocated the marker buoys, had pushed them away from the bars, rendering them inaccurate. He was afraid I was sailing too close to the edge of the channel. The steering cues were unnecessary. We only had a single barge string in the channel at once while moving toward New Madrid and I usually had the deep water all to myself. But the *Caroline N* didn't want to let us go, and once more I was bound to a captain and the immense, trembling stern of a tug cutting a path ahead of me. Swept up by the romance of sharing the river with the *Caroline N*, I was briefly tempted by the thought of following her wake all night, but we needed supplies and gas and I had already decided to spend a couple of days at New Madrid. At the top of the giant horseshoe bend, I turned in for the town landing, letting the *Patience* drift into the small, protected harbor behind the long New Madrid Bar. From the roof deck, I looked back over the stern and watched the *Caroline N* depart downriver.

It was late afternoon in early September. The sun was falling, but not below the horizon yet. The *Caroline N* was etched against the sky in the pale sunset.

The channel down the Mississippi curved southeast. The captain of the *Caroline N* gently advanced his throttles to just above idle, swaying his stern to starboard and pitching his forward barges out into the current, patiently waiting for the Mississippi's massive flow to catch his load and slowly point his barges south. Then, with a volcanic, purple-blue glow of heat rising from her stacks, the *Caroline N* powered up and churned back an immense, frothy wake. The whining of her turbines echoed off the Missouri banks and her wake broke in waves over the bars on New Madrid Island as the *Caroline N* slowly disappeared downriver. I was disconsolate, watching her go. I missed that captain already. I would miss him for weeks. With the *Caroline N*, our twenty-mile run down from the chute had been our most challenging, but dreamiest, day of sailing yet.

New Madrid is an old town, an old river town. Like Newburgh, or Natchez, it is a classic throwback to the flatboat era. In the 1780s, the Spanish governor of Louisiana, to create a bulwark against the newly independent American colonies, welcomed settlement at the top of the big Kentucky Bend by several breakaway bands from the Shawnee and other southwestern tribes, and even a few eastern tribes like the Delaware, most of whom had been disrupted by the American Revolution and were already pushing west. The small, displaced groups of native peoples more or less peacefully coexisted with a group of two hundred white pioneers organized by a former Revolutionary War officer from New Jersey, Colonel George Morgan, and a group of French fur trappers who had settled the area to trade with the tribes, forming a kind of multicultural haven on the Mississippi that was similar, but a lot more respectable and less raucous, than the mixed-race trading posts of Scuffletown and Shawneetown up on the Ohio. The town's location near the relatively calm shallows at the top of the Kentucky Bend, just sixty miles below the big confluence at Cairo, made New Madrid a popular reprovisioning and transshipment point, and by 1810, New Madrid was the largest port along the Mississippi between St. Louis and Natchez. But

disagreements over settlement with the Spanish authorities, the mosquitoes infesting the nearby swamps, and frequent flooding of the Mississippi
across the bayous and low prairies surrounding the town initially impeded
permanent development and gave the town a reputation for danger and
disease. Transience was New Madrid's predominant theme. It was a place
where the Kaintuckers pushed in, camped on their decks for a day or two,
trading and transferring their loads from boat to boat, and then pushed
off again, fighting the currents as they navigated the sandy banks between
frontier Kentucky and Missouri.

For a time, over the winter of 1811–12, New Madrid was the most famous town in America. Between December 1811 and February 1812, New
Madrid was the epicenter of three major earthquakes and more than two
hundred aftershocks that devastated a vast area stretching three hundred
miles into Missouri, Kentucky, and Tennessee. Seismologists now classify
the New Madrid earthquake that winter—with shocks registering up to
eight on the Richter scale and affecting an area ten times as large as the San
Francisco earthquake in 1906—as the largest seismic event in North American history. Huge open craters as long as a quarter mile scarred the new
frontier croplands throughout the three states, most of the buildings in
New Madrid and nearby settlements caught fire, and residents were forced
to the "safety," if it can be called that, of the nearby sandbars and bayous.
For a hundred miles in every direction from the epicenter at New Madrid,
plantation chimneys toppled and the foundations of manor houses and
barns collapsed. For three days, the seismic force of the event forced the
Mississippi to flow backward for one hundred miles, completely relocating
the banks in many areas and forming a twenty-square-mile body of water
called Reelfoot Lake, near Tiptonville, Tennessee, when the reversing river
mowed over the huge cypress forests along its east banks. It was said at
the time, and it is still repeated in published accounts today, that the shock
waves from the New Madrid quakes spread more than one thousand miles,
breaking windows in Washington, D.C., and ringing church bells all the
way to Philadelphia and Boston. It doesn't matter that there is no proof of
that. Myth is reality for most people and that is how the New Madrid shake
is still remembered.

At the time, no one kept records of the actual number of boats in transit
on the inland rivers, but the death toll from the earthquake on the lower

Ohio and the Mississippi must have been in the dozens, if not the hundreds. Along the stretch where the Mississippi flowed backward, water levels rose as high as thirty feet, suddenly catapulting flatboats upriver, capsizing many of them. Others were swamped not only by water, but by frightened settlers onshore jumping on board passing flatboats, under the belief that the river was now a safer place than land. A French priest riding a flotilla of flatboats carrying furs from St. Louis passed earthquake damage 250 miles south of New Madrid, and later wrote, "We saw dead bodies of several [on land] and afterwards drowned persons we saw floating in the river." John Bradbury, the Scottish botanist traveling the Mississippi that year during his survey of western lands, counted twenty-nine empty canoes, either washed up on the banks or floating downstream in the accelerated current created by the quakes. The canoes were the kind that many flatboats towed either to reach the shore or to escape a sinking flatboat during an emergency. Bradbury concluded that the empty canoes provided "melancholy proof" of the many boats that had gone down with their crews.

By the early 1820s, New Madrid had recovered, resuming its role as a vital river port along the Mississippi almost equaling Vicksburg or Natchez. In his 1828 *A Condensed Geography and History of the Western States*, Timothy Flint provided a rich description of the busy New Madrid harbor and its diverse boats, drawn from the several visits he had made there during his peregrinations along the Mississippi. He attributed the "fine eddy" of the town's harbor to the inner passage between the long sandbars along New Madrid Island and the riverbanks of Missouri, which created protected waters for boats both ascending and descending the Mississippi. Most of Flint's observations date from the early 1820s, before the widespread introduction of the steamboat. Flint called New Madrid "the central point, or the chief meridian of boats, in the Mississippi valley," and estimated that, through New Madrid, "nine tenths of the produce of the upper country, even after the invention of the steam boats, continues to descend to New Orleans in Kentucky flats." At the height of the spring freshets, Flint said, one hundred boats landed in New Madrid every day, and "the surfaces of the boats cover some acres."

Flint's description of the New Madrid harbor in the 1820s is one of the finest portraits of a river port at the height of the flatboat era. This passage from his *Condensed Geography* also evinces why Flint—now settled for good in Cincinnati and publishing the respected *Western Monthly Review*—was considered by literary travelers from England and the eastern states as perhaps the finest writer of the frontier West. (Frances Trollope, the mother of Anthony Trollope and herself a distinguished novelist and travel essayist, considered Flint "the best and most original of the American voices.") The misfit minister from the North Shore of Boston had found himself out west, becoming one of the most unique creations of the inland rivers frontier. At New Madrid, Flint discovered an American river town where both passengers and products had traveled hundreds and even thousands of miles to intersect, and he captures the personality, the economic clout, and the nation-making sweep of the flatboat era.

> The boisterous gaiety of the hands [at New Madrid], the congratulations of acquaintances, who have met here from immense distances, the moving picture of life on board the boats, . . . afford a copious fund of meditation. In one place there are boats loaded with pine plank, from the pine forests of the southwest of New York. In another quarter there are numerous boats with the "Yankee notions" of Ohio. In another quarter are landed together the boats of "old Kentucky," with their whiskey, hemp, tobacco, bagging and bale rope. . . . From Tennessee there are the same articles, together with boats loaded with bales of cotton. From Illinois and Missouri, cattle, horses, and the general produce of the western country, together with peltry and lead from Missouri. Some boats are loaded with corn in bulk, and in the ear. Others are loaded with pork in bulk. Others with barrels of apples and potatoes, and great quantities of dried apples and peaches. . . . Other boats are loaded with furniture, tools, domestic and agricultural implements; in short, the numerous products of the ingenuity, speculation, manufacture and agriculture of the whole upper country of the West. They have come from regions, thousands of miles apart. They have floated to a common point of the union.

At New Madrid, Flint would often stroll down to the waterfront to tour "the great confederacies" of flatboats, many of them eighty to one hundred feet long, lashed together as they floated down the Mississippi. Flint stepped from boat to boat across the harbor. "It was a considerable walk," he wrote, "to travel over the roofs of this floating town." The lashed-together fleet was a kind of vagabond, preindustrial service center, following the settlers downriver to supply every need. On a single tour across the harbor, Flint found, in addition to numerous store boats and dramshops, a slaughterhouse selling pork cuts and sausages to the surrounding boats, a completely equipped tin shop selling finished wares both wholesale and retail, and a blacksmithing boat, complete with its own forges and drop hammers, producing and selling axes, scythes, and other iron tools, but also containing several stalls for shoeing horses. The pioneers weren't so much venturing onto the inland waters to discover distant, unknown lands. The old, familiar America they already knew was traveling beside them, a floating civilization following the great migration down the inland rivers.

Most amazingly, as early as 1816, Flint found that many of these factory boats were powered down the river by a "paddle wheel"–style contrivance that anticipated the arrival of the steamboats a few years later. Treadmills powered by draft horses were connected to a shaft and gears, which in turn drove a "bucket wheel" assembly mounted on the side or the stern of the boat, providing enough locomotion to make headway and provide steerage in the Mississippi currents. During the same period early in the 19th century, many other writers described similar "horse power" store boats and shop boats that plied larger tributaries like the Wabash and the Muskingum. The Americans were energetic tinkerers, and improvements to these boats and their bucket wheels were made every year. "Indeed, every spring brings forth new contrivances of this sort," Flint wrote, "the result of the farmer's meditations over his winter's fire."

At night, the caterwauling of the crews echoed along the New Madrid waterfront. The more settled residents of town learned to avoid the riotous environs of the riverbanks after dark. The flatboat and shop boat crews scurried around the harbor in johnboat skiffs, alcoholically visiting from boat to boat. By midnight, however, Flint wrote, "the uproar is all hushed."

At dawn the next morning, to a great commotion of bugles, the fleet in the harbor became a frenzy of motion, and within half an hour the shop boats and settlers' arks were all underway and soon disappeared downriver. The waterfront was quiet again for several hours, until the harbor began to refill with new downriver flats in the late afternoon. Day after day during the high-water season, the cycle was repeated at river ports downriver. "The fleet unites once more at Natchez," Flint wrote, "or New Orleans."

That was life on the Mississippi in the early 19th century. I would read accounts like Flint's and feel like weeping because I had arrived two hundred years late, missing the antic pageantry of life then. But my regrets were premature. I would soon see that life on the Mississippi is just as bumptious in my own day.

We arrived at New Madrid at the beginning of the Labor Day weekend and I was delighted to experience an old river town in full holiday swing. As I idled in the small harbor behind the New Madrid bars, inspecting some large driftwood logs washed up on the riprap levee as likely candidates for tying up, the harbor was busy with flat-bottom johnboats and sleek, well-equipped bass boats darting about. The thirty-mile stretch of river below the big Kentucky Point bend at New Madrid is extensively rimmed with sandbars on both banks, with innumerable inlets, coves, and inner passages ideal for fishing, and the harbor was joyful with the noise of local families readying their boats for a long holiday weekend of angling. At the town landing, more boats were joining the fleet in the harbor every few minutes, with families cheerfully handing up ice chests, fishing gear, and folding chairs as the boats descended the cement ramp into the river behind pickup trucks. Everyone was curious about the *Patience* and raced over in their boats to ask about who we were and what we needed. It was a happiness assault.

The first couple that came beside the *Patience*, in a camo-painted johnboat, was out fishing with their fourteen-year-old son. They wanted to know how I planned to tie up.

"I was thinking of using those big drift logs there," I said.

"No. There's cable all along the riprap. It's strong. Barges tie up there," the woman in the boat said.

"Yeah, but how much water do I have there?"

The family on the boat shrugged their shoulders, looked into each other's faces, and laughed. They already knew that the steep pitch of the levee embankment provided more than enough water for me to park bow-in, but they wanted to reassure me. The camo boat raced off for the embankment.

"We've got a fathometer! We'll tell you."

After patrolling along the levee for a minute or two, the family in the camo boat raced back and told me that I would have three feet of water under my bow, right up to the embankment, and twelve feet behind me at the stern. When I told them that I had just come down the Ohio and was worried about the water depths changing throughout the night, they laughed again. I should have remembered, myself. I was on the lower Mississippi now. There were no locks and dams for the next one thousand miles, and thus no lockmasters raising or lowering water levels after dark. The stronger, natural flow of the river took care of depths. The water below me would remain fairly consistent overnight.

The camo johnboat pushed ahead of the *Patience* toward the embankment. The fourteen-year-old stripped off his shirt, dove overboard into the current, and yelled over his shoulder.

"Throw me your line! I'll tie you up."

Later, when I decided that I needed a stern line to the bank, too, the boy dove into the river again beside my kevel, took a line, and swam it to the cable on the embankment. For comfort, I threw an anchor and line off the stern. The *Patience* was now safely triangulated for the night.

The kindness campaign resumed as soon as we were out of bed the next morning and making breakfast in the galley in the bow. We were tied up thirty yards away from the town landing, just below the New Madrid waterfront park, and a lot of passersby saw us when they came down to the river. One couple, Toni Lynne Phelps, a schoolteacher, and her husband, Derrick Lawfield, pulled over in their pontoon boat. When I told him that I was interested in the surrounding area, because I had read about how that delta region of Missouri was being converted from cotton to flooded rice fields, Derrick scheduled me for an evening tour of his farm. Toni called her daughter on her cell phone and told her to drive over and take the *Patience* crew out food shopping.

A member of the Pentecostal church walked down to the boat and told us that the church's Labor Day picnic would begin at noon, and we were invited. Four very fun ladies from the New Madrid Garden Club, driving around town and fixing up public gardens in their shiny Kawasaki Mule, invited us for a pizza dinner that night. A geezer in a brimmed hat and a waterproof camo jacket steered his johnboat over to the *Patience* and idled his motor while he rested his boat against our side. He told us that his gray pickup was parked up on the levee.

"The keys are on the driver's seat," he said. "The vehicle is yours for the day."

The little town on the big bend in the Mississippi was just one exuberant Welcome Wagon.

The cordiality of New Madrid saved our trip down the lower Mississippi in another vital way. I was finally able to address my serious defi-
ciency in anchors, which I could already tell was going to be an important
issue on the faster, more treacherous Mississippi. I knew that I wasn't going
to be able to park in protected harbors or still-water island coves every
night. I needed anchors that could be deployed quickly in the fast currents
along the steep embankments and levees, both fore and aft, to hold the
Patience in place while a crew member from the boat jumped for the bank
and scrambled up the riprap to secure us with lines against the restraining
cables.

While I was drinking coffee in the stern, and enjoying the merry antics
of the New Madrid fishing fleet in the harbor, the geezer fisherman who
had offered me his pickup for the day drifted back to the *Patience*. Before
he shoved off for a day of fishing, he wanted to know if there was anything
else that I needed. I told him that I could use advice on better anchors
for the Mississippi. From the deck of his boat, he pulled up a homemade
anchor welded together from steel bar stock and ridged rebar rods that
are used to reinforce cement foundations and walls. The ends of the rebar
below the stem were bent out like spider legs to catch the Mississippi bottom mud.

The anchor looked stout enough to hold the lightweight fishing boats,
but it probably wouldn't be strong enough to restrain the heavy *Patience*
overnight. I could probably use it as a "stabilizing" anchor that would hold
me in place in a current while I ran lines to shore.

"Where can I get one of those?" I said.

"We just weld them ourselves," the fisherman said. "You can't find this
kind of thang at the Bass Pro Shop. Them people don't know nothin'. We
call them spider anchors, or Mis-ippi anchors."

Rummaging around in the bins on the sides of his boat deck, the geezer
pulled out another homemade spider anchor. The ends hadn't been bent
out yet, so he took a length of steel pipe from the same bin and used it as a
"cheater bar" to bend the bottoms out so they would fix against sand.

"Here, it's yours," he said, handing me the spider anchor over the gunwales of the *Patience*. "Just throw this baby out thirty or forty yards before

you hit the spot where you want to hold in the current and then tie up to the banks. Guaranteed. The thang'll catch."

I thanked the geezer and, after he left, I muscled up John Cooper's ungainly cement anchor, freed my two other lines, and let the *Patience* drift in the mild current in the inner passage behind New Madrid Island, experimenting with my new spider anchor. When I threw the anchor, attached to a nylon line, it dragged for twenty-five or thirty yards in the mud below the harbor, then caught firmly, holding me steady enough to have enough time to run lines to the shore. After it had done its job holding the *Patience* in place, the lightweight spider anchor was easy to pull back over the gunwales. This was a definite improvement, and now I only needed a second spider anchor to use for stabilizing the other end of the boat while a crew member scrambled up the riprap to secure lines.

I had already begun sketching a design for another, heavier style of anchor that I was pretty sure would work in the Mississippi mud to hold me overnight in the current, with the aid of lines tied to the shore. My idea was based on the "mushroom" style mooring anchors that I had seen used by small lobster and oyster boats that worked the tidal mudflats in the bays and rivers of Cape Cod and Maine. Mushroom anchors are disc-shaped, slightly convex on the bottom, providing some buoyancy when they are dropped from the boat, and thus sinking relatively gently. They are easy to either throw or to retrieve over the side. Once the discs reach the bottom, the convex surface fills with mud and nearly doubles in weight, providing more than enough heft to hold a boat like the *Patience*. But the mushroom shapes are easy to dislodge from the bottom by tipping them over by the line, or pulling them free with the motor, at which point the disc is suspended in the water and the mud slides off, making the lightweight anchors easy to pull back into the boat.

For the heavy currents of the Mississippi, I thought, I would probably need two "mushroom" bottoms for each anchor, stacked vertically on a single steel post. Two mushrooms welded to a single post would sink deep enough, and accumulate a load of mud sufficiently heavy, to hold the ten-ton *Patience* overnight.

I didn't know for sure, but guessed, that it would probably be best to use a style of harrow disc called the "frontier" disc, which has deep indentations around the circumference to enable them to dig deeper into hard sod. Now all I had to do was to find a local welder or farm shop, and a junkyard with plenty of cast-off frontier discs, to fabricate my new anchors. But I was pretty confident that I could manage that. During my wanderings in the Midwest and the West over the past thirty years, I had noticed that farm mechanization and consolidation had led to rapid depopulation of long stretches of farm country. The advent of Walmart and other big-box stores had shuttered most small towns, denuding them of the hardware stores and machine shops that were once their commercial lifeblood. Most of the farmers who had survived the economic crunch in flyover country had compensated by building well-equipped shops on their own farms, replacing the commercial facilities they had lost in town. It was hard to travel anywhere between the Appalachians and the Rockies without finding one of these farm shops within five or ten miles of where I needed one. Over the years I had modified or repaired numerous motorcycles, trailers, and even a mule wagon at these shops.

This was an odd piece of familiarity to have, but New Madrid already felt like my kind of town, and my confidence was soon rewarded. As I was finishing a second cup of coffee on the stern, the Garden Club ladies returned to the boat landing in their Kawasaki and were waving for me to come over. When I crossed the riprap to say hello, they introduced me to a trim, athletic retired farmer who lived nearby, Bud Henry. He perked up when I mentioned that I needed to have some anchors welded.

"My farm shop is just around the corner," he said, "and I've got a welder coming today. Are you going to the church picnic? Let's meet there. I can get those anchors made up for you."

I carried my spider anchor and my drawings for the mushroom anchors to the church picnic, which was only a short walk from the town landing. The picnic was held in a lovely town park opposite the Pentecostal church, across lawns that were arrayed with portable tables covered with plastic tablecloths, tall bowls of salad and cut fruit, and we all feasted on barbecued chicken and pork steaks, fried okra and macaroni and cheese. It was sunny and breezy on the hill above the river, and the church members regaled me with stories about life in southeastern Missouri. The event was crowded and everyone wanted to talk with me about our trip and ask about how they could help us. They wanted to know everything about me and I entertained them with stories about my boyhood summers in Pennsylvania.

There was an unspoken code of civility between us. Everyone seemed to sense that the Pentecostal picnic was not the time or the place to discuss politics with the visitors from the North. We were all Americans at a Labor Day picnic, not Yankee and southern Americans, enjoying the same barbecued ribs. But one porky Missouri buffoon, who identified himself as an insurance salesman, insisted on engaging me in a discussion about national health policy, "'bama care," he called it. He was dressed in baggy dork shorts, black socks, and a T-shirt that read I STAND FOR THE FLAG, AND KNEEL FOR THE CROSS. He considered it absolutely vital to explain to me that the "'nited states of 'merica" was being ruined by "librals and buree-cats."

I wasn't the least bit interested in this porcine Pentecostal's harangue. No one in the church group I was standing with was interested either, and they looked away or off to the sky, embarrassed by the lowborn fool and pretending not to hear what he was saying. A woman was crossing the grass with a tray full of plastic glasses filled with ice and sweet tea. The church lady standing next to me touched me on the elbow and spoke sideways into my ear, softly.

"Don't worry," she said. "That's his wife. This'll end as fast as a possum hit by a pickup."

The woman with the tray frowned at her husband while she handed us our drinks.

"Honey," she said, "shut your pie trap. This fella didn't come all the way down the river to listen to some loudmouth like you."

I was jubilant, and not only because the porcine Pentecostal immediately shut his pie trap and walked away. This is what I had come to the inland rivers to see. Along the big bend in the Mississippi, I was enjoying a Labor Day feast with some very fun and kick-ass church ladies.

After the picnic, I loaded my new spider anchor into the back of Bud Henry's pickup, and we drove over to his capacious shop nearby. I showed the welder my spider anchor and the crude sketches I had made of my mushroom anchor concept, and with Bud and his brother, Bill, we toured his extensive boneyard of rusty farm implements, old tractors, and pickup beds, cannibalizing several frontier discs from an old John Deere harrow. We found some square stock on an old Massey Ferguson three-way hitch. In the barn, I found some dry-rot mule harnesses hanging on the wall. On

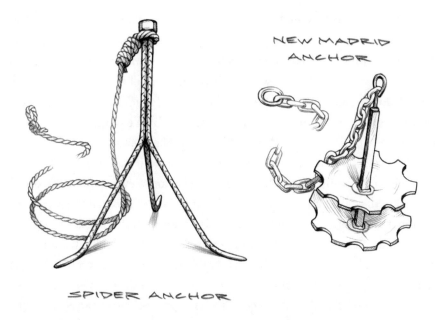

SPIDER ANCHOR

NEW MADRID ANCHOR

The "experts" on river travel gave us bad advice on anchors, so we designed our own. The "New Madrid" anchor (right) was welded from John Deere disc harrows, and the common Mississippi "spider" anchor (left) was useful for briefly holding the boat in the currents until we could tie up with lines.

the collar hames, the rings for holding the driving lines looked ideal for welding to the top of the anchors to attach my anchor lines. I pried them off the harness with a crowbar from Bud's pickup.

A breeze from the river picked up while the welder started working with our parts, and a low, puffy formation of cumulus clouds blew in from the west. I felt drowsy after my Pentecostal picnic feast and fell asleep in a plastic Adirondack chair under a shade oak, occasionally waking up from my nap to watch the sparks fly as my anchors took shape. The breeze carried over the pleasing, astringent smell of burning acetylene gas and welding rods fusing to hot steel. I dozed off again, happily reminded again of my boyhood days in Pennsylvania, falling asleep on the grass near the open doors of an Amish blacksmith shop.

When I woke, my new anchors were resting upright on the grass, shiny under the falling evening light where the welder had burnished the welds with a grinder.

Later, Derrick Lawfield drove me over to his extensive farm and gave me a tour of his cotton, rice, and corn fields. His uncle gave me a ride in the family's massive Claas combine and it was wonderful rumbling over the cotton while massive brown clouds of dust and chaff blew up and then drifted down past the river. At the American Legion dining hall, where Derrick bought me dinner, I decided to make a change of plans. I was going to end the trip right here and settle forever in New Madrid.

It was dark by the time Derrick drove me back to the town landing with my new anchors. But the lights of the large grain elevators and the docks along the Missouri banks lit the water behind the *Patience*, all the way down the inner channel beside New Madrid Island. I was exuberant about the day and wanted to test my new anchors. From the deck of the boat, I pulled in my lines and let the *Patience* drift backward with the current into the inner channel, down past the grain-loading docks. When I threw my new, stacked mushroom anchors, they dragged for twenty-five or thirty yards, and then my nylon line snapped tight, spraying off a shower of river water as the anchor caught. They worked perfectly, and would probably catch even sooner and deeper when I was dragging them against a stronger current.

I sat in the current testing my anchors some more, thinking about my day. I had begun this trip completely ignorant about anchors, unaware that I would have to fabricate new ones halfway through the trip. Preexisting knowledge, however, seemed to be overrated. I was just a sponge, a chamois cloth, a big old turtle shell constantly being filled with technology and information. My brain was so empty of the information that I needed to get down the river that I was thrilled every time I could replenish it with useful new knowledge.

Absorb, reabsorb. It was a pleasant realization and dreamily drew me back to the Kaintuckers, the gundalow travelers of the 19th century. They were constantly reabsorbing and reinventing—new ways to tie up against the trees on the bank, new leather cylinders and India rubber seals for their handmade pumps to bail out their wet hulls, new fruits to ferment for brew, new languages and songs. Nearly every day, they negotiated new bends on the river that had formed during the storms a month earlier, and were not yet charted on Zadok Cramer's latest map. Survival depended on adaptability, reabsorption, the new, a willingness to constantly self-educate and reinvent. The dogmatic, the closed-minded, the know-it-all with an inflated sense of self-worth didn't belong on the riverine frontier.

The New Madrid harbor was lit by the lights from the grain towers. I started the motor and gently puttered into the levee below the town landing. I threw one of my new anchors into the current and then climbed the levee and attached two bow lines to the barge cables. The *Patience* held securely all night, gently swaying in the current, and from my cot in the cabin I enjoyed the night sounds and sights from the Mississippi River town above. The teenagers in their pickups squealed off from the town landing, a few fireworks sounded, and, far off, the lights from the combines working the corn and cotton fields lit the night sky. And my new anchors were perfectly holding the *Patience.*

In New Madrid, the Mississippi delivered another message that I should have regarded as foreboding. Ever since the big 1927 flood, and subsequent inundations to this day, the Army Corps of Engineers has been spending billions securing the riverbanks in place with massive inclines, sometimes as high as forty or fifty feet high, constructed with treacherous riprap. The stone levees on the inland rivers are a metaphor of America. The stone is strip-mined from Minnesota to Tennessee and deliberately processed in giant crushers to render sharp edges, which resist water currents better, and then hauled downriver in barges to be dumped on the banks. The jagged riprap stones are anywhere from four inches to two feet in size. Because riprap levees are dangerous to descend or to climb, the Corps of Engineers' use of riprap has driven millions of Americans away from scenic riverbanks, and drastically restricted recreational boating along thousands of miles of the inland rivers. The federal agency, which is notorious for its arrogance and hated by many river-country residents, has never considered alternatives to sharp-rock riprapping and indeed considers the dangerous environment it has created to be an advantage. Riprap has cleared the riverbanks of weekend picnickers, bird-watchers, anglers, environmentalists, and recreational boaters. No one wants to visit a scenic river space where mothers with strollers or grandmothers in wheelchairs can't reach, can't see, the great waters without endangering themselves. But the Army Corps considers this an advantage. The only constituency the Army Corps wishes to serve—commercial barge companies—thrives without the annoying interference of the public.

On our second night in New Madrid, Deb Satterfield was returning from town after buying some groceries and ice. The *Patience* was tied up on the riprap levee about forty yards west from the cement landing below Riverfront Park. Deb hesitated about crossing the riprap in her flip-flops, but the bagged ice was melting, and she gingerly stepped across with heavy bags dangling from both arms. When she fell, she could hear the snap of bone as she landed on her arm.

I ran out across the riprap, helped Deb back to the boat, and then went back for the groceries and ice. She was in a lot of pain and it was obvious that she had broken her arm. We considered ourselves lucky that we had saved all of the numbers for the members of the New Madrid Garden Club. They rushed right over and drove her to the emergency room, where her arm was set in a cast.

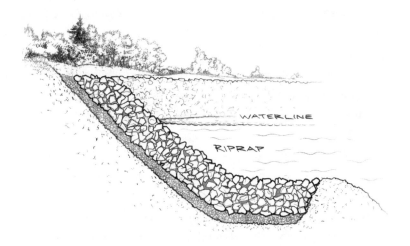

We had to tie up against the sharp-edged, treacherous "riprap" levees along the Mississippi most nights, a hazard of the trip that no one warned me about.

I spent the next two hours on the boat plunged in guilt. It was my fault that Deb was injured. I had deliberately tied up the *Patience* west of the town landing, along the riprap, to spend the night in the more placid waters behind the New Madrid bars. I could easily have tied up closer to the town landing, with tight lines, to protect my crew and visitors from having to scramble across the riprap. I had failed as a captain.

When Deb returned, she insisted that I should not blame myself. Her broken arm wasn't that painful, she said, and the hospital had sent her back with plenty of painkillers. She could continue to crew downriver, she insisted. In the morning her broken arm and cast would not prevent her from dogging the maps while I steered, and we would get down past Tiptonville to Memphis in fine shape. Now she just wanted to get into bed and sleep.

"Don't feel bad," Deb said as she disappeared for the roof deck. "It's just a broken arm."

I sat on the stern deck alone for another hour. My new anchors were holding well against the tug wakes. I decided to call my disc harrow design the "New Madrid" anchor. As the big line tugs moved by on the river, their running lights glowed off the beachy shoals of the New Madrid bars. In the fields north and west, the dry cornstalks rustled as they swayed in the river breeze, and gauzy moonlight reflected on the river behind me. A barred owl hooted in the trees beside the town landing. I could tell from the returning juvenile calls that she was teaching her fledglings to hunt.

I turned in for bed myself a little after ten o'clock. The *Patience* was contentedly swinging from her lines on new anchors in the harbor in the heart of the Mississippi River country. Timothy Flint! At New Madrid! I was gently bobbing on his old waters right now. The little town on the big bend, welcoming, generous, and kind, was embedded in my soul.

19

EVERY HOUR SPENT ON THE Mississippi was an intense suffusion of light, waterscape, and sand. The grand spectacle of the continent was racing by. The American harvest was underway and the trainloads of corn and beans off-loading onto the barges at the Caruthersville and Helena wharves were spewing giant clouds of dust that kited northeast across the bends. Immense flocks of American white pelicans were migrating south and, thousands at once, they rose over the Nebraska Point bars, shadowing the river in darkness when they flew between us and the sun. In the evening, while we were tying up, the catfish jumping beside the *Patience* were as large as dogs.

Enduring the river was also exhausting. Tense afternoons spent negotiating twenty miles of wing dams from the Linwood Bend to Island Number Twenty-One were followed by tense evenings scrambling up the riprap to tie up, then hauling the electric bike up the levee, climbing the second, backup levee, finding a road, and then driving into Ridgely or Osceola for gas. When I returned in the dark, I scrambled back down the riprap three or four times with 36-pound cans of gas. My sunburnt legs were pincushions of mosquito bites and my hands and knees had been kneaded by the riprap into steak tartare.

I had never known such weariness at night, but I had never known such satisfaction either. Scraping in between the buoys and the wing dams in the narrows beside Island Number Fourteen, only to find an immense string of grain barges blocking my exit from Little Prairie Bend, was exhilarating. From my fires at night, the embers rose high in the brisk wind and disappeared over the levees, orange witches against the moon. My emotions were raw, feral, stripped to a naked bipolarity. I just knew tired, tired, tired, but I also knew elation, elation, elation.

Our landing at Tiptonville, Tennessee, where I would wait for several days to be joined by my dream team crew and make one last modification to the *Patience* required for safely descending the Mississippi, was typical. Mike Binkley and I were crewing the boat, and we'd spent all day adjusting to the swift currents. We were moving downriver at one-third power, just enough to gain some steerage in the swift water underneath us, but still the wing dams and the bars were whirling by at more than 10 knots. We realized that we could easily do 60 or 70 miles downriver in a single day, and still have plenty of time to tie up early, build a fire, and make dinner. But the flow behind us, and the winds, even in the relatively protected shallows of coves and town boat ramps, were constant and ferocious, making every landing heroic.

I wanted to park the *Patience* close to the cement ramp at the public boat landing in Tiptonville, which would make it easier to load supplies, and to run back and forth for gas on the electric bike. As we raced past the Bixby Towhead Light I peered ahead with my binoculars and found a promising oak on the top of the levee just downstream from the ramp. We could tie our first bow line to the tree and, with a lot of power, keep the *Patience* stalled into the current long enough to throw a couple of anchors fore and aft and then triangulate some lines.

I was confident handling my poplar queen by now and knew how to land her in currents, which was boldly, as boldly as possible. The *Patience* was as stout as a Belgian draft mare. There wasn't a rock or a bar on the whole Mississippi, at least during the moderate water levels of the summer months, where I couldn't pin her by one side of the bow and then firewall the power to hold her while anchors and lines were thrown. But most of the crew members I had weren't aggressive enough and couldn't be convinced that the *Patience* was essentially a floating eight-ton dock, built for abuse, and they were too timid to land her properly. It was a lot better to land someone onshore first and to steer her myself from the wheel deck while the tie lines were thrown and the anchors set.

But now there was a new problem that I had to calculate every time I landed. I was spooked by Deb breaking her arm on the riprap back in New Madrid. I wasn't going to send the gentlemanly Mike, as fit as he was, scrambling up the riprap to secure a line to the oak. I didn't want to risk injuring another crew member.

As we raced past the Bixby Light, I told Mike my plan. We would stop forty or fifty yards north of the cement ramp, where I would jump off with a bow line to "walk the boat" to the landing. I wanted him to pin the *Patience* to the rocks just downstream of the landing while I scrambled the line up to the oak. I didn't want him to let the boat drift after that.

"Just pin her to the rocks at full power," I said. "You can lay her on the starboard side against the rocks if you want. Just don't let her drift. Then I'll come back and lay the anchors and the other lines."

Above the landing, I jumped into the water and briefly let myself drift with the current until I felt my feet touch the bottom. Once I got to the riprap, the boat was drifting downstream too quickly for me to scramble across the levee on my hands and knees, so I leapt from rock to rock with the line in my hand, following the *Patience* downstream. As we neared the landing, the river was breaking over some rocks set out in the current to slow the water down at the landing. There was plenty of water below the hull, but Mike was afraid that the bottom would run aground on the rocks. He steered farther out in the flow, the current caught the boat and it raced ahead of me, and I had no choice but to throw the line back into the river as it yanked out of my hands. We repeated this twice more and I had to throw the line back into the water, scramble along the riprap while the *Patience* drifted too far off the banks, and then jump back into the current to grab the line again.

But I was saved at Tiptonville by the barge cables lining the riprap. Halfway up the levee, I realized that I wouldn't have to reach the oak at the top after all. A barge cable was right there, and I quickly tied up the bow line and then used it as a kind of staircase banister as I stumbled back over the riprap to the boat. After pulling myself aboard, I threw my new anchors from the bow and the stern. The boat was still trying to drift downstream, but a wind from the south was pushing us toward the landing, and

I realized that if I triangulated my lines just right I could use the stalling effect of the wind against the current to hold the boat. Standing waist-deep in the water to carry more lines to shore, I had Mike tie two of my stoutest hemp lines together for extra length, and I ran this as a spring line from the port kevel on the stern, over the roof of the cabin, and then off the starboard side and all the way up the riprap to the big oak.

The *Patience* held relatively securely in the water while I finished tying up. My main spring line ran from the port kevel on the stern and over the roof to the starboard-side oak. To compensate for the downstream current, I ran my third shore line diagonally across the riprap, from the starboard kevel on the bow to a high barge cable on the port side. This was unorthodox and probably violated every boaters' manual ever written. I didn't care. Despite broadside winds of twelve to fifteen knots, and the strong current racing by the banks in the opposite direction, my oddball combination of New Madrid anchors and shore lines held us perfectly at a safe distance from the rocks.

As the sun went down, I sat on the galley deck at the bow, watching my lines and admiring the pastel light on the long Stewart Towhead Bar across the river. I made a few adjustments to the lines to let the *Patience* swing a little more between the current and the wind, relieving the pressure on my ropes. I tested my New Madrid anchors by pulling them one at a time back into the boat, and then throwing them back into the river to see how well they set. They worked perfectly. My predicament that night reminded me of Harlan Hubbard at the fans of the Wabash, rowing furiously with his wife around Wabash Island and then crashing to a landing in the trees. There wasn't a graceful way to sail the inland rivers, and there was no reason to aspire for that. I decided that the only thing I wanted out of this trip was beautiful sunsets over the sandbars, like tonight. I went to bed very tired but content.

Tiptonville became an important and mostly relaxing stop for me. While I waited alone on the *Patience* for my next crew to gather, I raced around on the electric bike, exploring the surrounding Tennessee and Kentucky countryside, visiting Civil War sites and canoeing Reelfoot Lake, the vast and mysterious universe of cypress swamps, now one of the world's great bird sanctuaries, created by the 1811 tornado. Earl Johnson, a farmer who lived just over the levees, visited the boat every morning to bring me groceries and ice. He was harvesting corn that week and clearing one of his wood lots, and I went over almost every afternoon to help him farm.

Camping on the river became an interesting social experience, exposing me to a broad cross section of Mississippi life. Even though the Tiptonville landing was in very remote country, everyone in town had heard about the wooden boat parked on the river and many of them came down for evening visits. A couple of nights, I pulled the *Patience* snug to the bottom of the cement landing so that people could safely walk down well away from the riprap, and lashed her hard to the barge cables to keep her from drifting. Then I threw down my front gangplank to welcome the crowd.

Many of my visitors were mothers who wanted to show their children a flatboat, but I also learned a lot about the different lines of work along the river. A local switch boat captain who worked the barges for a gravel operation downriver gave me tips on riding the shallows outside the buoys. A commercial fisherman who harvested only large catfish—seventy pounds or more—for a local cat food cannery told me all about that business. The local off-duty cops, of course, were appalled when they learned that I was traveling the river unarmed, doubly appalled when I refused their offers of free guns. Two card sharks came aboard, just to teach me card tricks. A diesel mechanic for the John Deere dealer in Union City warned me to be extremely careful when landing the *Patience* in low water at boat ramps. He told me that the public boat ramps along the Mississippi are popular places to dump cars, either for insurance fraud or to destroy evidence of a crime, and the river bottom just off the ramp was often a submerged junkyard.

As I had already seen, fear of the river—when it floods, when the currents are strong, when it is busy with tugboat traffic—permeates life in towns along the Mississippi, and it is interesting how that fear courses through the lives of families, anchoring them to a single, traumatic event that they can never expunge. The South tends to cling to families for several generations, everyone has either a relative or close friend who works on the river, and stories of the Mississippi violently rending a family's history are common. I was particularly touched by the story of Thomas Dial, a retired prison guard from Tiptonville, who came down to the town landing almost every afternoon to stare at the water and skip rocks across the Mississippi. He came over to the *Patience* one afternoon to tell me why hearing about my trip raised troubling feelings for him. We spoke for more than an hour on a sunny, breezy day, under the cool shadows of low cumulus clouds.

Dial is the son of a tugboat captain, and his father came from a rivermen's family. In the 1950s and 1960s, his father worked as a through-haul pilot, meaning that he spent a month at a time on his boat, pushing barges or other vessels all the way down to New Orleans, or all the way up to St. Louis, or Davenport or Rock Island in Iowa. Once, when he was a boy, Dial's father took him on one of his trips, and he rode the wheelhouse with his father all the way to New Orleans. When he was young, Dial thought that he would someday work on the river, too, and he took courses at the WoodenBoat School in Brooklin, Maine. But, for a variety of reasons, he decided to work for the state prison in Tiptonville instead. In his backyard near Reelfoot Lake, he has seven old wooden boats. He works on one of them, a Chris-Craft cabin cruiser, almost every day, and dreams about taking it all the way downriver.

"You are taking the dream trip I always said I would. I think about it all the time while I am working on my cabin cruiser. The big trip to New Orleans. But I know I will never do it."

Dial's uncle, Charles "Bud" Dial, lived downriver in West Memphis, and was a popular tug captain well known all along the river. He was a through-haul pilot who ran the full course of the river, just like Dial's father. Uncle Bud was barrel-chested and irrepressibly cheerful and loved to tell rivermen's stories and entertain his nephew with tales about his life on the Mississippi.

"Whenever Uncle Bud was coming through Tiptonville with a string, he'd call ahead and we'd go out to the landing to meet him," Dial said. "Sometimes we'd just stand on the landing and wave at him. Sometimes my dad would run me out to Uncle Bud's tug in our johnboat, and then Uncle Bud would let me ride the wheelhouse with him down to Caruthersville or Memphis. He'd let me steer the tug the whole way. My dad would drive down to run me home."

Early one morning in July 1984, Uncle Bud was running downriver

near Thebes, Illinois, on the tug *Helen Tully*, without a string, on a reposi-
tioning trip. It's unclear whether bad conditions on the river were a factor,
or whether he was having engine trouble, but apparently the *Helen Tully*
was adrift in the channel. Uncle Bud's last broadcast, before the *Helen Tully*
collided with the 26-barge string pushed by the tug *Maba Kelce*, was "I'm
getting run over."

Coast Guard rescue boats and helicopters searched for eight days. Dial
and his father joined the search, running the family outboard all the way
up to Thebes, glumly returning downriver when no sign of the *Helen Tully*
could be turned up. Eventually, when the tug was salvaged from the bottom
of the river, the body of the cook was discovered in the galley. But Uncle
Bud was never found.

"I still miss Uncle Bud a lot," Dial told me. "My father never got over
losing his brother on the river. Sometimes, when I come down to the landing, I have this sudden flash, 'Oh! There's Uncle Bud!' But then I have to
remind myself that he's not coming back."

It's interesting how, like the children and grandchildren who visit the
Lorraine American Cemetery in France, or the famous fiftieth reunion of the
Gettysburg veterans in 1913, people seem to need to return to the source of
their pain. I saw Dial at the Tiptonville landing almost every afternoon. He
was a river rat regular. He sat up on the levee and stared down at the river,
watching the big barge strings push out of the Cargill docks. He walked
down the ramp to skip rocks on the river. A couple of times, when the catfish
johnboats landed, he helped the crew carry their catch up the ramp.

But his relationship with the river wasn't going beyond that. During
our chats, Dial made it clear that he was never going to return to the river.

A considerable storm blew in from the southwest the second night I was
tied up in Tiptonville. The *Patience* swayed in the winds like the pendulum
of a grandfather clock, and the rain blew into the cabin through the window doors that I had kept open to cool the boat. In the middle of the night
my internal gyro woke me up on my cot—the boat was skidding violently to
starboard, probably because one of my lines had sheared. I pulled on some
pants and rubber boots, found a flashlight, and went forward to investigate.

On the bow, I could see that the nylon line running diagonally up the riprap from the port kevel was slack and had fallen into the water. I followed the line up the levee with the beam of the flashlight and could see that it had pinched against a sharp rock and severed, from the constant rocking pressure of the storm. It wasn't particularly advisable, on a night like this, to scramble the riprap to replace the line, but it was possible that the storm would sever other lines and I needed as many in place as possible. Walking back to my rope locker in the stern, I threw a sixty-foot coil of stout hemp line over my shoulder and headed forward again, tying one end of the coil to the bow kevel. I was tired and it was late. It never occurred to me to put on a life jacket.

Jumping into the current with a heavy coil of rope on my shoulder provided a useful educational experience. The waves from the storm slammed into my shoulder with the coil, providing a lot of buoyancy that kept my head above water. But the hemp quickly became saturated, too, and heavy, which dipped me down in the lulls between the waves so that my feet touched bottom. As I furiously sidestroked toward the levee, the line extending back to the kevel on the boat became taut, and that, too, was helping to suspend me in the water.

Uncoiling the rope from my shoulder as I scrambled up the levee on my hands and knees, I found the break in the old line and scrambled northeast, found the barge cable, and tied up. As I adjusted the line for tightness, I could just barely see through the rain how the *Patience* was riding the water and returning to the desired angle from the bank. I was worried about another line breaking in the storm and decided to cross the levee due south to check the other ropes. I used the barge cable near the top of the levee for support, standing up on the rocks to inspect the tension on the lines back to the boat.

In the dark, I didn't see the heavy limb blowing down from the trees on the top of the levee. One moment I was standing tall on the rocks, inspecting my knot on the spring line, and the next moment I was falling sideways as the limb swept through me at the shins.

As I went down, I thought, *You should have put on a life vest. You didn't even put on a shirt.* I landed on my right side on the sharpest side of a two-foot rock. *Crack.* I could feel exactly where the two ribs were snapped. *Damn it all, I have done it again.* I knew it would be a day or two before I felt any pain, and I was more annoyed at myself than hurt. If I had thought to wear a life vest, that would have cushioned my fall and I wouldn't have broken my ribs again.

I couldn't just lie there in the rain, dwelling on this. I had to get back to the boat. It took a lot of deliberate effort to get off the riprap and face backward on my hands and knees to shimmy down the levee. I found the water feet-first and used the bow line to steady me in the current before I hauled myself over the side to get back into the boat. My ribs stabbed with pain as I struggled over the gunwales and onto the deck. *Oooooo*, I thought, *maybe this is a different case of broken ribs.*

But it was a relief to be back on the *Patience*. I pointed the beam of my flashlight through the rain to check the lines, and the boat was holding securely at a forty-five-degree angle to the levee. We were good. Another line could break overnight and I probably wouldn't drift.

The *Patience* was a gorgeous tarnation that night. The wind and rain were pounding the poplar sides, rocking the boat, bouncing her back and forth on her lines, creating a commotion of rattling tin and glass on the galley deck. The Coleman lantern on the ceiling swiveled wildly, casting gyrating beams of light fore and aft. I wrapped myself in blankets and watched the storm through the open front door. Through the sheets of rain I could just make out the dark, brooding presence of the mountain of rock on the levee.

But I loved being inside my swaying poplar cave. I had broken my ribs again, but it was wonderful being in the dry cabin of my boat as it was tossed by the wind and the rain.

My best time on the river came the next day, although, technically, I wasn't on the river at all.

I drove into Tiptonville that afternoon to do laundry. My crew would be drifting back during the next day or two and I wanted to get my kitchen towels and bed linens tidied up. The laundromat was one of those rancid fiberboard shacks that you find in small towns in the South and Midwest, where the finicky washing machines have to be cycled two or three times just to get the laundry a few shades close to clean. But the evening wasn't so bad for someone who likes shabby small towns. I sat on a bench across from the Dollar General reading Harlan Hubbard's *Shantyboat on the Bayous*. Visitors to Tiptonville have to be quite patient while doing their wash and I got out of there late.

Riding the electric bike at night along the levee roads surrounding the river was spectral. Crickets screeched from the small stands of trees that had been planted for erosion control. Teenagers necked in pickups along dusty pull-offs. The roads into the levees curved sharply over the embankments. With my laundry bags and a can of gas loaded high on the bike, I had to swerve to miss a giant snapping turtle crossing the asphalt at a bend.

I didn't know how lost I was in the maze of featureless dirt roads behind the levees, which only made me more lost, because I kept turning onto another road thinking I could get it right. Then I started turning into cotton fields and running the bike down to the edge, where I thought I could see a way out through a break in the trees. In the ruts at the edge of the fields, the electric bike swayed violently and almost tipped over with its heavy load of laundry and gas. My ribs pierced with pain every time I hit another bump. The crickets screeching from the tree breaks and the raccoons waddling in the shadows reminded me of the spooky, sinister southern landscape where the three civil rights workers, James Chaney, Andrew Goodman, and Michael Schwerner, were killed in *Three Lives for Mississippi*.

Finally, I pulled up for a rest on a rise commanding a good view over the levees. I could see north over the vast cotton lands running north into Kentucky, and south over the sprawling Lake County of Tennessee. The long curve of the Mississippi bending northwest glowed under the moonlight.

One of the more charming features of the Mississippi at night is the constant presence of searchlights beaming toward the shore. The tugboats all carry large searchlights mounted outside of the wheelhouses so that the pilots can check the mile markers, daymarks, and buoys on dark nights, confirming their position, or scan the banks for barge fleets, moored boats, or other obstructions. From afar, the patterns cast by the constantly scanning searchlights give the river a pleasantly surreal appearance, resembling the eerie look of the giant searchlights probing the skies for bombers during World War II. The searchlights also reminded me of the soothing sensation of falling asleep on Cape Cod or along the coast of Maine, with the lighthouse beams softly crawling around my bedroom walls.

As I watched the light display on the river below, I realized that I could pick out many features from memory. *Oh*, I thought, *that tug is scanning the Bixby Towhead Light.* Far to the north, almost too far to see, another tug was scanning the coves just below the Mar Towhead Light. A down-coming tug with a full string of barges was scanning the grain elevator wharves across the river at Linda, Missouri. When I looked behind me, a couple of switch boats were searching with their lights while landing barges at the Cargill docks. The map in my head, from passing most of these spots a few days ago, was still fresh.

Okay, I thought, *the Tiptonville boat ramp is one and a half miles below the Bixby Towhead. So it must be right . . . there.* A screen of trees below was blocking my view of the landing, but I was pretty sure I could work my way down to a spot where there was a break in the trees. I would have to remain on high ground, traveling overland from high spot to high spot, so I could keep the river in sight. The searchlights on the tugs would bear me home to the *Patience* from there.

It was a rough ride at first. The cotton fields behind the levees are often separated by deep ditches, which required me to point the electric bike straight down and throw out my feet as stabilizing bars, and my load of laundry and gas crazily wobbled behind me and I shouted in pain every time my ribs throbbed over the bumps. I passed over a couple of dirt roads that I knew would lead back to the paved levee road, but I was more confident of navigating back to the boat via the river than trying to negotiate the confusing maze of dirt roads. As I dropped toward the river, there were fewer obstructions like trees and high ground to block my view, and I used the lights of the tugs out on the river as a reference to guide me back.

In the fields, my front wheel wobbled in the ruts. I probably traversed six or seven large cotton fields getting back. In the end, I was saved by the levees. At the last high point, where I could pick out the Bixby Towhead Light, I knew that the Tiptonville landing had to be just below me, over my left shoulder, but I couldn't see over the top of the mounded berm of the "backup levee" that angled northwest down there. I remembered that Earl Johnson had told me that most of the berm levees were topped with gravel roads. I could probably follow the berm back to the boat.

I pushed left through the ditch, walked the bike through a grove of young trees, and was pleased to find that the grass on the berm wasn't high. Maxing out the bike, and helping it along by pushing with my legs off the sides, I climbed the levee and reached the gravel road. I recognized where I was now—this was probably the same gravel road on the berm that dropped to the dirt road above the landing. After about one hundred yards, I could see the cement boat ramp and the *Patience* riding her lines.

It was agonizing getting everything back into the boat. To get the boat close enough to unload the bike, I had to wade into the current to loosen my side lines on the kevels, and then scramble the riprap up to the bow line to pull the *Patience* in. It was hell getting the gas can over the gunwales and my ribs raged with pain, but finally everything was aboard. In the shape I was in, I was never going to get the electric bike back on the boat, so I used a spider anchor and line to grapple the bike to a barge line.

Tired, tired, tired, elation, elation, elation. On the boat, I brought my old Amish rocker out to the galley deck and sat and watched a few more tugs pass, their searchlights probing the riprap and the trees on the top of the levees. I threw a handful of Tylenol pills into my throat and washed them down with bourbon. I angled my rocker on the deck for a view of the water, and the rising and falling of the boat gently swayed the rocker back and forth.

Finding my way back to the boat overland, by using the navigation points on the river, filled me with feelings of confidence and accomplishment. I had never been so lost in my life, but I had gotten through it. The elation of realizing that was both sensible and irrational.

I will never be lost again, I thought. We are never really lost. Saint-Exupéry wasn't lost in the Sahara after his big crash in 1935. The great Wilfred Thesiger wasn't lost in the Tigris-Euphrates marshes. Hooker's men weren't lost in 1863 when they climbed through the clouds to take Lookout Mountain. Lost isn't lost. It is man searching for a solution. I will never be lost again.

It had been quite a night and I now considered my transition to riverman to be complete. I was fully oriented to the river. I navigated on land according to the markers and the docks on the river, illuminated by the searchlights of the tugs. By the river, I had come through the cotton fields and over the levee to get back to my boat. My ribs didn't hurt that much if

I lay perfectly flat on my back. I slept well, a Kaintucker who had just found true north of soul.

At Tiptonville, Danny and I addressed the last remaining obstacle to safely descending the Mississippi. The river is a fuel desert. Along the long, lonely stretches of river between major ports—St. Louis to Memphis, or Memphis to Baton Rouge—there is not a single marina for over 400 miles. In between, even in the harbors or inland creeks of relatively large towns like Vicksburg or Greenville, Mississippi, where recreational boating is popular, buying gas along the waterfront is so inconvenient that most boat owners fill up by carrying cans of gas down to the slips in the trunks of their cars. The paucity of river facilities was dramatically worsened by a combination of events after 2008. The major national recession that year wiped out the savings of hundreds of thousands of boaters and decimated boat sales nationally, imperiling the finances of marinas on the inland rivers. Three years later, the record flooding during the spring of 2011 washed away many remaining marinas, or so destroyed waterfront facilities that most marina owners decided to close. The concatenation of disasters turned the Mississippi, once more, into a metaphor of America. Along the largest river in the richest country on earth, potentially a scenic and recreational national treasure, there is no fuel for boats. Except for a few scenic overlooks, and the occasional waterfront parks, the Mississippi is barred from the American public. The scarcity of fuel for boats is a major factor in driving people away from the river.

Danny and I had begun addressing the issue during our long layover for repairs in Newburgh, Indiana, when we were only about ten days from the Mississippi. We sat on our dock along the Ohio below the giant Mulzer Crushed Stone wharves, compiling equipment lists and drawing up plans. We spent a couple of afternoons driving around to marinas and boat dealerships, scouting used johnboats and small motors that we might be able to cobble together as a fuel tender, which we would tie behind the *Patience*. The idea was to pick up an inexpensive aluminum skiff or Zodiac dinghy that we would load with six- or ten-gallon fuel cans, giving us perhaps a hundred-gallon reserve for the long stretches between major cities where fuel would be unavailable. We would call it the Corjulo Fuel Tender.

Danny was adamant about it. He wasn't going to let the scarcity of fuel on the Mississippi interrupt our journey, and his infectious determination inspired me to find a solution. But I didn't want to be brash either.

"The whole world can't be wrong about this, Danny," I said. "Everybody says there isn't fuel on the river."

"You're forgetting something important here," Danny said. "We're not everybody."

We came up with a reasonable plan. After we got past the Wabash, Danny was flying home to return to work for a couple of weeks, and he would look on eBay for an inflatable boat and motor that we could afford, and then ship everything to Newburgh, where my pickup truck was sitting in the parking lot of Curtis Wasmer's shop. When Danny returned to the *Patience* for his next leg of the trip, he would drive the tender down to wherever I was with the boat and set everything up. When he got back to Connecticut and told his brother Clay about his fuel tender project, Clay told Danny that he had a perfectly serviceable Zodiac knockoff in his cellar in the Catskills. The boat was equipped with a five-horse Mercury motor, and Clay said that we were free to use it for the rest of the summer. The boat had sat in a friend's cellar for several years, deflated and folded up into a square. Clay thought that the rubber boat probably had some dry rot, and maybe some bad seams, but Danny went online and found a repair kit that he was pretty sure would work. There was one last touch that Danny loved. Someone had named the boat with bold Magic Marker lettering on the side.

"It's the *Honest Abe*," Danny said. "That's perfect."

Everything associated with the requisitioning of the *Honest Abe* became a classic Corjulo clusterfuck. After Danny decided to pick up the rubber boat at his brother's by flying over to New York State in his flying club's Cessna Skyhawk, he hit a flock of Canada geese while rolling out on the runway at the Kingston-Ulster Airport, and he spent the rest of the afternoon dealing with the Federal Aviation Administration and the aviation mechanic who had to be called in to inspect the plane. When he arrived back in Newburgh and loaded the *Honest Abe* onto my pickup, he discovered that the brake lines in my truck had rusted out and he made a perilous, two-hundred-mile drive south to Tiptonville by stopping at every auto parts store he passed in four states, to buy more brake fluid, and gingerly applying the emergency brake every time he had to stop at a light. The morning after he arrived in

Tiptonville, Danny spent a couple of hours on the cement boat ramp, cutting patches and applying epoxy glue to the bottom of the *Honest Abe*. He inflated the rubber hull by shit-rigging the exhaust pipe of a vacuum cleaner, which was hooked to our Honda generator. He left the rubber boat upside down on the ramp so the glue could dry in the sun.

When Danny was done, the landing ramp was a complete morass of tools, rubber patch remnants, and parts wrappers, and a heavy rain that afternoon washed most of this down to the Mississippi. The scissors that Danny used were stuck in the shut position by the epoxy, and permanently attached to the landing ramp by the glue.

But Danny was ebullient. Things that break, or accumulate dry rot in cellars, provide purpose to a devoted fixer-upper's life. Danny checked the spark plug and put clean fuel in the Mercury motor and mounted it onto the stern of the *Honest Abe*. I was puttering around on the *Patience* galley deck when Danny called from the ramp.

"Captain, vessel *Honest Abe* ready for her sea trials! Stand by to cast off!"

Curtis Wasmer had also driven down from Newburgh in his pickup, and he and Danny were now as thick as Tom and Huck. They would conduct the test voyage of the *Honest Abe* across the river together. I didn't consider braving a used rubber boat across the raging channel of the Mississippi to be advisable, but if anything happened the currents would probably push them into the massive Stewart Towhead bars on the Missouri side. I looked up and down the river for traffic, and the channel down to the Merriwether Light was clear, so perhaps they would be all right. I yelled over from the galley deck.

"Danny, Curtis! Life vests on, please."

"Aye-aye, Captain!"

They whined off across the river with the bow of the *Honest Abe* high in the air, flapping around in the wind like one of those jerky air-dancers in front of a used-car lot. They ran the *Honest Abe* over the top of the Stewart bar and pulled it twenty yards from the water so they could explore the vast expanse of sand. The bar was a display of the river's power—they saw massive driftwood trees, some as tall as forty feet, marooned on the ridges, kilned by years of sunlight to the color of bleach, and huge gravel screes dumped by the winter flow. The open, unobstructed airspace along the bar attracted large flights of low-flying ducks and terns that wheeled sideways toward the inlets and disappeared below the horizon. The sand was clingy and cumbersome underfoot and their boat shoes sank deeply into the sand with every step. At either end, the bar disappeared into blue air over the river, horizonless, disconnected from any context of surrounding landscape.

"You're on your own planet out there," Danny said later. "There is nothing else."

Danny Corjulo and Curtis Wasmer setting off to cross the Mississippi on the Honest Abe, *an inflatable dinghy that Corjulo hauled all the way to Tennessee to use as a fuel tender for the* Patience. *The* Honest Abe *sank that morning.*

As they raced back across the river, Danny noticed that something was awry with the *Honest Abe.* The rubber hull was disintegrating. Pieces of the patches he had just installed were flying past his head. Holes were flapping open in the raised hull and, through them, he could see the *Patience* on the approaching shore. Danny gunned the motor to keep the stern in the water and the bow raised, the only thing that was keeping the *Honest Abe* afloat. When he cut the power as he reached the shallows, the rubber dinghy was taking on water. The *Honest Abe* waddled over to the starboard side of the *Patience* half-submerged, sinking like a drowned poodle.

Amused, I watched from the galley deck as the Corjulo Fuel Tender sank. I threw Danny a line so that he could pull his rubber *Titanic* ashore. The water in the dinghy was already up to Danny's knees and all he had to do was walrus sideways to reach the water.

"Abandon ship! Abandon ship! Commence rescue and salvage operations!"

Curtis helped Danny pull his crippled tender to the bank. Then he sat on the riprap and laughed his ass off. I went for a bourbon. My ribs ached like hell and I didn't want to laugh and invite more pain. Danny stood on the riprap, disconsolate, staring down at the crippled *Honest Abe*, his body expressing the disappointment of failure. His jowls were low and his shoulders drooped.

"This certainly hasn't been my finest hour," he said. "But, hey. Winston Churchill made a lot of mistakes, too."

When he heard about the sinking of the *Honest Abe*, Earl Johnson drove over to console Danny. That night, as we sat by our fire on the riprap, Earl smoked while Danny self-medicated with gin and tonics.

"How do you think I felt in 2011 when the river carried away fifty acres of my farm?" Earl said. "I felt worse than a hound that's just poked his face into a porcupine. But you just gotta wake up the next morning and get back on the tractor."

When he left that night, Earl loaded the *Honest Abe* onto the bed of his pickup and hauled it home to his farm, where he dumped it onto a pile of junk in his greenhouse. As he drove off, the moonlight shining on the deflated and wrinkled dinghy made it look like a bouncing pile of old hose.

By the time we got to Memphis, 150 miles downriver, Danny and I had concluded that the horror stories about fuel were just another river myth. We already had the solution on board and just didn't know it. The electric bike and its cargo holders was our godsend. The bike proved adaptable to almost every condition, as long as we were willing and determined enough to use it. Even along the more remote stretches of the river, we could land on the riprap or in a small cove, haul the bike over the levee, and push through the trees and find a road. There was always a town within fifteen or twenty miles. There were plenty of boat landings with cement ramps, and there were always workers at the grain elevator docks who would help us tie up and get ashore. The farmers along the levees were harvesting corn and cotton that month. The fields were busy with combines and giant hopper trailers all day and, in the evening, when we pulled off the channel to tie up at a town landing or a cove, the farmers saw our big American flag fluttering out over the levees. They were about to park their tractors for the night anyway. They drove over to the river to see who we were in pickup trucks loaded with forty-five-gallon or sixty-gallon fuel tanks, both diesel and gas. They loved to linger on the roof deck watching the sun set while drinking Corjulo martinis, and they never let us pay for gas.

"Oh, hell, I probably got like sixty gallons of gas here," a farmer in Tunica, Mississippi, said when he drove over after we landed at the town ramp there. "Just take all you want."

The search for gas became part of the rhythm of the trip, part of the romance. On the electric bike, I rode for miles and miles in the dark through the moody, spooky southern row-crop fields of Bolivar and Claiborne counties, hunting for ice and gas. The screech of the insects was deafening. I swerved on the blacktop around the giant snapping turtles. My way was lit by the LED lights mounted on my John Deere cap. I didn't need a map. I never worried about being lost—getting over the levees at Tiptonville had vaccinated me for life from that. Every small town in the South can be found by the glow in the sky of the Dairy Queen lights. The gas station was right there, or nearby.

On my metaphoric boat on my metaphoric river, I went to bed every night tired but elated. I knew now that I wasn't sailing the Mississippi. I was sailing the River of Misinformation. In my homeland, misinformation is as American as apple pie, and I had to virally shed all of that to get to New Orleans.

20

THE MISSISSIPPI'S CULTURE OF MISINFORMATION was as powerful as the river's currents, and there was one last myth to debunk. All of the reenactors and the weekend anglers in their camo johnboats said the same thing: if I ran aground on the sandbars, my trip would be over. It would take weeks, even months, for the deeper winter flow to return and provide enough water over the bars to free my boat. I would have to abandon the *Patience* on the bar and then somehow haul my gear to the banks. In the meantime, under regulations devoted to maintaining the commercial waterways, the U.S. Coast Guard would declare my boat a "hazard to navigation," drag it away by salvage boat, and have it destroyed. I was even told that I could be prosecuted under federal laws forbidding abandoning a vessel adjacent to a commercial waterway. Boats left on the bars could be unexpectedly freed by a freak storm, float downriver, and then run adrift in the channel, imperiling barge traffic.

But now that I had spent two months traveling more than a thousand miles of the Ohio and the Mississippi, I considered this information suspect. In fact, the Army Corps of Engineers and the U.S. Coast Guard are inept at policing America's waterways and have never displayed much interest in maintaining either a safe or clean environment for boat traffic. The Ohio and the Mississippi are nothing but Superfund sites with water running through them. Vast stretches of the inland rivers, especially the banks near grain elevators, gravel quarries, and barge terminals, are littered with derelict wharves and abandoned barges stacked on top of each other, making it difficult to safely navigate the shallows nearby. There are mountains of oil barrels, abandoned boat motors, and heavy chains just beneath the surface at almost every location frequented by the big barge and tug companies. The nearby inlets and coves are junkyards filled with ditched dredging and mining equipment, leaking hydraulic oil, diesel fuel, and noxious chemicals in the rivers. Runaway buoys, half-submerged houseboats, and pyramids of refrigerators and shopping carts are compacted along the banks and under the bridge pylons of America's federally administered rivers. In 2014, University of Kentucky students conducted a visual survey of the debris floating by a single site, the town landing in Carrollton, Kentucky. Over twenty-four hours, they identified nineteen gas containers, forty-five tires, sixty-eight basketballs and footballs, and fifty-two fifty-five-gallon drums bobbling on the surface.

The federal government itself is America's largest polluter. Two-thirds of the country's designated Superfund sites are federal military bases, leaking gasoline, solvents, explosives, and refrigerator gas into the local rivers and water tables. The Pentagon recently estimated that, across 19 million acres of military bases, it maintains thirty-nine thousand contaminated sites.

So I wasn't going to worry about the Coast Guard or the Army Corps. They were obviously so busy supervising their existing flow of pollutants and rusty parts along the Mississippi that they wouldn't get to the *Patience* very quickly. Instead, as I spent afternoons looking ahead on my river charts and understanding the true nature of the river and its traffic, I realized that I had to reverse traditional thinking and fears and radically revise my seamanship. It was almost inevitable that I would face a situation where, to avoid getting run over by the barges, I would have to go up onto the bars. I would need a "refloat" strategy to get off.

The enormous flow of the Mississippi after its confluence with the Ohio has created a river that is endlessly serpentine, especially on the lower, southern reaches below Memphis. The constant motion of water slamming against the banks carves sharp, sudden turns on one side and moves massive deposits of sand to the opposite bank. This natural "oxbow formation" narrows the navigable channel of water as the river contracts to make a turn. Supplemented by the flow generated by the wing dams, the currents on the turn are fast.

The main difficulty on the sharp, oxbow turns is visibility. The barge string pushed by a tug typically contains six rows of barges, four across, which can stretch ahead of the wheelhouse a distance of 1,600 feet. The tall bows of the forward barges block the pilot's field of vision for another 600 feet. That's almost 2,200 feet of "blind space" in front of every rig moving on the river. The boat captains can usually locate boats ahead on their radar, but they can't visually "mark" that traffic for almost a half mile away.

My job on the *Patience* was to always position my hull so that captains either fore or aft could see my big American flag. The effort is similar to the way that an automobile driver following a truck should position their vehicle in the lane so the driver ahead can see trailing traffic in his rearview mirror. The strong flow of the Mississippi virtually guaranteed that a down-coming string, especially one with some empty barges, could quickly overtake us. On the straightaways I tried to cheat the bars on the edge of the channel so that the pilot behind could see me at an angle. I slowed down so he could pass me in the wider space. But if we were too close to a turn, where the navigable space narrowed, I powered up to speed away and wait for the next opportunity for being passed on a straightaway. This almost always worked and the down-comers were fun traffic.

Long strings moving upriver were much more dangerous, especially on the tight turns. If a tug and barge string ahead was already in the middle of the bend, splayed sideways across the channel to make the turn, the strong downstream flow was pushing against their massive length and slowing their hulls, turning them into an almost stationary obstruction. Meanwhile, the same current, behind me, was pushing me toward the string and I couldn't stop. The space between the forward bows of the string and the buoy I needed to cheat could be very narrow. Even if it looked at a distance that I could power up and speed through, the currents behind me were going to make my flat-bottom yaw sideways. The wing dams steering water from the shallows made conditions even worse. As the water came chuting back into the main channel at a high speed, usually at a sharp angle, it propelled my flat-bottom sideways, dramatically increasing my yaw. In this situation I could probably avoid being run directly over by the barge bows.

But my yaw angle could easily slip me sideways into the barges, in which case I would be just as dead.

The problem is multiplied by visibility. If a tug and barge string was already in the turn, I wouldn't see them until I came around the bend. The angling of the string to get around the bend would probably prevent the tug captain from seeing me as well, risking the possibility of one of the most dreaded scenarios on the river, a "blind collision." I had read about blind collision accidents where strings had run over small boats ahead and the crew of the tug didn't even feel a bump when their thirty-six thousand tons of loaded barges ran over a pontoon boat. When I looked ahead on my charts, I could see more than a dozen tight turns downriver where I faced exactly this possibility.

Reasoning logically, and looking ahead on the river charts at the obvious physics, I reached a conclusion. I could easily face an encounter with the barges where I would be safer, and the tugboat captains would be safer, if I elected to go up on the bars. I needed a contingency plan. I might have to climb the bars to get out of the way of a big upcoming string on a tight bend of the Mississippi.

During all this time I had also been making a study of tug wakes. At Cairo, surfing the wake at the stern of the tug effortlessly carried me through the narrows. At night, when I tied up against a tree or on a levee, I carefully triangulated my lines so that the wakes of the passing tugs actually helped me keep the *Patience* just the right distance from the banks. There were sideways wakes that pushed me in the direction I wanted to go. There were bow waves off the barge strings that created undertows that tried to suck me toward their hulls. Tug wakes were like being in love, or sitting down in the morning to write. I thought I knew what was going to happen, until I didn't.

I had observed for almost two months now that upcoming tugs, especially when coming out of a turn, threw massive amounts of water toward the banks. The wash of a wake over the wing dams or the bars could create an extra five feet of depth, two hundred yards away from the tug. If I had to run up on a bar to avoid a collision with the barges, and I managed to angle the bow downriver as I ramped up the sand, I would probably just have to wait five or ten minutes until the push boat moving upriver got abeam of my position. The water from its wake would lift me off the bar.

Landing on a sandbar, therefore, was not necessarily an emergency. It was simply a problem to solve—buoyancy must be restored. This was indeed the conception during the flatboat era. All of the significant river travelers in the 19th century—Zadok Cramer, Timothy Flint, Christian Schultz—wrote about running aground as a more or less expected event, and described the common strategies for overcoming it. The long "leviathan" flats were lashed together and floated as a single rig, creating a displaced mass so heavy that the flat-bottom on the edge of the tie-up, or those in the rear, was pulled over the bars near the banks by the weight and the momentum of the boats in deeper water. The Kaintuckers traveled in large collections of "floating villages," to guarantee a labor force large enough to jump over the side and free a stalled boat. There were many accounts of flatboat crews deploying for beached boats by canoe. Another tactic was called "slaving." Five or six boats were "slaved" together by ropes into a tandem row and then a long line was thrown to a stranded boat on a bar, quickly hooked up to the bow, and the stranded hull was slowly eased off. Paying passengers on keelboats and flatboats were frequently asked to go over the side to help free a boat. Getting off the shoals, by the variety of methods devised at the time, was called "bar jumping," or "jumping the bars."

Jumping the bars, or rescuing boats on the bars, became a big business during the flatboat era. Throughout the inland river country, especially after the steamboat was introduced in the late 1820s, running "lighters" was one of the most thriving trades. Lighters were flatboats with large crews that patrolled the shoals, looking for beached steamboats or responding to reports of stranded steamboats. Lighters floated over to the bars where a steamboat was trapped and its crews painstakingly unloaded the stranded vessel, staging the cargo on a safe bank nearby so that the boat was lighter and could be floated back into the river. Art historians consider George Caleb Bingham's *Lighter Relieving a Steamboat Aground*, which is now a part of the White House collection in Washington, D.C., to be one of his best compositions. The 1847 painting depicts a lighter crew, surrounded on the deck by heavy cargo boxes, floating downriver on their flat-bottom after unloading a steamboat beached on the Missouri River shoals near St. Louis. At river towns like New Madrid and Memphis, there were always several lighters in the parked fleet. Stranded boats being "lighted" was a common 19th-century scene on the rivers.

At Tiptonville, all of this reading about sandbars and boats prompted a strong mnemonic response, which I couldn't quite fathom at first. When I woke up on the *Patience*, I would see the face of Ted King. Ted King! Why was my nocturnal dream-processing cycling through Ted King every night, and then waking me up in the morning with the image of his face? Over two or three days I gradually accepted that my brain's memory function was working overtime to get me down the river. Ted King was one of the great bar jumpers of his day, in a great bar-jumping town on Cape Cod. Now that I needed him, he was returning from the past to help me get my bar jumping back in shape.

Ted was the father of my close boyhood friend, John King. John and I were inseparable as kids while growing up in northern New Jersey, and I often joined the Kings for two or three weeks during the summer at Chatham, Massachusetts, on the elbow of Cape Cod. John and I raced Sprites on Stage Harbor, prowled the Ocean Spray factory and fish pier docks, and took long bike rides over to Harding's Beach or the Chatham Light. Ted King ran the family business all week down in New Jersey and then commuted back to the Cape every weekend, when he sailed and relaxed and taught us the art of handling small boats.

Ted King was a skilled sailor, much beloved on the Cape. He was rakishly handsome and boyish, perpetually tanned, with thin legs that penciled down to his weathered boat shoes. He was a Yalie, Skull and Bones, and a former singer with the Whiffenpoofs. The Kings were actually Roman Catholics, mixed Irish and Portuguese, but like so many Catholic men of his day, Ted preferred to "pass," condensing into one personality every virtue and vice of a faux WASP. He was caustic and sarcastic and then suddenly lovable and benevolent, then bigoted and snide again, a great man for kids, until he decided that he wasn't. He was a snob who was the friendliest man alive. My father was the same way. John and I used to argue about whose father was more aggravating, his or mine.

Ted was devoted to sailing instruction and legendary as an organizer of sailing competitions and training programs for young sailors, and would later be awarded sailing's most prestigious award, the Nathanael G. Herreshoff Trophy. He was a connoisseur of the small tricks that a sailor could deploy to large effect. He taught us to lie as low as possible in the boat, below the freeboard, to reduce the drag we were presenting to the wind. At the downwind buoys, he taught us to approach at an angle, and then come around hard, so we could accelerate upwind on the next leg.

Chatham, like Marblehead to the north or Annapolis, Maryland, is a famous sailing town, but the elbow of the Cape is considered a great training ground for a unique reason. The Atlantic waters off Chatham are among the most dangerous in the world, laced with shoals and tricky currents. Captains experienced in rounding the outer Cape waters were prized during the 19th century. The outer waters along Nauset on the Atlantic side are called an "ocean graveyard," littered with more than 1,000 wrecks, from Chatham to Provincetown. But inside the barrier islands, the waters from Nantucket Sound to Pleasant Bay, challenged sailors in other ways. On summer days, powerful southwest breezes of twenty-five knots or more were common. The low-water shoals are as big as a cornfield and constantly shifting.

On Saturday afternoons, Ted took us out into these challenging waters, usually over to Monomoy Island, a mystical planet of sand serrated with endless dunes and salt marshes with brooding colonies of sandpipers and terns, where we roamed and picnicked for hours. His boat was an American classic, specifically designed for the western Nantucket Sound Cape waters, a sleek, gaff-rigged wooden sloop called the Wianno Senior. The Wianno was a famous boat. Jack and Teddy Kennedy were frequently pictured in *Life* magazine, as bronzed and as handsome as movie stars, heeling over in their Wiannos as they raced on the Sound. In his red hull, the *Tailwind II*, Ted had raced out of Harwich Port and built his reputation as a skipper. But the Wianno hull was built for the deeper waters of the Sound out past Hyannis, where its pointed bow and heavy centerboard keel were ideal for slicing through chop in stiff winds. It was not the perfect hull for the tricky waters off Chatham, where its draft was often too deep for the shoals. Ted was determined to use his limited time off on weekends to take us all out to Monomoy for a picnic, and he loaded the *Tailwind II* like the family station wagon, stuffing eight or nine kids and their friends into the cramped oval cockpit.

The prevailing winds in Chatham were from the southwest and landing on Monomoy was difficult. In the shallow waters, the wind was behind us, pushing us toward the beach, and the barrier island offered no protection, requiring a notoriously tricky "lee shore" approach. Chatham produces such unstable conditions for sand that the bars around Monomoy were constantly changing. Depending on the tides, we never knew their exact location. We slammed into the bars a lot, beaching the boat at a list, and lurching to a halt. Suddenly, eight or nine kids were compacted together in the front of the cockpit, the sails luffed, and from below we could hear the lead weights stacked around the keel loudly clinking together, like bottles on a beer delivery truck.

But we were always game for this. Beaching the Wianno was just a part of our day with Ted King.

"John, Rinker, Sam," Ted would say. "Over the side. Push us off."

Lighting the *Tailwind II* off the bar was fun, but hard work. Usually, two of us were staged at the bow, two at the stern, and we rocked the boat end to end to try to work it off. Sometimes we had to wait for a current or an incoming tide to help lift the boat. A couple of times we stood with our backs to the boat and pushed hard with our feet against the sand walls of the shoal. Once the boat was freed, Ted wanted to get underway immediately so he could tack toward deeper water. He would yell at us to get back into the cockpit, and it was hard getting back over the sides of a moving boat. Panting for air, clawing at the rail of the cockpit, we pulled ourselves back in. It felt like a miracle every time I was recovered to the boat.

I still don't fully grasp why my memories of Cape Cod emerged right after I got to the Mississippi. Confronting a massive string of barges at the bars along the Mississippi was a lot more hazardous than beaching the *Tailwind II* off Monomoy. Perhaps my brain was simply reminding me, "You have done this before." It was certainly the case that I had learned, in some of the toughest waters of the world, to bar jump with the best. I should be ready.

My Sharpsburg, my Vicksburg siege, arrived at Mile 821 on the river, twenty-five miles below Caruthersville, Missouri, where the Wrights Point bars form a massive sand barrier protecting the banks just above a sharp northwest turn in the river called Tamm Bend. We were running the *Patience* down through the oxbows at half power, enjoying the lovely, low stratocumulus clouds and the cooling gusts blowing over our faces from the southwest.

Cynthia Lee, center, and Deb Satterfield, rear, were so reliable at steering the Patience *and navigating that I often left them on the roof deck to handle the boat by themselves.*

I couldn't have been happier that day. My dream team was aboard and everything was running perfectly on the boat. While I steered from the roof deck, Deb Satterfield sat beside me on our poplar bench, following on the map and looking ahead with binoculars, as meticulous as a nun grading school papers. When I asked about our position, she would say, "Mile 840. The daymark is out but I can see the buoys. That's Island Eighteen ahead." Cynthia Lee, who is quite good at reading water, was standing behind us, offering steering tips. "I don't like the way that the water is curling around that buoy." Cynthia had concluded that the buoy was probably in the wrong place and she directed me to steer wide around it.

New best friends Danny and Curtis were below, wailing with laughter and goof-boy behavior as they cleaned the cabin and galley. At Caruthersville that morning, they had vowed to spend a few hours thoroughly scouring the *Patience* with water and bleach. There were mushrooms growing in the cracks in the floorboards, a family of juvenile snakes crawling around, and the galley walls and floor were grimy with a patina of chopped onions, pepper seeds, spices, and flour where Danny had cooked the night before. I had overheard them talking that morning.

"Rinker is such a pain in the ass," Danny said. "I cook him all of these great meals and then he complains that the floor is dirty. What am I, his bitch?"

"Humor him," Curtis said. "The captain has a lot on his mind."

As we came past the mouth of the Obion River and entered the bend, I saw the forward bows of a long string of barges splayed across the narrow channel ahead. The captain was maneuvering to starboard to pitch his string for entering the next bend, throwing a lot of wash to the Tennessee banks, and I knew I couldn't go there because his stern was just off the bank. I couldn't go to the Arkansas banks either because the captain had his forward bows pointed toward the end of a long wing dam that extended into the channel.

I was being pinched. When we got there, a half mile ahead, there might be just enough space between the barges and the wing dam to squeeze through, but this was suicidal to consider. I couldn't possibly predict my yaw angle in these currents and the chances were good that I'd slide sideways either into the barges or the wing dam. This was exactly the kind of scenario I had worried about and I had to act soon.

I decided to turn right, pointing the bow directly at the buoy marking the Wrights Point bars. I was betting that I could beat the bows of the first barges to the buoy with a comfortable margin and then firewall downriver to get away from the string. If I was betting wrong, I would have to run the *Patience* up on the bar, which would at least avoid a fatal collision. My big mistake that morning was having failed to alert Deb and Cynthia that I might have to jump the bar somewhere to avoid a barge string, and that I had a plan for getting us off the bar afterward.

As I angled toward the sandbar, they could see the peril. Beside me, Deb kept repeating, "Left, left, left," to go left of the buoy. Cynthia was urgently telling me to look at the water ahead. The ripples on the surface told her that we were headed for low water near the buoy.

A quarter mile out, I could see that we weren't going to beat the barges to the buoy. My space between the barges and the buoy was narrowing by the second. There was no time left. I couldn't even yell to Deb and Cynthia that I was going up the bar. I just had to do it.

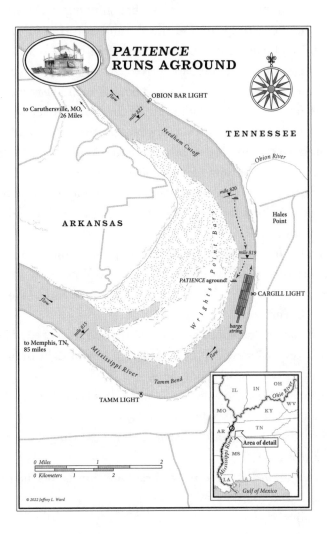

The *Patience* performed beautifully that morning. As we entered the rippled water I firewalled the throttle and pulled hard to starboard on the wheel. The bow lifted and gouged out a sand track as we bumped over the edge and then I turned to port to try to get us on the bar facing downriver. The engine roared, but it now had only half of the hull to push—the rest was up in the air—and we skittered around nicely, landing with a hard bump facing just about due south. There was still water around us, but only a few inches. Our hull was planted, firmly, on the bar.

As I put the motor in neutral, I was surprised by how calm and relieved I felt. There are two steps to bar jumping, I thought—getting onto the bar, and getting off. On the fly, and not even knowing what I was doing, I had just executed a nearly perfect phase one. And I could see from the wash the tug just downriver was producing that phase two could be quite successful, too. I looked behind me to see where the captain was going. The bend at the mouth of the Obion River was mild, and the captain had a five-mile straightaway after that. He could easily play with his stern to give me plenty of water and still position his string away from the banks. By the time he was abeam of my position on the bar, he could swing to his port to mid-channel, or even all the way over to my Arkansas side, feeding me a great deal of lifting wash. I would be off this bar in five minutes.

Deb and Cynthia were concerned, perplexed. They couldn't believe that we'd just run aground and worried that we'd never get off the bar. I told them to remain calm and just relax. I had a plan and needed to talk to the captain downriver.

I knew that the captain ahead couldn't see me yet. His barges were splayed blocking his view. But I had a decent line of sight to his tall radio antenna and we could work from there.

"Tugboat and string at Mile 817, Point 5, this is the flatboat *Patience*."

The captain hailed me right back and asked where I was.

"Flatboat *Patience* is on the bar just above the wing dam at Mile 818. Your channel is clear."

"Ah, yeah, okey-dokey. I thought I saw sumthin' go off the river on my radar. Tankee. Did you steer off for me?"

"Affirmative."

"Tankee, yeah, tankee. Let me just get straight again and see where you are."

"Your mark is the American flag. We've got a big American flag."

"Stand by."

I was pretty sure that I knew what the captain was doing now. He was staring ahead with his binoculars, and looking at his radar paint of the banks ahead, to see how much maneuvering room he had to point his barge string. His iNav screen would be showing him that the layout ahead of his string was favorable for getting me off the bar.

After about five minutes, when the tug lumbering upstream finally had its string mostly straight and the captain could see out his port window, he came back on the radio.

"Flatboat *Patience*. Mark. Dem are nice Stars and Stripes."

I explained to the captain that I was aground on the bar, but only a few yards from the deep-water channel. I needed the wash from his wake to get off.

"And you're goin' to git it. Stand by."

The captain came on a minute or two later and gave me his plan. When he got abeam of my position he would go to max on his turbines, swing his stern to port, and flood the bar. He wanted me to go off the sand in reverse because that was my shortest direct path to deep water in the channel. He suggested that I steer straight across the river for the Cargill docks from there, so that I wouldn't risk yawing back toward the bar. I was to be patient and wait until he was well past me so there was no danger of us colliding. He didn't want me to back off the bar until he said "Go."

"Affirm. The *Patience* is standing by."

While all of these conversations were taking place, I asked Cynthia to get below and use our "fathom stick" to measure the depth of water around the stern. A fathom stick was a length of tree limb or milled lumber that the Kaintuckers used, marked with heights, to probe the water around their boats so they could call back to the tiller and give their captains an idea of how deep the water was nearby. I had bought our fathom stick—a twelve-foot section of one-inch dowel—at Home Depot and marked it with height levels with red spray paint.

We still had plenty of water around us, just not enough to float the hull. Cynthia came back up to the roof deck and told me that there were spots off the *Patience*'s bow and sides where we had two feet of water. We were just barely aground.

The first barges of the string were beginning to pass us on the port side when Danny excitedly leaped up the stairs to the roof deck. He had been sitting on the toilet below when we ran up the bar and ran above so quickly that his shorts were still down to his ankles. I had briefed him days before about the possibility of running aground, but the event itself delivered to him the perfect excuse for a classic Corjulo meltdown.

"Mayday! Mayday! Hull aground! Hull aground!"

"Danny," I said. "Shut your pie trap."

"Aye-aye, Captain."

I told Danny to get below to the stern deck and tilt the main motor out of the water. I also needed him to start the backup motor and let it idle out of the water. Curtis could operate the tilt switch on the main motor. When the tug downriver passed us and its wake began to flood the sandbar, they would have to tilt both motors back into the water and then run the backup motor at full power in reverse. We were going to back off the bar to reach the channel.

Danny feverishly belted up his shorts and ran back to the stairs.

"Activate emergency power! Activate emergency power! This is not a drill! This is not a drill!"

It was beautiful, and I was moved almost to tears, as I watched the big tug lumber upriver, pushing its heavy load. Every minute or so a black puff of smoke exited the tug's stacks, and the stern swung toward the Arkansas banks, as the captain tested pushing his wash over the bar, before he straightened back out. The wake broke over the bar below us in large whitecaps, flooding west for sixty or seventy yards. Once, a flock of white pelicans and terns, foraging on the bar, flew up and wheeled south as the tug's wash flooded their position.

I waited, working at being patient. The bow waves from the barge string were washing over the bar now and I could feel the *Patience* responding. She was lighting, almost lifting off the bar. When I knew that I had just a minute or so left, I walked over to the side of the roof deck, out from underneath the bimini, and waved to the captain. The captain's wheelhouse door was open and, holding his wheel with his far hand, he stood up and waved back with his cap.

Just past us, but still abeam, the stern of the big tug wheeled over to face the bar. The stacks roared with black exhaust and then purple and yellow heat. I leaned down to the radio speaker to make sure that I could hear the tug captain's broadcast.

"Go!" he shouted.

It was the most magnificent feeling, elation, elation, elation, because the *Patience* was already afloat in the wash and we were drifting backward off the bar. I yelled down to Danny.

"Go!"

We effortlessly backed off the bar and recovered the channel in just a few seconds and then, elation, elation, elation again, I was pointed toward the Cargill docks and well clear of the tug before I turned south with the flow.

"Tug at Mile 819, flatboat *Patience* is underway and no longer a factor. Thank you, Captain."

"We're good, Capt'n. That's a beautiful flag."

Cynthia and Deb were clapping their hands and slapped me on my shoulders. Danny was screaming yahoos from the stern deck. When I looked down he was standing with both arms raised high, Sylvester Stallone at the top of the stairs of the Philadelphia Museum of Art.

"Mission accomplished! Mission accomplished! Hull underway!"

I yelled for him to shut down the auxiliary motor.

"Aye-aye, Captain! Deactivating emergency power! Deactivating emergency power!"

We were good to go downriver. The weather was ideal for the rest of the day and we moved quickly with the flow as the white pelicans rose in the thousands beside us. That night, we camped in an inlet on the bars along the Arkansas side, opposite the Chickasaw Bluffs. At sunset, the sandstone cliffs glowed pink, lavender, and Osage orange.

I fell asleep profoundly content. Another river myth had been put to rest, another milestone passed, and I was now a jubilant Kaintucker, an alligator-horse at rest. The *Patience* had jumped the bars, once more defying all the prophecies of doom.

21

AS SOON AS I BEGAN reading about the flatboat era, I knew that I had to get to Natchez, Mississippi. The charmingly preserved town sits majestically on the tall bluffs 250 miles above New Orleans, and for much of the 19th century it was one of the most fabled places in America. Natchez was mystical and lyrical and famously bipolar, a glorious clash of Creole suave and upriver crude. At the base of the bluffs, a shantytown called Natchez Under-the-Hill sloped down a cramped gravel bar to the river. As many as two hundred flat-bottoms were parked there every night, and the Kaintuckers drank and gambled and whored until dawn. The fistfights were so rough that men bit off the end of their opponent's noses. Above the bluffs, on Natchez On-Top-of-the-Hill, the cotton millionaires of the South lived grandly, building sumptuous mansions with the alacrity of an Ottoman collecting wives. They were called the Natchez nabobs and they were perhaps the most famous and envied oligarchs in the world. The Forks of the Road slave market just outside town was the second largest in the country, supporting the extraordinarily cruel extension of slavery into the Deep South. All of the fractious contradictions of America were concentrated on the Natchez bluffs.

In the 19th century, Natchez had the reputation of being a place where anything could happen, and often did, and the landing of the *Patience* there proved this point. I was sailing that day with my most memorable crew member, a burly, Whitmanesque continental wanderer named Jamie Buckley. Jamie was a veteran thru-hiker who had walked thousands of miles of ridges along the Appalachian Trail, the Pacific Crest Trail, and the Continental Divide Trail, and I met him along the river while he was nearing the end of a 2,300-mile kayaking trip down the Mississippi. In Vicksburg, I suggested that he lash his kayak to the stern kevel of the *Patience*, to rest and relax for a few days while continuing his voyage down the river. He settled into a living space amid the cots on the roof deck and was still with me three hundred river miles later, when the *Patience* reached New Orleans.

Since the flatboating days, most of the acreage of the old Under-the-Hill gravel bar has been carried away by storms, and there is no inlet or even a break in the levees to provide protection from the flow while landing. On the afternoon in early October when we got to Natchez, we had a strong southwest wind pushing us from behind. I asked Jamie to jump off the *Patience* and threw him a line to tie us up on one of the barge cables on the levee. But the boat was being pushed so hard by the current and the wind that it was impossible for Jamie to run beside it and secure a line. He stumbled several times on the riprap. The only way to stop the *Patience* was to ram the bow onto the levee near the remains of an old casino landing. I scrambled up the riprap myself and found a barge cable to tie us up. Then I had to wait for half an hour on the boat, until enough tug wakes reached the old casino landing and floated me off the rocks, to secure the *Patience* with lines in a few feet of water.

That afternoon, after a pleasant tour of the mansion district and the national cemetery out past the bluffs, I was standing on Silver Street above Under-the-Hill and enjoying the river views when a paddle wheel–style cruise ship, the *America*, wheeled in from the channel and parked at the old casino landing, about thirty feet from where the *Patience* was riding her lines. The boat lowered a long gangplank to the cement ramp at the landing and passengers began filing off to have meals and see the town.

At Memphis and Vicksburg, cruise ships and Coast Guard boats had parked right beside me and I had spoken to the captains. I knew the drill. Even though I had priority because I had landed first, it was considered good manners to ask the cruise boat captain if I was in his way and to offer to move my boat. When I walked down and yelled up to the captain, he stepped to the edge of the deck high above.

"You're okay where you are," the captain said. "But if you'd like to help, it would be better if you moved fifty or sixty feet down the levee."

Jamie was inside the Magnolia Grill on Silver Street, commencing a taste test of the martinis in town. He wasn't going to be much help moving the boat, so I walked across the levee by myself, laboriously resetting all of my lines, pulling up my anchors, and then starting the *Patience* to move her down the levee. After I reset my anchors, I waited on the boat for a few minutes to see how she settled in the current. The captain of the *America* was standing on his gangplank as his passengers got off and thanked me as I went by.

It was getting dark as I walked up the embankment to Silver Street, where I noticed a police car with its blue lights flashing, parked sideways into the driving lane, partially blocking traffic. Police officers are so addicted to obstructing traffic with their patrol cars that it must be required in their operating manuals. They would do it out of loyalty to protocol even if it wasn't required. Natchez must be a great town, I thought.

The cop was walking toward me with an angry expression on his face. He was one of those hideous mannequins of redundancy with multiple walkie-talkies and shiny pouches of handcuffs, pepper spray, and mace hanging from his belt.

I took one look at him and thought, *Oh, here we go. The rogue cop.* There's always at least one on every trip.

"Is that your boat down there?"

"That's my boat."

"Take it away. Homeland Security regulations. You're not allowed within two hundred fifty feet of a cruise ship."

I started off softly, even though I didn't feel like displaying an ounce of politeness toward this Attila. I explained that I was the first in the harbor, and that the cruise ship had parked after me. I had already moved my boat for the cruise ship captain. I had parked close to cruise ships before and, in Memphis, the Coast Guard had boarded my boat while I was parked next to a cruise ship and never said a thing. There was no other room in the harbor and I didn't consider it safe to operate in a commercial channel at night.

"You're not in Memphis," the cop snarled. "You're in Natchez. Homeland Security regs are Homeland Security regs. Move your boat or I'm calling the Coast Guard to tow you away."

I asked the cop where he suggested that I move my boat. The landing area in Natchez is quite small.

"That's not my problem," the cop said. "Move your boat or I'm calling the Coast Guard."

I knew that this bonehead was bluffing and, later, when I called the section office in Vicksburg, the Coast Guard said that the only thing they would have done was to call the captain of the *America* and ask him if I was a threat to the cruise ship. They didn't even have a boat available that night. But the cop wasn't looking for a solution. He was looking for a confrontation to appease his deep inner need to exercise authority, reasonable or not.

A deep sadness for my country sinks inside me whenever I have to deal with another rogue cop. I always have the same thought. If this guy is hassling my white privileged ass, how is he treating everyone else? But I wasn't in the mood for crying for my country that night. My ribs ached, and I was exhausted from sailing all day and then tying up twice in one afternoon. I was pondering what to do.

"Let's call the police chief, or your desk sergeant," I said to the cop. "I'm not sure you're correct about the regulations."

"Not going to happen. I'm not calling anyone for you. Move your boat or I'll have it towed."

A group of tourists and motorcyclists who were visiting Under-the-Hill, and several passengers from the cruise ship, had gathered on the green lawn beside us overlooking the river, to watch my fracas with the cop. It was gratifying to hear their comments. One of them yelled to the cop, "He's already moved his boat, you jerk," and another said, "Welcome to Mississippi, home of dumb cops." But they weren't making any progress with this moron either.

While I was still getting nowhere with the cop, I noticed two men who looked to be in their early twenties standing on the edge of the crowd, occasionally adding their own insults to those yelled out by the crowd. One of them, a chisel-faced man in cowboy boots, walked over and motioned me away from the cop. His name was Garrett Yelverton. Garrett was a kind of modern-day Natchez nabob. He was a member of a prominent business family in town. He told me that the cop was well known around Natchez for being a troublemaker. Garrett owned a small company that

reprovisioned the tugs running on the river with groceries and other supplies. He had his own dock across the river in Vidalia, Louisiana. I could
park the *Patience* there as long as I wanted. I was immediately tempted by
his offer because parking in a protected slip across the river would be a lot
better than the *Patience* hanging out in the current on the Natchez side.
But I was worried about running at night, which I had vowed not to do.

Garrett motioned with his chin across the river.

"The whole way is lit. That's my dock right there, and there's lights under
the bridge. I run at night all the time, supplying the tugs. I'll go with you."

I didn't have much choice, and it seemed like the better decision.

"All right, thanks," I said. "Let me just say good night to this asshole."

"Suit yourself," Garrett said. "But just remember what my father says.
The assholes are never worth it. It's better to leave them in the dark."

I liked that. Garrett asked the young employee who was with him to
meet us over in Vidalia with his pickup. I looked back as we turned to walk
down the levee toward the *Patience*. The cop was still standing on Silver
Street, scratching his head while the blue lights from his cruiser flashed on
his walkie-talkies and mace, still drawing insults from the crowd.

Garrett seemed like a pretty capable riverman. He told me to get up to
my console, start the *Patience* motor and put it in reverse, to hold the boat
gently against her lines while he freed the ropes. I picked him up on the
banks and he gave me careful instructions for getting around the stern of
the *America*. In the chill night air, we had a nice run across the river, with
the headlights from the cars on the Natchez-Vidalia Bridge casting spooky
shapes, and our motor reverberating loud echoes when we got underneath
the span. We tied up at Yelverton's dock and drove back across the river.

When we returned to Silver Street, the cop and his obnoxious blue
lights were gone, and Under-the-Hill seemed festive with tourists. College
students and middle-aged motorcyclists with their helmets on their laps
sat at tables on the outdoor patios of the bars, laughing, enjoying the river
view, feeding leftover chicken wings and sliders to their dogs. I decided
that I liked Natchez—it was going to be a nice respite after more than two
months of running on the rivers.

Natchez was also going to be a land of instant friendships, and I could
tell I was going to enjoy several nights carousing with Garrett and his
friends. When we pushed through the door of the Magnolia Grill, Jamie

was seated at a table by the window with the best view of the river. He and his best new friend, the town attorney, were enjoying their third martini.

Natchez was one of those wilderness intersections that grew because of the accidents of history. The cleared bluffs developed as a river port before the American Revolution because of its strategic location, just a few days' sail from New Orleans. The low country inland from the bluffs also stood at the beginning of an old Indian trail, which would eventually be called "The Natchez Trace," and led 450 miles north to the Tennessee and Cumberland rivers and the prized hunting and trapping lands of Kentucky. Initially, the Natchez Indians, a mound-building tribe who were successful farmers and trappers, acted as intermediaries for the other southwestern tribes, brokering Cherokee, Chickasaw, and Choctaw pelts, dried fish, and vegetables to be sent downriver, which turned the Natchez bluffs into a busy trading and canoeing center. The endless conflict and pitched battles of the fur-trapping era after 1760 scattered the tribes and destabilized the region. But the fur era also filled western Mississippi with roving bands of native and mixed-race men, as well as French and British trappers, who began to rely on Natchez as a kind of Scuffletown on the next river, a rendezvous point with good river access for moving product from the interior to points south. The French and Spanish colonial authorities unwittingly contributed to the growth around Natchez by perpetually ceding the lands of western Mississippi back and forth as the spoils of war, drawing in new blood, and new traders, with each change of power. During this period, when frontier North America was administered as an extension of the endless wars between the European powers across the Atlantic, no one was really in control, or at least not for very long. Order was maintained, and goods shipped through, according to a Hobbesian state ruled by local trading and fur-trapping warlords and their bands of men. The frontier along western Mississippi was, essentially, a violent melting pot that worked because the system, however chaotic it was, continued to deliver the furs and dried goods that the rest of the world wanted. At the Natchez bluffs, lawlessness begat prosperity.

Natchez boomed anew during the Revolution and then the War of 1812, as boatloads of soldiers, gunpowder, and contraband flooded up and down the Mississippi to supply the fighting. This created the host environment for the next wave of development, the boisterous Kaintuckers drifting south in ever greater numbers after 1800. The waterfront areas of the crude ports along the Ohio and the Mississippi—Pittsburgh, Steubenville, Wheeling, Memphis, and St. Louis—had always had unsavory reputations, but among the river Gomorrahs, Natchez was the most notorious. Below Silver Street, wandering groups of Cherokee and Chickasaw men, trappers, Kaintuck boatmen, card sharks, Creole sailors, and amazed Hoosier farm boys freely mingled in the bustling shantytown that began to be known as "Under-the-Hill." The flatboat crewmen were bored after six weeks floating downriver and easy marks for the prostitutes and the cockfight promoters. Decisions by colonial administrators only made things worse. In 1798, the Spanish governor Manuel Gayoso de Lemos panicked about the conditions in Natchez and decreed that, henceforth, boatmen passing through the Natchez district were no longer allowed into the gridded section of town above the bluffs. After the Louisiana Purchase in 1803, American territorial officials and then town officials pursued a similar plan, organizing sheriff's raids and making tax collection visits to bars and whorehouses that they wanted to run out of town. It was a beautiful example of the unintended consequences of government reform. The taverns and the whores were simply chased down the bluffs, where they marvelously concentrated their offerings into a depraved port for the growing population of flatboaters.

The growth industry of sin was a brilliant economic development plan for Natchez Under-the-Hill, just like meatpacking along the Cincinnati waterfront or shipbuilding in Marietta. Business at Under-the-Hill also benefited from the reluctance of steamboat owners to operate very far upriver before the 1820s, because very few river towns had dredged for harbors or installed landing ramps or wharves that could accommodate steamboats. But steamboat service from New Orleans to Natchez began in 1814, giving Natchez a head start. An estimated twelve thousand flatboat crewmen disembarked every year to congregate in traveling groups before returning north on the Natchez Trace. A few days of aggressive womanizing and drinking before departure became embedded in the flatboating culture.

During his famous birding tour down the Mississippi over the winter of 1820–21, John James Audubon counted between 150 and 160 flatboats a night on the Natchez waterfront. Depending on crewing levels, that guaranteed between 750 and 1,000 sex-deprived, alcohol-needy, fistfight-loving Kaintuckers cruising the limited space between the bluffs and the waters of the Mississippi every night. The steamboats probably delivered another five hundred cater-wauling boatmen every week. In the Under-the-Hill community, there were at least fourteen clapboard and cedar-shingle grog shops, with names like Kentucky Tavern and Under-the-Hill, a quarter track for horse races, gambling pits, shanties for fighting cocks and pit bulls, a flea market for guns and pow-der, a slave auction, stalls for selling jewelry and knives, and cobblers who sold "Spanish-style shoes with brass buckles." The whorehouses slanted down from the bluffs in pods and continued right down to the river, where "gun boats" swayed from their lines in the current. The fighting was constant and often in-cluded hair-pulling, ear-boxing, and biting off a portion of an opponent's nose.

In the 1830s, the rapid expansion of steamboat travel, and the more so-phisticated travelers that steam power brought to the river, did little to improve conditions at Natchez Under-the-Hill. This 1833 description of Under-the-Hill, by the Scottish explorer and British army officer Captain J. E. Alexander, paints a river scene that was typical for Natchez until the Civil War.

> In the evening a steamer stops at Natchez to land or take in goods, and pas-sengers observe several houses lighted up, and hear the sounds of fiddles and merriment, and they run up to see what is going on; they find men and women dancing, gambling, and drinking, the bell of the steamboat rings to announce that she is about to continue her voyage, the lights in the houses of entertainment are immediately extinguished, and the passengers rush out, afraid of being too late for the boat, and run down towards the land-ing; ropes are drawn across the road, the passengers fall heels over head, a number of stout ruffians thrown themselves upon them, and strip them of their money and watches, and they get on their board in doleful plight, and of course never see or hear more of their plunderers.

During Audubon's fabled 1820 trip, a servant left a portfolio contain-ing fifteen drawings of birds and ducks on the banks of Under-the-Hill. Audubon knew that it was useless to go back and search for his sketches and thus some of America's most priceless art was lost. At Under-the-Hill, the "flat boats and houses [are] filled with the lowest of Caracters [sic]," Audubon lamented. "No doubt My Drawings will serve to ornement their Parlours or will be Nailed on Some of The Steering Oars."

Audubon was supporting himself by selling his artwork, and the loss imperiled his journey. As he continued downriver, he comforted himself by observing the riverscape below Natchez.

"We passed to day A Long Line of Bluffs exquisiting grand to the sight."

On the top of the bluffs, quite a different reality was emerging. By the 1830s, Natchez was commencing one of the grandest building sprees in American history, becoming not only one of the best mansion districts along the river, but one of the most renowned house-proud towns in the world. The architecture and style of what eventually became known as Natchez On-Top-of-the-Hill mirrored the opening acts of the young country's development, defining America as an economic order based on stark inequalities. A system that relied either on slave labor or the sweatshop toil of desperately poor immigrants produced extraordinary wealth for those at the top.

In the late 18th century, under Spanish administration, Natchez's natural advantages as a shipping location along the Mississippi had drawn a small but determined cadre of traders, commodities brokers, and plantation owners who had established their outpost on the bluffs as a kind of upriver extension of New Orleans. The adventuring sons of French and Spanish aristocrats, ambitious British and Scottish entrepreneurs, and a few outliers from old Virginia families had initially been drawn to the Natchez bluffs through contacts with merchant firms in Baltimore and Philadelphia, which were now probing the inland rivers during and after the American Revolution. The East Coast traders had occasionally made considerable profits supplying gunpowder and foodstuffs for the Continental army, and later for Mad Anthony Wayne's Northwest Indian Wars in the 1790s, and now they were establishing networks for river trading after flatboat traffic picked up in the 1790s. Meanwhile, ocean traders from Boston and New York, who were primarily rum, spice, and sugar brokers with strong ties to the merchant dynasties in New Orleans, were hoping to extend their trade routes upriver. The Natchez bluffs were ideally located as a nexus for a great deal of this traffic. Natchez was also conveniently located in the center of the alluvial plains that were rapidly being developed for cotton and sugar plantations.

Natchez was also ideally positioned to take advantage of one of the most significant developments after the American Revolution. In the 1790s, the economy of tidewater Maryland and Virginia, and the dissolute aristocracy that exploited it, was collapsing. The Virginia planters had always lived beyond their means by lavish spending and borrowing against future crops from their London creditors, but now the disruptions of the Revolution and the depletion of their tobacco lands had turned the proud and haughty Jeffersons and Randolphs into some of the best-dressed debtors in the world. They could no longer afford wine cellars filled with Madeira and port, the shiny broughams imported from London and Paris, or their overspending and underachieving children. The introduction of the cotton gin and the shifting of the textile and clothing industries toward short staple cotton had drastically altered the geography of farming. Short staple cotton, which produced a more durable cloth, grew best in the low-country coastal regions of the Carolinas and Georgia, or along the floodplains of the Mississippi around Natchez. The economic center of gravity was rapidly moving southwest. By the early 19th century, the tidewater of Virginia had become, as historian Alan Taylor describes it in *Thomas Jefferson's Education*, a "landscape of decay," with long stretches of country roads now lined with fallow tobacco fields and tree saplings pushing up through the porches of abandoned plantations. Planter-politician John Randolph lamented the decline of the country that had birthed so many leaders of the Revolution. "Nothing . . . can be more melancholy than the aspect of the whole country on tide-water," he wrote to a friend in 1814, "—dismantled country-seats, ruinous churches, fields forsaken, and grown up with mournful evergreens,—cedar and pine."

Virginia's loss was Natchez's gain. Many scions of the old Virginia families were now migrating to Mississippi and Louisiana to plant the new strains of cotton, or to join the boom in sugarcane production along the river. The rise of "King Cotton," during which the exporting of cotton would grow from 720,000 bales in 1830 to 5 million bales in 1860, had begun. Short staple southern cotton would eventually dominate the American economy, representing 60 percent of all exports and playing a mighty role in New England's industrial revolution. The 19th-century boom in sugar production was just as staggering. After 1795, when Jean Etienne de Boré, a Creole who had migrated to New Orleans from the Kaskaskia River in Illinois, invented a granulation process, sugarcane production would make the Louisiana banks of the Mississippi the single richest agricultural region on earth. By the Civil War, Louisiana was producing almost 500,000 barrels of sugar a year. It was a stunning achievement that dramatically transferred a huge amount of capital and resources to the Louisiana banks of the Mississippi. In the 19th century, the global demand for sugar was insatiable, not only as a food preservative and sweetener, but as a base material for the fermentation of whiskey and rum. Before 1800, America wasn't even a player in sugar—most of it came from the European colonies in India, the Caribbean, and Brazil. By 1850, Louisiana was producing one-quarter of the world's supply. "King Cotton" and the "white gold" of sugar, shipped down the river, rocketed America to global dominance.

Natchez, where fortunes could quickly be made by investing in plantation lands, or in supplying the rapidly expanding cotton and sugar empires that lined the banks of the Mississippi, became the hot place to be. The city on the bluffs gained a reputation as a cosmopolitan town where the remnants of old Virginia and Maryland planter families joined their destinies with ambitious, colorful migrants from Europe, or with the olive-skinned and fastidiously dressed Louisiana Creoles. A large contingent from Philadelphia and New York, looking for opportunities along the frontier, but unwilling to rough it in the crude pioneer villages, joined the march to Natchez. The elite social class formed from this global mixing became known as the Natchez "nabobs." The nabobs considered themselves existing in a world of their own, an elite defined by a shared code of manners and style. There were few good roads into town across the swampy bayous, and the entire social and economic order was defined by the exotic European and Asian fabrics, cuisine, and furniture reaching the bluffs via the river. The town's outlook was global, substantially European and Creole, and not local, specifically not American, because that's where its elites and most of its supplies originated.

The nabob style was sui generis, a blending of Paris, New York, and the old James River plantations in Virginia. Natchez became a tiny Venice hermetically sealed off from the rest of the frontier. The nabob men wore European-style waistcoats and Spanish straw hats, and the nabob wives and teenage daughters spent weeks planning their dresses for the fall cotillions, fussing over bolts of lush satins and laces imported from Belgium and France. Their children were assigned liveried slaves their own age and rode around town in upholstered carts pulled by donkeys or white pony mules. The nabob families adopted a style of absentee plantation management that had long been practiced by European colonials, or along the sea islands of South Carolina and Georgia, a system that had created the man-sion districts of Charleston and Savannah. To avoid the heat and insects of the swampy lands along the river, nabob tycoons built elaborate mansions along the breezy bluffs in town, turning the management of their sultry, distant plantations over to professional "masters" who supervised day-to-day affairs. The holdings were staggering—the planter and judge John Perkins, a migrant from tidewater Maryland, owned eighteen thousand acres of cotton fields in Mississippi and Louisiana, controlling it all from a graceful mansion with a wide porch with Doric columns, overlooking the bluffs, called the Briers. You weren't a pedigreed nabob until you had fretted over a mansion-building project or two. When Thomas Henderson, a wealthy planter and cotton broker descended from Scottish pioneers, built Magnolia Hall at the corner of Pearl and Washington Streets, he hired a Massachusetts architect who specialized in creating the "brownstone" look of the fashionable homes that were all the rage at the time among the Knickerbocker blue bloods in New York. The imposing features of the Greek Revival masterpiece were achieved, in part, by importing New York stonemasons expert in laying brick, then coating the facade and porch col-umns with a rich veneer of luxe stucco the color of chocolate.

Over on Main Street, Henderson also built an attractive brick warehouse as a headquarters for his new cotton exchange, which remains today as an outstanding example of commercial architecture in the South. The nabobs typically extended their business empires by investments in related fields, building cotton and tobacco exchanges, cotton gin facilities, metal plants that fabricated cotton-baling equipment and, later, after the introduction of steam power, cotton looms and barge and tow companies. Politically and so-cially, the nabobs considered themselves above petty regional or party affilia-tions. They were Natchez nabobs, not southern planters. They rarely married outside their own elite group of families, often sent their children north for Ivy League educations, and vacationed every summer with their wealthy northern counterparts at Newport, Rhode Island. Natchez was believed to have more millionaires than any other town in America. The nabob families never numbered more than one hundred, but their influence was considera-ble. In early 1861, when Natchez voted on whether or not Mississippi should secede from the Union and join the southern Confederacy, the nabobs pre-vailed and the town officially remained neutral.

The mansion district of Natchez was eventually named Ellicott Hill, after the U.S. Army major Andrew Ellicott, who defied the old Spanish regime in 1797 and raised the American flag over the bluffs, claiming the Natchez territory for the United States. Initially, the houses facing the Spanish Esplanade along the bluffs were built in the style of the Creole "cottages" of New Orleans, with wide, long porches facing the river and filigreed cast-iron grillwork mounted at the corners, or as porch railings. Later, the porch ceilings were raised to allow light into second-floor ballrooms and bedrooms, and the crazes of the Greek Revival and Victorian movements were indulged with fluted columns, cupolas, and bay windows with scalloped shingles. Because of its location on the river, Natchez also benefited from the postbellum boom in cast-iron facades, and the city is considered one of the best locales for studying metal adornments. The bluffs protect Ellicott Hill from flooding, and Natchez's Unionist sympathies largely protected it from damage during the Civil War. Today there are over 1,000 buildings in the city listed on the National Register of Historic Places. That's a lot of preserved architecture for a relatively small town, and Natchez is now a mecca for art and architecture students, and a new house-proud class, similar to the Savannah characters described in John Berendt's *Midnight in the Garden of Good and Evil*, has moved in. The wealthy couples from New York and California, songwriters, art collectors, and software tycoons trade the old Creole cottages and columned manses back and forth like expensive paintings, or yachts. In this way, the old nabobs are still there and Natchez retains its identity as a refreshing outpost of cosmopolitism in the South.

Natchez lay at still one more intersection that would determine the future of the country, the extension of slavery into the Deep South, under terms that made it a considerably harsher institution over the course of the 19th century. As tidewater Virginia and Maryland declined and the Mississippi plantation country boomed in profits from cotton and sugar, a massive "slave deficit" in the South could only be supplied by the new surplus of slaves up north, especially after the importing of slaves from Africa and the Caribbean was outlawed in 1808. Over the next fifty years, at least a million tidewater slaves were sold "down the river" and brutally transported to plantations along the Mississippi

banks, creating one of the ugliest chapters in American history, and one that
has been assiduously ignored by professional historians and schoolteachers.
In his magisterial *The Half Has Never Been Told*, Cornell historian Edward E.
Baptist has begun the task of reversing a century and a half of official neglect
of the "Black Trail of Tears." Initially, in the 1790s, the slaves were carried south
to the Kentucky frontier as soon as the Monongahela and the Ohio could be
reached, because overland routes provided too many opportunities for escape.
"Once enslavers got their captives through the mountains and onto the Ohio
River," Baptist writes, "these escape attempts declined. The flatboats didn't stop
until they reached the growing frontier port of Louisville." By 1820, Natchez
was the busiest port along the frontier, and conveniently located for the
end-buyers, the owners and managers of cotton and sugar plantations.

It's not hard to see today why this huge stain on the history of the
country was never taught in the schools. The marching of the slaves between Virginia and the Mississippi was so brutal that it would be hard to
get children to recite their Pledge of Allegiance after they learned about it.
As they were loaded onto flatboats that would carry them on the first leg
of their one-thousand-mile route to the sugar coast, or at the trailheads of
the routes they would follow over the Appalachians, the female slaves were
fitted out with neck halters and connected by a rope in a tandem line. Male
slaves were considered a greater escape threat. They were met at departure points on the river by a blacksmith who fitted them with a thick iron
neck band that couldn't slip off, and manacles for their wrists, which were
attached by chains to the slave who would march ahead of them. Often,
padlocks were attached to each neck band, and rings were welded on, so
that a single heavy chain could be slid from the front to the back of the line.
Groups of forty or fifty slaves chained together this way were called "coffle
lines," a term that is believed to have derived from the Arabic word *cafila*,
for the caravans of slaves traded in Africa and the Middle East.

Between 1790 and 1850, at least a million African American slaves were
transported one thousand miles to the interior South or the Sugar Coast in
coffle lines, under conditions of exceptional brutality. A variety of routes
were followed. Sometimes, after an overland route over the Appalachians,
the flatboats transporting the slaves, who remained in coffles for the entire
trip, stopped in Louisville, where the slaves were disembarked for the long
march to plantations and slave markets in interior Kentucky or Tennessee.

The conditions were abominable. The slaves in the coffle lines were marched in the searing heat up to twenty miles a day, flanked by mounted slave traders armed with rifles. The few slaves who managed to escape, or attempted escape, were immediately executed when caught, to set an example for the others. At night, when the march was stopped, the slaves slept while still in their coffle chains out in the open, or all crammed together in a single, squalid tavern room. They shared a dinner of cornmeal mash served in cast-iron pots, which they ate with their hands. Cholera outbreaks were common in the cramped, unsanitary conditions of the coffle line transport.

The cruelest aspect of the system delivering an expanded slave labor force to the Deep South was the sudden, unexpected separation of families. On the old tidewater plantations, slave families had lived together for several generations. The new cotton and sugar plantations along the Mississippi generated a large demand for relatively young, fit field-workers, and the slave traders traveled north with lists demanding young men below the age of twenty-five, or teenage girls. Candidates for transport were selected regardless of family ties—young fathers were abruptly separated from their families, mothers were separated from children, brothers and sisters were sent off in coffles in separate groups to cross the Appalachians for the Ohio, and would never see each other again. Baptist and other scholars estimate that at least a third of the families working on the old tidewater plantations were broken up to satisfy the insatiable needs of the expanding agrarian economy of the South.

Initially, the rapid growth of flatboat travel down the Ohio helped to keep the extent of the coffle line transport system hidden from the American public, because slave traders generally avoided the dense floating villages of settlers and cargo flats, to reduce the possibility of slaves escaping. But as Ned and Constance Sublette point out in their *The American Slave Coast*, the slave transport system became harder to ignore after the rise in steamboat traffic in the 1830s, when the coffle lines were transferred to steamboats. Americans learned to look the other way. The Sublettes quote from the autobiography of William Wells Brown, a mixed-race slave who escaped from a plantation in Kentucky and crossed the Ohio River when he was nineteen, eventually settling in Boston and Europe, where he became a successful essayist, novelist, and abolitionist. In the 1830s, before he was sold to the Kentucky plantation, Brown "worked out" for his owner on Missouri River steamboats.

"A drove of slaves on a southern steamboat, bound for the cotton or sugar

At their former plantations in tidewater Maryland and Virginia, African American slaves were chained together by a blacksmith into "coffle lines" and then carried in flatboats and marched a thousand miles to the Mississippi Sugar Coast.

regions," Brown wrote, "is an occurrence so common, that no one, not even the passengers, appear to notice it, though they clank their chains at every step."

On arrival at their new cotton and sugar plantations along the Mississippi, the slaves were confronted by a ruthlessly efficient system of managing forced labor, which is why so many African American chattel dreaded being sold downriver. Quotas for each slave's daily harvest—so many baskets of cotton, so many wagonloads of sugarcane—were enforced by keeping records with chalk and slate, and slaves who fell short were regularly whipped. A "pushing system" that determined how many acres each slave was supposed to plant and keep free of weeds all season was gradually increased from five to ten acres. Slave-on-slave discipline was enforced by assigning "captains," who goaded the labor gangs to move more quickly through the field. The intensification of the labor system showed results. At the beginning of the 19th century, on the old tidewater and North Carolina plantations, slaves were expected to pick twenty-eight pounds of cotton a day. By 1828, Baptist writes, "in Alabama, the totals on one plantation ranged up to 132 pounds, and by the 1840s, on a Mississippi labor camp, the hands averaged 341 pounds each on a good day."

Productivity gains like this only increased the demand for slaves transported south, and Natchez's favorable position at the bottom of the trace, at the port below the bluffs, soon made it one of the largest slave-trading centers of the South, second in size only to New Orleans. During the early years of American territorial control after 1803, slave markets were haphazardly organized, as in many other southern cities, with auctions taking place at Under-the-Hill and on many street corners above the bluffs. But the nabobs, many of whom were originally northerners or educated Europeans, who didn't mind making profits off slavery, were uncomfortable being known for it. They soon placed restrictions on the sale of slaves within their oasis of brick walks and mansions. A cholera outbreak in Natchez also built resentment about the trading of slaves. In a series of town ordinances passed after 1830, slave trading was severely limited on city streets, which gradually drove the trade to an open space just east of town, which came to be known as the Forks of the Road.

The cluster of buildings at the busy intersection of Liberty Road and Washington Road had long been a busy slave market, probably because America's largest slave trader, Franklin and Armfield, had established its southern headquarters in Natchez in 1819. From its northern headquarters in Alexandria, Virginia, Franklin and Armfield sent overland coffles down the Natchez Trace, and delivered additional slaves down the Atlantic and through New Orleans. Under the supervision of partner Isaac Franklin, the Forks developed into one of the most profitable and unique markets in the country. Instead of the usual practice of auctioning off slaves individually to the highest bidder, Franklin encouraged visits by plantation owners or their representatives by selecting choice slaves from the one thousand or more detained at the Forks into large "field groups." He negotiated the sale of these groups with each buyer, eliminating the pricing uncertainty of auction bidding. Alternately, a planter traveling to Natchez in search of, say, six or seven female slaves for housework or as seamstresses, could negotiate a separate deal for them. Franklin drummed up interest every morning, and emphasized his large selection, by conducting a circus-like march on the open grounds in front of the Forks sales buildings. Joseph Holt Ingraham, a young writer and former seaman from Maine, who collected his observations about the South in an 1835 book, *The South-West by a Yankee*, described the spectacle every morning at the Forks of the Road.

"A line of negroes . . . extended in a semicircle around the right side of the yard. . . . Each was dressed in the uniform of slaves, when in market, consisting of a fashionably shaped, black fur hat, roundabout and trousers of coarse corduroy velvet, precisely such as worn by Irish laborers. . . . Good vests, strong shoes, and white cotton shirts, completed their equipment."

When the parade was over, buyers from throughout the neighboring plantation country walked down the lines, inspecting each slave. Then they could step inside and see the field groups organized by Franklin's workers, and negotiations could begin. Once they were sold, the slaves turned their fur hats and corduroy suits back in at the Forks clothing lockers. They would be worn by a new group of parading slaves the next day.

In 1863, as Ulysses Grant's Army of the Tennessee worked its way down the Mississippi, gradually splitting the Confederacy in two, Union troops dismantled the Forks slave market, using the lumber to expand nearby Fort McPherson. The old Forks market lay abandoned and virtually ignored for the next 160 years. Recently, however, with the encouragement of a new mayor, the Forks has been developed by the National Park Service into a major visitors site, on three acres of land donated by the city. Eventually, with federal funds, the Forks of the Road area will be developed into an eighteen-acre park with a large interpretive center, outdoor exhibits, and a memorial to the hundreds of thousands of slaves who were processed through Natchez in the 19th century.

When I drove up on the electric bike to visit the Forks, the old slave market area east of town felt deserted, with car traffic droning past the few interpretive signs. The quiet at the Forks contrasted sharply with the crowds of tourists, delivered by the cruise boats, thronging in the mansion district downtown. Even with a new federal park on the way, the site will be a reminder that, at too many historic shrines, there is nothing of consequence left to see, and only words can describe what the place once meant. Now, at least, there's a new generation of scholars like Edward Baptist, finally exploring the truth about how "the coffle chained the early republic together."

"So enslaver-generals took land from Indians," Baptist writes in *The Half Has Never Been Told*, "enslaver-politicians convinced Congress to let slavery expand, and enslaver entrepreneurs created new ways to finance and transport and commodify 'hands.'"

After five days of plantation tours, rides up to the Forks, and lavish dinners at the Monmouth Inn, I felt relaxed, ready to take on the last, arduous leg into New Orleans. My ribs pierced with pain whenever I coughed or laughed, and the roof deck was hot under the unrelenting Mississippi sun. But I was overjoyed about the bonus I had just received. Obsessing on the flatboat era had delivered me to the hidden history of my country, the truths that for too long too many feared to teach. Natchez was a miniature of a more troubled America, a more iniquitous America, than the country I was raised to love. But the truth about our past is also the truth about our present and I was reckoning with the America that is.

As I left the Vidalia docks and swung out into the channel beneath the bridge, I looked east to the bluffs below town. The low clouds nearby seemed to meet the rim of the cliffs and extend them into the sky, and the morning sunlight had turned them into sharp bands of bronze, matte black, and salmon pink. They were indeed, as Audubon wrote, exquisiting grand to the sight.

Maintaining safe clearance from the commercial barge traffic was especially challenging as we got closer to New Orleans. We often shared the channel with almost a dozen ships and barge strings.

22

OUR RUN DOWN THE MISSISSIPPI after Natchez was our dreamtime on the river, an Eden of long, spacious sandbars and scenic bends so sharp that the water pushing sideways at the stern yawed us effortlessly around each turn. Life on board the *Patience* was carefree and relaxed and I was enjoying the rewards of my random selection of crew. Deb Satterfield had returned to the boat and was so precise at keeping track of our position that I glided through the bends without ever looking at a chart. Jamie Buckley had become expert at setting bow lines. The bayous of Louisiana surrounded us on both banks and there were long stretches without vegetation or trees, so I could see the tugs and their strings of barges miles away across the bends, and easily steer for traffic. We stopped each night at a sandbar, cooking dinner in the galley while the *Patience* gently swayed from her lines in the currents, well off the commercial channel. Even my dreams about my mother were peaceful. She was sitting on her porch in Maine looking down on Damariscotta Harbor, which was now the Mississippi River, sipping tea and discussing how much she had enjoyed watching my boat move south.

At Baton Rouge, we parked on the large gravel bar just south of the Horace Wilkinson Bridge, reprovisioning for the last run into New Orleans and picking up our final dream crew. Danny came back on board, a hypomaniac frenzy of tightening antennas that had wobbled on their mounts in the breezes, and rearranging all the cooking utensils in the galley, annoying and uplifting me at once. We both enjoyed it when a group of inner-city Black kids from over the banks strolled down the beach, collecting bottles and cans for recycling in town, and came on board the *Patience* to see the boat and talk. We spent a fun hour with the kids, telling them about our trip. One of the kids wanted to know what kind of "heatas" we were carrying for personal protection on the boat.

"We're not carrying weapons," I said. "We don't think we need them."

"Man, you crazy," the kid said as his friends nodded in agreement. "Dem kay-juns down there is going to murda your ass. You need some guns!"

Danny and I found this hilarious and depressing at once. The tragicomedy of America was expressing itself on our boat. Upriver, the off-duty cops and redneck river rats who had come aboard implored us to get weapons because the Blacks in Vicksburg and Baton Rouge were going to pour over the banks to rob the boat. Downriver, the Black kids were convinced that the rednecks were going to get us. The race-blind solution for all was the same: America, Get Guns.

At Baton Rouge, we also brought on the ultimate dream team crew. Reed Hillen, a lawyer from Tupelo, Mississippi, and his friends Rick Maynard and Will Denton were all members of a fabled whitewater group from Alabama, Locust Fork Expeditions. Twenty-five years ago, the group had built a cabin and a paddling camp above the scenic cliffs of the Locust Fork of the Black Warrior River in northern Alabama, to spend time with their sons on river trips. This had evolved into organizing weekend rafting trips for Boy Scout and church groups and eventually the Locust Fork paddlers ran expeditions along the Salmon and the Snake rivers out west. They had also hiked major peaks around the world, from Mount Kilimanjaro in Africa to Mont Blanc in the French Alps.

The Locust Fork boys were skilled rivermen who were always game first thing in the morning and knew just what to do. After camping that first night on the Baton Rouge bar, Reed, Rick, and Will walked over to the *Patience* at dawn, threw their gear over the gunwales while Danny was starting coffee and breakfast, and looked to me on the roof deck for instructions.

"Okay, Reed, I've got just enough water under the prop to steer out," I said. "You come aboard and pull my anchor. Rick and Will, untie the bow lines and pull me in so the bow is facing downriver and my port side is on the gravel. Then jump in with your lines."

Our launch that morning was the best of the trip and, as I pulled away from the bridge and entered the current, I looked down to the bow. Rick and Will were already coiling the lines and then carrying them to their hooks on the stern.

We camped that night thirty-five miles downriver on the Bayou Goula Towhead, an immense sandbar at the edge of the sailing channel, opposite Point Clair in Louisiana's Iberville Parish. I was immensely satisfied that night because we had burned almost no fuel all afternoon, surfing the wake of the immense *American Heritage* tug, which was throwing back so much water that we could just ride on top of the foamy curl in front of us and skitter around the bends holding just one-third power. The Locust Fork boys were always on top of the maps and Will Denton, in particular, was as precise as a Bible whacker citing chapter and verse.

"That's the Plaquemine Bend daymark there on the starboard bank, Mile 210," Will said. "Actually, no. It's Mile 210.4"

When we landed on the Bayou Goula Towhead that night, I had nothing to do. I held the bow of the *Patience* against the bar with half power and calmly walked down to the bow. I didn't have to say a word.

"I'll drop an anchor off the stern," Reed said. "Don't worry. I'll leave some slack."

"Rick," Will said, "see that big pile of driftwood over there? Tie the port line there. I'm going to angle out wide and tie my line to that big driftwood tree over there."

That night was one of the few on the trip when I was rushed by feelings of personal progress, and knew it at the time. I had begun this trip almost four months ago having no idea what to do. Every day I was immersed in the frustrations of a maniacally incompetent reenactor, or one of his pals, screaming exactly the wrong directions at the top of their lungs. Now, at the helm, under dazzling pastel twilight, I was calm and confident, speechlessly overseeing a perfect landing and tie-up, with the help of an experienced, river-worthy crew.

We made a driftwood fire on the beach and bathed the profile of the *Patience* with flashlights to make us visible to the passing tugs, even though we were clear by a wide margin from the commercial channel. Danny was in a rush to make dinner that night. Reed had brought along some frozen rabbit for us to cook and Danny considered this a challenge. He was determined to show these "southern wussies" how to cook by making homemade pasta and sauce, which he would fashion into a gourmet dish with the rabbit. Danny had his chef's apron on and the galley deck was strewn with pasta bits, powdery flour, and vegetable shavings.

"Danny, slow down, slow down," I said. "Let's relax on the sandbar. We don't have to eat right away."

"Rinker, we don't tell the pasta when to eat. When the pasta is ready, it tells us."

"Oh, Christ. Who told you that? Grandma?"

"Rinker, you are the worst kind of Irish. An Irish who can pass for a WASP. You've got to learn to let some of my Italian in."

So, we ate early. Afterward, we brought chairs out from the boat and arranged them around our fire on the bar, watching the orange and purple cinders rise against a black and gray cirrus sky.

We were Kaintuckers that night, or at least I imagined so. We were a mixed flatboat crew gathered from several points in the country—New England, tidewater Maryland, Alabama, and Mississippi—powerfully drawn together and toward storytelling after a day spent on the river and then landing on the bar. The night was black and the coals of the driftwood fire glowed cobalt and orange. The Locust Fork boys told tales about climbing Mount Hood and Mount Whitney. Danny told a story about landing his Cessna on the winter ice at Lake Winnipesaukee in New Hampshire. Jamie had a great tale about Mount Kilimanjaro. I felt tired after a day in the sun and sleepy from drinking bourbon and felt no need to join the storytelling, to top everyone else's tale with one of my own.

The coals from the fire warmed my legs and just before I fell asleep in my chair I remember thinking, *You know, you don't have to be fighting a current all the time. You can take a vacation from achieving. Stop pushing so hard. Stop fighting boredom. Sometimes, everything you want just comes to you.*

The "You're going to die" theorists had apparently lost interest in the voyage of the *Patience* by the time we got below Baton Rouge, which was ironic, considering that our final push into New Orleans would be the most hazardous leg of the trip. The fifty-four miles of river between Baton Rouge and New Orleans is managed as a single Port of South Louisiana and is essentially a commercial sea-lane, congested with large oceangoing vessels, operated between the banks of the Mississippi. The river below Baton Rouge is America's export granary—60 percent of America's grain exports exit for global markets through this single stretch of the Mississippi. The hundreds upon hundreds of grain barges that we had seen moving south for the past four months mostly end up here, and are unloaded by conveyors into giant cement silos that line the banks, where the grain awaits pickup by 950-foot Panamax ships. (Panamax cargo ships, carrying 52,500 tons of grain, with drafts of 40 feet, are designed to fit inside the locks of the Panama Canal.) More than 56,000 barges are pushed through this space between Baton Rouge and New Orleans every year, and 3,600 large oceangoing vessels call on the silos annually. Loading and unloading at several large container ports, a dozen major oil refineries, giant oil storage tanks, and chemical plants turn this stretch of the Mississippi into a swirling maze of switch boats, crew ferries, massive barge strings tied together, and Panamax and container ships.

The landscape beside us changed dramatically below Baton Rouge. The Elysium of long sandbars and picturesque river bends, with moody bayous stretching off to the horizon on both banks, was transformed, within just a few miles, into a gritty, endless wall of giant silos, massive oil tanks, and refineries spewing exhaust from a shiny maze of pipes and stacks. The plumes of exhaust billowing skyward seemed larger than the clouds above. The *Patience* seemed miniaturized against this colossal industrial space.

The first few hours were fine. For a couple of miles ahead of us there were always three or four barge strings in sight and it wasn't that difficult to steer around them. But I had a lot less negotiating room than I had enjoyed upriver. At every grain wharf and refinery there were moored fleets of barges waiting to be emptied or towed away, sometimes parked eight across. This substantially narrowed the channel, especially when two strings were moving in opposite directions, which tended to force me to the edge because I didn't want to sail between two strings and run the risk of getting pinched if a captain decided to angle his load for the next bend. But then a large ship or two would appear ahead, which tended to push the traffic to the edges. The long Panamax ships consistently occupied the middle of the channel, where the channel was deepest, and the tugboats could either see them coming on their radar or were listening on their radios. Even when I was in a sharp bend and couldn't see very far ahead on the river, I began to sense by the way the tugs and their barges were making room in the middle that another big ship was just a mile away.

The marine radio channel was virtually useless in this mayhem. There were long pauses of quiet interrupted by a sudden cacophony of broadcasts, as several captains at once were talking to their traffic, often in an indecipherable Cajun English that was impossible to understand through the blare of static. I decided to ignore the radio entirely and just "read" a route ahead of me by anticipating how the tug ahead of me was going to play the next bend, and always trying to avoid the middle of the channel in case another big ship was coming through.

I didn't understand why I was so calm. A summer spent steering around barge traffic must have hardened me, and I was reassured by Rick Maynard and Will Denton beside me at the steering console, calling out waypoints and the miles, even though the banks were now so dense with docks and industrial buildings that it was hard for them to get a fix. I could see Jamie on one of the cots ahead of me, with a sleeping bag pulled over his head, and so I concluded that the constant roar of traffic all around us must have been frightening. But I was concentrating so hard on my positioning, on the tug ahead of me, or on the oncoming barge string, that this must have eliminated the distraction of fear.

I started to devise a variety of short-term solutions that I would follow for four or five minutes, before I moved on to another solution. It was reassuring and seemed to keep me calm, living minute by minute like that. A tug ahead of me that was angling its load against the banks was probably clearing the middle of the channel for another ship, so I powered up and stayed with his wake through the bend. A summer of riding tug wakes allowed me to be comfortable there—my experience, I thought, was paying off. When there were no tugs around, but I couldn't see around the bend to check for a ship, I tried to find a fleet barge along the bank with full barges, low in the water. I knew that a loaded barge drew nine feet of water, plenty of draft for me. If there was no traffic near the moored fleet, I powered up quickly and sped over to the barges, hugging them downriver for a half mile. If there was traffic nearby, I lingered upriver at low power until the barges were clear. There was one stretch after the Luling Bridge so thick with fleeted barges on the right bank that I was able to hug the parked hulls for almost three miles, well clear of a barge string and a massive ship moving upriver at the same time.

Good, I thought, *that's three more miles behind you. Now look for the next excuse to concentrate on something you know will work.*

Another feature of the mile-marking into New Orleans was reassuring. Upriver, at a sharp bend south at Mile 130, we saw on the map that we were at "35-mile Point." This was confusing at first, until I remembered that New Orleans was one hundred miles upriver from the Gulf of Mexico, and so "35-mile Point" must be our distance from New Orleans. Ahead, there was both a "26-mile False Point" and the actual "26-mile Point," followed by a "12-mile Point." I timed our progress between the points and realized that, in the monstrous flow near the bottom of the river, we were doing over ten knots. *Good*, I thought, *only two hours to go.* I began mentally breaking down our time to New Orleans into twenty-minute segments. I remained calm by constantly reassuring myself.

"Okay, good, you just got through that twenty minutes. Now just do another twenty minutes."

That's how I steered the last thirty miles into New Orleans, mile by mile, minute by minute, always looking for the next traffic solution that calmed me by being a sure bet.

I would have been almost fine following this variety of stratagems, except for the switch boats. They were constantly darting out from the open spaces between the barge fleets, seemingly impervious to traffic, dropping off full barges to be unloaded at the docks, racing off with empties that would be attached to the long strings moving upriver. They darted cross-river to find their barges, weaving in and out of the long barge strings, apparently trusted by the long-haul pilots to stay out of their way. Meanwhile, the parade of massive oceangoing ships in the middle of the channel was now constant—we could always see two or three ahead, and one or two behind. I had worked my way over to the right bank, seeking shelter against the barge fleets, and now I would have to stay there because I couldn't risk crossing the river against the ship traffic. I was now restricted to half of the river. Whatever was there, I would have to deal with it.

I had been dealing with another drama ever since Baton Rouge. My plan after reaching New Orleans was to follow the Industrial Canal, which runs five miles from the Mississippi at New Orleans to Lake Pontchartrain, where I had reserved a slip for the *Patience.* But in Baton Rouge I learned that the locks leading into the canal, which were over one hundred years old, were broken, and the canal was indefinitely closed. On the gravel bar at Baton Rouge, we met a fun couple walking their dogs, Linda and Jim Marchand, who commuted between homes in Baton Rouge and New Orleans. They offered to make calls to see if they could find a dock or slip space and, during our last day on the river, they called to tell us that the administrators at New Orleans's vast Audubon Park had agreed to let us land at their excursion dock. We could stay as long as we wanted. The situation wasn't ideal—at the Audubon dock, we would be well off the commercial channel, but still in the strong flow of the Mississippi. But that's where we would land in New Orleans. The dock was just upriver from 6-mile Point.

Exhaustion, exhaustion, elation, elation. Now I could see the skyscrapers of downtown New Orleans and the neat rows of houses in suburban Jefferson Parish fanned east in a grid of streets lit bright by the sun. A ceiling of nimbo-cumulus clouds with dark bottoms seemed to be pressing us down onto the river. When I looked ahead, there were three Panamax ships and more barge strings than I could count racing down the straightaway to the Carrollton Bend. In between them, switch boats, some with a barge or two, some solo, were racing between the moored fleets on both banks. Ahead of me there was nothing but a maze of boats and boat wakes, colliding to form the shape of an open scissors, along five miles of the straightaway.

All right, calm, calm, you're going to get through this, just six miles to go, force yourself to remain calm. I powered back to delay meeting all of the traffic ahead. *You're living now encountering ship and barge string, just to encounter the next ship and barge string. That is your reality now. Remember Cairo and Mile 820.*

As I came around the Carrollton Bend I considered cutting sharply to port, to reposition myself on the left bank for landing at Audubon Park, but just as I did a huge ship behind me sounded his horn, an immense bassoon wail so powerful that I could feel the sound waves vibrating against my back. I wasn't sure that the captain was sounding for me, but he probably was, warning me to remain in my space on the right bank, well away from his path in the middle of the channel. I was more annoyed than rattled. I could have easily crossed the channel and remained clear of the ship, but there was too much traffic on the straightaway downriver for me to know where I would go after that.

Behind me, I saw the white, curling bow wave of a down-coming fifteen-barge string about a quarter mile behind me. The tug pilot was easing toward the right bank to make way for the big ship. I was pretty sure there was enough room for both of us to pass through the cement revetments on the banks, but I wanted to talk to that captain. I pushed my mike switch when there was a pause in the radio traffic.

"String at Mile 109. I'm the wooden boat to your starboard. I'll hug the right bank. Can you give me enough space?"

"Wooden boat, affirm. We're good."

A minute later, the captain came back on.

"Wooden boat, can you see that gray barge in my string coming on your port?"

"Affirm."

"I'm going to power back a little. You power up. Just stay in the middle of that gray barge and I'll block for you down through the straightaway."

"Good, Captain," I said. "I'll remain on that gray barge."

It was a wonderful fifteen minutes on the river. The captain of the tug pushing the string beside me seemed joined to me on the *Patience*, a soul mate on the river. The big ship behind us passed in the middle of the channel. Two more huge ships, and a string of barges, passed going upriver, but I was shielded in my space on the right bank by the string beside me. I never did get that captain's name, or the name of his tug. But I didn't care. The satisfaction of the captain protecting me down my last stretch of river must have been just as pleasing to him as it was pleasing to me.

As we got to the bottom of the straightaway, I called Jamie and Reed and Rick to the roof deck. I told them that, in the currents, and all of this river traffic, our landing on the Audubon docks might be hard—more of a "bow plant" against the dock than a graceful sideways landing. I didn't care about graceful. I needed them on the Audubon Park dock as soon as we got there and cleating us against the current. We had only one chance to get this right. Turning back for the shipping channel and tangling with the traffic again would be a disaster.

At the Carrollton Bend, I had to power back and let the string beside me pass, so I could cut across the wake of the tug and head for the Audubon dock on the left bank. But I couldn't see over his string of barges. I began to power back, letting the gray barge overtake me.

"Captain, am I good for the left bank?"

"You're good. There's a Panamax at the point. Steer hard left and you'll be fine. Nice knowing you, wooden boat."

"Thank you, Capt'n," I said.

As I cut across the wake of the tug toward the left bank, the big Panamax ship the captain had mentioned was racing directly toward us. There were only a hundred yards between us and the approaching ship, and as I turned hard left for the dock I screamed to Jamie and Reed that this was not going to be a docking so much as a crash. As soon as we hit the dock, they had to jump off and immediately cleat up with their lines to make way for the passing ship.

"We're going to hit hard," I yelled above the noise of the motor. "Get on the dock and cleat us!"

Jamie was off the boat first, with a bow line. He pulled it tight at the first cleat he found on the dock, and Reed and Rick jumped from the gunwales in the rear and found cleats alongside the aluminum stern. We were down and hard, secured with ropes, in New Orleans.

When I woke the next day, I carried my coffee down to the porch of the Park View Hotel and stared across the broad lawns of Audubon Park, down to the river. The St. Charles Avenue streetcar rumbled along the median, clanged its bell, and an attractive group of students from Tulane and Loyola got out, dispersing for their classes. Tall, springy mothers in yoga pants jogged by, pushing their babies in three-wheel strollers. The light and the breeze from the park, the exotic flora of the uptown neighborhood gardens, and the metallic echo of the streetcar wheels were enchanting, a benign reentry into civilization. Still, I was missing something. The porch didn't sway on its lines and there were no tugboat wakes rocking the floor-boards.

I was exhausted and dehydrated from the trip and felt a deep torpor inside, and for some reason the absence of activity and the movement of a boat made my ribs ache even more. But Danny, Jamie, and I dove into New Orleans according to the prescribed tourist plan. We watched a lot of pre-Halloween parades, stood on the corners of the French Quarter while high school kids played with their brass bands, and ate at most of the better restaurants. I spent hours hiking the Garden District and discovered Magazine Street. Families strolling through Audubon Park, curious after seeing the *Patience* down on the river, came down to the river landing, and became new best friends, river family. They invited us home for dinner, but my ribs were so painful, I passed out at the table whenever someone made me laugh. Because the Industrial Canal in New Orleans was closed for repairs, I sailed the *Patience* down the Harvey Canal instead, parking it at a boatyard in Lafitte until I decided what to do with the boat. Friends of friends lent me their boathouse over on Lake Pontchartrain, and Jamie and I spent a couple of afternoons unloading the contents of the *Patience* into my cargo trailer, walking across the edge of Audubon Park with armfuls of rope, wooden chairs, and cots. I was indefinite about leaving for home.

People kept asking me if the trip had changed me, and I was exasper-ated about not having a reply. Even after a long, fruitful experience, we are all pretty good about following our old selves around, and I didn't feel different, just maybe more experienced, and a little vain about proving that I could handle a boat. When Mike Binkley and others complimented me about being "tough" and "persistent," I corrected them and said that I had merely been stubborn. Continuing the trip without pausing after I broke my ribs certainly was stubborn, but even that wasn't quite accurate because there really wasn't any way to stop our journey down the river after it had begun. Gradually, I accepted a new truth. My thirst for new experience, for following history, was so great that I placed myself in situations where I *had* to be stubborn to finish the project. Or, and this is just as likely a con-clusion, my threshold for boredom is so low, my need to test myself against the unknown is so high, that foolhardiness comes naturally to me. In that sense I hadn't changed at all. I ended the trip to New Orleans just as con-fused about myself as when I began.

I was changed intellectually, however. The litany of "You're going to die" scenarios I heard along the river—the whirlpools that were going to separate me from my underwear, the torrents at the mouths of the tributaries, the barge strings that would force me onto the wing dams—were all untrue, but what was salient about these dangers was that I believed them a lot longer than I should have. Shared falsehood, endlessly repeated, is more powerful than the truth. In fact, all of these dangers were just problems to solve, a chain of circumstance that, taken apart link by link, could be overcome. But we don't want to take things apart piece by piece—that's too laborious, and too lonely. The human mind defaults toward the herd, believing the endlessly repeated lie more than the truth. Perhaps that is what my trip ultimately meant. We have to travel right past the edge of the alleged hazard and find out for ourselves.

The same is true for history. American children have been raised for more than two hundred years on the cherished rubrics of the Declaration of Independence, "all men are created equal" and the inalienable right to "life, liberty, and the pursuit of happiness." But the founders who gave civilization these words, especially the Virginia aristocrats, also lusted for the West. Once they got it, they unleashed a march over the mountains and then a flatboat ride down the rivers and the tributaries that freed ambitious people to build countless waterwheels, river locks, and one-hundred-ton leviathans that, collectively, within a span of eighty years, propelled a young country toward unimaginable wealth. But the flatboat era that carried the pioneers downriver to clear the lands also empowered Andrew Jackson to forcibly remove the native people who were in the way, and encouraged the agricultural magnates of King Cotton and the Sugar Coast to carry a million slaves to labor in the unbearable conditions along the banks of the Mississippi. Surely, Jacksonian democracy liberated "the common man." But shouldn't the concomitant history—the destruction of the five civilized tribes, the severity of slave life on the cotton and sugar plantations—also be told? That was the meaning of my trip, too. The myths of American history are also more powerful than the truth. My trip to New Orleans liberated me to reject the myths.

But I was also the beneficiary of the truth. Harlan Hubbard, Timothy Flint, Asbury Jaquess, and Christian Schultz, like so many of the flatboaters, had all shared two invaluable traits. They didn't believe what they hadn't seen yet, and, even in a vacuum of knowledge, they were relentless. Following their diaries as I moved downriver instilled in me a belief in historical experience and confidence in the power of words. Zadok Cramer was an inexhaustible compiler of fact. He proved to a generation of river travelers that meticulously detailed maps and topographic descriptions are the foundation of progress, and then he proved, by endlessly updating his gazetteers year to year, that facts, like a river course, often change. I learned over the course of two thousand miles along the Ohio and the Mississippi that the advice of my contemporaries was usually wrong. Instead, I stood on the shoulders of the historic chroniclers who passed the same space more than two centuries earlier, teaching myself that the past is often far more valuable to know than the present.

In New Orleans, because I was pondering these things, I felt more reflective than victorious. The exhaustion and elation of the trip had delivered me not just to New Orleans but to enlightenment.

In late October, I drove Jamie and his kayak downriver for almost a hundred miles, to Venice, Louisiana, a remote fishing hamlet ten miles north of the Gulf of Mexico. Jamie wanted to ride his kayak down the last, lonely stretch of the Mississippi and complete a "toe touch" with the Gulf waters, to be able to say that he'd completed the length of the river. It was a pleasant day for me, given over to tourism instead of running a boat, when all I had to do was drive my pickup and enjoy the scenery. After leaving the suburbs south of New Orleans behind, we drove down through a spare, narrow floodplain with cattle fields, citrus orchards, and a few oil refineries and fishing docks.

I dropped Jamie off at the pullout of a small National Wildlife Refuge off Highway 23. We hoisted his kayak and gear over a breakwater and I was impressed with the confident way that he dropped into his kayak, mounted his GPS unit in front of him, and organized his maps and gear on either side of his legs. Bobbing in the wakes of some fishing boats, Jamie gamely wiggled across the water toward the edge of a cypress swamp, which he would follow into the Mississippi and the last Grand Pass section of the river into the Gulf. He seemed lonely and brave in his blue kayak as he disappeared into the cypress grove, with each stroke of his paddle reflecting light from the sun.

It was the first time I had been alone for months and I luxuriated in the solitude of a wildlife sanctuary just a few miles above the Gulf, which I had all to myself in late October. Pathways led to interpretive signs about hurricane damage, all the species of wintering birds, and statistics about the number of boats and the tonnage of cargo carried from the Mississippi to the globe. There was a comfortable spit of sand overlooking a bird-viewing area and I laid my head on my daypack and took a nap in the sun.

Jamie reached the Gulf in a few hours and then hitched a ride with a fishing boat back to the Venice marina, getting in just before nightfall. We ate a fish dinner at the marina restaurant and then drove back to New Orleans, talking about the summer together, what Grand Pass looked like, and the stories he'd been told by the fishermen who picked him up. I was too drowsy when we reached New Orleans to drive another twenty minutes over to Lake Pontchartrain and I suggested that we detour instead to Audubon Park and the *Patience* at her dock. We had done this a few nights before and left our sleeping bags and two cots on the boat.

Jamie went right up to sleep on the roof deck, but I wanted to linger for a while on the port side of the galley deck, where I had sat so many nights before. The flow from Carrollton Bend toward 6-mile Point was so strong that I could hear the water splashing against the poplar sides. The *Patience* jerked against her lines and then bounced back on the rope bumpers I had made back in Tennessee. I had a bourbon or two and became dreamy, and I was happy to be alone. The lights from Bridge City and Westwego across the river were twisting in the boils out in the river like Japanese lanterns in the wind. A tug pushing a work barge with a gantry crane whined by, going upriver, turning toward the Audubon banks to make way for a Panamax ship coming down. The combined wakes didn't settle for a couple of minutes and the *Patience* rocked hard against the dock. I tried to remember the first time I had experienced the enchantment of tug wakes—was it in Elizabeth, Pennsylvania, before we even launched, or somewhere in West Virginia? Or was it during my first camp on the *Patience*, back on the Cumberland River in Tennessee?

Regardless, the satisfaction of the lullaby wakes had followed me all the way down both rivers. I felt like I had lived for years in Newburgh,

Shawneetown, and New Madrid. I'd had to be a hard-ass for four months to get to the bottom of the rivers, but now I was sentimental and almost weepy. I wished I knew the name of the tug captain at Tamm Bend who had swung toward the banks and pushed all of that water to get me off the bar. That night in Tiptonville, lost in the cotton fields, it was just an accident that I looked down and saw the river and could get back to the boat. The mistakes that you exploit define you.

But memory was but a distraction and I had vowed when beginning this trip to appreciate the moment, to live for what you have just now and not pine for something grander. I was on a familiar bend in the river at the bottom of the country, not far from the levees where Walt Whitman had come to reinvent himself, in the city of New Orleans. I was glad that I had followed him there.

ACKNOWLEDGMENTS

SAILING A WOODEN FLATBOAT TWO thousand miles to New Orleans renewed my conviction that collaboration is the mother of adventure. The countless river rats, tugboat captains, and mothers who drove down to the banks with their children to see the *Patience* formed a spontaneous support group that sustained us from Pennsylvania to Louisiana. And my research on the flatboat era and what it means for a true understanding of American history relied on a wide congregation of scholars, writers, and diarists, both living and long dead, without whom I could not have written my narrative.

I have described Dan Corjulo as someone who proves that the bonds of friendship can yield both our highest moments of pleasure and our deepest pits of rage. But Danny meant much more to the voyage of the *Patience* than that. Tireless and inventive, he spent almost a year before we left researching river navigation, fuel requirements, Coast Guard regulations, and, being Danny, everything he could learn about outfitting a flatboat for cooking and fine cuisine. He found our electronics and radio gear, and a great deal of other equipment, on eBay, saving me hundreds of dollars. Danny's most salient trait is his refusal to be discouraged by adversity and momentary failure. On the Ohio and the Mississippi, he proved every day that adversity is merely a speed bump encountered along the way toward success.

I made it clear in my text how much I valued the contributions of crew members Deb Satterfield and Cynthia Lee. Deb is one of the best navigators I have ever worked with and was adept at such tasks as laying anchors and lighting the boat at night to avoid conflicts with passing barge strings. Cynthia, an experienced angler and river traveler, taught me a great deal about how to read water surfaces and judge important factors such as tributary flow, channel markers, and the impact of man-made obstructions. She is also a friend of considerable warmth and wisdom. I believe firmly in the concept of parallel, nonbiological family; Cynthia is my sister. Curtis Wasmer can fix or restore anything, tie up in a raging current, and has perhaps the best sense of humor this side of the Mississippi. Jamie Buckley is one of America's most experienced mountain hikers and a great boatman and storyteller. Mike Binkley was an ideal crew member and companion, and so youthful and congenial that all he has to do is stand near a highway with an empty gas can at his feet and his thumb out. The motorists back up beside him on the road shoulder, squabbling over who gets to run him into town for supplies. Brady Carr and Jay Rotkin were particularly helpful getting the trip underway in Pennsylvania, making repairs and shepherding us through the locks, and setting up camp every night. Driver Jason Alford of Manchester, Tennessee, and his assistant, Cornelio Alvarez, did a superb job hauling the *Patience* north despite multiple blowouts on our trailer tires.

Travel to Elizabeth, Pennsylvania, someday and meet Mayor Barry Boucher, and your faith in local politics will be restored. Barry kept us fed and sheltered in Elizabeth and on our first day out gave me an introductory lesson in river navigation and steering around commercial barges along the Monongahela River. He taught me how to negotiate the locks. His common sense and good judgment influenced me for the rest of the trip.

The Locust Fork Expedition group from Mississippi and Alabama— Reed Hillen, Will Denton, and Rick Maynard were calm hands during our last leg in the chaotic, congested water space below Baton Rouge, and have become fast friends and supporters since then. Another member of the Locust Fork group, the incomparable West Pointer and historian Jak Smith, steered me toward research, historical sites, and museums that helped me to interpret how 19th-century events influenced the flatboat trade.

A four-month trip down the inland rivers produced memorable events practically every day, but a writer has to be disciplined about keeping his book to readable length and choosing characters and moments that move the story forward. Several crew members who made important contributions to the trip do not appear in the final book. Porter and Clay Davis were welcome boatmates and able tie-up hands during the early phase of our journey down the Ohio. Paul Cannizaro and Mary Parrott helped me for several days of scenic cruising below Memphis. My friends Cindy and George Rousseau traveled to Tennessee to help me build the *Patience*, and George expertly built the wooden window shutters that protected us from rain all the way south. Mike Russell, a logger and alligator hunter from Battletown, Kentucky, joined us several times along the Ohio and the Mississippi in his airboat, reprovisioning us with motor and radio parts, whiskey, alligator chops, and venison sausage. Camping with him and his family along the banks became a vision of what 19th-century alligator-horse life must have been like.

My old friend and falconer Bob Spiering joined me for two long stretches along the Ohio. He was expert at handling the boat and his outdoor skills were vital. When a swarm of mayflies descended overnight on the *Patience* near Cave-in-Rock, Illinois, Bob plucked a few mayflies from the sides and placed them on his fishhooks, catching enough catfish to feed us for several days. Skyjumper Billy Richards performed a most valuable service, encouraging me to realize that I could handle the flatboat alone without a crew.

Two friends from Maine, Doug Fowle and the late Terry McClinch of the Boothbay Harbor Shipyard, provided critical help when I needed advice on flatboat construction. Billy Smith and Barclay Shephard of the Woodchucks firewood group helped sustain me while I was planning the trip. Sailmaker Nat Wilson of East Boothbay provided essential guidance on sails for flatboat designs and was a font of advice on 19th-century hulls. Polly and Bill Vaughan of Newcastle; Barnaby and Susan Porter of Damariscotta; and Drew and Erica Peck of Boothbay were wonderfully supportive friends and kept me fed during my long months of research in Maine. Chloe Deblois of the Maine Coast Book Shop ordered me several obscure titles that I needed to research flatboats. Molly Bolster of the Gundalow Company in Portsmouth, New Hampshire, gave me a tour of the group's replica gundalow, the *Piscataqua*, and introduced me to the history of the Piscataqua River gundalows and their role in accelerating America's industrial revolution. A single sentence that Molly said—"The gundalows were the semitruck of New England"—framed my approach toward understanding the role of flat-bottom scows in American history. My brother Nicholas sternly warned me not to undertake a long river journey without learning how to tie nautical knots and cheerfully accepted that I ignored his advice.

John Cooper of Gallatin, Tennessee, provided the basic service I required—building me a boat that would reach New Orleans. The difficulties I encountered securing all of the features I needed on the boat are described in my early chapters. I was a novice at boatbuilding, and Cooper is a reenactor unfamiliar with the requirements of an authentic trip.

Not surprisingly, the drama continued after my trip was over. In New Orleans, Cooper and I had a contract dispute, and when I refused to pay for the boat to be delivered back to Tennessee until our financial differences were resolved, he sued me in the Tennessee courts. The case was settled out of court and Cooper then gave the *Patience* to Scott Mandrell, who assumed the cost of transporting it to Illinois.

I will never be able to list all of the people who assisted the journey of the *Patience*. Pastor Derrick Jackson of First Baptist Church in Gallatin, Tennessee, and his congregation, welcomed me to their services and embraced my quest to reach New Orleans. I found their support, and attending services at First Baptist, wonderfully inspirational. Photographer and river traveler John Guider of East Nashville was skeptical about my trip but nevertheless offered me advice that proved useful. Dentist and veteran reenactor Bryant Boswell of Star, Mississippi, helped me understand the inadequacies of the "river guide" that John Cooper had recommended to me. Photographer Robert Mitchell of Boothbay, Maine, traveled to Tennessee while I was building the boat to document construction and is a wonderfully supportive and fun-loving friend.

Mayor Howard E. "Bubba" Miller and marina owner Lynn Robinson of Weirton, West Virginia, were very helpful when we stopped there to refuel and buy new gas cans during the first week of our journey. Steelworker Philip Kincaid of Barboursville, West Virginia, stopped beside the *Patience* and offered to run us into town for food shopping, delivering an interesting lecture on the industrial history along his section of the Ohio. The members of the Shawnee Boat Club in Portsmouth, Ohio, waved us in from the river and insisted that we spend the night at their delightful marina. They ran Dan

Corjulo into town for his nightly food-shop, filled our coolers with ice, bombarded us with cheeseburgers and drinks, and insisted that we take showers at the marina facilities—my first after ten days on the river. The captains of the push boats the *Donna York* and the *Marathon Kentucky* guided us southwest along the Ohio through the fog, from the mouth of the Scioto River to Vanceburg, evincing the legendary helpfulness of Ohio River tug crews. The proprietors of Fatboy's Dream Floating Restaurant and the Lovely Lady Marina in Felicity, Ohio, and, just downriver, the residents of Augusta, Kentucky (Rosemary and George Clooney's hometown), not only live in one of the loveliest districts for antebellum architecture in America, but are marvelously entertaining and hospitable. In Brandenburg, Kentucky, river rats Don Richardson and Bill Matthews were helpful and generous with their time.

Jack A. Brown and his friends at Rocky Point, Indiana, were also wonderfully hospitable and described to me the many foibles of the reenactors who they saw sail down the river celebrating Lewis and Clark and other voyages. Jeff and Lacey Wright of Grand Chain, Illinois, guided me through the Olmstead Locks and Dam section of the Ohio. The captain of the *Caroline N* helped steer me through the big "Kentucky Bend" into New Madrid, Missouri. I have described in chapter 18 the friendliness of New Madrid and particularly the helpfulness of Toni Lynne Phelps and Derrick Lawfield. Earl Johnson of Tiptonville, Tennessee, drove down to the town landing every morning to make sure I was provisioned with food and ice. Cutting hay and logging on his property was one of the most enjoyable diversions of the trip. The staff of the U.S. Fish and Wildlife Service's Reelfoot National Wildlife Refuge walked me through the creation of Reelfoot Lake during the New Madrid Earthquake in 1811–12 and helped me find a canoe so that I could tour that magnificent natural wonder and wildlife paradise.

I consider Natchez, Mississippi, one of the great finds of the trip. It is an informative place to visit to learn about the King Cotton economy of the Deep South, the iniquities of slave trading, and the flowering of architecture in antebellum America. Garrett Yelverton and Austin Doughty rescued me from a rogue lawman the night we landed in Natchez and were perhaps the most enjoyable "best new friends" I've met in years. Michael Scott Alexander Smith—the famed "Cricket" of downtown Natchez—is one of the most well-informed tour guides I have ever met and our long conversations about southern history and antebellum architecture were the intellectual highlight of my trip. Mimi Warren Miller of the Historic Natchez Foundation was very helpful and provided me with a wealth of 19th-century letters, contemporary accounts, and biographies of the old Natchez "nabobs" and the Forks of the Road slave market. The collection at the First Presbyterian Church in Natchez is probably the best photography archive in America. It is worth traveling to Natchez just to spend a day observing the extraordinary images captured by postbellum photographers of both nabob and African American families. Braxton and Carol Hobdy welcomed me to their splendid house along Cemetery Road, where I spent several evenings on their breezeway overlooking the majestic Giles Island stretch of the Mississippi.

In New Orleans, Dr. Daniel Gremillion and Jennifer Gremillion of Nashville became fast friends and rushed to support what I was trying to accomplish with my trip and as a writer. I met them first at the Savannah Writer's Conference. They introduced me to Kurt and Linda Sims of New Orleans, who fed, housed, and then helped me sail the *Patience* south after we learned that the Industrial Canal was closed, and assisted me on innumerable projects while I was closing down the boat and preparing my cargo trailer to haul all of my gear north. Their friends, Bob and Judy Quinildy, let me stay for a month in their boathouse on Lake Pontchartrain until I was ready to leave New Orleans, which saved me a lot of worry about living costs. Linda Friedlander and Jim Marchand, who I first met on the waterfront at Baton Rouge, arranged for me to land at Audubon Park in New Orleans and were enormously helpful afterward. Once I was settled in New Orleans, the staff of Octavia Books in the Magazine District was resourceful in helping me track down titles about 19th-century flatboats and adjust to life in the city.

Tracing the evolution of the basic gundalow during the 18th-century colonial era became one of the delights of my research. There are a number of primary books documenting the spread of the gundalow flat-bottoms: Richard E. Winslow III's *Workhorse for a Tidal Basin Empire*; Jack Brubaker's *Down the Susquehanna to the Chesapeake*; and Mathew Schropp Henry's *History of the Lehigh Valley*. Seth C. Bruggeman's master's thesis for the College of William & Mary, "The Shenandoah River Gundalow and the Politics of Material Reuse" (2000), is not only a superb read, but a reminder that prominent historians often do exceptional work while still graduate students. The Durham Historical Society in Bucks County, Pennsylvania, maintains an exquisite replica of the Durham boat used along the

Pennsylvania rivers, and the archives of Washington Crossing Historic Park trace the widespread use of the Durhams before and after the American Revolution. I visited a number of museums both during and after my voyage on the *Patience*, picking up valuable scraps of information on the history of the flatboat, including the Ohio River Museum in Marietta, Ohio; the Mississippi River Museum in Memphis, Tennessee; and the Tennessee River Museum in Savannah, Tennessee.

One of the advantages of the digital age is being able to find on the web detailed graduate theses that previously could be read only by personally visiting university libraries—assuming that you knew the work was there. My knowledge of the flatboat era was measurably enhanced by Michael Kern Sr.'s "Morgantown's Legend," a history of colonial development in West Virginia. From Thomas E. Redard's "The Port of New Orleans: An Economic History, 1821–1860" (1985), a 550-page doctoral dissertation for the graduate school of Louisiana State University, I found excellent descriptions of dockside New Orleans in the 1820s and the three-hundred-ton "hayboats" that regularly sailed during the 19th century from the Wabash farmlands in Indiana to the forage-needy city of New Orleans. From another marvelous graduate thesis available from the LSU Digital Commons, John Amos Johnson's "Pre-Steamboat Navigation on the Lower Mississippi River" (1963), I gleaned such details as flatboats rarely carrying anchors, because they drifted day and night, and I was able to examine cross sections of Durham boats, keelboats, and flatboats commonly in use during the heyday of river transport before the Civil War. I am indebted to the digital library JSTOR, which makes available to writers like me such monographs as T. W. Records's "Flatboats," from the *Indiana Magazine of History*, or *Recollections of the Early Settlement of the Wabash Valley*, by Sandford C. Cox. JSTOR was also a wonderful source for other, geographically specific studies, such as John A. Jakle's "Salt on the Ohio Valley Frontier, 1770–1820," and Steve C. Gordon's "From Slaughterhouse to Soap-Boiler: Cincinnati's Meat Packing Industry, Changing Technologies, and the Rise of Mass Production, 1825–1870," which allowed me to trace the role the flatboat played in the development of basic industries along the early 19th-century frontier. I found too many other monographs on JSTOR to name them all. In almost all of these cases I tried to follow the standard practice of attributing my sources in the text.

I have also come to rely over the years on the excellent offerings of the Gilder Lehrman Institute of American History in New York. Gilder Lehrman offers one of the best repositories of first sources, essays, and broad interpretations of subjects in American history and has proven invaluable to researchers and writers like me.

The required reading for a book like mine also created the joyful experience of discovering so many significant historians beyond the traditional pantheon of "must reads." The devotion of historian Archer Butler Hulbert to river history (*The Ohio River: A Course of Empire*; *The Paths of Inland Commerce*; and his twelve-volume opus on the American rivers, *Historic Highways of America*) introduced me to the importance of apprehending rivers as America's primary avenue of growth. A most excellent scholarly book, published by the Johns Hopkins University Press, *Western River Transportation: The Era of Early Internal Development, 1810–1860* (by Erik F. Haites, James Mak, and Gary M. Watson) is packed with useful research like wages paid to flatboat crews. It also contains perhaps the best essay on the flatboat era, "The Persistence and Demise of Old Technologies," which explains why flatboats were never entirely replaced by steamboats and indeed continued in use until World War I. John Francis McDermott's *Travelers on the Western Frontier*, published by the University of Illinois Press, a compendium of maps, diaries, and contemporary engravings documenting the progress of Americans across the inland water and then the prairies, is infinitely entertaining and useful. Collections like McDermott's allow writers like me to offer "primary source" descriptions and events, so that readers are confident that they are reading about flatboating as it was depicted at the time.

I was intrigued to discover that New York publisher Holt, Rinehart and Winston, in collaboration with William Hodge and Co., of London and Edinburgh, enjoyed one of the most successful franchises in American publishing history by releasing the sixty-five-volume series, Rivers of America, between 1937 and 1974. (I relied most heavily on two books from the series, Hodding Carter's *Lower Mississippi* and R. E. Banta's *The Ohio*.) The founding editor of the series, Constance Lindsay Skinner, who died at her desk while editing her beloved river books, preferred that each book be written by poets or literary figures, not historians. When she launched the series, Skinner declared her purpose with such conviction and grace that it bears quoting here. It aligns with my own reasons for writing this book, and my belief that citizenship requires all of us to be widely read, perpetually self-educating, and thoughtfully informed.

"This is to be a literary and not a historical series," Skinner wrote in 1937. "The authors of these books will be novelists and poets. On them, now in America, as in all lands and times, rests the real responsibility of interpretation. If the average American is less informed about his country than any other national, knows and cares less about its past and about its present in all sections but the one where he resides, it is because books prepared for his instruction were not written by artists."

Michael Allen's *Western Rivermen, 1763–1861* and Leland Baldwin's *The Keelboat Age on Western Waters* are standard texts for anyone interested in the flatboat era. More seriously afflicted book turds like me will also enjoy and profit from Ronald E. Shaw's *Canals for a Nation: The Canal Era in the United States, 1790–1860*; Charles Henry Ambler's *A History of Transportation in the Ohio Valley*; Marquis Childs's *Mighty Mississippi: Biography of a River*; and Paul Schneider's *Old Man River: The Mississippi in North American History*. Richard Campanella's *Lincoln in New Orleans: The 1828–1831 Flatboat Voyages and Their Place in History* is a great Lincoln and flatboat book.

I also relied on a trio of surveys of American economic history. Isaac Lippincott's *Economic Development in the United States*; George Rogers Taylor's *The Transportation Revolution, 1815–1860*; and, most especially, Seymour Dunbar's *A History of Travel in America* are monuments of American scholarship.

It is impossible to understand America's Golden Age without knowing Walt Whitman, and David S. Reynolds's *Walt Whitman's America: A Cultural Biography* is triumphant. A number of scholars have lately begun to realize that Whitman the prose stylist was as significant as Whitman the poet, and his period of composing vivid and conversational sketches of the American scene began with his famous trip to New Orleans in 1848. Whitman's prose works are collected in a number of editions by the Library of America or Funk & Wagnalls (with annotations and scene-setters by Justin Kaplan or Malcolm Cowley), usually titled *Walt Whitman: The Collected Prose*. From his descriptions of amputated Civil War soldiers teaching themselves to write left-handed to his sketches of the jammed

commercial wharfs of New Orleans, Whitman was one of the best journalists working in America in the 19th century and readers can still profit
mightily from consuming his prose work. I also relied on Reynolds's *Waking Giant: America in the Age of Jackson* for its capacious survey of American history during the flatboat era.

I have long been disappointed that the Ivy League "deans" of American
history so assiduously steered their scholarship toward promotion of
American myths instead of toward research of events that authentically
reflected what happened in our past, and how these events affected the
common man. They are what I call "Wall Street historians," more interested
in the bank wars or tariff disputes of financial elites, and their servants in
the U.S. Congress, than the real-life conditions facing farmers or frontier
mechanics. We cannot understand American history without reckoning
with the extermination of the tribes or the brutalization of slavery during
the flatboat era. Fortunately, a new generation of historians has emerged
to counteract the habitual myopia and bias of the 19th- and 20th-century
American history establishment.

I relied on the following books for an accurate account of Indian Removal in the 1830s and the intensification of the brutality of the American
slavery system as it moved south from tidewater Virginia to the slave coast
of the Mississippi after 1800. *Unworthy Republic: The Dispossession of Native
Americans and the Road to Indian Territory*, by the University of Georgia's
Claudio Saunt, is the best history of the genocide of the five civilized tribes
in the 1830s. *Indian Removal*, by David S. and Jeanne T. Heidler, provides
very useful primary-source accounts of what happened to the Cherokee, the
Creek, and the Chickasaw during the removal period. Walter Johnson's *Soul
by Soul* takes readers inside the antebellum slave markets of Natchez and
New Orleans during the flatboat era. *Empire of Cotton: A Global History* by
Sven Beckert, and *Cotton: The Biography of a Revolutionary Fiber* by Stephen
Yafa are essential reading for anyone interested in the role that King Cotton
played in the American economy before the Civil War. *The Sugar Masters:
Planters and Slaves in Louisiana's Cane World, 1820–1860*, by Richard
Follett, is an excellently written account that provides a detailed look at how
the Mississippi coast plantations brutally managed their captive, forced-
labor populations to enhance annual increases in productivity.

Jill Lepore's *These Truths: A History of the United States*, like Howard

Zinn's earlier *A People's History of the United States*, is helping to drive readers toward a more honest conception of our country's past. The work of the University of Virginia's Alan Taylor (*The Internal Enemy* and *Thomas Jefferson's Education*) has radically changed not only how we understand African American slavery, but the prejudices and hypocrisy of the Constitution writers from Virginia. Edward E. Baptist's *The Half Has Never Been Told: Slavery and the Making of American Capitalism* is one of the most well-researched and magisterial books of American history.

Frederick Law Olmsted's *The Cotton Kingdom: A Traveller's Observations on Cotton and Slavery in the American Slave States, 1853–1861* is a great travelogue and observation on the southern states before the Civil War and explains how cotton and flatboats (and later steamboats) emerged as significant factors leading to the Civil War.

A number of former southern plantations open to visitors now devote their tours to understanding the cotton agronomy from the perspective of slaves, and after reaching New Orleans I was able to visit one of the best of these, the Whitney Plantation in Edgard, Louisiana. The National Park Service maintains more than two dozen highly informative interpretative sites along the Trail of Tears National Historic Trail, across nine states in the Ohio and Mississippi valleys, many of which I visited at stops along both rivers, where I learned, for example, that local physicians and boat captains were often recruited to man the U.S. Army removal expeditions to Oklahoma, and that river transportation played a major role in the displacement of the tribes. National Archives documents and artifacts from the Trail of Tears are housed at the Museum of the Cherokee Indian in Cherokee, North Carolina. The staff of the Trail of Tears Interpretive Center in Pulaski, Tennessee, was quite helpful in assisting me in tracking down maps and contemporary accounts of the removal routes through Kentucky, Tennessee, and Arkansas.

Scholars have long believed that the "first frontier" along the inland rivers has received less attention than the much later Oregon Trail in the 1840s and 1850s because of a relative lack of river journals and diaries. I was delighted to discover that this was untrue. Historical and genealogy societies, state university archives and presses, and county museums that I visited from Morgantown, West Virginia, to St. Francisville, Louisiana, were a surprising trove of pamphlets, tracts by local historians, and reprinted journals describing the flatboat migration through their areas. I have indicated in my text the sources of the journals that I relied on most: Asbury C. Jacquess's "The Journals of the *Davy Crockett*" and John Calvin Gilkeson's "Flatboat Building on Little Raccoon Creek," both published in the *Indiana Magazine of History*; and "A Tour in 1807 Down the Cumberland, Ohio and Mississippi Rivers from Nashville to New Orleans," by John R. Bedford and Johannes Sappington, published by the Tennessee Historical Society. Editor Harry G. Enoch's *Bound for New Orleans!: John Halley's Journal of Flatboat Trips from Boonesborough in 1789 & 1791* contains an informative digest of other late 18th-century flatboat trips to New Orleans. I often relied on the summaries in the Redard and Johnson dissertations in the Louisiana State University archives for confirmation of basic facts about flatboat building and travel. W. Wallace Carson's "Transportation and Traffic on the Ohio and the Mississippi Before the Steamboat," published in 1920 in the *Mississippi Historical Review*, was also a rich source of contemporary accounts of the "broad horns" developed on the Ohio River frontier.

The Wreck of the America *in Southern Illinois: A Flatboat on the Ohio River* (Southern Illinois University Press) describes how a team lead by archaeologist Mark J. Wagner meticulously unearthed a pre–Civil War flatboat preserved in the mud along the Ohio north of Cairo, Illinois. Wagner's measurements and conclusions about building methods confirm many details we know about the "vernacular" design of flatboats.

I have always believed that good books should direct readers toward other good books, especially gems of the past that have been forgotten over time. *The Navigator* series of river gazetteers by the redoubtable Zadok Cramer, and Samuel Cumings's *The Western Pilot: Containing Charts of the Ohio River and of the Mississippi, from the Mouth of the Missouri to the Gulf of Mexico for 1829* (republished in 1848) are rewarding reads, if only for the peculiarities of 19th-century syntax. Joseph Holt Ingraham's two-volume *The South-West: By a Yankee* is a classic 19th-century narrative. The *Journal of John James Audubon, Made During His Trip to New Orleans in 1820–1821* is wonderfully eccentric and contains beautiful descriptions of landscapes and birds, as well as descriptions of the frontier river towns along the water route to New Orleans. Morris Birkbeck's 1819 *Notes on a Journey in America from the Coast of Virginia to the Territory of Illinois* and John Bradbury's *Travels in the Interior of America in the*

Years 1809, 1810 and 1811 are epic. Christian Schultz's 1807 *Travels on an Inland Voyage Through the States of New York, Pennsylvania . . .* [to] *New Orleans*, available in several reprinted editions, depicts the perilous passage down the Ohio and the Mississippi during the formative years of the flatboat era. Thomas Bangs Thorpe, whom I quote in chapter 13, is now sadly forgotten, but he was one of the great humorists and naturalists of the 19th century. *A New Collection of Thomas Bangs Thorpe's Sketches of the Old Southwest* (edited by David C. Estes), published by the Louisiana State University Press, is a prerequisite for anyone interested in truly understanding 19th-century history and prose.

The best of all of these was Timothy Flint, whose colorful if uneven career in the West after 1815 made him one of the most paradigmatic Americans of the 19th century. His *Recollections of the Last Ten Years, Passed in Occasional Residences and Journeyings in the Valley of the Mississippi* and *The History and Geography of the Mississippi Valley: To Which Is Appended a Condensed Physical Geography of the Atlantic United States, and the Whole American Continent* were frequently republished in America and Europe in the 1830s and were credited with driving thousands of adventurers and pioneers west. Numerous reprinted editions are available today, the best of which is the reissue by the Southern Illinois University Press, with biographical introductions by George R. Brooks and John Francis McDermott. A weekend spent with Flint's *Recollections* provides a most rewarding reading experience, delivering a highly entertaining sweep of the 19th-century American experience.

I occasionally experience another frustrating but ultimately useful exercise when composing my books. I spent several fruitful days exploring the uniquely preserved and biodiverse Duck River of Tennessee with a local historian and mapmaker from Columbia, the late Joe Brooks, who spent a quarter century documenting how the flatboat helped foment a lively industrial revolution along that tributary before the Civil War. I also became obsessed with how the ease of carrying heavy structures on the rivers spawned one of America's most signature industries. In the 1840s, the Pullis Brothers' Mississippi Iron Works and the Mesker Brothers Iron Works turned St. Louis, Evansville, and Owensboro into global centers for manufacturing distinctive cast-iron building facades, hundreds of which can still be found all over the country. Because of space concerns, both of these sections had to be cut from the book. However, in the ineffable and vaporous ways that writing often works, the words taken out somehow enrich the words left in. Readers interested in these subjects can consult a classic of American mechanical history, given to me by Joe Brooks, *The Young Mill-Wright and Miller's Guide*, by a brilliant Revolutionary-era inventor and engineer from Philadelphia, Oliver Evans. The fascinating subject of metal facades, and the ways that inland river commerce contributed to their growth, can be found in *A History of Cast Iron in Architecture*, by John Gloag and Derek Bridgwater, or Margot Gayle's excellent *Cast-Iron Architecture in America*.

I could not have finished this book without the strong publishing team that stands behind me. Sloan Harris and Julie Flanagan of International Creative Management are always there when I place a call. Jofie Ferrari-Adler of Avid Reader Press is the most superb line editor in the business, a fast friend, and a sympathetic listener, who knows just when to push for chapters. At parent company Simon & Schuster, despite his increased responsibilities, Jon Karp remains wonderfully engaged with his writers and their books. Alexandra Primiani, Meredith Vilarello, and Caroline McGregor are the best marketing and publicity team I have ever worked with, and Jonathan Evans and Paul Dippolito are a superb production team. Carolyn Kelly is always on top of the details and I would have been lost getting this book ready without her. Thanks also to Ben Loehnen, Lauren Wein, Katherine Hernández, and Julianna Haubner. Felice Javit gave the book an expert legal vetting.

Lifelong collaborator Michael Gellatly has provided the illustrations and now the covers for most of my books and it was a delight working for the first time with cover designer Alison Forner. I have spent more than a half century now communing with my oldest companion in books, Alexander Hartley Platt, who is always a rich source of reading tips and interpretations of American history, and who graciously took the time to read my entire manuscript and make several useful suggestions. Tugboat pilot Jason Roberts of Lawrenceburg, Tennessee, spent hours answering all of my questions about commercial barge traffic on the inland rivers.

A book is really just an ad hoc community created over time to deliver 150,000 words of intellectual content to the right audience, and I am grateful to all of these friends for their help. Most of all, they have patiently put up with me.

INDEX

NOTE: Page references in *italics* refer to figures and illustrations.

ABOUT THE AUTHOR

RINKER BUCK began his career in journalism at the *Berkshire Eagle* and was a longtime staff writer for the *Hartford Courant*. He has written for *Vanity Fair*, *New York*, *Life*, and many other publications, and his work has won the PEN/New England Award, the Eugene S. Pulliam National Journalism Writing Award, and the Society of Professional Journalists Sigma Delta Chi Award. He is the #1 *New York Times* bestselling author of *The Oregon Trail*, *Flight of Passage*, and *First Job*. He lives in Tennessee.